Comparative Perspectives on *Shari'ah* in Nigeria

Comparative Perspectives on *Shari'ah* in Nigeria

edited by

Philip Ostien, Jamila M. Nasir and
Franz Kogelmann

Spectrum Books Limited
Ibadan
Abuja •Benin City •Lagos •Owerri

Spectrum titles can be purchased on line at
www.spectrumbooksonline.com

Published by
Spectrum Books Limited
Spectrum House
Ring Road
PMB 5612
Ibadan, Nigeria
e-mail: admin1@spectrumbooksonline.com

in association with
Safari Books (Export) Limited
17 Bond Street, 1st Floor
St Helier, Jersey JE2 3NP
Channel Islands
United Kingdom

© Philip Ostien, Jamila M. Nasir and Franz Kogelmann

First published 2005

Publication of this book has been made possible by a grant from the Volkswagen Foundation, Kastanienallee 35, 30519 Hannover, Germany, www.volkswagenstiftung.de.

The map on the front cover is used by permission of Global Mapping International, 15435 Gleneagle Drive, Suite 100, Colorado Springs, CO 80921 USA, www.gmi.org.

All rights reserved. This book is under copyright and no part of it may be reproduced, stored in a retrieval system, or transmitted, in any form or by any means, electronic, mechanical, electrostatic, magnetic tape, photocopying, recording, or otherwise, without the prior written permission of the copyright owners.

ISBN: 978-029-547-X

Printed by Printmarks Ventures, Ososami, Ibadan

Contents

Preface
    Monday Y. Mangvwat vii

Introduction
    Philip Ostien, Jamila Nasir and Franz Kogelmann ix

KEYNOTE ADDRESSES

Women's Rights in Shari'ah: A Case for Codification of Islamic Personal Law in Nigeria
    Saudatu Shehu Mahdi 1

Which Road Leads Beyond the Shari'ah Controversy? A Christian Perspective on Shari'ah in Nigeria
    Danny McCain 7

PAPERS AND COMMENTARIES

The Demand for Shari'ah in African Democratisation Processes: Pitfalls or Opportunities?
    Abdulkader Tayob 27
Commentary:
    Warisu O. Alli 57
    J. Isawa Elaigwu 66

Rethinking the Role of Religion in the Public Sphere: Local and Global Perspectives
    Rosalind I. J. Hackett 74
Commentary:
    Muslih T. Yahya 100

The Enforcement of God's Law: The Shari'ah in the Present World of Islam
    Ruud Peters 107
Commentary:
    Joseph Kenny 135
    Auwalu Hamisu Yadudu 139

Nigeria's 'State Religion' Question in Comparative Perspective
    W. Cole Durham, Jr. 144
Commentary:
    Musa A.B. Gaiya 168
    Ibrahim Na'iya Sada 174

Freedom of Religion and Its Limitations: Judicial Standards for Deciding Particular Cases to Maintain the State's Secular Role in Protecting Society's Religious Commitments
    John C. Reitz 178
Commentary:
    Jamila M. Nasir 244

The West and the Rest: Reflections on the Intercultural Dialogue about Shari'ah
    Sanusi Lamido Sanusi 251
Commentary:
    Umar H.D. Danfulani 275
    Is-Haq Oloyede 292

Religion: Source of Conflict or Resource for Peace?
    Gerrie ter Haar 303
Commentary:
    J.D. Gwamna 320

The Future of Shari'ah and the Debate in Northern Nigeria
    Abdullahi Ahmed An-Na'im 327
Commentary:
    Ali Ahmad 358
    Andrew F. Walls 373

About the Authors 383

Index 389

Preface

Many readers of this book will have heard of the terrible outbreaks of civil strife that occurred in Jos in September 2001 and again in May 2002. Although the underlying causes almost certainly had nothing to do with religion, it was religion that defined the two sides in the fighting, Christians vs. Muslims. The university of Jos, unfortunately, was in the thick of the fighting, simply by virtue of its location within Jos City. The university was closed for the duration, its staff quarters filled up with refugees, and many were lost – students and staff. It was a terrible time for Jos and for the University of Jos.

It was with some trepidation, therefore, that we in the university's administration decided, less than two years later, to go ahead with plans to host a conference on *shari'ah*. The question was whether, given the contentiousness of the topic, the many hundreds of interested persons coming in from all over the North to discuss it, and the much-subsided but still subsisting tensions in Jos, the conference would come off peacefully. We thought that it would, and that if it did, it would be a very positive step forward for the city and for the university. I am delighted to say that in this we were proved right. The conference attracted, as main speakers and commentators, first-rate scholars from Europe, America, and around Nigeria, giving the audience the opportunity – all too rare in our university in recent years – to hear and participate in high-level scholarly discussions of the most recent developments in law and religion and the relations between law and religion around the world. The religiously-mixed audience was large – over 900 people signed the registration books – and the debate was sometimes hot, but the proceedings were orderly and passed entirely without conflict. Besides their participation in the conference, some of the speakers also scheduled seminars, lectures, and colloquiums in their respective faculties or departments within the university while they were here, providing academic stimulation and cross-fertilisation greatly beneficial to our undergraduate and postgraduate students and to our academic staff as well. Our foreign visitors also had much to learn, from each other and from their extended interactions with Nigerians inside and outside the conference hall. In sum, the conference was an unqualified success and a large step forward for Jos and for the University of Jos. On a larger scale, the conference was a step forward for Nigeria – a constructive example of dialogue, in an academic setting, between Muslims and Christians, and others neither Muslim nor Christian, about *shari'ah* as seen in a global perspective, with a view to enhancing peaceful coexistence and creating an environment where peoples of all faiths can live together in harmony. On behalf of the University, I express my heartfelt thanks to all concerned – the sponsors, – the organisers, the speakers, and the members of the audience one and all.

The papers that were presented at the conference – main papers and commentaries on them – have now been revised and prepared for publication in this book. The book is a permanent contribution to the literature on law and religion in Nigeria, valuable to judges and lawyers, scholars and students of many disciplines, clerics and laypersons throughout the country. May it play a positive role in bringing unity and peace to our great nation.

Professor Monday Y. Mangvwat
Vice-Chancellor, University of Jos

Introduction

Philip Ostien, Jamila M. Nasir and Franz Kogelmann

This book is one product of a year-long project of scholars from the University of Jos (Nigeria) and the University of Bayreuth (Germany), under the title "The *Shari'ah* Debate and the Shaping of Muslim and Christian Identities in Northern Nigeria." The entire project, including the conference at which the papers collected in this book were first presented, was funded by a grant from the Volkswagen Foundation, headquartered in Hannover, Germany. That fact, and other things about the project and the conference in Jos which marked its close, stirred up suspicion and controversy in Northern Nigeria. We wish to take this opportunity to address some of the issues that came up. This will permit us not only to introduce the volume and the papers in it, but to provide some information, especially for our Nigerian readers, about the academic grant-making process of which our project was a beneficiary, and to give readers from outside Nigeria some further insight into "The *Shari'ah* Debate and the Shaping of Muslim and Christian Identities in Northern Nigeria."

ORIGINS OF THE PROJECT

Everyone will agree, we think, that the various steps taken, beginning in late 1999, to implement *shari'ah* in twelve of Nigeria's northern states, were by far the most important and most controversial changes in Nigeria's laws in many years. Grant that this is so. But precisely because *shari'ah* implementation was so significant and so controversial – both locally and globally! – it was bound to attract the attention, not only of politicians, the press, and partisans to the controversies it generated, but also of *scholars* – academicians interested in *studying* it, not as something good or bad, not as something to be praised or condemned, not as something to be supported or opposed, defended or attacked, but rather as a complex set of fascinating legal and sociological and world-historical developments to be documented, analysed, and understood – "in the same way as any other important trend in society, such as the economy, education, or public health."[1]

It so happened that during the academic year 1999-2000, just as *shari'ah* implementation was taking off, there were several scholars based at the University of Jos whose prior work had already involved them in the study of the application of Islamic law in Nigeria, Muslim-Christian relations, and religion and politics generally,[2] and who were well-prepared and ready to turn their attention to the new developments. One of these scholars was Professor Frieder Ludwig, then of the University of Bayreuth,[3] a theologian and historian of religions, who, in furtherance of a long series of exchanges between Jos and Bayreuth, was spending the year at Jos as a visiting professor. When *shari'ah* implementation started, Ludwig and others at Jos began collecting and exchanging information about it and discussing its ramifications. Some information was gleaned from the Nigerian newspapers – but the stories in the press were often conflicting often very obviously biased or confused, and always frustratingly incomplete. The papers presented at several of the early *shari'ah* conferences were obtained and studied[4] – but these tended to be more the literature of religious exposition and apologetics than of academic research and scholarship. Some journeys were made to some *shari'ah* states, at personal expense, to try and gather more complete and more accurate information about developments on the ground, including the new laws – but the scope of these efforts was limited by the cost. Grants were applied for, from the University of

---

[1] Ter Haar, this volume, 306.
[2] Ludwig, 1997, Nasir, 1999; Ostien, 1999.
[3] Professor Ludwig moved to Luther Seminary in St. Paul, Minnesota in 2002, where he teaches Mission and World Christianity.
[4] E.g. from the "National Conference on Sharia and Constitutional Process", organised by the Centre for Islamic Legal Studies, Ahmadu Bello University, held at Zaria, 17th-18th Nov. 1999; "National Conference on the Application of Sharia" held at Bayero University, Kano, 1st-3rd December, 1999; "National Conference on Shariah and the Nigerian Federation", organised by 24 Islamic organisations in Borno State, held at Imam Malik Islamic Centre, Maiduguri, 31st January-2nd February, 2000; "National Seminar on Shari'a", organised by Jama'atu Nasril Islam, held at Arewa House, Kaduna, 10th-12th February, 2000.

Jos, in hopes of getting the funds needed to carry out more extensive research — but this was just at the time when research grants from Nigeria's universities were drying up almost completely. These early efforts did bear some scholarly fruit;[5] but by late 2000, when Ludwig returned to Germany, it was quite unclear where money might be found to finance the more thorough-going study of *shari'ah* implementation that we all wanted to do.

THE BIG FOUNDATIONS

Scholars seeking funding for their research often turn to the great private foundations which became fixtures of civil society in the West in the 20th century. Nigerians will be familiar with some of the names. The Ford Foundation, one of the largest, currently with assets of $9.8 billion, has been working in West Africa since 1958, when its first grant was made for training public service professionals in Nigeria. Since then, Ford's West Africa office, located in Lagos, has made over 600 grants totalling approximately $250 million to institutions and individuals throughout the region.[6] In April 2000 Ford, along with the MacArthur and Rockefeller Foundations and the Carnegie Corporation (with assets of $4b, $3b, and $1.8b, respectively) launched their "Partnership to Strengthen African Universities," committed to investing $100 million in African universities in the first five years of the Partnership's work. MacArthur and Carnegie are investing in Nigeria: after sifting through applications from many of the country's universities, they have now made grants totalling $14 million to six of them. The aim of these grants is to bolster institutional reforms, strengthen the universities in various other defined ways, and to implement gender equity projects.[7] MacArthur, which like Ford has an office in Nigeria

---

[5] E.g. Danfulani, 2000; Ludwig, 2001; Ostien, 2000 and 2002; Danfulani, Ostien, and Ludwig, 2002.
[6] www.fordfound.org/about; www.fordfound.org/global/office/index.cfm?office=Lagos. These and all other websites cited in this introduction were last accessed in September and October 2004.
[7] See www.carnegie.org/sub/news/africanuniversities.html; www.macfdn.org/programs/gss/nigeria.htm. MacArthur has made three-year grants of $3 million each to the University of Ibadan and Ahmadu Bello University and of $2 million each to Bayero University and the University of Port Harcourt; Carnegie has

(in Abuja) has been making grants here since 1989. According to its website,

> [t]he core element of [MacArthur's] work in Nigeria is to strengthen nongovernmental organizations, universities, independent institutes, some government agencies, and individuals as they work toward improvements in higher education, population and reproductive health, human rights, and the challenges in the Niger River Delta.[8]

And to take just one more example, consider the Bill and Melinda Gates Foundation, far and away the world's largest, currently with assets of $32 billion. According to its website, the Gates Foundation

> works to promote greater equity in four areas: global health, education, public libraries, and support for at-risk families in Washington state and Oregon. * * * The foundation's Global Health Program is focused on reducing global health inequities by accelerating the development, deployment and sustainability of health interventions that will save lives and dramatically reduce the disease burden in developing countries. * * * Preventing deadly diseases among poor children by expanding access to vaccines, and developing vaccines against malaria, HIV/AIDS, and tuberculosis, are central priorities.[9]

Consistently with these goals, in November 2000 Gates announced a grant of $25 million to the Harvard University School of Public Health (HSPH) for an HIV/AIDS prevention programme in Nigeria. Called APIN – AIDS Prevention in Nigeria – the initiative in its first phase has focussed on Lagos, Oyo, and Plateau States, working with and through universities, government institutions, and community organisations. Identification of high-risk groups in each state was an important first step: "Nigerian health researchers and physicians believe high-risk groups may vary regionally within Nigeria and that they may differ markedly from such groups in other countries in Africa."

---

made three-year grants of $2 million each to the University of Jos and Obafemi Awolowo University.
[8] www.macfdn.org/programs/gss/nigeria.htm.
[9] www.gatesfoundation.org/MediaCenter; www.gatesfoundation.org/Global Health.

HSPH researchers will also work with Nigerian colleagues to standardize screening and data collection, so that the information gathered about seroprevalence is accurate. They will also help upgrade laboratory facilities for sexually transmitted diseases (STDs) in the . . . states chosen and will provide STD treatment, particularly among commercial sex workers, and determine the impact of prevention on HIV spread. The initiative will also provide screening for pregnant women and antiretroviral treatment for those who test positive. Findings on levels of infection among these women and on the strains of HIV identified will be shared with Nigerian colleagues and will inform public education efforts.[10]

The Jos University Teaching Hospital has been a beneficiary of this grant. It is an APIN centre; several staff of the University's Faculty of Medical Sciences are actively involved in the project; and many sufferers from HIV/AIDS and other STDs from Plateau State and elsewhere in the North are receiving treatment.

Let us now sum up very briefly some salient facts about the private grant-making foundations and the way they operate.

- There are a great many private foundations. According to the Foundation Center of New York City, as of 2002 there were 57,834 of them in the USA alone, with combined assets of $364.1 billion and total "giving" of $30.4 billion.[11] About half of these totals, however, are controlled by the 200 biggest foundations – including Gates, Ford, MacArthur, Rockefeller, and Carnegie. The numbers for other countries are smaller, but the institution of the private charitable or philanthropic foundation is apparently universal. In Muslim lands it is known as the *waqf* – the Islamic pious endowment–"a phenomenon that is present in virtually all

---

[10] www.hsph.harvard.edu/apin/.
[11] www.fdncenter.org/fc_stats/index.html, and the many tables available there. To get some sense of how much $364.1 billion is, consider that Nigeria's estimated GDP for 2003, at purchasing power parity, was $110.8 billion, see www.indexmundi.com/nigeria/

Islamic societies and which has a high prestige in social, religious, political, cultural and economic terms."[12]

- Private foundations are non-profit organisations – usually incorporated in the West as charitable trusts – that distribute private wealth for public purposes, or "in the public interest." Their endowments often (but not always) derive from private fortunes made in business: the names of Ford (cars), MacArthur (insurance, real estate), Carnegie (steel), and Gates (computer software) are indicative. The grantor or grantors convey money, stocks or other property (the endowment) by deed of trust to named trustees, who are responsible for administration of the endowment and its proceeds according to directives given in the trust instrument. The endowment is invested; the money given away comes from the profit on the investments. Everything is regulated by the laws of the place where the foundation is domiciled.[13]

---

[12] Hodgson, 1974, 124. On *awqaf* see also Bendjilali, 1998, Ghanim, 2004, Kogelmann, 1999 and 2004, and Peters, 2002. The articles in Weiss, 2002, focus on *awqaf* and other means of social welfare in Muslim societies in Africa specifically. For a more general survey of philanthropy in the world's traditions, see Ilchman, Katz, and Queen, 1998, which includes articles on precolonial Africa (Feierman, 1998) and on the Muslim world (Arjomand, 1998 and Kozlowski, 1998). Salamon et al., 1999, give detailed information about private foundations and other elements of the non-profit sectors in many countries. As has already been indicated, a great deal of current information about foundations and their work can be found on the Internet. Most foundations have their own websites. For more general information, see (for instance) the websites of: the Association of German Foundations, www.stiftungen.org; the European Foundation Centre, www.efc.be; the UK Association of Charitable Foundations, www.acf.org.uk; the Japan Philanthropic Association, www.philanthropy.or.jp; and the Foundation Center (US), www.fdncenter.org.

[13] For the law in the US, see, e.g. Hopkins and Blazek, 1997 and Barber, 2002. Among other things regulated are the taxability of donations to foundations, of their other income, and of donations made by them; management of investments; minimum mandatory annual giving; allowable administrative expenses; self-dealing by foundations or by those who control or work for them; and reporting requirements. All private foundations in the US must file an annual report, Form 990PF, which reveals the foundation's entire list of grants given during each year and the endowment's investment portfolio in complete detail, including prices of stocks when purchased, when sold, current book value, and dividend earnings. The forms 990PF are public records and are the

INTRODUCTION

- Within the broad parameters laid down by the law of charitable trusts, foundations are free to set their own grant-making agendas and to run their programmes as they see fit. Some administer their programmes themselves, others make grants to other charities, public or private, which spend the money on to the desired ends. Some foundations concentrate on assisting defined population groups;[14] others fund activities in specific subject areas;[15] some fund "think-tanks" dedicated to the analysis of public policy issues. Within the world of academic grant-making, foundations may support academic institutions, or individuals at different stages of their educations, or they may fund research in particular fields: law, medicine, the physical sciences, the social sciences, etc., and within those fields research aimed at specific goals, for instance finding a vaccine against malaria or a cure for HIV/AIDS.

- Because there are so many foundations funding such a wide variety of activities, a whole separate industry has grown up of helping grant-*seekers* to find grant-*makers* who might be willing to fund their projects, and then helping the grant-seekers to write "winning proposals." The Internet is a rich source for such materials; we give a small sample of books on the subject in our list of references.[16]

- Some grant-making is directed abroad, as we have seen.[17] Presumably a wide variety of foreign foundations – not just the ones we have mentioned – are funding activities in Nigeria. They no doubt have many different agendas, not all of which would be approved by all Nigerians. This brings us to our final point.

---

source of a great deal of information about foundation activity, much of which is published by the Foundation Center's annual *Foundation Grants Index*.
[14] E.g. the poor, the disabled, widows and orphans, children and youth, the aged, women, specified ethnic groups, specified religious groups or their institutions such as schools, churches, or mosques, veterans of the armed services, victims of disasters, etc.
[15] E.g. education, libraries, museums, the arts, other cultural activities, health, sports and recreation, community development, governance, the environment, animal welfare, etc.
[16] Schneiter, 1985; Ries and Leukfeld, 1995; McIlnay, 1998; Glass, 2000.
[17] On international grant-making by US foundations, see Renz, 1997.

- The work of private foundations is sometimes controversial. Their grant-making programmes are defined by *their* visions of the public good – and these may not be shared by everyone. In the 1950s, for instance, the Ford Foundation helped to fund the movement for civil rights for American blacks. This offended Southern conservatives, who didn't think civil rights for American blacks were such a good idea, and who proceeded to launch two separate Congressional investigations into alleged "subversion and Communist penetration" of America's philanthropic foundations.[18] Today there are recognisably "left-wing" foundations supporting such causes as human rights and environmental protection, and "right-wing" foundations devoted to dismantling the welfare state. Coming closer to home: all Nigerians can support Ford's training programmes for public professionals, and Gates's APIN. But what of Carnegie's efforts to promote its "liberal Western" ideas of gender equity here, or MacArthur's efforts to strengthen Nigerian NGOs and independent institutes? Some people hate the very name of "gender equity." And some governments, especially in the third world, actively discourage NGOs and independent institutes (along with other elements of civil society), as being rival centres of power with which the governments would rather not have to contend.[19] In sum, the work of foundations sometimes involves them in political controversy, even political struggle. This is neither surprising nor a bad thing. It is part of the healthy ferment and debate that always go on in societies where economic and political power are diffused in many hands and where many different visions of the public good are free to contend.

---

[18] Kiger, 2000 and Downie, 2001 discuss these and other official investigations into foundation activities.

[19] This has been a problem also in many Muslim countries since independence, see Kogelmann, 2004, 383: "The state tried to control and regulate, if not directly suppress, previously autonomous endowments [*awqaf*], among other things. The centralised pious endowment administration, or the ministry created for this purpose, are given–in addition to the responsibility for safeguarding the religious infrastructure–the task of propagating a state-sanctioned form of Islam, and the pious endowments were intended to provide the means for achieving this goal."

THE VOLKSWAGEN FOUNDATION

With current assets of $2.6 billion and total giving of $122 million a year,[20] the Volkswagen Foundation ranks in size between Rockefeller and Carnegie among the foundations we have mentioned. In short, it is among the world's biggest. Its endowment, however, did not derive from the gift of one or two wealthy individuals.

> It owes its existence as well as its name to a contractual agreement between the Federal German Government and the State of Lower Saxony which put an end to the controversy concerning the ownership of the Volkswagen company after 1945. Following lengthy discussion, it was decided in the late 1950s to transform the Volkswagenwerk GmbH [the car company] to private ownership by issuing so-called 'people's shares' and use the proceeds from the sale of these shares to establish the Stiftung Volkswagenwerk [the Foundation], as it was called until 1989. * * * By means of prudent and profitable management of its portfolio the Foundation has since increased its initial endowment capital fourfold.[21]

Notwithstanding the origin of its endowment and its name, the Volkswagen Foundation is in no way affiliated to the Volkswagen car manufacturing company. It is separately incorporated under German private law, is economically independent, and is completely autonomous in its decision-making. The fourteen members of its Board of Trustees, appointed to five-year terms, half by the German Federal Government and half by the State of Lower Saxony, are fully independent and are bound only by the Foundation's statutes. They govern the Foundation and decide on its funding initiatives and the distribution of its funds.[22]

The Volkswagen Foundation's funding is directed entirely to higher education and research.

---

[20] See www.volkswagenstiftung.de/english.html, page on Foundation Capital. We have converted euros to dollars at 1.22/1, the prevailing rate at the time of writing.
[21] Ibid., page on Brief History of the Volkswagen Foundation.
[22] Ibid., pages on Foundation Capital and Foundation Structure.

> The Volkswagen Foundation provides financial support to academic institutions in Germany, as well as other countries, and funding is available for projects in all disciplines. Another important part of its mission is to provide support for aspiring young academics, promote international exchange and to enhance the structural conditions for research and higher education. * * * [The Foundation's] support is spread among a great diversity of fields, ranging from interdisciplinary investigation into materials technology to research into endangered languages and to innovative processes in the corporate sector and society, for example.[23]

By defining its own funding initiatives, Volkswagen itself takes a hand in setting the academic research agenda, with a decided emphasis on the *new*:

> The work of the Volkswagen Foundation is not restricted to the mere allocation of funds at applicants' request. The aim of the Foundation is to make the utmost of its funding opportunities, and to inject new impetus into the world of research. * * * [G]enerating impulses which are to have a lasting effect is no easy matter: it can only be accomplished by concentrating the allocation of funds onto a relatively select number of issues. The Volkswagen Foundation has therefore applied the strategy of focusing its efforts on selected funding initiatives. * * * The main thrust is to stimulate new interdisciplinary developments, to assist in creating highly-qualified research capacity, and to establish new, path-breaking fields of research. * * * Whereas the main concept remains stable, the scope of actual funding is changing constantly. Individual funding initiatives are terminated once they have achieved their goal in generating the originally sought for impetus. This makes way for new ideas and initiatives. [This] practice . . . ensures that the Foundation's efforts are constantly turning to new challenges. Thus, only one aspect of the support provided by the Volkswagen Foundation always remains constant – the process of innovation.[24]

---

[23] Ibid., Home Page and page on Foundation Capital.
[24] Ibid., pages on The Foundation, Funding, and Mission and Profile.

Is there anything in this that Nigerians might find controversial? Perhaps so. If you believe, as some seem to, that all essential elements of human knowledge were defined and completed long in the past; that the proper work of scholars now is not to search out new knowledge but rather to preserve and interpret what has come down from of old; that "there is no progress in the history of knowledge, but at most a continuous and sublime recapitulation;" that innovation – in thinking perhaps most especially–is sinful arrogance;[25] – if you believe these things, then you might well regard the Volkswagen Foundation and its mission with the greatest suspicion. Its passion for innovation, its persistent pursuit of progress, of the new, mark it as a creature of the modern West, facing squarely toward the future, not the past.

VOLKSWAGEN'S FUNDING INITIATIVE ON INTER-CULTURAL IDENTITY-SHAPING

In the early 1990s the Volkswagen Foundation announced a new funding initiative, on the subject of "The Foreigner and the Native – Problems and Possibilities of Intercultural Communications." For some years this initiative

> focused on issues of (inter)cultural competence and interaction, especially with respect to the internal German problem areas of relations with migrants (including schools, municipal districts, the police, the judicial authorities).[26]

The aim was to encourage academic research "to utilize its potential and opportunities to establish improved prerequisites for intercultural under-standing, communications and conduct."[27]

---

[25] The quotation in this sentence and some of the other phraseology are from Eco, 1983, 199. Eco puts these views in the mouth of a Christian theologian of the early 14th century, looking back to the work of the Hebrew prophets, the early Christian evangelists, and the fathers and doctors of the Catholic Church. "[B]eyond that there is nothing further to say. There is only to continue meditation, to gloss, to preserve."
[26] www.volkswagenstiftung.de/foerderung/foerderinitiativen/schwerpunkte_e.html, page on Information for Applicants, I.
[27] Ibid.

By the year 2000, the Foundation had concluded that this funding initiative should be reconceived.

> [T]he impending changes at both the academic and the sociopolitical levels are providing new challenges for research. This is particularly the case with regard to the structural change discussed in terms of the keyword 'globalisation', and the attendant transnational interconnections, which bring about ever new forms of conceptualisation, combination and intermixture of 'foreign' and 'native'. Thus, for example, the question arises as to what extent identities can emerge within the framework of the globalisation trends beyond territorial and cultural loyalty and which relevance is, in this context, ascribed to ethnic minorities. Questions of transnationality and transculturalism are also on the agenda.[28]

The reconceived initiative was given a new name: "How Do We Perceive or Shape 'Foreign' and 'Native' Cultural Identities? Research on Processes of Intercultural Dissociation, Mediation and Identity-Shaping." In 2000 the Foundation announced that "it wishes to support research analysing [these] processes." Its call for proposals said, among other things, that:

> Investigating these processes [of intercultural dissociation, mediation, and identity-shaping] and their momentum of change, analysing their premises, conditions, framework, structures, and effects theoretically as well as empirically and with the necessary historical reflection, and thus illuminating them in a problem-oriented perspective – this is the thematic scope of the reconceived priority area. Accordingly, projects which pursue these objectives and address these central points of interest will be given priority. * * * The Foundation is particularly interested in international/intercultural and – insofar as necessitated by the subject matter – interdisciplinary cooperation. * * * It is important to the Foundation that project results are discussed within the framework of an interdisciplinary symposium involving German and non-

---

[28] Ibid.

German representatives from the respective academic and practical fields. In addition, the presentation and conveyance of results in university teaching and to the public is particularly desired.[29]

The reader will observe how broad, how unspecific, one may even say how vague, this call for proposals is: re-read the last several paragraphs and see. Nothing here about Christian-Muslim relations, or Nigeria, or *shari'ah* implementation in Northern Nigeria: these in particular, although no doubt highly relevant to the more general study of "processes of intercultural dissociation, mediation, and identity-shaping," were not Volkswagen's priorities, but ours.[30] For, back in Germany after his year's visit to Jos, Frieder Ludwig saw Volkswagen's new call for proposals, and thought this might be just what he and his colleagues in Jos had been looking for: a source of funding for the deeper study of *shari'ah* implementation in Northern Nigeria that we all wanted to do. Certainly, we were an international and intercultural group of scholars, with diverse national, ethnic, and religious backgrounds and opinions, and we were interdisciplinary as well, coming from the fields of law and religious studies. If our project could be shaped to fit Volkswagen's new funding initiative, we might just have a winning proposal.

THE PROJECT ON "THE *SHARI'AH* DEBATE AND THE SHAPING OF MUSLIM AND CHRISTIAN IDENTITIES IN NORTHERN NIGERIA"

Two people were primarily responsible for the research proposal that our group submitted to the Volkswagen Foundation – Professor

---

[29] Ibid., II, III.
[30] Volkswagen funded a total of 40 projects under the initiative "How Do We Perceive or Shape 'Foreign' and 'Native' Cultural Identities? Research on Processes of Intercultural Dissociation, Mediation and Identity-Shaping": ten in 2000, twelve in 2001, five in 2002 (including ours), twelve in 2003, and only one in 2004, when the initiative was closed out. The entire list of universities receiving grants and their project titles is given at www.volkswagenstiftung.de/foerderung/foederinitiativen/schwerpunkte_e.html, pages on Grants. Some readers may like to review the list and observe the very wide range of countries and topics covered, only one of which–ours–has anything to do with *shari'ah* in Nigeria.

Ulrich Berner, Chair of Religious Studies I, University of Bayreuth, who led the application process and subsequently oversaw administration of the grant, and Frieder Ludwig, who was the principal architect of the proposal. Our special thanks go to both of them. Writing such proposals is no small thing. Far in advance of the project's actual execution, you have got to describe what work you and your colleagues intend to do, in concrete detail, month by month for as long as your project will last. You have got to prepare a budget that corresponds to your workplan and that foresees every expense you will incur – because only rarely can you go back later for more. You must explain what you expect to achieve, and why, from the point of view of the current state of scholarship in your field, that achievement will be worthwhile. Not least, you must show that your project fits the funding objectives of your hoped-for grant-maker – because if it does not it will be rejected out of hand, no matter how worthwhile it may otherwise be. Our own proposal went through several drafts which were discussed and revised via e-mail between Jos and Bayreuth. Finally submitted to the Volkswagen Foundation in February 2002, it was approved in June, much to our gratification, and work began in October 2002. The budget for our projected one year of work was 159,907 €. This was to fund, *first*, an extensive programme of information-gathering and analysis in Nigeria, and to a lesser extent in Europe and America, on *shari'ah* implementation in the North since 1999, its effects on the shaping of Muslim and Christian identities in Nigeria, and its perception abroad; *second*, an academic symposium to be held in Jos half-way through the project, attended by about twenty-five scholars from Nigeria, Europe, and the US, to discuss results so far; and *third*, a second academic symposium to be held in Bayreuth at the end of the project, again attended by about twenty-five scholars from Nigeria, Europe, and the US, to discuss "Religious Tensions in Northern Nigeria: Their Local and Global Dimensions." It was contemplated that one book would emerge from the project; in the end there will be three, of which this is the first to come to press.

Why did the Volkswagen Foundation agree to fund this project? This question was raised later, as part of the controversy surrounding the Jos conference:

Admittedly, Volkswagen Foundation (VF) has an impressive record in funding research and teaching in science and technology, yet one [may] legitimately ask why is VF recently intruding into sensitive issues that matter a lot in the lives of peoples, without cross examining the intricacies that make the project valid, meaningful, and worthwhile.[31]

Muslims find it difficult to understand the reasons behind the massive interest of the West in *shari'ah* implementation, considering the West's open hostility and aversion to Islam and the Muslims especially after the 9/11 incident.[32]

The agenda-setting posture of the West is also evident from the topic of the main study . . ., "The *Shari'ah* Debate and the Shaping of Muslim and Christian Identities in Northern Nigeria." Muslims argue that the topic appears to be an intuitive articulation of the real goal of the study [i.e. to actually shape identities, rather than to study their shaping]. It is observed that secularism, which has de-Islamised the Muslims in the south-western part of Nigeria for instance, does not attract such study, but the very recent development of implementation of the *shari'ah* is so disturbing to the West that many [projects and] conferences have to be funded apparently to nip it in the bud.[33]

While we are not contesting why the University of Jos is the main co-host of the project, but it is apt to ask why other critical universities located at the heart of the *shari'ah* projects are not selected. Or is the conflict-ridden multi-religious Jos society neutral for this kind of research project? Would the project represent their hopes and aspirations? Certainly not.[34]

After what has come before, our responses to these comments and questions can be brief. *Why was the University of Jos selected as the Nigerian co-host of the project?* Because three scholars from the

---

[31] Chairman, Kano State Shari'ah Implementation Advisory Committee, 2004.
[32] Sada, this volume, 177.
[33] Oloyede, this volume, 293-94.
[34] Chairman, Kano State Shari'ah Implementation Advisory Committee, 2004.

University of Jos, together with two colleagues from the University of Bayreuth, went to the trouble of preparing and submitting a research proposal that the Volkswagen Foundation agreed to fund. Scholars from "other critical universities located at the heart of the *shari'ah* projects" were and are free to prepare and submit their own proposals to Volkswagen or any other grant-maker. *Whose project was it?* Not "the West's," and not the Volkswagen Foundation's, but the Jos and Bayreuth scholars' who conceived and executed it. *Why did Volkswagen agree to fund this particular project?* Because it made good sense as a doable, worthwhile, and relatively inexpensive package of academic research and analysis, it fit well with Volkswagen's funding initiative on the study of "processes of intercultural dissociation, mediation, and identity-shaping," and it met the additional criteria of involving international, intercultural, and interdisciplinary cooperation among scholars. *What was the project agenda?* See the first paragraph of this section.

The information-gathering aspect of the project, particularly in Nigeria, went very well. A "Nigeria Team" was constituted – including five Muslims, four Christians, and one "free-thinker."[35] Detailed lists of documents to be sought for, people to be interviewed, and questions to be asked, were prepared. Over thirty trips were then made, to all twelve *shari'ah* states plus Adamawa, Benue, Enugu, Lagos, Nasarawa, Plateau, Taraba, and the Federal Capital Territory of Abuja. Interviews – of which detailed records were made – were conducted with state officials, religious leaders, and laypersons, men and women, Muslims and Christians. Thousands of pages of primary documents were collected, including the reports of several of the state *Shari'ah* Implementation Committees and Councils of *Ulama* on various aspects of *shari'ah* implementation, all *shari'ah*-related legislation enacted by the Houses of Assembly in all twelve *shari'ah* states, many of the *shari'ah*-related bye-laws enacted by Local Government Councils, materials relating to *hisbah* groups and the collection and distribution of *zakat*, the decisions of the courts in

---

[35] The members of the Nigeria team, besides two of the editors of this book, were Dr. Umar H.D. Danfulani, Dr. Musa Gaiya, Mr. Muhammad Daud Abubakar, Miss Rahmat Awal, Dr. J.D. Gwamna, Dr. Sati Fwatshak, Alhaji Muhammad al-Khamis Idris, and Hajiya Khadijah Abdullahi Umar. For their hard work and dedication to the project we extend our warmest thanks.

several important cases,[36] crime statistics covering several years before and several years after *shari'ah* implementation, and more. A great deal of secondary literature was also collected – writings by Nigerian Muslims and Christians on *shari'ah* implementation as they understand its purposes and its effects. We are grateful to the hundreds of people throughout the North and elsewhere in Nigeria who took the time to talk with us at length, freely answered our many questions, and unstintingly gave us the documents we sought. Only rarely in our travels did we encounter any suspiciousness or reluctance to cooperate, and this was usually quickly overcome. Our only regret is that we have not yet found the time to prepare for publication the documents (many of them already hard to find in 2003) and other information we collected. The book containing them, tentatively to be entitled *Shari'ah Implementation in Northern Nigeria 1999-2003*, when it comes out, will be a valuable historical record of this phase of Nigeria's history and a resource for scholars for years to come.

As planned, a conference was held half-way through the project, but for various reasons it met in Bayreuth instead of Jos. Holding on 11 and 12 July, 2003, the Bayreuth conference attracted some forty scholars from Nigeria, Europe, and the US. Its primary aim was to offer members of the project's Nigeria Team the opportunity to present first results of the ongoing research, and eight out of ten were able to attend and made presentations. The project also brought over Dr. Ibrahim Na'iya Sada, the Director of the Centre for Islamic Legal Studies at Ahmadu Bello University,[37] and representatives of two influential NGOs – Mrs. Saudatu Shehu Mahdi, the Secretary-General of the Women Rights Advancement and Protection Alternative (WRAPA),[38] and Dr. Yusufu Turaki of the International Bible Society; all three of these persons also presented papers in Bayreuth and took active parts in the discussions. Another Nigerian contributor was Sanusi Lamido Sanusi, an independent scholar (and a banker in his "day job") who plays an active role in the discussions among Nigeria's Muslims about *shari'ah*. This was the first opportunity many of the rest of the Bayreuth conferees had had to

---

[36] Including the decisions of all tne courts that decided the two controversial *zina* cases of Safiya Husseini and Amina Lawal.
[37] Also a contributor to this volume, 174-77.
[38] Also a contributor to this volume, 1-6.

meet Sanusi; his presentation on "The *Shari'ah* Debate and the Construction of a 'Muslim' Identity in Northern Nigeria"[39] so impressed us that we promptly invited him to be one of the main speakers at our project's Jos conference, which was then in the planning stages. Five other scholars also presented papers in Bayreuth, including Frieder Ludwig. A number of interesting insights emerged from the lively, informative, and sometimes provocative debates that followed each presentation. The papers presented at the Bayreuth conference are also being prepared for publication, under the editorship of Professor Ludwig and Drs. Danfulani and Gwamna of our Nigeria Team.

After the Bayreuth conference, our field research continued in Nigeria, though at a much reduced rate, and attention turned to organising the Jos conference – first set for late December 2003, but later moved to 15 to 17 January, 2004.

THE JOS CONFERENCE

According to our research proposal, the Jos conference should have been another small symposium for academicians: twenty-five or so scholars gathered in a room for two or three days reading papers to each other and talking about them. But it turned out quite otherwise: the Jos conference developed into something much larger, much more open and inclusive not just of academicians but of people from all walks of life – and much more controversial – than we had originally envisioned. Fortunately, prudent management of our project budget meant we had some unspent funds that could be reallocated to the costs of the larger conference. But even so, we still found ourselves short – a problem whose solution only generated additional controversy before and during the conference itself.

Ideas behind the conference

Several related ideas lay behind the enlarged scope of the Jos conference.

- *Freshness.* By late 2003, all of us associated with the project had attended or read the proceedings of any number of *shari'ah* conferences held at venues around Nigeria, seeing the same

---

[39] Sanusi, 2003.

people, hearing the same speakers from the Muslim side and from the Christian side expressing the same ideas and arguments over and over again. We wanted to try for something fresh this time, something that might inject new perspectives, new concepts, new ideas and analyses into the Nigerian discourse about *shari'ah* and perhaps help move the public discussion ahead. This thought led to the invitation mostly of foreign scholars to be main speakers – which definitely brought in new perspectives, ideas, and analyses, but also generated a great deal of controversy at the time of the conference itself.

- *Discussion of neglected topics.* We had some specific ideas about topics we thought were highly relevant to the Nigerian discourse but were being ignored or overly simplified. For instance, the issue of separation of religion and state. Nigerian Christians, arguing against *shari'ah*, have tended to take a strongly separationist view – inspired at least in part by the belief that strict separation of religion and state is what obtains in "modern" or "developed" states – i.e. in the predominantly Christian West. But this is very far from being the case. We thought it would be helpful if an expert on the comparative study of law and religion were brought in to talk about what obtains elsewhere, in hopes of complicating Nigerian thinking and discourse about this issue. In the end, in fact, this matter of the variety of relations between religion and state, and the ways these relations are changing in the present day, became a central theme of the Jos conference.

- *Conference title.* In accordance with the foregoing, we decided to give the conference the title "Comparative Perspectives on *Shari'ah* in Nigeria." If asked, we would have emphasised the *'comparative perspectives'* part of this. Others, however, as we discovered later to our chagrin, saw only the *'shari'ah in Nigeria'* part: a conference on *shari'ah* in Nigeria, and most of the speakers are foreigners! But the focus was never intended to be on Nigeria itself, so much as on the broader global community of which Nigeria is a part – from which "comparative perspectives" on Nigeria are possible. No doubt we did not explain this nearly as clearly as we should have in the lead-up to the conference.

- *Inclusion of a wider audience.* In the tradition of most *shari'ah* conferences in Nigeria, we agreed we should invite the public to attend, rather than limiting the proceedings to a relatively few academicians. This also fit with Volkswagen's objective of "the presentation and conveyance of results in university teaching and to the public," and with our own aim of injecting new perspectives into the Nigerian discourse. to this end we hoped to attract a large audience of both Christians and Muslims from all walks of life.

- *More time for main speakers.* Finally, we decided to abandon the usual rule at academic conferences, according to which speakers (who may have flown half-way around the world to attend) are given only twenty minutes to present their papers. We decided to allow our main speakers forty-five minutes to present, giving them time to develop their themes at greater length; each would be followed by two commentators on their papers and then take questions from the audience.

Main speakers and their themes

Once these basic decisions had been taken, we were able to put together a really first-rate roster of internationally renowned scholars as our main speakers—the authors of the eight papers that form the core of this book.

Cole Durham, of Brigham Young University, a leading expert on religion/state relations around the world, agreed to talk on "Nigeria's 'State Religion' Question in Comparative Perspective." His paper, at pp. 144-167 below, with its valuable taxonomy of religion-state relationships along two axes and its wealth of comparative constitutional information and analysis, will now become essential reading for anyone – judges, lawyers, and laypersons alike – thinking about Section 10 of Nigeria's constitution (barring any "state religion") and its interpretation, as well as for all those interested in knowing more about the wide variety of religion/state relationships that human societies have evolved.

Rosalind Hackett, Distinguished Professor in the Humanities at the University of Tennessee and well known as a scholar of religion in many of its manifestations, spoke on a topic closely related to Durham's – the changing role of religion in the "public sphere." Her paper, "Rethinking the Role of Religion in the Public Sphere: Local and Global Perspectives," at pp. 74-100 below, shows that the impetus for a wider role for *shari'ah* in Nigeria is part of a world-wide drive, in virtually all societies of whatever religious complexion, to "claim recognition for, and the possibilities for implementation of, religious ideas, values, practices, and institutions in the governance of nation-states and the lives of their citizens."

Ruud Peters, of the University of Amsterdam, a leading Western authority on Islamic law, was invited to give a survey of *shari'ah* implementation in the Muslim world today – to frame the drive for *shari'ah* implementation in Nigeria in its wider Islamic setting. His paper, "The Enforcement of God's Law: The *Shari'ah* in the Present World of Islam," at pp. 107-134 below, discusses the nature of *shari'ah* as religious law and as jurists' law, its "Westernisation" in the 19th and early 20th centuries, and finally the current situation: some Muslim societies whose legal systems have been completely secularised, some in which aspects of *shari'ah* are applied within the framework of Westernised legal systems, some now re-Islamising, and some completely Islamised.

Abdullahi An-Na'im, Professor of Law at Emory University, who proved to be our most controversial speaker, gave a searching meditation on "the public role of *shari'ah* in present Islamic societies." His paper, "The Future of *Shari'ah* and the Debate in Northern Nigeria," at pp. 327-357 below, explores the question "how to reconcile the profound and consistent commitment of Muslims to *shari'ah* with the needs of present and future Islamic societies at home, as well as their need for peaceful and cooperative international relations with other societies." His conclusion, that *shari'ah* has a vital role to play "for its foundational role in the socialisation of children, sanctification of social institutions and relationships, and the shaping and development of those fundamental values that can be translated into general legislation and public policy through the democratic political process," but *not* "as a normative system to be enacted and enforced as such by the state as positive law and public policy," will continue to generate heated debate in Nigeria and elsewhere for years to come.

Abdulkader Tayob, of the International Institute for the Study of Islam in the Modern World in the Netherlands, brought these issues of religion/state relationships down to concrete cases, speaking on "The Demand for *Shari'ah* in African Democratisation Processes: Pitfalls or Opportunities?" His paper, at pp. 27-57 below, explores the controversies and crises – very different from country to country

– that have arisen over demands for the implementation of Islamic law, in one form or another, as an element of the processes of democratisation still going on in Kenya, South Africa, and Nigeria.

John Reitz, Professor of International and Comparative Law at the University of Iowa, like Cole Durham was invited to speak on a legal topic central to the Nigerian debate about *shari'ah* – the constitutional guarantee of freedom of religion. There is virtually no Nigerian case-law on this subject. Reitz's paper, "Freedom of Religion and Its Limitations: Judicial Standards for Deciding Particular Cases," at pp. 178-244 below, discusses the analytical tools – the judicial standards – which the European Court of Human Rights, the Canadian and U.S. Supreme Courts, and the German Constitutional Court have developed to guide them in resolving difficult issues about claimed rights to engage in sometimes controversial forms of religious practice. Reitz's paper will become a text-book for students of the comparative constitutional law of religious freedom.

Gerrie ter Haar, of the Institute of Social Studies, the Hague, viewing religion from the social science perspective, as "a human construct, something which has grown among human communities and serves human interests" – a view not intended to contradict the theological or "insider's" perspective on religion but to complement it – examined religion's potential for use as "a tool in the hands of human beings that can be used for good or not-so-good purposes, for constructive or for destructive aims and objectives." Her paper, "Religion: Source of Conflict or Resource for Peace" at pp. 303-320 below, discusses uses of religion for good or ill in a variety of historical, social, and religious settings, in the end placing the responsibility squarely on each of us "to help steer its course in one or the other direction."

Sanusi Lamido Sanusi, active in the Nigerian debates about *shari'ah* but also much exposed to the international scene, was invited to talk about the intense interest foreigners have taken in *shari'ah* implementation in Nigeria. His paper, "The West and the Rest: Reflections on the Intercultural Dialogue about *Shari'ah*," at pp. 251-274 below, in fact analyses three poles of the conversation: (1) "the totality of discourse in contemporary Muslim Northern Nigeria," dominated by politicians, traditional rulers, and religious scholars, including "the declaration of *shari'ah* by a number of state governments and the various real and cosmetic signifiers of this declaration," (2) "the opposition voices from Europe and America, in the form of governments and [NGOs], which have stridently condemned the implementation of *shari'ah* in the name of dogmatic adherence to a Western conception of universal human rights and political values," and (3) the progressive Muslim critics of the Northern discourse, "a group that seems to hang somewhere between the Muslim world and the West" – critical of various aspects of the official Northern discourse on *shari'ah* but equally "suspicious of Western powers and critical of the West's strategic approach to the Muslim world." Sanusi's sophisticated critical analysis of the positions of all sides demands and will repay serious study by all concerned.

Keynotes and commentaries

Our commentators too were a distinguished group in their own right – all but one of them Nigerians or long-time residents of Nigeria, in order to provide Nigerian perspectives on the perspectives brought in from outside; half Muslims and half Christians, in order to ensure balanced representation of the views of both sides. Their presentations, scattered through the pages that follow,[40] not only shed more light on the main papers and the themes they address, but also provide windows onto the preoccupations and concerns of Nigerians at this point in their history.

The two keynote speakers make substantive contributions of their own:

Saudatu Shehu Mahdi, a prominent Nigerian women's rights activist concerned particularly for "the weak and vulnerable, especially women in *shari'ah* jurisdictions," at pp. 1-6 below makes "A Case for Codification of Islamic Personal Law in Nigeria." Mahdi argues that "local customs, laws, and negative value systems continue to encroach upon the implementation [in the *shari'ah* courts] of the pure principles of *shari'ah*," to the detriment especially of women. The remedy she proposes is codification, which "will provide the opportunity for development of *shari'ah* personal law in a manner consistent with the Qur'an and the *hadith* [and will] dispel pressure for its compliance with standards set by parameters other than Islam."

---

[40] Except for three that we have unfortunately been unable to include.

Danny McCain, the other keynote speaker, has lived and taught in Nigeria for many years. His paper, "Which Road Leads Beyond the *Shari'ah* Controversy? A Christian Perspective on *Shari'ah* in Nigeria," at pp. 7-26 below, surveys the roads of mass conversion, confrontation, segregation, and secularism, and rejects them all as being either impossible or undesirable. Arguing that the only real option for Nigerian Muslims and Christians is the road of consensus, McCain makes a series of concrete recommendations for religious leaders on both sides, including the valuable suggestion, illustrated by a programme McCain himself has initiated, that Christians and Muslims begin working together in an organised way to attack such societal ills as HIV/AIDS and corruption.

We fall under suspicion

We spread the word about the conference, and invited people to come, through advertisements in the newspapers and the distribution of many hundreds of invitation cards to people in all parts of the North and elsewhere as well. Here, as we have indicated, we did not do as well as we might have. In the newspapers, speaking as the Faculty of Law and Department of Religious Studies of the University of Jos, we announced a conference on "Comparative Perspectives on *Shari'ah* in Nigeria," "the culmination of a year-long programme of research and writing carried out in conjunction with the Department of Religious Studies at Bayreuth University and sponsored by the Volkswagen Foundation," and we identified the main speakers by name and institutional affiliation. But, the cost of newspaper advertising being what it is, we did not expand on the ideas behind the conference, or explain why these particular speakers had been selected, or even give the titles of their papers. More information went out with the invitation cards – we included with them the full conference programme, which included the titles of the main papers, the names of all the commentators, and, at the back, several paragraphs of information about our research project and its sponsor. We thought that all this information, especially perhaps the titles of the main papers, which reinforced, we thought, the "comparative perspectives" part of the conference title as against the "*shari'ah* in Nigeria" part, and the names of the commentators, including many well-known Nigerian scholars on both sides of the religious divide, would allay suspicions about the conference and our motives in staging it.

But it was not to be. What stuck out, especially to Northern Muslims, was: *foreign – nay, Western – sponsor; Western academics brought in as main speakers; even Western organisers planted at the University of Jos; all presuming to come to preach to us about shari'ah in Nigeria.* There was more. From their names, it was clear that three of the eight main speakers came from Muslim backgrounds. But two of them were well-known to Nigeria's Muslims, and what was known was not much liked. Sanusi Lamido Sanusi, a scion of the house of the Emir of Kano and unquestionably an orthodox Sunni Muslim, was nevertheless considered to be "Westoxicated"– spoiled in his mind by his Western education[41] – and of course had been a long-time gadfly of the Northern Muslim establishment. Abdullahi An-Na'im was worse: not only thoroughly Westernised, but in his religious beliefs a follower of the distinctly unorthodox Mahmoud Mohamed Taha, proclaimer of "The Second Message of Islam" and hanged as an apostate by the government of Sudan in 1985.[42] And then what of Ruud Peters – already known as the author of a book on *shari'ah* in Nigeria critical of its criminal law aspects on human rights grounds.[43] It looked, with some justification, as if the conference deck was stacked against the proponents of *shari'ah* implementation in Northern Nigeria. This was not our intention – as we believe the actual conference and this book demonstrate – but we can see how and why this impression was created and we regret our failure to communicate more clearly in advance what we were about.

And then there was also one more thing again. The immensely increased expenses of the enlarged conference have been mentioned. Savings effected on other parts of the project made up some of this. But we were still short of money. It occurred to us that the Cultural Affairs Section of the US Embassy in Abuja might be willing, under its speakers programme, to sponsor one or two of the four main speakers coming from universities in the US. We proposed this, giving the Embassy full information about the conference (which was then already set) and its principal sponsorship by the Volkswagen

---

[41] Sanusi, this volume, 271.
[42] An-Na'im, this volume, 331 and 354.
[43] Peters, 2003.

Foundation. The Embassy eventually agreed to assist us by sponsoring one of the US-based speakers – in the end this was Professor Durham. This was a great help to us because it freed money we would otherwise have had to spend to bring Durham over, for other conference uses. Durham then spoke not only at our conference, but also, subsequently, in Zaria and Kano, before returning to the US.

So far so good. But now the Embassy, as is usual, put out its own announcement of the fact that it was bringing Durham over, and the announcement got badly garbled in the press. Here it is as it appeared in *ThisDay*, a national daily, a week before the conference:

> **US Embassy**
> The United States Embassy, University of Jos and the National Orientation Agency are organising an International Conference on Sharia. Nigerian and American scholars at the University of Jos will attend the nine-day conference titled "Comparative Perspectives on Sharia in Nigeria."
>
> According to information from the public affairs section of the US Embassy, American scholar Professor Cole Durham of Gates University will participate at the Jos conference by putting an international comparative perspective to the current debate on Sharia in Nigeria.[44]

This little news item is laughably confused – no doubt by some junior *ThisDay* staffer – but many people were not laughing. They thought they detected lies on our part, about who was sponsoring us and our conference, and as the conference came on, this gave them further reason for suspecting that the whole thing was in reality just another manifestation of a Western agenda to subvert Islam.

> Again why one asks, there is the invisible hand of the US Embassy in the project based on the information coming from its Public Affairs [Section] . . . as contained in This Day, Friday, January 9th, Vol. 9, No. 3183, page 3. This calls for deeper probe.[45]

---

[44] *ThisDay*, 9 January, 2004, 3.
[45] Chairman, Kano State Shari'ah Implementation Advisory Committee, 2004.

Muslims in Nigeria are almost unanimous in suspecting the motives of the organisers, particularly when the USA's involvement is alleged. * * * Muslims consider the West as generally hypocritical, deceptive, exploitative, and unjust.[46]

The organisers, the sponsors, the main speakers (seventy percent of whom are Westerners, the others Western bred Muslim apologists) make the conference suspect to Muslims. Only two or three discussants and the participants were to speak for Islam so one wonders what perspectives are in the conference.[47]

The keynote address supposedly from the Muslim side should have been from a well-learned and open-minded person not from others with undue Western influence on 'fabricated' Women's Rights Projects. Clearly, as the Muslim's interest may not be catered for by the proposed keynote speaker, she is undoubtedly not a match to her Christian co-keynote speaker.[48]

The organisation of such and related conferences must always consider basic imperatives to ensure the promotion and integrity of scholarship which we feel the organisers have systematically destroyed and have *undoubtedly said good bye to intellectual integrity, objectivity and fairness.*[49]

[T]he Westerner does not necessarily organise, sponsor or attend a conference such as this in order to understand the Muslims perspectives and perhaps accord it better understanding and respect but to sell his own perspectives and standards. The tuition of Western scholarship, propaganda and indeed entertainment at what ever level and form at all times does not go beyond or fall short of the unavowed goal to prove that the Western races and their civilisation are superior to anything that has or could be produced in the world, and so

---

[46] Oloyede, this volume, 293 and 296.
[47] Al-Wasewi, 2004, 2.
[48] Chairman, Kano State Shari'ah Implementation Advisory Committee, 2004.
[49] Tanko, 2004, Part II, 12 (emphasis in original).

to give a sort of moral justification to the Western quest for domination and material power.[50]

The concern of the European Union and Western multinational corporations is . . . not for the so-called victims of Shari'ah Laws but how to ultimately make European libertarian values universal values. So that religiously inspired laws will become obsolete and for example same sex marriages will become acceptable. People will become Europeanised and eventually justify western dominion and looting of the resources of Africans and other oppressed peoples. Volkswagen Foundation and the US Government supported the conference not for academic reasons but for ideological reasons.[51]

And it wasn't only the Muslims who were suspicious of us either. There was also a groundswell of opinion among Christian indigenes of Plateau State – at least in and around Jos – of which we heard from security agents, that far from being anti-*shari'ah*, the conference was actually part of an Islamic agenda to bring *shari'ah* to Plateau State.[52] Fortunately this idea was quelled before it did any damage.

The Jos conference

Muslim suspicions might have led them to boycott the conference, but instead the opposite happened: Muslims turned out in large numbers from all over the North.

[S]ome states like Kano, Jigawa and Bauchi published the conference over their local radio stations and urged Muslims to attend and make positive contributions to defend the cause of shari'ah . . .[53]

On the day the conference started, the Kano State Shari'ah Implementation Advisory Committee took out a full-page advertorial in the *Daily Trust*, a national daily read widely by Muslims, to express

---

[50] Al-Wasewi, 2004, 2.
[51] Ado-Kurawa, 2004, 4–5.
[52] Also remarked in Garba, 2004, 25.
[53] Tanko, Part II, 12.

its concerns, several of which have been quoted above, and to remind everyone that

> Shari'ah is a deeply seated and fundamental pillar in the lives of Muslims. It is not a trivial matter. The conference should open up dialogue and transparent understanding for all religions and cultures. * * * The project should not stir up controversy, misgivings or mistrust. The project on "Shari'ah Debate" should not be presumptuous based on the premise of either demonising or deconstructing the structure and process of worship (Shari'ah) of millions of Muslims that populate this great nation.[54]

We hope and believe that we lived up to these admonitions. The Kano State government also sent a delegation led by Shaykh Ibrahim Kabo, the Chairman of its Shari'ah Implementation Advisory Committee; several members of this delegation, including Shaykh Kabo, took active parts in the proceedings. Altogether, over nine hundred people signed the registration books, and we reckon that there were an average of five or six hundred in the hall at any given time. Besides the large turn-out of Muslims, many Christians also came, from many parts of the country but predominantly from the various seminaries and colleges in and around Jos; and of course many students and staff of the University of Jos, Christians and Muslims, also attended. We also had a smattering of Europeans and Americans (in addition to the invited speakers), some of whom came great distances just to attend the conference. Our thanks go to all these people, not only for braving all hazards to come, but for their spirited participation in the discussions.

Besides exceeding our wildest expectations in terms of attendance, how successful may we judge the conference to have been? Let us ask the question this way: how open were the audience to the often complex ideas and analyses articulated by the speakers? – Not: how open to *accepting* them, necessarily – this is not the point – but how open at least to *understanding* them and grappling with them on more or less their own terms?

---

[54] Chairman, Kano State Shari'ah Implementation Advisory Committee, 2004.

By this measure the conference was only a modest success. Some in the audience, of course, came already "knowing" what they would hear, with minds firmly shut and a determination only to resist. The larger problem, however, was different: it was the novelty of the academic discourses which many in the audience – on both sides of the religious divide – were encountering for the first time: the *refusal* of the speakers to simplify, trivialise, demonise, or presume; their insistence, rather, on complexities, uncertainties, and the seriousness of the subjects at hand; their use of concepts and methods of thinking, distinctions and abstractions unfortunately all too foreign to Nigerian discourse at any level. The Nigerians have a saying: "Too much English!", and this was very true of our conference. Even for the most open-minded, the papers presented difficulties of comprehension that only further reading and study can hope to overcome.

Nevertheless, for many, particularly the students in the audience, the conference was "a lovely and fantastic effort towards boosting learning."[55] And as one of our reviewers said,

> For the sake of intellectual life in Nigeria, where a number of no-go areas need to be opened up, it was clearly worth the effort and the heat of arguments provoked.[56]

And furthermore: all the more reason for this book! For despite their difficulties, the papers presented at the conference, now revised, edited, and published here, deal with issues with which Nigerians must eventually come to terms in ways more complicated and informed than they are doing now. Our hope is that this book will succeed, more than the conference from which it stems, in helping to bring this result about.

THIS BOOK

In conclusion, two brief comments on the book itself.

Spelling of Arabic words. We have adopted a perhaps old-fashioned system of spelling Arabic words: *shari'ah* instead of *shari'a* or just plain *sharia*, for example. We did this because the system adopted seems to

---

[55] Garba, 2004, 25.
[56] Harneit-Sievers, 2004, 8.

be the one preferred in Nigeria. But in proper names, titles of publicatons, and quotations we have left spellings as we found them.
Lists of references. We have placed lists of references at the end of each contribution – main papers, commentaries, this introduction. There is in fact very little overlap among the lists of references, and we considered that on balance it was preferable that an author's references be identified with his or her paper rather than merged in a general list at the back of the book.

REFERENCES

Note: websites referred to in the footnotes are not mentioned again here.

Ado-Kurawa, Ibrahim, *Jos international conference on comparative perspectives on the Shari'ah in Nigeria*, Kano: Trans West Africa Limited, 2004.

Al-Wasewi, Ibrahim Harun Hasan, "The international conference on comparative perspectives on shariah in Nigeria and a closer look at the views of a western Muslim in *Islam at the Crossroads*", 2-page paper distributed at the conference on "Comparative Perspectives on S*hari'ah* in Nigeria", copy with the editors.

Arjomand, Said Amir, "Philanthropy, the law, and public policy in the Islamic world before the modern era", in Ilchman, Katz, and Queen, 1998, 109-132.

Barber, Putnam, *Accountability: a challenge for charities and fundraisers*, San Francisco, Ca. : Jossey-Bass Publishers, 2002.

Bendjilali, Boualem (ed.), *La Zakat et le Waqf: Aspects historiques, juridiques, institutionnels et économiques*, Djeddah: Institut Islamique de Recherches et de Formation (IIRF), 1998.

Chairman, Kano State Shari'ah Implementation Advisory Committee, "Cause for concern over a lopsided and unbalanced 'International Conference on Comparative Perspectives on Shari'ah in Nigeria'", advertorial appearing in the *Daily Trust*, 15 January 2004, 33.

Danfulani, Umar, "Expected obstacles and attendant problems in the execution of shariah in Northern Nigeria: a critical analysis", *HUMANITY: Jos Journal of General Studies*, November 2000, 1-15.

Danfulani, Umar, Philip Ostien, and Frieder Ludwig, "The sharia controversy and Muslim-Christian relations in Nigeria", *Jahrbuch für Kontextuelle Theologien 2002*, 70-95.

Downie, Mark, *American foundations: an investigative history*, Cambridge, Mass: MIT, 2001.

Eco, Umberto, *The Name of the Rose*, New York: Harcourt Brace Jovanovich, 1983.

Feierman, Steven, "Reciprocity and assistance in precolonial Africa", in Ilchman, Katz, and Queen, 1998, 3-24.

Foundation Center, *Foundation grants index*, New York, N.Y. : Foundation Center, annual.

Garba, Ahmad, "A critique on the Jos international conference on *shari'ah* in Nigeria", *New Nigerian*, September 24, 2004, 25.

Ghanim, Ibrahim al-Bayumi (ed.), *Nizam al-waqf wa'l-mujtama` al-madani fi'l-watan al-`arabi*, Bairut: Markaz dirasat al-wahdah al-`arabiyyah/al-Amanah al-`ammah li-l-awqaf bi-daulat Kuwait, 2004.

Glass, Sandra A., ed., *Approaching foundations: suggestions and insights for fundraisers*, San Francisco, Cal.: Jossey-Bass, 2000.

Harneit-Sievers, Axel, "Encounters and no-go areas in the Nigeria sharia debate", *Daily Trust*, January 30, 2004, 7-8.

Hodgson, Marshall G.S., *The venture of Islam: conscience and history in a world civilization*, vol. 2, *The expansion of Islam in the middle periods*, Chicago: University of Chicago Press, 1974.

Hopkins, Bruce R. and Jody Blazek, *Private foundations: tax law and compliance*, New York, N.Y. : John Wiley, 1997.

Ilchman, Warren F., Stanley N. Katz, and Edward L. Queen, II, eds., *Philanthropy in the world's traditions*, Bloomington, IN: Indiana University Press, 1998.

Kiger, Joseph C., *Philanthropic foundations in the twentieth century*, Westport, Ct.: Greenwood Press, 2000.

Kogelmann, Franz, *Islamische fromme Stiftungen und Staat: der Wandel in den Beziehungen zwischen einer religiösen Institution und dem marokkanischen Staat seit dem 19. Jahrhundert bis 1937*, Würzburg: Ergon, 1999.

_____, "Some aspects of the development of the Islamic pious endowments in Morocco, Algeria and Egypt in the 20th century", in Randi Deguilhem and Abdelhamid Hénia (eds.), *Les fondations pieuses (waqf) en Méditerranée enjeux de société, enjeux de pouvoir*, Kuwait: Kuwait Awqaf Public Foundation, 2004, 343-393.

Kozlowski, Gregory C., "Religious authority, reform, and philanthropy in the contemporary Muslim world", in Ilchman, Katz, and Queen, 1998, 279-308.

Ludwig, Frieder, "Christlicher Revival und Islamische Erneuerung in Nigeria", *Dialog der Religionen* 1997/1, 79–85.

_____, "Religion und Politik im Kontext multireligiöser afrikanischer Staaten am Beispiel Nigerias", *Hallesche Beiträge zur Orientwissenschaft* 31, 2001, 249–270.

McIlnay, Dennis P., *How foundations work: what grantseekers need to know about the many faces of foundations*, San Francisco, Ca.: Jossey-Bass, 1998.

Nasir, J.M., "CEDAW and women under sharia", *Current Jos Law Journal*, 5/5, 1999, 20-33.

Oloyede, Is-Haq, "Commentary" on Sanusi Lamido Sanusi, "The West and the Rest: Reflections on the Intercultural Dialogue about S*hari'ah*", this volume, 292-302.

Ostien, Philip, *A study of the court systems of Northern Nigeria, with a proposal for the creation of lower sharia courts in some northern states*, Jos: Centre for Development Studies, University of Jos, 1999.

_____, "Islamic criminal law: what it means in Zamfara and Niger states", *Journal of Public and Private Law* (University of Jos) 4/4, 2000, 1-18.

_____, "Ten good things about the implementation of *shari'ah* in some states of Northern Nigeria", *Swedish Missiological Themes*, 90/2, 2002, 163-174.

Peebles, Jane, *Handbook of international philanthropy*, Chicago, Il.: Bonus Books, 1998.

Peters, Ruud, "Waqf", in P.J. Pearman, Th. Bianquis, C.E. Bosworth, E. van Donzel and W.P. Heinrichs (eds.), *The Encyclopaedia of Islam New Edition*, Volume XI, W-Z, Leiden: Brill, 2002, 58-63.

_____, *Islamic Criminal Law in Nigeria*, Ibadan: Spectrum Books Limited, 2003.

Renz, Loren, *International grantmaking: a report on U.S. foundation trends*, The Foundation Center in cooperation with the Council on Foundations. New York, N.Y.: Foundation Center, 1997.

Ries, Joanne B. and Carl G. Leukfeld, *Applying for research funding: getting started and getting funded*, Thousand Oaks, Ca.: Sage, 1995.

Sada, Ibrahim Na'iya, "Commentary" on W. Cole Durham, Jr., "Nigeria's 'State Religion' Question in Comparative Perspective", this volume, 174-77.

Salamon, Lester M. et al., *Global civil society: dimensions of the nonprofit sector*, Baltimore, MD : Johns Hopkins Center for Civil Society Studies, 1999.

Sanusi, Sanusi Lamido, "The *shari'ah* debate and the construction of a 'Muslim' identity in Northern Nigeria: A critical perspective", www.gamji.com/sanusi.htm, 2003.

_____, "The west and the rest: reflections on the intercultural dialogue about *shari'ah*", this volume, 251-74.

Schneiter, Paul H., *The art of asking: how to solicit philanthropic gifts*, Ambler, Pa.: Fund-Raising Institute, 2nd edition, 1985.

Tanko, Sani B., "Comparative perspective on shariah", *Weekly Trust*, Part I: February 7-14, 2004, 12; Part II: February 14-20, 2004, 12.

Ter Haar, Gerrie, "Religion: source of conflict or resource for peace?", this volume, 303-320.

Weiss, Holger (ed.), *Social welfare in Muslim societies in Africa*, Uppsala: Nordiska Afrikainstitutet (The Nordic Africa Institute), 2002.

Women's Rights in *Shari'ah*: A Case for Codification of Islamic Personal Law in Nigeria

Saudatu Shehu Mahdi

I am honoured and humbled by the invitation to deliver a keynote address before the august and rich community of scholars and researches assembled here today. I also want to commend the organisers, the Faculty of Law and the Department of Religious Studies of the University of Jos, and the sponsors, the Volkswagen Foundation, for facilitating an open and constructive dialogue aimed at bringing about a broader understanding and enhanced implementation of the *shari'ah* legal system in Nigeria. The conference topic, "Comparative Perspectives on *Shari'ah* in Nigeria" is not only apt at this stage of the implementation of *shari'ah* in Nigeria but an opportunity for all stakeholders in *shari'ah* matters (implementing jurisdictions, scholars and researchers, the judiciary, the Muslim *ummah* and adherents of faiths other than Islam) to be availed with perspectives and practices of *shari'ah* beyond our own territories. The benefits of such an interaction would among others be to objectively crystallise what the issues around *shari'ah* are, what we in Nigeria have done so far, how other *shari'ah* jurisdictions in Africa and the East are doing it, and above to all draw appropriate and compatible lessons that will enhance our own *shari'ah* practices in Nigeria.

Comparative perspectives of *shari'ah* must take cognisance of the basic Islamic framework for the system, which is not limited or moulded by geography or culture. It must also bear in mind the different contextual (political, social, and economic) issues in the different jurisdictions, which ultimately fashion the parameters for enjoyment and enforcement of its provisions. The periodic reform of the law (based on knowledge and dialogue) is another factor. This accommodates change and provides for the adoption of new and progressive provisions that sustain the universality of Islam. There must also exist the basic framework for the application of *shari'ah* law, which is *social justice* underscored by fundamental Islamic values of justice, benevolence and compassion (*'adl, ihsan* and *rahmah*).

Shari'ah or Islamic law, in Nigeria and indeed in the Muslim world, is an issue that is inseparable from the declaration of Islam as a faith. However, what has emerged in time is its graded application, variously, in totally Islamic, semi-secular, or totally secular states. The historical evolution of states, the struggle for identity by their citizens, global secular trends, and internal and external political pressures have to a large extent determined the level of application of *shari'ah* law or even the practice of Islam.

In the Muslim world today, states can be characterised into four groups by their varying use of Islamic law. First, there are states in which religion is separated from law in virtually all areas. A good example is Turkey, where there has been almost a complete separation of law and religion since the 1920's. Second are the states that apply non-religious law in all areas with only a few limited exceptions. In these states, Islamic courts exist, but generally have jurisdiction only over consenting Muslims who have family or inheritance law disputes. Examples include Indonesia, Jordan, Oman, Ethiopia (except in Oromo region), Tunisia and Morocco. Nigeria was in this category until 1999-2000 when 12 of its 36 states expanded the jurisdiction of *shari'ah* to include criminal law. Third are states that apply Islamic law universally except in one or more specific areas, such as certain forms of capital punishment and/or certain areas of the *shari'ah* that regulate business activities. Examples include Kuwait, UAE, Qatar, and Libya. Fourth are the states that apply strict Islamic law with no exceptions. Examples include Iran, Saudi Arabia, Sudan and Somalia.

Reforms in *shari'ah* law must of necessity be continuous and informed by research and recognition of changes in the social setting. Over time, Muslims have struggled in countless ways to reinterpret, protect, deconstruct, modernise or stabilise their faith in response to sometimes overwhelming pressures from an outside world intent on ceaseless material and social adventure. A majority have opted for a broadly conservative stance that tolerates technological and political change, but frowns on any radical reworking of social or intellectual structures, much less of religious or religio-legal forms. Others, fewer in number, have attempted a more far-reaching re-think of how

Muslim communities should live, seeing modernity as a challenge that offers Islam the possibility of deep internal renewal. Reforms in these communities rely on *ijtihad* (i.e. exerting oneself in knowledge and application) to address contemporary issues where no precise guidance was available in the Qur'an and Prophet's Sunnah. What does the above imply for the weak and vulnerable, especially women in *shari'ah* jurisdictions? The balance between theory and practice is of great concern. This is compounded by the rigid stance of those who view emerging proposals to accord women recognition as "alien" and at worst as anti-Islamic. Some even go so far as to reject provisions in national, regional and international statutes that are based on the same principles in Islam which accord human dignity and certain rights for women. As Ali Asghar Engineer has said:

> The greatest resistance, in the name of *shari'ah*, is manifested by men when it comes to according better status to women. In this respect the *shari'ah* becomes sacred and immutable and arouses great passions. The Islamic world, if it has to understand the dynamic spirit of Qur'an, and enact it in real life, will have to enact changes in the *shari'ah* laws and accord women an equal status.[1]

Improvement in the lot of women under *shari'ah* jurisdictions entails reforms through development especially of personal law in a manner consistent with the Qur'an and the *hadith* augmented by *ijtihad*. Development of *shari'ah* personal law has occurred in many Muslim countries through the enactment of codes. Some were a reaction to the social changes that have come with the modernisation of economies and political systems. Other reforms were effected in the quest for the pure application of Islamic law by governments, enhancement of the administration of justice as well as access to justice by all especially the vulnerable members of society, women and the poor. Of thirty-eight countries with predominantly or very substantial Muslim populations only seven (18%) have not codified any part of their personal status laws.[2] Twenty-five (66%) have

---

[1] Engineer, 2003, 9-10.
[2] Nigeria, Bahrain, Gambia, Oman, Qatar, Saudi Arabia, and the United Arab Emirates.

codified all parts of the law regarding personal status for their Muslim citizens.[3] The remaining six (16%) have codified the Islamic personal status laws in part.[4] These numbers show that the majority of countries have completely codified, or have begun to codify, their personal status laws. In codifying, these countries have created codes that encompass the classical jurisprudence of their respective schools of law (either Hanafi, Maliki, Shafi'i, or Hanbali) and have made provisions that take contextual realities as factors for the administration of Islamic personal law.

In Nigeria only Islamic criminal law is codified. It is a settled fact that *shari'ah* provides women full human, social, and economic rights and in many situations provides special means to ensure that the rights are respected. However, local customs, laws, and negative value systems continue to encroach upon the implementation of the pure principles of *shari'ah*. The personal status laws as currently practised in Nigeria breach both the letter and the spirit of *shari'ah*. An avenue for improvement is the codification of Islamic personal law in order to enhance the level of enjoyment of the rights of women, which are most vulnerable in the area of domestic relations. Codification in accordance with the tenets of the Qur'an and *hadith* is imperative for the following reasons:

1. It will provide greater understanding of rights and responsibilities regarding marriage, maintenance, divorce, and custody within the family and society.
2. It will ensure that women enjoy the rights granted to them by Allah within the framework of *shari'ah* at all levels and in all instances of family life.
3. It will ensure that implementation of the law as is truly Islamic and not an arbitrary hybrid of principles derived from non-authoritative interpretations, traditions and customs, and the whims of individuals.

---

[3] Algeria, Egypt, Iraq, Jordan, Kuwait, Bangladesh, Libya, Morocco, Indonesia, Israel, Kenya, Lebanon, Malaysia, the Philippines, Singapore, Palestine, Somalia, Sri Lanka, Sudan, Syria, Pakistan, Tunisia, Yemen. Senegal and Tanzania have incorporated classical Islamic family law into their civil codes.

[4] Brunei, Ethiopia, Ghana, India, Iran, and Maldives. Ghana has codified only matters relating to the registration of marriage and divorce.

4. It will provide standards, consistency and enhance the administration of justice. Judges (especially at the lower courts) will be guided by the well-researched code thereby reducing the constraints of scarce literature, which even where available is in classical voluminous Arabic texts.

In sum, it will provide the opportunity for development of *shari'ah* personal law in a manner consistent with the Qur'an and the *hadith*. Through this, the principles of *shari'ah* personal law will be brought to bear to dispel pressure for its compliance with standards set by parameters other than Islam. The purity of Islamic law will be preserved and safeguarded from encroachment by extraneous influences that most times fail to put value to the peculiarities in different jurisdictions.

Ladies and gentlemen, I am not a paper presenter; therefore I want to conclude thus. There is currently a struggle going on for the preservation of Muslim identity, indeed of Islam itself and its laws and practices, in a world led by global "security," political, economic, and secular considerations. We here in Nigeria are playing our parts in this struggle, and we must and will continue to do so. My point is simply that as we do, we must not lose sight of the need to focus on the entrenchment of the fundamental Islamic values of human dignity and justice for all. I hope that the presentations and discussions that take place here at this conference will contribute to that happy outcome.

Thank you for your kind attention and I wish us a happy and successful conference.

REFERENCES

Engineer, Asghar Ali, "Islam, women, and gender justice", a paper presented at the International Conference on *Shari'ah* Penal and Family Laws in Nigeria and in the Muslim World: A Rights Based Approach, organised by the International Human Rights Law Group, (GLOBAL RIGHTS) Abuja, with support from the German Embassy, held in Abuja, 5-7 August, 2003.

Gravelle, Kent Benedict, *Islamic Law in Sudan: A comparative analysis*, http://www.nsulaw.nova.edu/student/student_organizations/ILSAJournal/issues/5-1/Gravelle%205-1.htm.

Ladan, Mohammed Tawfiq, "Legal pluralism and the development of the rule of law in Nigeria: issues and challenges in the development and application of the *shari'ah*", a paper presented at the International Conference on *Shari'ah* Penal and Family Laws in Nigeria and in the Muslim World: A Rights Based Approach, organised by the International Human Rights Law Group, (GLOBAL RIGHTS) Abuja, with upport from the German Embassy, held in Abuja, 5-7 August, 20u3.

MacEoin, Denis, "Deconstructing and reconstructing the *shari'ah*: The Babi and Baha'i solutions to the problem of immutability", http://bahai-library.com/id.php?id 1441, posted 26 October, 2003.

Mahdi, Saudatu, "The need for codification of *shari'ah* personal law in Nigeria", a brief to the Attorneys General of Sokoto and Zamfara States, 2003 (unpublished).

_____, "Women's rights and access to justice", a paper presented at the International Conference on *Shari'ah* Penal and Family Laws in Nigeria and in the Muslim World: A Rights Based Approach, organised by the International Human Rights Law Group, (GLOBAL RIGHTS) Abuja, with support from the German Embassy, held in Abuja, 5-7 August, 2003.

Which Road Leads Beyond the *Shari'ah* Controversy? A Christian Perspective on *Shari'ah* in Nigeria

Danny McCain

"Blessed are the peacemakers, for they will be called sons of God" (Matthew 5:9). These were the words of Jesus during his first major address. Although there are many things Jesus could have stressed in the early part of his ministry, he stressed peace.

This scripture means that whenever there is a controversy between two persons or within a family or in the society, the Christian response should always be to seek for a peaceful solution. And Jesus says a special blessing is promised to those who seek peace.

The road we have travelled since the introduction of *shari'ah* in twelve Northern Nigerian states has been a rough one. It has not improved the peace in this region. Christians have responded to *shari'ah* with resignation, fear, frustration, and anger that has sometimes boiled over into violence. But Jesus calls us to peace. So what must we do to make sure there is peace in our society?

I believe our experiment with *shari'ah* here in Northern Nigeria has led us to a junction from which five roads lead. Which of those roads will lead to that peace that both Christianity and Islam teach? We have travelled down all five roads a bit but have not yet chosen one and excluded the others. In this address I want to present a Christian perspective on these five roads.

CONVERSION

The first option is the road of conversion. One of the last things Jesus said was "go and make disciples of all nations, baptising them in the name of the Father and of the Son and of the Holy Spirit, and teaching them to obey everything I have commanded you" (Matthew 28:19-20). One of the main convictions of Christianity is that

Christians should share the good news of God's kingdom with all the nations of the world and try to persuade everyone in the world to become a follower of Jesus. Islam has similar convictions.

And herein lies much of the tension between Christianity and Islam. Both religions are evangelistic in nature. Both are attempting to solidify their positions in Nigeria and to gain more ground. Islam is pushing hard to win Nigeria's Middle Belt for Islam and Christians are aggressively evangelising Muslims, even in the core North.

Although conversion to one religion or the other would solve the *shari'ah* debate, it is not a realistic possibility in the foreseeable future. Both Christianity and Islam are very firmly rooted in Nigeria and neither is going away. We must recognise that the immediate conversion of all those in other religions is unrealistic. Thus, we must embrace one of the other options.

CONFRONTATION

The most visible response to the *shari'ah* debate that Nigeria has experienced to this point has been the road of confrontation. The perception of many Christians is that *shari'ah* was not introduced through the mosque, so Muslims could truly practice their religion. It was introduced through politics so Muslims could marginalize Christians in Muslim-dominated areas and embarrass and put pressure on the "Christian" government.

The response by Christians has all too often been to shout at Muslims and even abuse Islamic images, including the word '*shari'ah*.' This kind of confrontation has often escalated and led to physical violence. The catastrophe which Kaduna experienced in February 2000 is a good example of what happens when there is this type of confrontation. Hundreds of lives were lost; thousands of homes and businesses were destroyed. Almost a thousand churches and mosques were destroyed, damaged or defaced during that confrontation. Unfortunately, the Kaduna crisis, which was directly linked to proposals to introduce *shari'ah* in Kaduna State, has fuelled the rumour mills in parts of Northern Nigeria with horrible stories of atrocities and this has led to other crises.

Although this may not be obvious to the average Muslim in Northern Nigeria, this kind of violent confrontation is not a legitimate option for the Christian. Although warfare was allowed and even authorised by God for the Jews in the Old Testament period, when Jesus came to this world, he instituted a new kind of kingdom. This was a kingdom that was to be superimposed upon other nations without replacing them. Individual nations would maintain their sovereignty. They would field armies and police forces that confront evildoers and mete out justice but Jesus made it clear that individual Christians were not to defend his causes with violence.

Jesus' statements about violence are well known. Perhaps the most well known is where Jesus said, "You have heard that it was said, 'Eye for eye, and tooth for tooth.' But I tell you, do not resist an evil person. If someone strikes you on the right cheek, turn to him the other also" (Matthew 5:38-39). Jesus not only taught about non-violence, he practised what he preached. When his disciples produced a sword to defend him while being arrested, Jesus said, "Put your sword back in its place . . . for all who draw the sword will die by the sword" (Matthew 26:52).

Some Christians have attempted to justify a violent response to violence by appealing to Jesus' words in Luke 22:36: "He said to them, 'But now if you have a purse, take it, and also a bag; and if you don't have a sword, sell your cloak and buy one.'" Anyone versed in Semitic languages and culture knows that this was a common Hebrew way of telling his disciples to prepare for violence. It is an idiom similar to Jesus' statement, "If anyone comes to me and does not hate his father and mother, his wife and children, his brothers and sisters – yes, even his own life – he cannot be my disciple" (Luke 14:26). This statement certainly did not mean one was literally to hate his family members. It was a Semitic way of showing that one should be more committed to Christ than to his family. A fundamental rule in communication is that we interpret figures of speech in light of clear passages. Therefore, Jesus' statements about taking up a sword, in light of all his clear teachings on violence, simply mean his disciples should prepare themselves for the coming violence that would result from being a new minority religion.

Although Jesus very clearly taught against violence, unfortunately the Christian Church has not always followed his teachings. These inconsistencies are well known. However, these historical shortcomings do not excuse us from applying Jesus' teachings in our own situation.

Though Jesus did not remove from governments the responsibility to protect their citizens, with violence if necessary, he did remove that right from individual Christians.[1] Therefore, for a Christian to respond to the *shari'ah* issue by attacking Muslims or destroying mosques is not a legitimate option for the Christian. In fact, the Bible consistently teaches that violence is evil and wrong. It not only destroys the society but ultimately hinders the progress of the Christian church.

All Christians and Christian leaders in Northern Nigeria should fully embrace Jesus' teachings about peace and violence and teach them to their followers. We must reject violence in all its forms. However Christians may choose to respond to *shari'ah*, the teachings of Jesus make clear that violence is not an option.

SEGREGATION

The third road leading from the junction at which we find ourselves is the road of segregation. Because of violence and discrimination, some Christians are moving to predominantly Christian areas and some Muslims are moving to predominantly Muslim areas. Christian families who have lived for generations in Northern Nigeria no longer feel safe there and are leaving. In a similar way, some Muslims have sensed a new antagonism in the South and are moving North. Of course, the ultimate example of segregation would be the division of Nigeria with one country being made out of the Christian South and another country made out of the Muslim North.

Is segregation what we want? Is segregation what is best for us? Is segregation what our religions teach? I will allow my Muslim colleagues to explain what Islam teaches about the responsibility of Muslims toward those who practise a different faith. I will say a few words about the Biblical response to this issue.

---

[1] Christian theologians have differed on the issue of personal self-defence. Some insist on total passivity. The majority position, however, would teach that it is legitimate for an individual Christian to defend himself or his family against an armed robbery or other personal attack or threat.

Old Testament Legislation about Aliens

In the Old Testament period, the Mosaic law demanded that the nation of Israel should be hospitable and treat fairly those non-Israelites among them. Exodus 22:21 says, "Do not mistreat an alien or oppress him, for you were aliens in Egypt." An even stronger statement is found in Leviticus 19:34: "The alien living with you must be treated as one of your native-born. Love him as yourself, for you were aliens in Egypt." One of the reasons the prophets condemned Israel in its later history was because she had ignored this command. Malachi 3:5 says,

> "So I will come near to you for judgment. I will be quick to testify against sorcerers, adulterers and perjurers, against those who defraud labourers of their wages, who oppress the widows and the fatherless, and deprive aliens of justice, but do not fear me," says the Lord Almighty.

It is amasing that God considered mistreating aliens in the same category as sorcery, adultery, perjury, abusing labourers and taking advantage of widows and orphans.

We must recognise that though Christianity accepts both the Old and New Testament as authoritative, we no longer have a sacred nation of which we are a part. Jesus came to introduce a new kind of kingdom – a spiritual kingdom that would be superimposed on other nations without interfering with the governments of those nations.

How do we Christians interpret and apply the Old Testament? We look for principles that were part of the nation of Israel, which can be applied to our modern world. The Old Testament principles related to aliens imply that God expected His followers to accommodate and be fair to anyone living among them who was different.

New Testament Teachings about "Non-Christians"

Does the New Testament support this teaching? Because of the nature of the kingdom Jesus came to introduce, the New Testament reveals that there is even greater flexibility in interacting with "unbelievers." Jesus recognised that, at least at first, Christianity would be a minority religion. The emphasis that Jesus and the early apostles made was that Christians were to be a positive influence on any society that was non-Christian. Jesus said that we were to be "in the world" but not really "of the world" (John 15:19; 17:11; 14-16). In other words, we were to be part of the mainstream part of society but we were not to allow the evil influences of the world to be a part of us.

Jesus raised the standard even higher than it was practised in the Old Testament period. He reiterated the teaching, "love your neighbour as yourself" (Leviticus 19:18; Matthew 19:19; 23:39) but was even more specific. "Love your enemies, do good to those who hate you, bless those who curse you, pray for those who mistreat you" (Luke 6:27). He added later, "But love your enemies, do good to them, and lend to them without expecting to get anything back." Even if we consider our neighbours to be our enemies, there is to be no segregation. We should treat them with kindness.

Jesus spent much time visiting non-Jewish areas, including Tyre, Samaria, Decapolis and other predominantly Gentile places. This shows his interest in the whole world. One of his most well-known stories is about a Samaritan who is presented in a very positive light, even though he would have practised a different kind of religion than the Jews. These kinds of positive statements about those who were not Jesus' followers demonstrate the kinds of attitudes Christians should have toward non-Christians.[2]

Segregation is not in the best interest of Christianity. It is not in the best interest of Nigeria. And I do not believe it is in the best interest of Islam either.

---

[2] The issue of potential segregation along ethnic lines did arise in the early church period. One hundred percent of the early Christians were Jews. And the Jews wanted to continue the policy of separation they had practised for generations. This was illustrated by their insistence on making circumcision a requirement for Gentile believers. Even some of the apostles were temporarily swept up into this very narrow position (Galatians 2:11-14). Had this issue been allowed to continue, it would have led to the segregation of the Jewish part of the church from the Gentile part of the church. See the Book of Galatians and the Jerusalem Council (Acts 15) for the way the early church resolved this problem and avoided segregation.

SECULARISM

A fourth road available to Nigeria is the superhighway of secularism. Secularism has been defined as "a system which seeks to interpret and order life on principles taken solely from this world, without recourse to belief in God and a future life."[3] In a popular sense, secularism refers to the separation of religious practices from public life. This implies little or no overlap between the church or mosque and the state. Secularism is usually promulgated for one of at least two reasons. First, if one does not believe in God or believes God is irrelevant to society, naturally that person would promote secularism.

Second, secularism, as it was originally developed in America, was promoted to protect religion, particularly the minority religions. If one religion is recognised and funded by the government, this means that the minority religions help to finance the majority. This is viewed as inherently unfair to the minority religions in Western countries.

An African application of this is to say that, in a multi-religious society such as Nigeria, it is not government's responsibility to underwrite the expenses of the *hajj* or pilgrimages to Jerusalem. The government's responsibility is to make sure that there is no obstacle in the way of anyone wanting to make a religious pilgrimage. The government should expedite the production of passports and foreign exchange for pilgrims. However, pilgrimages are purely religious affairs. It is unfair to require Christian taxpayers to help underwrite the expenses of Muslims going to Mecca or for Muslim taxpayers to help underwrite the expenses of Christians going to Jerusalem or for those who do not believe in either to help fund religious pilgrimages.

Although that is certainly a reasonable position, the modern application of separation of church and state in the Western world usually goes much further than that. For example, in the last forty years, secularism in the USA has led to the removal of prayers, religious teachings and even religious symbols from schools, courtrooms and other public facilities. The recent legislation in France that bans the wearing of head coverings by Muslim school children is a demonstration of how this kind of secularism is now

---

[3] Cross and Livingstone, 1983, 1255.

applied in some Western countries. Secularism has too often ceased being non-religious and become anti-religious.

Although the second reason for promoting secularism has a noble objective, secularism is not really an option for Christians. Jesus said,

> You are the salt of the earth . . . You are the light of the world. A city on a hill cannot be hidden. Neither do people light a lamp and put it under a bowl. Instead they put it on its stand, and it gives light to everyone in the house. In the same way, let your light shine before men, that they may see your good deeds and praise your Father in heaven (Matthew 5:13-16).

This passage teaches us that Christianity is not to be separated from the world but we are to engage the world. Christianity is not just a religion that is to be practised on Sunday and ignored the rest of the week. Christianity is that which affects the totality of our being and must be practised twenty-four hours a day, even when we are in public. Christians are not called to impose our faith on others, but neither are we expected to compromise or hide our faith when in the public. That makes secularism an impossibility if Christians are to truly practise their faith. It would be a serious mistake for the African church to embrace secularism in reaction to *shari'ah*.[4]

Little needs to be said about Islam and secularism. The very *shari'ah* debate itself demonstrates that secularism is not an option for Islam. In fact, Christianity has many things it can learn about secularism and holistic theology from observing the way Muslims view life holistically and their willingness to submit themselves to the teachings of their sacred writings, regardless of how modern secular society views them.

---

[4] See Smith, 2003, 65-79 for a thoughtful discussion of Islam, Christianity, and western values. On pages 77-78, he makes this insightful observation: "Nothing could be more tragic than for the churches of Nigeria to simply repeat the terrible mistakes made by Western churches in relation to modernity in the past two hundred years through an uncritical embrace of technology and the acceptance of a system of economics cut adrift from moral restraints and principles."

Secularism is not a realistic option for Africa either. John Mbiti, a Kenyan expert on African Traditional Religions, once said, "Africans are notoriously religious."[5] When Islam and Christianity came to Africa, they did not meet a religious vacuum. The fervour and commitment to the traditional religions were transferred to the new religions of Christianity and Islam. Religion in Africa is considered a very real part of life and is not restricted to private life. Separating one's religious life from his or her public life is a foreign concept in Africa and must be rejected.

Although Islam has led in the opposition to secularism, Christians should stand shoulder to shoulder with their Muslim brothers and sisters and oppose it because it is not in the best interest of our society and it is certainly not in the best interest of either Christianity or Islam. An English proverb states that sometimes a person will "cut off his nose to spite his face." Christians must not so react against *shari'ah* that we hinder our own ability to publicly practise our religion. It is better to make some concessions to accommodate Muslim convictions and preserve the opportunity to practise our own religion publicly than to lose our religious soul to the godless forces of political correctness and secularism.

CONSENSUS

If these roads will not lead to the peace and harmony we all seek, which road will lead us forward? Although it is rather narrow, there is very little go-slow on the right road because not many people travel that direction. In fact, the road is a rather dangerous place because travellers on this road tend to get shot at from both sides. The road I speak of is the narrow path of consensus. The word "consensus" includes several concepts including respect, cooperation, compromise and unity, practices that must be a part of the *shari'ah* discussion.

Christianity and Islam are both "voluntary" religions. God is not interested in our worship if it is forced or contrived.[6] Thus, there

---

[5] Mbiti, 1970, 1.
[6] All aspects of Christianity are voluntary, including the initial personal commitment to God, prayer, fasting and worship. Jesus referred to hypocrisy, which is insincere worship, at least 20 times in his teachings.

must be no compulsion in religion. If God only accepts voluntary worship, then giving others the right not to worship or to worship in a different way is an essential belief of our two religions. Thus, it is the principle of voluntarism that demands Christians and Muslims give one another the freedom to practise their religious faiths whenever they find themselves living together.

Within the Christian community, there are standards of behaviour and ethics. Christian members who violate those standards are often subjected to "church discipline." The ethical standards and the punishments apply only to voluntary members. If *shari'ah* were voluntarily practised only within the Muslim community and did not have the threat of state enforcement, most Christians would have little objection to its implementation.

From a Christian point of view, it would be most ideal if everyone lived by the Ten Commandments and other Christian principles. However, where the Christians are in the majority, the non-compulsion tenet of our faith demands that we give non-Christians the right to practise their religion to the extent that it does not infringe upon the rights of others. Where Christians find themselves in a minority, particularly where there is a Muslim majority, Christians should attempt to "live at peace with everyone" (Romans 12:18) and respect not only the laws of the land but the cultural traditions of that society. The Apostle Paul underscores this point:

> Though I am free and belong to no man, I make myself a slave to everyone, to win as many as possible. To the Jews I became like a Jew, to win the Jews. To those under the law I became like one under the law (though I myself am not under the law), so as to win those under the law. To those not having the law I became like one not having the law (though I am not free from God's law but am under Christ's law) (1 Corinthians 9:19-21).

Where Christians reside in a place where the laws of the land require them to do something that will violate their faith or prohibit them from doing something demanded by their faith, they, like the Apostle Peter, must choose to "obey God rather than man" (Acts 5:29). If it ever becomes necessary for Christians to practise civil disobedience in order to preserve their consciences, they must do so respectfully and peacefully and be fully willing to accept whatever consequences accompany that decision.

There is no good example in the New Testament of Christians working closely with non-Christians. However, once Jesus' disciples came to him and said (Mark 9:38-40), "Teacher . . . we saw a man driving out demons in your name and we told him to stop, because he was not one of us." Here is Jesus' response: "Do not stop him . . . No one who does a miracle in my name can in the next moment say anything bad about me, for whoever is not against us is for us." Though this story does not suggest Christians and Muslims should remove all their distinctives and create one amalgamated religion, it does suggest that there should be mutual respect for and an absence of antagonism toward those who have different opinions about the best way to worship God.

Christians and Muslims must come together and mutually work out the best way for Muslims to observe the tenets of *shari'ah* without infringing upon Christian rights. This should be done in a spirit of peace and harmony not suspicion and anger. When we shout at one another, we become angry. When we interact peacefully, we come up with workable solutions.

In light of these observations, what should be the response of Christian and Muslim leaders? I make the following recommendations:

RECOMMENDATIONS FOR CHRISTIAN LEADERS

1. Stop giving silent consent to violent "Christians."

Jesus is abundantly clear about violence. Christian leaders have the responsibility to teach and defend Jesus' teachings. Christian leaders have found it convenient to "look the other way" when their church members have failed "to turn the other cheek." An old proverb says, "two wrongs do not make a right." You will never stop *shari'ah* or spread Christianity with violence.

If your feel fellow Christians have had their rights violated, you should first try to resolve the issue by using Jesus' principles of reconciliation.[7] If that does not work, you are free to use the court system. Until the Nigerian court system gives a definitive ruling on the constitutionality of *shari'ah*, we will not know the extent to which *shari'ah* can be implemented in Nigeria.

2. Stop rumours among your constituents.

Thousands of people have lost their lives in Nigeria – both Christians and Muslims – because of unfounded rumours. Rather than reading only what your Christian colleagues are writing about *shari'ah*, give the courtesy to your Muslim colleagues to read and listen to them. Whenever there is a rumour of some pending "crisis" fomented by Muslims, be courageous enough to go see your Muslim counterparts for clarification. The entire Bible condemns gossip and rumour-mongering (Proverbs 16:28; 20:19; 26:20; Romans 1:29; 1 Timothy 5:13; James 4:11). Whenever we participate in it or even tolerate it, we are undermining the very Christianity we are pledged to support. It is evil to slander and spread lies, even against one perceived to be your enemy.

3. Focus on the positive.

The Apostle Paul declared in Philippians 4:8, "Finally, brothers, whatever is true, whatever is noble, whatever is right, whatever is pure, whatever is lovely, whatever is admirable – if anything is excellent or praiseworthy – think about such things." Even from a radical Christian point of view, not everything about *shari'ah* is bad. In fact, much of *shari'ah* is consistent with Christianity. For example, both Christianity and Islam (*shari'ah*) condemn drunkenness and

---

[7] In Matthew 18:15-17, Jesus outlines a three-step process to resolve problems. 1) Go to the offending person alone and attempt to resolve the problem; 2) Go to the offending person with one or two others; 3) Take the matter to the public. Jesus specifically mentions taking the matter to "the church." However, the word translated church (*ekklesia*) can also be translated assembly. Where all parties are Christians, the church is the logical place to solve problems but where all are not Christians, there are neutral courts that will help resolve problems. Jesus also made a very strong demand that his followers should be reconciled as quickly as possible even with their enemies (Matthew 5:25-26).

immorality. Both promote strong family values. Both encourage compassion toward the poor and needy. Both practise prayer and fasting. If Christians and Muslims refused to listen to the gossip of their members and focused on the positive elements their religions share, it would be easier to reconcile the areas of disagreement.

4. Establish wholesome relationships with your Muslim counterparts.

As community leaders, you should work at reconciliation without compromising your own doctrinal beliefs. You owe it to your constituents to develop positive relationships with the imams and other Islamic leaders. You will find you have much in common with them. These relationships can also be helpful in preventing crises and in bringing peace in times of tension.

In addition, where Christians have offended Muslims, Christian leaders must lead in seeking forgiveness. Also, pastors and other Christian leaders must teach their people to practise what Jesus taught about forgiving others. If Jesus made any statement more radical than "turn the other cheek", it was the one he made in response to Peter's question, "Lord, how many times shall I forgive my brother when he sins against me? Up to seven times?" His startling reply was: "I tell you, not seven times, but seventy-seven times" (Matthew 18:20-21). This means even if Muslims have been violent against them, our Christian duty is to forgive and be reconciled.

RECOMMENDATIONS FOR MUSLIM LEADERS

1. Reign in the radicals.

In the last three years, the peaceful nature of Islam has been greatly tarnished by those who practise violence. And, unfortunately, from the Christian perspective, this has been done with little vocal opposition from the leaders who represent the great majority of Muslims. If you want to promote Islam, you must present a more positive peaceful image than what has been presented to the world since September 2001. If Bin Laden does not represent your understanding of what Islam is, then you need say so publicly.

Muslim leaders must condemn everything that the Qur'an condemns, including violence against non-Muslims.

2. Push religious leaders to the forefront in the *shari'ah* debate.

At a recent national conference of religious leaders in Abuja, a Catholic bishop said, "If the *shari'ah* issue had been introduced by known religious leaders, we Catholics would have supported it. However, the fact that it was introduced by politicians meant that its real objective was political and not religious." Whether the thesis or the application of the statement is true or not is unknown. However, what is true is that the perception most Christians have is that *shari'ah* was introduced primarily by political leaders to promote political ends. If this perception is wrong, it must be the religious leaders who come to the forefront to clarify that point.

3. Apply *shari'ah* equally and fairly.

One of the primary arguments of the *shari'ah* proponents has been that the religious courts would be able to function more quickly and more fairly than the government courts. This is a noble objective because the perception in society is that there is much inefficiency and corruption in the court system, whether those courts have been led by Christians or Muslims. Certainly there have been some positive examples of cases being resolved quickly in the *shari'ah* courts. However, the perception in the Christian community is that the implementation of *shari'ah* has been very unfair. It is cow thieves and unwed mothers who have so far experienced the *shari'ah* penalties. What has been missing is highly placed political and business leaders feeling the sting of *shari'ah*.

Shari'ah proponents have gotten some very bad media coverage through the Amina Lawal case. If you want to get Amina Lawal off of the front pages of the world's newspapers, you need to start taking some of the "big people" in society to the *shari'ah* courts. When the *shari'ah* courts start punishing those big people who have stolen billions of naira and the rich men who prey upon young schoolgirls to be their "sugar-daddies" with the same kinds of penalties that cattle thieves and unwed mothers receive, Christians will start viewing *shari'ah* much differently.

Here is another question: How has *shari'ah* been applied to those committing religious violence? What have the Kaduna *shari'ah* courts done to those young men who were apprehended burning churches and destroying property of Christians after the Miss World debacle? If you want *shari'ah* to be accepted by Christians, let it be seen that *shari'ah* implementation is so fair it will defend even the rights of Christians and will punish Muslims who practise violence against non-Muslims. I suspect the single biggest way you can remove Christian opposition to *shari'ah* is to implement its laws as fairly and consistently as they were originally intended to be implemented.

4. Leave Christians out of *shari'ah*.

The proponents of *shari'ah* continue to state publicly that Christians have nothing to fear from *shari'ah*. However, it is obvious that some of the "*shari'ah*" laws are being applied to everyone. Apparently prostitution laws and even alcohol laws apply to everyone in some states, regardless of their religion. This is certainly not a call to excuse Christians who participate in such social vices. However, the proponents of *shari'ah* must clarify what does and what does not apply to Christians. Surely, the recent closing of churches and the refusal to allow the teaching of Christian Religious Knowledge in public schools in core Northern states must not be a part of *shari'ah*. These kinds of practices have hurt the credibility and fairness of those promoting *shari'ah*.

In addition, those responsible to implement *shari'ah* must train the *shari'ah* policemen and enthusiastic supporters of Islam to treat Christians with respect. Christians must be left out of the *shari'ah* unofficially as well as officially. Remember, it is not just the official implementation of *shari'ah* that creates the perception of *shari'ah* in the society. That perception is also shaped by the actions of those reckless Muslims who, without any legal authority, have taken upon themselves the responsibility to enforce what they perceive to be God's mandate for their communities.

RECOMMENDATIONS FOR CHRISTIAN AND MUSLIM LEADERS

1. We must move beyond government solutions to religious solutions.

Our tendency in Nigeria is to look to the government to solve all our problems. However, *shari'ah* is primarily a religious issue. The state legislators in the *shari'ah* states have done their part in crafting legislation they think is appropriate in their respective states. The *shari'ah* courts have made some good attempts at implementing these laws. The media have presented blistering attacks against *shari'ah* and brilliant defences of *shari'ah*. Although we all look to the federal government for the ultimate solution, it has been remarkably passive in this debate so far.

If we are going to solve this problem, it is likely going to be solved by the respective religious bodies themselves. It is now time for the national religious leaders to act, with or without the mandate or funding of government. Whenever there is a national problem, most governments are looking for good ideas and solutions and are open to those that come from the religious community. As indicated earlier, whenever religious leaders in Nigeria approached the government, both at the state and federal levels, with ideas about fighting the AIDS battle through a faith-based programme in secondary schools, they found that government was not only willing to listen but also willing to accept and implement such ideas.

Religious leaders should take the initiative and appoint a national religious coalition (or adapt an existing one) that will make recommendations to government for solving this and other religious problems. Representatives from the various religions and their respective religious scholars should come together in Nigeria's version of the *loya jerga*.[8] This committee should lock themselves into some venue, if necessary, and stay there until they arrive at a solution we can all live with.[9]

---

[8] A *loya jerga* is a traditional council of elders from very diverse backgrounds in Afghanistan that meets to solve problems. A *loya jerga* was recently conducted to draft and approve Afghanistan's new constitution.

[9] What are the steps this committee needs to take? Four are given in the continuation of this footnote on the next page:

If we are going to solve this problem, all parties are going to have to make painful concessions. No group is going to get everything they want. However, by constructive cooperation among religious leaders on this issue, we will get much closer to the ideal than we will by sponsoring demonstrations, writing inflammatory editorials and feeding destructive rumours.

We also must be patient. Solving religious problems takes time. Northern Ireland has struggled with religious differences for thirty years and those are differences among Christians.

This conference is a wonderful step in the right direction. However, courageous religious leaders must walk that narrow path of consensus and cooperation and lead their followers beyond the laudable theories of academia to real reconciliation, observable peace and a brighter future.

2. We must move beyond the *shari'ah* debate to active cooperation on other issues.

It is an unfortunate reality that Nigeria experienced religious tension even before the recent introduction of *shari'ah*. Therefore, even if we are able to totally solve the *shari'ah* problem, that would still not resolve the religious tension in the country. I believe the time has come for Christians and Muslims to go beyond dialogue about

1. ***Identify specific problems.*** The things about *shari'ah* that offend Christians do not include more than four or five specific issues. Also Muslims should identify things Christians do in their communities that are particularly offensive to them. These also need to be addressed and resolved.
2. ***Work out a solution for each problem.*** As long as we view the problem as *"shari'ah"* itself, we will continue to have problems. Therefore, we must work at a solution for each of the specific problems raised by the *shari'ah* debate.
3. ***Present recommendations to the government and the religious communities.*** If religious leaders work out a solution, government will listen. And if religious leaders promote these recommendations publicly and privately, their constituents will follow.
4. ***Pledge to defend and promote the solutions.*** Religious leaders must be seen as leading the way in resolving these issues. They must pledge to renounce violence and resolve all problems peacefully.

shari'ah to active cooperation on issues of common interest. There are many things that we believe jointly. In fact, Christians and Muslims have more common beliefs than they have divergent beliefs.[10] Most of the social ills in society such as prostitution, drunkenness and corruption are taught to be wrong in both the Bible and the Qur'an (though unfortunately adherents to both religions have often practised these). Poverty and disease and illiteracy affect Christians and Muslims alike. Rather than focusing on the few areas where we disagree, we must focus on those areas where we agree and work together.

One positive thing that has happened in recent years in Nigeria is the cooperation of Christians and Muslims in creating the "Faith-Based AIDS Awareness Programme for Senior Secondary Schools." In 1999, Christian and Muslim members of the Department of Religious Studies, at the University of Jos, in response to the growing AIDS crisis here in Nigeria, came together to create some themes on human sexuality for the Christian and Islamic studies curricula in the public secondary schools of Nigeria. Our reasoning was if we, the people of faith, do not come together and create a faith-based approach to the AIDS problem, the secular NGO's, who have no place for God in their projects, are going to create a programme for us. Our convictions about the issue of human sexuality are much closer to one another than they are to the secular approach.[11] Because of that conviction, organisations as diverse as the Fellowship of Christian Students and the Jama'atu Nasril Islam joined in this initiative to develop a faith-based plan for fighting the HIV/AIDS battle. This public school project promotes sexual abstinence as a way to fight AIDS. To do this, we had to produce joint material. In addition, we jointly conduct five-day workshops for teachers of

---

[10] For a discussion of the foundational teachings of Christianity that affect society, see McCain, 1995. In this paper, I present eight basic principles of Christianity that should provide the foundation to societies. I believe that Islam shares these same eight convictions. These include: 1) sacredness of truth; 2) dignity of labour and work; 3) sacredness of human life; 4) the importance of justice; 5) respect for individual human rights; 6) compassion for the poor; 7) peaceful co-existence of people of diverse backgrounds; 8) preservation of the environment.

[11] For an overview of the faith perspective on HIV/AIDS, see McCain, 2003.

Christian and Islamic Religious Knowledge, guidance counsellors and health officers in the public schools of Nigeria. We have so far conducted this project on a state-wide level in three of Nigeria's states, including Plateau, Nasarawa and Benue States. Kaduna and Bauchi States are planned for implementation within the next few months.

Not only is this project making a contribution to the AIDS battle, it is also making an impact upon Christian-Muslim relationships. We are not just talking to each other about our differences; we are actively working together. That kind of cooperation produces understanding, respect and friendship. At our most recent workshop, which was conducted in Benue State in mid-December 2003, one of the Christian participants came to me and said, "Sir, this is the first time I have ever been in a workshop with Muslims. I pray that your organisation will continue to do this. This has helped me understand Muslims more than anything else I have done." Several Muslims participants expressed similar sentiments.

Is AIDS the only issue on which we can work together? Why cannot Christians and Muslims, whose religions teach similar things about theft, work together to create positive approaches to dealing with corruption in society? Why cannot we create faith-based approaches to protect our society from pornography and other media that undermine our social morals?

If Nigeria wants to get beyond the *shari'ah* debate, we need to move beyond just talking to active cooperation. It is only as we work together that we will understand one another. It is only as we understand one another that we will have the peace that both Christianity and Islam teach. Let us unite to wage war against our common social and moral enemies and then separate to practise our respective religions.

CONCLUSION

Christians must not deny Muslims the right to practise their religion to the extent those rights do not infringe upon the rights of non-Muslims.[12] And Muslims must not alienate themselves and their

---

[12] This paper focuses primarily on the relationship between Christians and Muslims. However, there are still many who practise one of the varieties of

religion from others by demanding the implementation of laws that create the perception of injustice, intolerance, discrimination and violence.

Shari'ah is not the death knell for Nigeria. In fact, I believe the *shari'ah* debate is a powerful assignment, given to us by God Almighty, to provide us an opportunity to learn to solve problems and live together. If we cannot solve the *shari'ah* problem, our children will continue to experience hatred and violence and the unfortunate distortion of their religions as they kill and destroy in the name of God. However, if we rise to the challenge and find the right road around this and other difficult religious and moral problems, we will have assured a much brighter future for all who love and serve God. And, in so doing, we will be able to teach the rest of the world about how to live successfully in a multi-religious society.

REFERENCES

Cross, F. L. and E. A. Livingstone, *The Oxford Dictionary of the Christian Church* (2nd edition), Oxford, UK: Oxford University Press, 1983.

Mbiti, John, *African Religions and Philosophy*, New York: Anchor Books, 1970.

McCain, Danny, "Christianity: a moral foundation to Nigeria", a paper presented to the Tenth Annual Conference of the National Association for Biblical Studies in Owerri, Nigeria, on 25 October 1995.

———, "The Christian-Muslim perspective on HIV/AIDS", in: *Answers to Questions on HIV/AIDS*, Abuja: UNICEF, 2003.

Smith, David, *Against the Stream*, Leicester, UK: Inter-Varsity Press, 2003.

African Traditional Religions and their views and convictions must also be considered in any solution to the *shari'ah* controversy.

The Demand for *Shari'ah* in African Democratisation Processes: Pitfalls or Opportunities?

Abdulkader Tayob

INTRODUCTION

During the last decade of the twentieth century, attempts have been made to increase the levels and extent of democratisation in a number of African states. After the collapse of the Berlin Wall and the end of the cold war between East and West, dictatorships and minority regimes from Pretoria to Kinshasa to Bamako could no longer count on international support for their disregard of the basic democratic rights of their citizens. One of the effects of the resulting wave of democratisation and relaxation of the public sphere has been religious revival in many countries. The emergence of religion in the public sphere is an important part of the democratisation process, but not without some contradictions between the nature of religious loyalty and organisation, and democracy. This paper explores the controversies and crises over Islamic law as an element of the democratisation process. The organisation and implications of democratic forms of government are evident in the conceptualisation of Islamic law in a number of different countries.

There are at least two models for the proper role of religion in pluralist democratic contexts. In the modern period, the first model can be traced back to Jean Jacques Rousseau before the French Revolution, then to Durkheim's model of religion as society, and then to Robert Bellah's revival of Rousseau and Durkheim in the second half of twentieth century. Their notion of civil religion suggests that there exists a general symbolic system for the state derived from existing religions, but one that avoids their sectarianism:

> The dogmas of civil religion ought to be few, simple, and exactly worded, without explanation or commentary. The

existence of a mighty, intelligent and beneficent Divinity, possessed of foresight and providence, the life to come, the happiness of the just, the punishment of the wicked, the sanctity of the social contract and the laws: these are its positive dogmas. Its negative dogmas I confine to one, intolerance, which is a part of the cults we have rejected.[1]

From another angle, Durkheim's thesis of a religion as society may be regarded as the model of religion that suits this conception of civil religion. Rather than thinking of the distinction between church and state as Rousseau argued, Durkheim's theory posited the essential nature of religion as civil religion. According to Durkheim, society as such had a unique mysterious element. As an embodiment of the collective mind:

> [S]ociety has its own mode of existence which is peculiar to it; correspondingly, its own mode of thought. It has its passions, its habits, and its needs, which are not those of the individual, and which leave their mark on everything it conceives . . . . [S]acred things are those whose representation society itself has fashioned [including] . . . all sorts of collective states, common traditions and emotions, feelings which have a relationship to objects of general interest, etc.; and all those elements are combined according to appropriate laws of social mentality.[2]

For Durkheim, religion and society were indistinguishable. The civil religion thesis received another boost after the Second World War. Robert Bellah in the 1960s argued that liberalism had prospered at the expense of public morality, both important pillars of democratic government.[3] In order to redress the imbalance, he argued for a general system of symbols that created commitment and confidence among citizens. In different forms, this notion of a symbolic system that supports the political culture of a society has a long history in

---

[1] Rousseau, 1973, 276.
[2] In Pickering, 1975, 95.
[3] Bellah, 1980.

Western sociological reflection.[4] David Chidester has argued cogently that the symbolic power of religion has been taken over by the state. The national narratives, the sources of authority, the ceremonies and the systems of control operating in modern states mirror religious systems.[5] In African studies, this idea of a civil religion has been an attractive model in terms of which to understand the role of religion in pre-modern societies, as well as in contemporary states.[6]

There has been considerable criticism levelled against such an over-arching system of symbols. The undemocratic nature of symbols imposed from above, and the tendency for their abuse, have been evident in both religious states and their modern reformulations in nation states. Against the totalitarian character of a grand symbolic order, many scholars of religion have suggested that religions ought rather to play their role in the development of a public philosophy. The influence of Habermas has been evident in these proposals. The most systematic proposal for this approach remains Casanova's,[7] who suggested that the role of religion is best played in the sphere of civil society and not in political society. Religions ought neither to play a role in the formation of political parties nor the elaboration of a general symbolic system. Rather, religions have an important role to play in the formulation of moral and public philosophies that are geared towards good government and human fulfilment. Regretting the abandonment of a public moral calling among religious traditions, Casanova's vision of the constructive role of religion is clear:

> What I call the deprivation of modern religion is the process whereby religion abandons its assigned place in the private sphere and enters the undifferentiated public sphere of civil society to take part in the ongoing process of contestation, discursive legitimation, and redrawing of the boundaries.[8]

Among Nigerians, Illesanmi's critique of Olupona's approach to religion and state through a civil religion model fits in this

---

[4] Beckford, 1992.
[5] Chidester, 1988, 1996.
[6] Tayob, 1995; Olupona, 1991.
[7] Casanova, 1994, 58-63.
[8] Casanova, 1994, 65.

perspective.⁹ Similarly, Gifford's review of Christianity in public life in a number of countries¹⁰ may be placed within this category as well.

These two models of religion in public life seem a good starting point for examining the meaning of the implementation of *shari'ah* in a number of African states. I would like to use them as a framework to understand some of the crises, but also as a basis of critique of both those who oppose and those who support the introduction of the *shari'ah* in some form or the other. The models avoid the debate about the nature of a secular state that seems to underlie many objections to the implementation of the *shari'ah*. Opponents of *shari'ah* in Nigeria, for example, have often upheld the ideal of a secular state against the implementation of religious laws.¹¹ And yet, the role of religion in the symbolic system of the state (civil religion) or in the development of a public philosophy seems to make some concessions to the meaning of religion in social and public life. At the same time, the models also provide the elements of tolerance and public philosophy against which to examine the demands for *shari'ah*. Supporters of the implementation of *shari'ah* seem oblivious to the ramifications of *shari'ah* in national contexts characterised by pluralism and freedom of expression. For both supporters of and objectors to *shari'ah*, the models present alternative lines of debate and reasoning.

Going beyond the models, however, I would like to suggest a third option for religion in public life that does not necessarily reject the other two models. This third option takes into consideration the history of the implementations and implications of *shari'ah* in a number of African states. While the Durkheimian model has focussed on the state, and the Habermasian model on civil society, I think that the experience of the *shari'ah* in African plural societies suggests careful consideration of a pluralistic legal culture. Arguing for the *shari'ah* in the legal structure does not mean that other forms of religious effects in the state and civil society can be ignored. In fact, the legal demands are often enmeshed in debates that rage in the civil and political spheres.

---

⁹ Illesanmi, 1995.
¹⁰ Gifford, 1998.
¹¹ Okike, 2000; Kenny, 1996.

The option that I am talking about can be seen in *shari'ah* demands in Nigeria, Kenya and South Africa since each of these countries has democratised its polities and public spaces. In the following, I want to sketch the contexts of these demands in each of the countries. As will become clear, each country is unique in terms of the different Islamic background, the legal and constitutional history, and the issues being addressed. I will begin with the South Africa case and work towards the north. In each case, my analysis will consider, in turn: the legal and constitutional changes in which the issue of the *shari'ah* has become an issue; the issues being addressed; and the outcome of such deliberations and conflicts. I will then conclude with a general discussion under the rubric of the two models and my third option of religion in the public sphere.

SOUTH AFRICA: THE RIGHTS IN SHARI'AH

When negotiations began in 1990 between the white minority regime and the African National Congress, Muslims almost immediately began to discuss their future in relation to these political and social changes. A National Muslim Conference was held in the same year to discuss how Muslims should respond to the negotiations. There was no consensus at the conference, but discussions revealed the widely differing class, racial and religious backgrounds of the participants. The transition to a more open society and democracy opened the floodgates to views and perceptions. The increased freedoms including both freedom of religion and freedom of expression led to intense debate among the many voices of Islam in the country. And the place of the *shari'ah* in the constitution was one such issue that came up for discussion in a very short period of time.

The most dramatic provision for Islam in the constitution was the recognition of Muslim marriages *or* a complete system of Muslim personal law. Section 15, entitled *Freedom of Religion, Belief and Opinion*, included such a provision in its subsection (3):

(3)(a) This section does not prevent legislation recognising
   (i) marriages concluded under any tradition, or a *system* [my emphasis] of religious, personal or family law; or

(ii) *systems* [my emphasis] of personal law and family law under any tradition, or adhered to by persons professing a particular religion.

(b) Recognition in terms of paragraph (a) must be consistent with this section and the other provisions of the Constitution.

This constitutional provision has been the subject of active debate and development since its first promulgation. Immediately after the first elections in 1994, the government appointed a Muslim Personal Law Board to propose a system of Islamic law as provided by paragraph 15(3)(a). The body consisted of members drawn both from the religious leadership and from youth organisations that were active against apartheid. The Board collapsed by April 1995 when its members could not reach agreement.[12] In a second attempt, a project committee was appointed by the South African Law Commission under the chair of Mr. Justice M. S. Navsa of the Supreme Court of Appeal. At the end of 2001, this committee produced for public discussion a proposed draft bill for recognising Muslim marriages, and in June of 2003, after receiving input from the public, presented a revised bill to the Minister of Justice for presentation in Parliament.[13] The Law Commission committee appears to be enjoying greater success than the Muslim Personal Law Board. The process leading to its draft bill provides an opportunity for understanding how Muslims have responded not only to legal reform but to religious freedom and freedom of expression.

The Muslim Personal Law Board set about to discuss the system "of personal law and family law" allowed by subparagraph (15)(3)(a)(ii) of the constitution. As I will shortly show, there is an important difference between subparagraphs (i) and (ii) of paragraph (a). Most contemporary Muslims see Islam as a system, and the discussion naturally veered in this direction. The members reached agreement on the desirability of recognising Islamic personal law by the state, but split into two camps on the nature and context of Islamic law. Women's interest groups and progressive Islamic

---

[12] Moosa, E., 1996.
[13] See statement issued by the South African Law Commission, wwwserver.law.wits.ac.za/salc/media/IslamRep.doc.

organisations insisted that subsection 15(3) should be read in its entirety. For them, the crux of the matter rested on the fact that the system of Islamic law must be consistent with the "other provisions of the constitution." They believed that the system of Muslim personal law in South Africa should be interpreted with this condition in mind. And most importantly, this condition would ensure an interpretation of Islamic law that would not disadvantage women. The leading and most articulate spokesperson for this new interpretation of Muslim personal law was Ebrahim Moosa. In both academic and newspaper articles, he argued that many traditional provisions in the *shari'ah* should be regarded as *fiqh*, constructed and produced by scholars whose interpretations need no longer be considered valid.[14] He has taught and inspired students and activists to revisit traditional issues in Islamic law. Reflecting this approach, Najma Moosa, a member of the project committee, argued that "Muslims can only give practical legal effect to the constitution if due recognition is given to a *reformed* MPL [Muslim personal law] and its implementation."[15]

On the other hand, the opponents of this reformist group believed that Muslim personal law, as a component of the *shari'ah*, was divine and thus not susceptible to change and interpretation, particularly with regard to issues clearly stated in the Qur'an and the Sunnah of the Prophet. In response to the argument that the *shari'ah* "system" should be subject to the Bill of Rights, some of the proponents of this more traditional view insisted that a system of legal pluralism should be adopted by the South African constitution. Toffar, a religious scholar from Cape Town, rejected outright the secular constitution which made provision for an Islamic juridical system, arguing that "it is ludicrous to suppose that our family and personal law will function properly according to *shari'ah* in the present set-up."[16] Citing the model of Singapore, he called for a completely separate judicial system for Muslims under a regime that did not impose its secularism on them:

---

[14] Moosa, E., 1991, 1996.
[15] Moosa, N, 1998 (emphasis added).
[16] Toffar, 1422, 18.

This is practical, guaranteed, just and fair minority rights in action and avoids the application of the abuse and cruelty of the democracy of numbers – a seemingly inherited phenomenon in virtually all democracies. One may wonder why the aforementioned system [of Singapore] is not considered seriously. Instead, systems of a secular imposed value and administrative system appears to receive apparent favour.[17]

Without calling for a separate parallel system of Muslim personal law like Toffar, other Muslims have appealed to Section 36(1) of the constitution, which allows for limitation of the rights provided in the Bill of Rights:

> The rights in the Bill of Rights may be limited only in terms of laws of general application to the extent that the limitation is reasonable and justifiable in an open and democratic society based on human dignity, equality and freedom.

They usually argued that a system of law should be codified directly from the books of *fiqh* for the South African courts, and that the limitation clause should apply to such codification. The interim constitution may have given the impression that customary or religious laws pertaining to personal maters would not be subject to the Bill of Rights. Toffar believed that the absence of a specific clause such as 15(3)(b) guiding the interpretation of Muslim personal law in the interim constitution implied the exemption of such a law from the jurisdiction of the Bill of Rights. This particular model was followed in Zimbabwe where personal laws originating from customary practices were exempt from equality provisions in the rest of the constitution. According to Najma Moosa, a member of the second committee mentioned above, such a presumption was plausible from

---

[17] Ibid. The appeal to legal pluralism is shared by others as well, e.g., Ebrahim Moosa, 1996. According to Cachalia, another activist who has made a significant contribution to the debate, a parallel legal system would not avoid bringing the "potential conflicts between women's rights and religious rights into focus," see Cachalia and Albie, 1991.

the interim constitution.[18] To clear any such presumption, the final South African constitution specified the limits of customary legal tradition including the Islamic one.

The new committee was entrusted with the difficult task of formulating a solution. From the perspective of many progressive organisations, moreover, the committee consisted mainly of individuals who supported a more traditional interpretation of Islam, including some women. The committee was formed by the Ministry of Justice that was responsible to the state and to uphold the constitution. It eventually produced a document that appears consistent with the constitution, agreeable to most members of the religious bodies, and responsive to the concerns of women's groups.[19]

The proposed bill demands an explanation of how the project committee was able to arrive at a compromise between radical reform and tradition. The debates among the Muslims will probably continue, but the approach of the committee seems to indicate a unique stance towards the constitution and the general problem of the non-recognition of Muslim marriages. The committee gave up the attempt to propose "legislation recognising systems of personal or family law" (Section 15(3)(a)(ii)), as the earlier Muslim Personal Law Board had done. Such an approach had opened up ideological differences that could not easily be settled. They were reflections of global Islamic debates that had no immediate resolution within the South African nation.[20] Instead, the committee opted to develop the second provision for "legislation recognising marriages concluded under any tradition" (Section 15(3)(a)(i)). There is a subtle different between the two and the constitution has an important disjunction (or) between the two clauses. The earlier attempt of the Muslim Personal Law Board was bogged down in the representation of a comprehensive *system* of personal law. Such a system, widely assumed in modern Islamic discourses, has failed many an attempt at

---

[18] Moosa, N., 1998.
[19] The South African Law Commission has collated some of the responses on its website: http://wwwserver. law.wits.ac.za/salc/issue/issue.html.
[20] Apart from Toffar's, no systematic arguments for the exclusion of Muslim Personal Law were presented. It was simply assumed that the divine nature of the *shari'ah* precludes any discussion. Instead, attention was focussed on those who argued for a different approach.

elaboration. According to Najma Moosa, a member of both the first board and the second committee, nothing short of a complete code would have been desirable: "MPL should be codified into a separate code of law which would form part of the statutory law of the South African legal system" and the best solution lay "in codifying Islamic law and enacting a comprehensive bill or 'uniform Muslim code'."[21]

The new committee, it seems, avoided the gigantic task. It directly addressed the critical problem of Muslim marriages in South Africa, a source of great social problems. Muslim marriages conducted by imams in the mosques were not recognised until the promulgation of the new constitution. Even in the new dispensation, effective court decisions were hamstrung in the absence of legislation. In the apartheid days, Muslim marriages were considered "potentially polygamous" and hence repugnant to the Western norms adopted by South African courts. In a legal review of these issues, Rautenbach underlined the continued challenge of non-recognition:

> [The] consequences of non-recognition are particularly unfair to women. She has no claim for support if the husband is killed; she has no claim for maintenance against her husband after their divorce; she is not a beneficiary after the death of the husband in terms of the In testate Succession Act; she may be compelled to give evidence against her husband in criminal proceedings; and she has no claim for financial support during their marriage.[22]

Rautenbach argued that recognition of Islamic personal law should not be exempt from the provisions of the Bill of Rights, but her review of the legislation points to the severe handicaps suffered particularly by women in the non-recognition of Islamic law. By abandoning or side-stepping the ideological debate in favour of the actual needs of citizens, the proposed bill seemed to have charted a different course. So far, I have not seen any evidence that this was a conscious decision. It was an approach forced upon the participants, between a complete overhaul of the Islamic legal system and the

---

[21] Moosa, N., 1998, 201, n. 36.
[22] Rautenbach, 2000, 46.

rejection of any recognition of Islamic marriages. I believe the compromise has produced a solution that has far-reaching consequences for thinking about popular demands for *shari'ah* in Muslim societies. This approach confirms an important democratic principle of working from concerns and issues that affect people. The ideological debates were important, but they tended to ignore the issue of *recognition* that the constitution sought to address in the first place. The case study in South Africa demonstrates that the recognition of Islamic law in matters of personal relations must be addressed by legislation in order for justice to be done. Such recognition affects the lives of a large number of Muslim relations.

At this point, I would venture to say that the models of religion from Rousseau and Habermas do not adequately address these issues. The small number of Muslims in South Africa probably precludes the emergence of a perception or potential for Islamic symbols as part of the political or civil space. Some of the objections to the development of a system of Islamic personal law in conformity with the Bill of Rights may be interpreted in light of the place of Islam in the political space. Outside South Africa, particularly in Nigeria, this fusion of legal and political demands becomes clearer. The reactive nature of the South African debate has so far avoided the second possibility of the civil debate. Issues in Muslim personal law, bogged down in the divine or human nature of the issues, have not entered the general debate as such. But the legal dimensions of equity and justice in addressing the needs of ordinary citizens cannot be ignored. They seem to be bypassed by those who argue that religion (Islam) should occupy a pre-eminent place in the symbolic system of the state, or that the principles or equity and justice should prevail in the civil sphere.

KENYA: AMENDMENT TO THE CONSTITUTION

Debates about legal provisions in the constitution have also emerged in Kenya in the context of the writing of a new constitution in the closing years of the 20th century. In Kenya, the place of religion in the legal structure has enjoyed attention and invited criticism from both Muslim and Christian groups. A review of the process again reveals the entanglement between religion and a pluralist democracy in the legal sphere.

Immediately after independence, the ruling party KANU (Kenya African National Union) moved quickly to eliminate or neutralise political opposition in the name of national unity. Opposition to the concentration of power at the centre persisted, and accelerated after the death of Jomo Kenyatta. However, the demand for greater democratic reforms within the country did not receive much attention from outside until the fall of the Berlin Wall and the end of the Cold War. Then, in an international climate more conducive to democratic reforms, The Constitution of Kenya (Amendment) Act (No. 2) of 1991 repealed the constitutional prohibition on forming new parties.

The greater degree of freedom in the public space led to the formation of political parties. In addition, a civil society initiative from lawyers, human rights activists and religious representatives spearheaded the demand for more human rights protection, greater devolution of powers to the regions, and a new constitution. The initiative was called the Ufungamano and involved the organisation of regular meetings that insisted that parliament listen to the demands of people in the different regions of the country. This major civil society initiative finally had the desired effect. The Constitution of Kenya Review (Amendment) Act of 2001 and the Kenya Constitution Amendment Act of 2001 formed the Kenya Constitutional Review Commission (KCRC) and gave it 24 months to obtain extensive views from the general population and to produce a draft constitution.[23]

The KCRC produced a draft constitution reflecting the demands of the public. Most of the demands were directed at the devolution of power from the centre, and better government. However, one of the issues that came to the table was a demand that the existing *qadi*'s courts be reformed to make them more efficient and to make them more responsive to the demands of those who sought redress from them. The British colonial authorities had established *qadi*'s courts as part of their agreement with the Sultanate of Zanzibar when they took over administration of the Kenyan coastal strip. The courts were

---

[23] www.kenyaconstitution.org.

carried over from the colonial regime into independent Kenya as part of a regional agreement. Since independence, the services of the courts seem to have been sought by Muslims all over Kenya, but more particularly women.[24] However, a number of criticisms had been laid at their methods of operation, efficiency and relation to the national courts.

The KCRC heard recommendations to improve the workings of the *qadi*'s courts some of which were incorporated into the draft constitution. *Qadi*s were to be trained in both Islamic law and common national law. A requirement was included that, in addition to their Islamic credentials, they should have a common law degree and experience that would qualify them to be advocates. Secondly, it was pointed out that more women had recourse to the courts than men. Women approached the courts with grievances against their husbands or male relatives in divorce, custody, and inheritance matters. The KCRC recommended that women should be represented on the boards that would appoint the *qadi*s. There seemed no acceptance among Kenyan Muslims that women should also be represented on the *qadi*'s bench itself. Thirdly, the recommendations included provisions for a new "Kadhi's Court of Appeal" to hear appeals from the judgements of the lower *qadi*'s courts; only after passing through the Kadhi's Court of Appeal would cases from the lower *qadi*'s courts be heard in the national higher courts. The KCRC also included a recommendation to expand the jurisdiction of the *qadi*'s courts to hear minor cases of financial claims. The *qadi*'s courts were regarded as more accessible and more efficient at dealing with such issues.

These recommendations generated great controversy in the country, and instigated an intense debate over religion and state in general, and Muslims and Christians in particular. Both Muslim and Christian positions were articulated. They are worthy of reflection and analysis in the light of the models and options for religion in public life discussed in this paper. There was one particular Christian response from the Kenya National Church that claimed to represent 80% of the Kenyan population. Other Christian views were also expressed in national and religious media. The Muslim responses

---

[24] Hirsch, 1998.

seemed less coordinated. A group of Muslim lawyers responded to the objections of the Kenya National Church in its particular legal ramifications.[25] But Muslim responses from religious representatives were more diverse and reflected the competition over the identity and content of the state's relations with religions. Both the Muslim and Christian responses may be evaluated in light of the religion and public life debates that I have outlined above.

The Kenya Church issued a statement in December 2002 outlining its responses to the proposals of the KCRC. I will first look at the Church's objections with respect to the *qadi*'s courts and then come to its general recommendations that impact on the nature of religion-state relations. The Kenya Church demanded that all mention of *qadi*'s courts be completely removed from the constitution, including the provision for women membership on the boards appointing *qadi*s. Such provisions, it felt, meant that one particular religion was being privileged in the constitution, which violated the principle of the separation of religion and state. Making provision for *qadi*'s courts which were Islamic in origin created a state religion. Furthermore, the Kenya Church also presented Islamic justifications for its objections. Its paper argued that there was "no personal law in Islam, as Islam is a way of life" and that Muslims do not need to be mentioned in the constitution as they "have their own constitution (embodied in the Qur'an and *hadith*s) and religious processes, just like other religions."[26]

But – although the Kenya Church's objections to the *qadi*'s courts overshadowed its other objections to the constitutional proposals – the Church's responses did not deal only with the *qadi*'s courts. And its other objections were no less revealing about its vision of relations between religion and state. They bear important evidence for its view on the symbolic capital of the state. The Kenya Church said it was concerned to "ensure that the final constitution not only reflect[ed] the wishes of Kenyans, but also the eternal purposes of God." It insisted that the first clause of the constitution should mention God. Instead of beginning only with the words "We, the people of Kenya," it should go on, "recognising the supremacy and

---

[25] Advocates, n.d.; Bashir, 2003.
[26] The Kenya Church, 2002.

sovereignty of the Almighty God of all creation." A similar demand was made to include mention of God in another clause. Instead of:

> Kenya is founded on the Constitution and the rule of law and shall be governed in accordance with the Constitution,

the following was suggested:

> Kenya is founded on the supremacy of God, and shall be governed in accordance with the constitution and the rule of law.[27]

These recommendations make it very clear that the Kenya Church did not support a secular state. It clearly argued that the symbols of the civil religion of the Kenyan state should be pervaded by the supremacy of God. God and nationalism in this view were closely linked. And one may venture to suggest that the symbolism of *qadi*'s courts was more objectionable than the legal issues that were being debated might suggest. The place of religion in the broader symbolism of the state was acceptable, but the symbolism of a specific religion like Islam was unacceptable.

The Muslim responses were varied and should also be separated between arguments focusing on the legal dimensions of *qadi*'s courts and the civil religion issues reflected in the Kenya Church statement. Muslim advocates made legal and constitutional arguments why *qadi*'s courts should be provided for in the constitution. These arguments – similar to those made in South Africa – reflected the need to address the legal problems arising out of Islamic legal cases emerging within Kenyan society. They merit more reflection because they represent a grassroots demand for a well-functioning system to adjudicate disputes that need to be addressed through some recognition of Islamic law. In Kenya, for social and historical reasons, the *qadi*'s courts were dealing with this class of cases, and the proposed constitutional amendments tried to redress some of the grievances that had arisen with respect to these courts.

---

[27] All quotations in this paragraph from The Kenya Church, 2002.

Another set of responses, however, echoed the Christian response from the Kenya Church. They were not as clearly formulated, but they can be identified with the demand that Muslim religious symbols be recognised in the civil religion of Kenya. Muslim reaction to the Kenya Church was quick to point to the anomaly between the Church's demand for separation of religion and state and its demand for a religious justification for the state. Many saw the Kenya Church's objections to any constitutional provision for *qadi*'s courts in terms of the already-close relationship between the national leadership and the Christian churches. Parliamentary members were regularly blessed at religious ceremonies and special breakfast meetings, which for Muslims spelt a close relationship between Christianity and the state.[28] One can see evidence of this even in the Muslim advocates' information sheet. One of its explanations revealed its perception of the role of Christianity in the national courts:

> Christians do not need to have separate courts. This is because the laws of Kenya are mainly Judeo-Christian in nature. This is more so in relation to family. The principles upon which the Matrimonial Causes Act is based are Christian principles and therefore Christians are confident that if they do present their family law disputes before a judge or magistrate (who in all probability will be Christian), the dispute will be settled in accordance to his or her religious values, albeit in a round about manner.[29]

Other Muslim responses were not satisfied with pointing out the close relationship between Christianity and the judiciary. The Kenya Church objections to the proposed provisions for *qadi*'s courts provided an opportunity to point to the absence of any symbolic representation for Muslims in the Kenyan state. In fact, the *qadi*'s bench was regarded as an obstacle to the symbolic representation of Muslim interests. The following summary by one commissioner of

---

[28] The Kenya Church's complete rejection of the *qadi*'s courts was regarded as a confirmation of the subordinate status of the Muslims in the country in general, see Brown, 1994, Constantin, 1993, O'Brien, 1995, Oded, 1996.
[29] Muslim Advocates, n.d..

the KCRC reveals the desire for Muslim representations at the state level and not at the judiciary:

> The Chief Kadhi and other kadhis have often assumed nonjudicial roles such as leading prayers in mosques, giving sermons therein and for the Chief Kadhi, he has been holding himself out as the spiritual leader of the Muslims and their spokesperson when he has not been elected or appointed as such. It is common knowledge that a lot of controversy arises among the Muslims during the month of Ramadhan when the Chief Kadhi purports to issue edicts directing when the moon was sighted and when the Idd will be. It would have been more practical for this role to be left to an elected Islamic leader of the Muslims or a mufti who should be an advisor to the government on Islamic affairs.[30]

The particular issue that Hassan referred to related to a dispute in the closing years of the twentieth century between the Chief Kadhi and the imam of the Friday mosque in the capital of Nairobi. Imam Ali Shee, the holder of the office, had objected to the Chief Kadhi's role in announcing the festival days. Another related issue around Islam and state in Kenya emerged earlier in 1992. Then, an "Islamic Party of Kenya" emerged in Mombassa in the wake of the liberalisation of the political space.[31] From this particular quarter, the absence of Islamic symbols in the Kenya state was a sore point, but one that had nothing to do with the *qadi*'s courts. Both the emergence of the Islamic Party of Kenya and the ambition of the imam in Nairobi pointed to important implications for the nature of Islam-state relations. But like the Kenya Church, they were more closely related to the competition over national symbols for the civil religion in Kenya, than the legal issues around the proposed new constitution.

Before moving to examine the Nigerian case, it may be useful to reflect on the South African and Kenyan cases. In both cases, it seems that the legal provision for Islamic *shari'ah* cannot be avoided. They seem to be addressing the needs of citizens that went beyond

---

[30] Hassan, 2002.
[31] Oded, 1996.

the objections that might be raised by the advocates of secularism. Moreover, it is also clear that the *shari'ah* needs in both cases were rooted in the historical experiences of Muslims in each country. However, it is also clear, more so in Kenya than in South Africa, that the competition over the religious symbols in the state is intense and varied. In Kenya, Muslims were particularly sensitive to the close relationship between churches and state officials. The response of the Kenya Church to the constitutional amendments reveals their investment in this regard. Muslims were themselves hoping to enjoy similar access and prestige but the models of an "Islamic Party of Kenya" or a "National Mufti" seemed inept for Kenya. The *shari'ah* in recent years had become the symbol par excellence for such a symbolic representation. But the Kenyan debate reveals that solution of the concrete problem – the actual working of the *qadi*'s courts – might fall victim to both some Christian and some Muslim representations. The immediate legal issues stood to lose most in the competition over national religious symbols for the state.

NIGERIA: EXTENSION OF THE *SHARI'AH*

Nigeria's turbulent history of military rule ended with multi-party elections in 1999. Soon thereafter, on 27 January 2000, Ahmed Sani, the governor of Zamfara State, officially announced that *shari'ah* legislation would be extended from personal law to all aspects of life including criminal cases. The initiative taken by Zamfara spread to eleven other Northern states in the next two years. The crisis in the Nigerian state deepened as *shari'ah* courts began issuing judgments on the basis of hastily passed codes.[32] The most alarming cases, involving sentences of death by stoning for adultery, were brought to Appeal Courts, while floggings and amputations were carried out.[33] The crises poured out on to the street as imams demanded that the governors dare not step down from their announcements, and youth groups pressurised the police and judges to conform to the new codes. Clashes between Muslim and Christian groups broke out in

---

[32] Peters, 2003, 13-15.
[33] Peters, 2003, 19-21.

Kaduna (February 2000 and 2002) and Jos (September 2001) leading to the worst clashes since the Civil War of the late 1960s. Compared to South Africa and Kenya, it seems that the Nigerian situation produced a crisis of major proportions. Nevertheless, the tools of analysis applied to the other more benign cases may shed light on the situation in Nigeria. In fact, I would like to argue that without the benefit of these cases, the situation in Nigeria appears catastrophic for inter-religious harmony and the quest for justice. My analysis will use the tools to examine the nature of the *shari'ah* demands. In the following, I will argue that the demands for *shari'ah* should be located within the democratisation process. In terms of this analysis, however, the issue over the *shari'ah* is mostly contested within the political sphere and not the legal nor the civil spheres. Some governors seem to have promised their electorates that they would restore the glory of Islam in all aspects of life. But the main protagonists of *shari'ah* are a new class of Muslim youth groups, imams and intellectuals who aim to invest the civil religion of Nigeria with Islamic symbols. They seem to view their involvement in the political space of Nigeria in direct competition with Christians. Products of post-independence Nigeria, their interests lies not so much in the *shari'ah* as a legal system, but as a symbolic presence of Muslims in the national public space in competition with their Christian counterparts. The legal possibilities of *shari'ah* in the Nigerian system, and better relations between Muslim and Christians, are the real victims in this battle over the content and form of civil religion.

Governor Ahmed Sani's election promise and then later promulgation has been a good indication that the *shari'ah* may have been an important means by which the Northern elite could maintain power. In this case, it seems that *shari'ah* demands represented forces that resisted the further democratisation of Nigeria. A number of scholars have advanced the thesis that *shari'ah* has been employed to muster support for corrupt politicians. The *shari'ah* laws were an ideal means to maintain the patriarchal structure of the North against the pressure of democratisation.[34] Furthermore, the implementation of *shari'ah* laws in criminal matters allowed the spotlight to be placed on

---

[34] Joda, 2001.

petty crimes and sexual morality instead of the appalling record of Northern politicians in terms of service delivery and public fraud. According to Sanusi, religious identity politics pre-date the recent *shari'ah* and are a reflection thereof:

> The construction of a specific "popular-Islamic" or "popular-Christian" identity in contradistinction to the demands for altering this collective pathetic condition has enabled the dominant classes among Muslims and Christians [to] appropriate large numbers of the deprived as cannon-fodder in their competition for political and economic space – with the Nigerian State as the principal arena.[35]

In addition to these contextual critiques, there are many others who suggest that the promulgation of the *shari'ah* is an indication of the essentialist nature of Islam and Muslims to take control and subjugate non-Muslims to second-class citizenship. In this regard, the Nigerian governors and politicians were simply fulfilling the religious mandate coming from Islam.[36] In my opinion, the essentialist interpretations of this crisis can only be sustained if differences among Muslims, for and against *shari'ah*, are ignored, and if one chooses to place Muslims out of history. This is not to deny that Muslim discourses that denigrate the other have no historical effects. In order to unmask them, however, we need to understand them in both religious and historical contexts. To argue that a politician and a poor peasant both support the implementation of the *shari'ah* for the same reason seems to me preposterous, and avoids the scholarly tasks of analysis and interpretation.

The more substantial historical critique of the employment of *shari'ah* is clearly valid, and should be taken more seriously. But even this view seems only partially correct, because it ignores the fact that the governors like Ahmed Sani were also responding to the demands for *shari'ah* in the first place. The demand for *shari'ah* seems to predate its use or abuse by politicians. Ahmed Sani's election promises were an indication that the demand for *shari'ah* was already there. Thus

---

[35] Sanusi, 2003.
[36] Harnischfeger, 2003; Kukah, 1996; Okike, 2000; Turaki, 2003.

Murray Last, a leading historian of the Sokoto Caliphate, pointed out the important popular dimension of the *shari'ah* in a number of other states:

> [T]he politicians in power were not in favour of reintroducing the full Shari'a; it was a popular movement they were unable to resist without appearing to be publicly apostate.[37]

If we accept this argument, and reject the full implication of the essentialist and political critique, then we still have to show what the *shari'ah* means to people who support it. And for this comparison, I would like to explore the meaning of the *shari'ah* for the many supporters that do not form part of the Northern political elite.

The identity of the state, and here I restrict the term to the nature of its civil religion, can be a useful tool for analysing the meaning of the *shari'ah* for Muslims. And the first place to begin is to raise the question of the extent of secularity of the Nigerian state. Many Christians have argued that Nigeria is a secular state where church and state were completely separated. According to a perceptive analysis of Ostien and Gamaliel,[38] however, Nigeria does not have a disestablishment clause comparable to that of the constitution of the United States of America. Nigeria's clause (Section 10 of the constitution) remains ambiguous: "The Government of the Federation or of a State shall not adopt any religion as state religion." Christian critics have asserted that the extension of *shari'ah* law to include criminal jurisdiction creates a state religion. On the other hand, supporters have argued that the implementation of the laws follows Nigerian law and constitution going back to 1979. Ostien also seems to be of the view that notwithstanding the real crises on the political and civic levels, the promulgation of *shari'ah* has followed legal procedures.[39] It seems that the Nigerian case may best be compared with other European cases where some churches are officially recognised. The Nigerian case certainly cannot be compared with situations where Islam is the state religion like many North

---

[37] Last, 2002.
[38] Ostien and Gamaliel, 2002.
[39] Ostien, 2005.

African countries, or where Islam constitutes the foundation of the state as in Iran.

Religion is not completely disestablished in the Nigerian state. In fact, in many ways, both Muslim and Christian groups enjoy special privileges from state resources. The practice of supporting Muslims to go on *hajj* seemed to have been begun by British colonial practice, and has been continued since.[40] In some states, Nigerian Christians have received the same privilege of being sponsored by the state to go on pilgrimage to Jerusalem. Moreover, religious broadcasting has been actively supported by the state.[41] In this area, Muslims in the Niger Delta region envy the success of the Christians at taking advantage of the media opportunities provided by state television: "It has not been easy for Muslims to live peacefully under the well-packaged and numerous Christian church programmes aimed at winning more 'souls for Christ'."[42] Christians in the Muslim-dominated North complain of exactly the same marginalisation: "We cannot air our programmes on the State Radio and Television simply because we are Christians. We cannot even advertise. Nevertheless, the State Radio and Television broadcasts more than 90% of purely Islamic programmes."[43] The competition over state resources indicates the high degree to which religious symbols have become part of the political competition that politicians engaged in to the advantage of one or the other religious group. In the Northern states, Christian minorities suffer the disadvantages of public support for religious symbols. And the extension of the *shari'ah* is regarded with certain justification by Christians as part of this marginalisation. Political leaders seem to be tapping into this competition.

But the demand for religious symbols and values is not restricted to political circles. Over the last two to three decades, historians and students of religion have pointed to the dominance of Christian influences in the public sector, and the emergence of a Muslim voice. It is the Muslim voice that I would like to focus on without forgetting the role played by Christian churches in shaping the course of national life. It is in the context of this new Islamic discourse that we

---

[40] Tangban, 1991.
[41] Kilani, 2000.
[42] Ibid.
[43] The Christian Association of Nigeria (CAN), 2001.

can identify the demand for *shari'ah*, not as a source of laws and values but as a symbol of the state. Justice Ambali, a defender of the *shari'ah*, has identified this struggle succinctly:

> Essentially, beyond the controversy on the two sides are *da'wah* on the part of some Muslims who support the application of *shari'ah* and evangelism on the part of some Christians who oppose it because they regard the successful application of *shari'ah* as growth of Islam at the expense [of] Christianity.[44]

I would argue that the competition between Muslims and Christian is not restricted to the competition over individual souls in Nigeria, but over the national soul of the state.

A new Islamic group, variously referred to as Islamists or fundamentalists, have lobbied intensively for the place of religious symbols and Muslim interests in particular in the state. Products of the increased schooling offered by the independent Nigerian state, they have argued for a dominant role of Islam in the state.[45] Loimeier's study of Gumi follows the transformation and evolution of Muslim interests from one concerned with preserving Northern Muslim interests to the representation of Islam in the national state. Gumi began his career as an advisor to Ahmadu Bello and eventually became Grand Kadi of the Northern Region. He represented the image of Islam in power in Nigeria. At the same time, he also played a real and symbolic role in the direction and concerns of the 'Yan Izala movement. In the latter regard, Gumi was more interested in the purging of local African and Sufi influences from Muslim religious practices, and in the political representation of Muslims in the national state.[46] His challenges to the Sufi groups constituted a reformulation of Islamic practices on the basis of the texts and prescriptions of the sources of the Qur'an and Islamic law. In this regard, he can be compared with similar Islamist visionaries in the Muslim world. On the other hand, his decision on voting in Nigerian

---

[44] Ambali, 2001,4.
[45] Reichmuth, 1993.
[46] Loimeier, 1997.

elections during the *hajj* period indicates his clearly nationalistic aspirations. Umar and Barkindo have documented the popular dimension of this trend in Nigerian Muslim life.[47] What is very clear in this regard is that during the period of independence, the Islamist vision of society has emerged as a third grouping within Islamic public life alongside Sufism and the judiciary.[48]

And it seems that this group has led the demand for the Islamisation of the society through the judiciary. Islamists and now governors threaten to use and do use the *shari'ah* as a means of further Islamisation. Governors employ *shari'ah* as a symbol of political life in comparison with Christians invoking God at meetings and other political functions. The decision to pass laws on public transportation in Zamfara clearly is an indication of this attempt to impose a particular vision of morality on the civil space. More ominously, the pressure that is being put on Christian minorities in the affected states indicates that the *shari'ah* extensions go beyond the judiciary. As a religiously based law, the *shari'ah* is dragged into the competition over religious symbols in the national state.

But the introduction of *shari'ah* as a form of Islamisation has had at least one unexpected outcome. It has forced the issue of religion from the political space to the judiciary. The Nigerian Islamists have ended up in a dilemma which is beginning to unravel. On the one hand, the extension of the *shari'ah* is an important part of the demand for Islamisation. On the other hand, the extension of the *shari'ah* is justified in the constitution of the country. And the latter has brought to the fore Muslim and secularist voices to the debate. In the Nigerian case, the constitution clearly demands due process of law in the implementation of the *shari'ah*. The federal government has not challenged the question of the *shari'ah* as such, but insisted for proper process in the different codes to be used and in the process from the local courts to the federal courts. In this space, women's activist groups and other Islamic voices in Nigeria have insisted that rights are protected within the ambit of the law, and that includes the implementation and extension of the *shari'ah*.[49] In a short period of

---

[47] Umar, 1993, Barkindo, 1993.
[48] Christelow, 2002.
[49] Imam, 2003.

time, they have become active in the formulation of a strategy of providing defence lawyers, raising awareness of rights within an Islamic legal framework, and ensuring due process in the various stages of the legal process.[50] The enhancement of this process and the high level of judicial awareness seem to have taken shape in the open political process in Nigeria. In this regard, one can see a comparable situation with South Africa where a system of Islamic law or a system of recognition of Islamic law came under the general framework of the Bill of Rights.

CONCLUDING REFLECTIONS

The comparative analysis of *shari'ah* in South Africa, Kenya, and Nigeria has the advantage of highlighting aspects more dominant in one country than another. In all the countries, to a greater or lesser extent, it seems that the demands for some recognition of *shari'ah* arise from relations within Muslim society itself. Rather than regarding the state imposition of *shari'ah* regulations from the top down, one should also look at the bottom up needs of justice and the regulation of social relations. This does not mean, of course, that certain social actors do not see the benefit of *shari'ah* for their own political or religious ambitions. This ambition has been clearest in Nigeria for the political benefits of Islamisation of the political space. A closer study would reveal other interests involved in the other countries as well. Moreover, the Nigerian case also shows the close relation between movement for Islamisation in the political space and its judicial aspects. Firstly, one should see this in its competition with similar Christian ambitions for religion in the public domain. More importantly, one should not forget important Islamic voices that confine *shari'ah* to its judicial application. Women's rights groups, with a strong interest in progressive Islamic interpretation in South Africa and Nigeria, are clearly interested in the particular aspects of the *shari'ah*. For these groups, the role of *shari'ah* within the limits of the constitution in each respective country holds promise for communities and personal relations. So far, their contribution seems to be reactionary in that harsh punishments and unjust judgments

---

[50] Mahdi, 2003.

have to be mitigated by an appeal process that allows the alternative interpretations of Islamic law to emerge. However, the experience of the *qadi*'s courts in Kenya suggests the effective ways that women's rights may be protected in an efficiently run system of *shari'ah* courts. But this can possibly only be achieved when the issue of the *shari'ah* is taken out of its political dimensions.

The analytical rubric of religion and public life between the civil and political spaces has been a useful and illuminating window into the complex *shari'ah* issue. It is clear that in the post-colonial African state, Muslims are using the *shari'ah* in order to define the symbolic nature of the nation state. They see Christian influence in the very nature of the state and law. Deeply embedded within the nation state, Christianity appears to them prefigured in the marital laws of Kenya or the nature of the secular state in Nigeria. Furthermore, Muslims see the close relations between Christianity and government officials as an advanced position in the political competition. The political space, even in the absence of strong religious parties, seems impregnated with religious competition. In this religiously contested political sphere, the extension or recognition for *shari'ah* seems like a reasonable demand to make. Again, however, the *shari'ah* in the political competitions tends to sacrifice the legal needs of justice and equity.

The entrapment of the *shari'ah* issue in the political sphere ignores its important role in the judiciary. The demand for justice in Muslim personal relations becomes the victim of political competition with Christians, and the Islamisation of society. The latter two cannot be disentangled from each other. The loss of justice, however, is an important witness to the futility of the latter. In both South Africa and Nigeria, in spite of these limitations, the emergence of progressive voices for the due process of law indicates the possibly constructive role of religion in society. However, in my view, this positive contribution can only take place if the competition in the political sphere can be unmasked.

The possible contribution of the legal dimension in the broader debate about religion and public life still needs to be seen. The controversies in Kenya and to some extent in South Africa, have clearly demonstrated the need for progressive Islamic legal intervention. Secular laws that deny recognition to alternative systems of justice usually deny justice. In this challenge, the role of religion in the judiciary seems a reasonable third option that needs greater consideration. It fits neither in the political sphere of civil religion nor in the public discourse of civil society. It can easily be employed in the competition over civil religion, clearly demonstrated in Nigeria and to a lesser extent in Kenya. The debate over Islamic law may be employed fruitfully in the civil discourse, but then it would need to be recognized in some way in the judiciary in order that its benefits reach citizens. The possibilities, in my view, are there for the democratisation and the extension of rights through an unlikely ally.

REFERENCES

Ambali, Honourable Justice M. A., "Application of Islamic personal law in Nigeria", paper presented at the Second Symposium of the Islamic Law in Africa Project, Dakar, 29 June-1 July 2001.

Barkindo, Bawuro M., "Growing Islamism in Kano City since 1970", in: Louis Brenner (ed.), *Muslim Identity and Social Change in Sub-Saharan Africa*, London: Hurst & Company, 1993, 91-105.

Bashir, Amina, "Why do kadhi's courts need to be in the constitution?", paper presented at the ICJ Public Lecture, Grand Regency Hotel, Nairobi, 29 April, 2003.

Beckford, James, "Religion, modernity and post-modernity", in: Bryan Wilson (ed.), *Religion: Contemporary Issues*, London: Bellew Publishing, 1992, 11-23.

Bellah, Robert N., "Religion and the legitimation of the American republic", in: Robert N. Bellah and Phillipp E. Hammond (eds.), *Varieties of Civil Religion*, San Francisco: Harper & Row, 1980, 5-23.

Brown, Beverly B., "Islamic law, qadhi's courts and Muslim women's legal status: the case of Kenya", *Journal Institute of Muslim Minority Affairs* 14/1-2, 1994, 94-101.

Cachalia, Firoz and Albie, Sachs, *The Future of Muslim Family Law in South Africa*, University of the Witwatersrand: Occasional Paper 12. Johannesburg: Centre for Applied Legal Studies: University of the Witwatersrand Press, 1991.

Casanova, Jose, *Public Religions in the Modern World*, Chicago, London: The University of Chicago Press, 1994.

Chidester, David, *Patterns of Power: Religion and politics in American culture*, Englewood Cliffs, New Jersey: Prentice Hall, 1988.

──────, "The Church of baseball, the fetish of Coca-Cola, and the potlatch of rock 'n' roll: theoretical models for the study of religion in

American popular culture", *Journal of the American Academy of Religion*, 54, 1996, 743-65.

Christelow, Allan, "The persistence and transformation in the politics of sharia in Nigeria, 1958-2002: in search of an explanatory framework", paper presented at the Third Symposium of the Islamic Law in Africa Project, Cape Town, 11-14 March, 2002.

The Christian Association of Nigeria (CAN), Zamfara State, "Peace and democracy in Nigeria", no publication information given, 2001 (copy in the possession of the author).

Constantin, Francois, "Leadership, Muslim identities, and East African politics: tradition, bureaucratisation and communication", in: Louis Brenner (ed.), *Muslim Identity and Social Change in Sub-Saharan Africa*, London: Hurst & Company, 1993, 36-58.

Cruise O'Brien, Donal B., "Coping with the Christians: the Muslim predicament in Kenya", in: Holger Bernt Hansen and Michael Twaddle (eds.), *Religion and Politics in East Africa: The period since independence*, London: James Curry, 1995, 200-219.

Gifford, Paul, *African Christianity: Its public role*, London: Hurst & Co., 1998.

Harnischfeger, Johannes, "Sharia, ethnic hegemony, and land conflicts in Northern Nigeria", paper presented at the conference on The Shari'a Debate and the Shaping of Muslim and Christian Identities in Northern Nigeria, Bayreuth, July 10-12 2003.

Hassan, Ahmed Issack (Commissioner), *Working Document for the Constitution of Kenya Review Commission on the Kadhi's Courts, Chief Kadhi and Kadhis*, 2001 Constitution of Kenya Review Commission, 2002 [cited September 3 2003]. Available from http://www.kenyaconstitution.org/docs/07d046.htm.

Hirsch, Susan F., *Pronouncing & Persevering : Gender and the discourses of disputing in an African Islamic court*, Chicago: University of Chicago Press, 1998.

Illesanmi, Simeon O., "The civil religion thesis in Nigeria: a critical examination of Jacob Olupona's theory of religion and the state," *The Council of Societies for the Study of Religions Bulletin*, 24/3-4, 1995, 59-64.

Imam, Ayesha, "Please stop the international Amina Lawal protest letter campaigns", Mailing list: AfricaDemocracy@yahoogroups.com, 2003, cited May 1, 2003.

Joda, Asmau, "The citizenship of women: some Nigerian Muslim interpretations", paper presented at the Second Symposium of the Islamic Law in Africa Project, Dakar, 29 June-1 July 2001.

Kenny, Joseph, "Sharia and Christianity in Nigeria: Islam and a 'secular' state", *Journal of Religion in Africa*, 26/4, 1996, 338-64.

The Kenya Church, "Recommendations to the Constitution of Kenya Review Commission on the proposed Draft Constitution of the Republic of Kenya", Nairobi: The Kenya Church, 2002.

Kilani, Abdul Razaq, "Islam and Christian-Muslim relations in Niger-Delta (Nigeria)", *Journal of Muslim Minority Affairs*, 20/1, 2000, 129-36.

Kukah, Matthew Hassan and Falola, Toyin, *Religious Militancy and Self-Assertion: Islam and politics in Nigeria*. One of "The Making of Modern Africa" series, Abebe Zegeye and John Higginson, series editors. Aldershot, Brookfield, Hong Kong, Singapore, and Sydney: Avebury, 1996.

Last, Murray, "The shari'a in context: people's quest for justice today and the role of courts in the pre-and early colonial Northern Nigeria", paper presented at the Third Symposium of the Islamic Law in Africa Project, Cape Town, 11-14 March 2002.

Loimeier, Roman, "Islamic reform and political change: the example of Abubakar Gumi and the 'Yan Izala movement in Northern Nigeria", in: Eva Evers Rosander and David Westerlund (eds.), *African Islam and Islam in Africa*, London: Hurst and Company, 1997, 286-307.

Mahdi, Saudatu S., "Shari'a implementation in Nigeria: implications for women's rights", paper presented at the conference on The Shari'a Debate and the Shaping of Muslim and Christian Identities in Northern Nigeria, Bayreuth, July 10-12 2003.

Mohammed, Abubakar Siddique and Sa'idu Hassan Adamu, *The Living Conditions of the Talakawa and the Shari'ah in Contemporary Nigeria*, Zaria, Nigeria: Centre for Democratic Development, Research and Training (CEDDERT), 2000.

Moosa, Ebrahim, "Religion and human rights: taking rights religiously", paper presented at a conference at the University of Natal, Pietermaritzburg, Natal, 1991.

―――, "Prospects of Muslim law in South Africa: a history and recent developments", in: Eugene Cotran and Chibli Mallat (eds.), *Yearbook of Islamic and Middle Eastern Law, Volume 3*, London: Kluwer Law International, 1996, 130-55.

Moosa, Najma, "The interim and final constitutions and Muslim personal law—implications for South African Muslim women", *Stellenbosch Law Review Regtydskrif*, 9/2, 1998, 196-206.

Muslim Advocates, No title: questions raised on kadhi's courts in the constitution, 5 pp., Nairobi, n.d. (copy in the possession of the author).

Oded, Arye, "Islamic extremism in Kenya: the rise and fall of Sheikh Khalid Balala", *Journal of Religion in Africa*, 26/4, 1996, 406-15.

Okike, Benedict Ohadughiro, *The Practice of Sharia in Nigeria: A democratic secular state*, Owerri, Imo State, Nigeria: Amamihe Publications, 2000.

Olupona, Jacob Obafemi Kehinde, *Kingship, Religion, and Rituals in a Nigerian Community : A phenomenological study of Ondo Yoruba festivals*, Stockholm Studies in Comparative Religion: Stockholm: Almqvist & Wiksell, 1991.

Ostien, Philip, "Ten good things about the implementation of *shari'a* in some states of Northern Nigeria", *Swedish Missiological Themes*, 90/2, 2002, 163-174.

———, "An opportunity missed by Nigeria's Christians: the *shari'a* debate of 1976-78 revisited", in: Benjamin Soares, ed., *Muslim-Christian Relations in Africa. Islam in Africa* series, volume 5. Leiden and Boston: Brill, forthcoming 2005.

Ostien, Philip and Gamaliel, J.D., "The law of separation of religion and state in the United States: a model for Nigeria?", in: S.O.O. Amali et al. (eds.), *Religion in the United States*, Ibadan: American Studies Association of Nigeria, 2002, 14-32.

Peters, Ruud, *Islamic Criminal Law in Nigeria*, Ibadan: Spectrum Books Limited, 2003.

Pickering, W. S. F., *Durkheim on Religion: A selection of readings with bibliographies*, London: Routledge & Kegan, 1975.

Rautenbach, Christa, "The recognition of Muslim marriages in South Africa past, present and future", *Recht van de Islam*, 17, 2000, 36-89.

Reichmuth, Stefan, "Islamic learning and its interaction with 'western' education in Ilorin, Nigeria", in: Louis Brenner (ed.), *Muslim Identity and Social Change in Sub-Saharan Africa*, Bloomington: Indiana University Press, 1993, 179-97.

Rousseau, Jean Jacques, *The Social Contract and Discourses*, London: Dent, 1973.

Sanusi, Lamido, "The shari'a debate and the construction of a 'Muslim' identity in Northern Nigeria: a critical perspective", paper presented at the conference on The Shari'a Debate and the Shaping of Muslim and Christian Identities in Northern Nigeria, Bayreuth, July 10-12 2003.

Tangban, O. E., "The hajj and the Nigerian economy, 1960-1981", *Journal of Religion in Africa*, 21/3, 1991, 241-171.

Tayob, Abdulkader I., "Civil religion for Muslims in South Africa", *Journal for the Study of Religion*, 8/2, 1995, 23-46.

Toffar, A. K., "The Qur'anic constitution and its expression in law—a legal dilemma in a non-Muslim state", *Occasional Journal of ICOSA*, 2, 1422 [2001/02], 1-20.

Turaki, Yusufu, "The shari'a debate in the northern states of Nigeria: implications for Muslims, Christians and democracy in Nigeria", paper presented at the conference on The Shari'a Debate and the Shaping of Muslim and Christian Identities in Northern Nigeria, Bayreuth, July 10-12 2003.

Umar, Muhammad Sani, "Changing Islamic identity in Nigeria from the 1960s to the 1980s: from sufism to anti-sufism", in: Louis Brenner (ed.), *Muslim Identity and Social Change in Sub-Saharan Africa*, Bloomington: Indiana University Press, 1993, 154-78.

Commentary

I.

Warisu O. Alli

Professor Abdulkader Tayob has carried out a very critical analysis of the growing demand among the Muslim communities across Africa for the implementation of the *shari'ah* using the three African states of Republic of South Africa, Kenya and Nigeria as case studies. He concludes that these demands are fuelled by the democratisation process in these countries and that the demands have actually manifested themselves in different forms concerning the jurisdiction *shari'ah* would have and the structures for its implementation. Still another reason he gives for these demands for *shari'ah* is the need felt by the Muslims in these countries for some Islamic religious symbols as part of the political and civil space hitherto since the colonial period "impregnated with religious competition and the dominant role of Christian symbols in the state and public sphere," and because of these he argues that "the extension or recognition for *shari'ah* seems like a reasonable demand to make." He notes certain differences in the demands for *shari'ah* in these countries. While in South Africa the demands were for the adoption of Muslim personal law for Muslims, and in Kenya for the reform of the *qadi* court system, in Nigeria it was for the comprehensive implementation of the *shari'ah*, particularly in several Northern states.

SOUTH AFRICA

In South Africa for example, the Muslims wanted, as their contribution to the post-apartheid constitutional reform, the introduction of Muslim personal law, for very practical purposes like for example recognition for marriages conducted by imams in mosques. Some Muslim groups insisted on a reformed system of Islamic law, which should be consistent with the provisions of the constitution and subject to the Bill of Rights such that it would not disadvantage women. Others argued that as divine laws, the *shari'ah* should be taken directly from the books of *fiqh* and should not be susceptible to change, thus preferring instead a system of legal pluralism which will not impose secularism – a kind of "abuse and cruelty of the democracy of numbers"– on Muslims.

In the end, the South African constitution achieved a compromise between radical reform and tradition allowing for a Muslim personal law "consistent with the constitution" and recognising marriages "concluded under any tradition," thus allowing for a plural legal system and "implying the exemption of Muslim personal law from the jurisdiction of the Bill of Rights." Such marriages have been a source of many problems particularly for women in relation to divorce, and other claims on the husband before the courts or on inheritance, before the promulgation of the South African constitution.

However, this South African approach is unique and as has been rightly observed by Professor Tayob, "has far-reaching consequences for thinking about the demands for *shari'ah*" by Muslims in other societies and "confirms an important democratic principle of working from concerns and issues that affect the people.

KENYA

In Kenya, according to the author, this demand, which was for the reform of the *qadi*s, whose services seem to have been sought by Muslims all over Kenya, grew out of a general campaign for democracy attendant upon the collapse of the Berlin Wall and the end of the Cold War. This new climate led to the repeal in 1991 of the former constitutional prohibition on forming new political parties, which in turn led to the Unfungamano Initiative, a pro-democracy civil society initiative, leading to the formation of new parties, campaigns for greater freedom, respect for human and religious rights and greater decentralisation of power. By 2001, the agitation led to the Constitution of Kenya Review (Amendment) Act of 2001 and the formation of the Kenya Constitution Review Commission, which was given 24 months to collate the views of the population and produce a draft constitution.

It was this draft constitution which brought out the demand for the reform of the *qadi*s who had served the Muslims of Kenya since the colonial period. Islam was the dominant religion in East Africa well into the 20th century, and *shari'ah* had been in Kenya, particularly the Kenyan coastal strip, for centuries before the arrival of the Europeans and Christianity. It was colonialism that suppressed Islam and the *shari'ah* in Kenya, allowing only Muslim personal law.[1]

Some of the recommendations for the constitutional review were for better training for the *qadi*s and the demand that they possess, apart from Islamic credentials, also legal degrees. There was a recommendation that because more women than men approach the *qadi*s with grievances against their husbands or male relatives, women should be represented on the boards that would appoint the *qadi*s, a demand not particularly supported by Kenyan Muslims, according to the author. There was also a recommendation for a Kadhi's Court of Appeal through which decisions of the lower *qadi*s on minor cases of financial claims for which the *qadi*s were considered efficient, could pass to higher national courts for further deliberations.

The responses to these recommendations by both the Christians, represented by the Kenyan National Church (KNC), and a diverse group of Muslims constituted the platform for the analysis of the *shari'ah* issue in Kenya. The KNC objected to the inclusion in the constitution of provisions on the *qadi*s and on women taking part in the appointment of *qadi*s, claiming such provisions "violated the principle of the separation of religion and state." However, the KNC also argued that the first clause of the constitution should mention God. The body also wanted the addition of another sentence "recognising the supremacy and sovereignty of the Almighty God of all creation." – all these from a body claiming to be fighting for the secularity of the state. As Professor Tayob beautifully observed, it seems in Kenya, "the place of religion in the broader symbolism of

---

[1] Bakari, 1993, 82.

the state was acceptable, but the symbolism of a specific religion like Islam was unacceptable."

The Muslims supported the recommendations, arguing that there was need for the constitution to address the problems of the *qadi*s and to create appropriate constitutional mechanisms for addressing legal problems arising from the Islamic legal cases emerging within the Kenyan society. Responding to the objections of the KNC, the Muslims argued that the Christians did not need to have separate courts because the laws of Kenya are mainly Judeo-Christian in nature.

The *shari'ah* issue in Kenya is therefore an attempt to use the opportunity of the constitutional review to address some of the grievances of the Muslims particularly against the inadequacies of the *qadi*s. According to Bakari, there were big gaps in the available manpower for the *qadi*'s courts, and furthermore most *qadi*s were mosque-trained and not sufficiently qualified for the roles expected of them.

> The *shari'ah* law graduates from Medina, Al-Azhar and suchlike institutions often do not have even a working knowledge of English, and consequently, feel themselves at the periphery of the secular society and also feel themselves as totally incapacitated to contribute to legal, economic and social debates within the country.[2]

The other issue at stake in Kenya was the dominant visibility of the KNC in the political system and national affairs and the high level of interaction between the church and prominent government officials and consequently "between Christianity and the state."

Ironically, it was the opposition of the KNC to the recommendations that alerted the Muslims to the degree of absence of Islamic symbols in the Kenyan state. This thus became an opportunity for them to ask for the symbolic representation of Muslim interests in the Kenyan state which may be partly solved by an improvement in the constitutional provisions for the working of the *qadi*s. However, the author did not show that Kenyan Muslims

---

[2] Ibid., 83.

actually demanded for the implementation of *shari'ah* comprehensively or in part despite their obvious need for it. Thus the struggle of Kenyan Muslims revolves around the desire to have an improvement in the work of the *qadi*s and for greater representation and for more visibility and actually more Islamic symbols in the political space of Kenya.

NIGERIA

Shari'ah has always been part of the legal system in Nigeria. In fact *shari'ah* was already being fully implemented in Nigeria before the arrival of Christianity with the Europeans. It was well entrenched as the operating legal system particularly in Northern Nigeria and despite pressures for reforms and its being ousted from one legal subject matter after the other in other parts of the Islamic world, it survived in Northern Nigeria more or less intact before independence, thanks to the Fulani *jihad* and the orthodoxy it represented.

However, all this came to end in 1960. Under what Ostien has called "The Settlement of 1960,"[3] Islamic criminal law was abrogated, the judicial powers of the Emirs were curtailed, while the alkali courts became less traditionally Muslim. The Settlement of 1960 came about because, in preparation for Nigerian independence, the leadership of the predominantly Muslim Northern region agreed to drop some aspects of the *shari'ah* in deference to the clamour of minorities in the region and the pressures from the British. The Muslims were left with a new Sharia Court of Appeal. The judgements of this court on matters within its jurisdiction were made final. In addition, the *qadi*s of the Sharia Court of Appeal had a seat in the three-man panels of judges of the Native Courts Appellate Division of the High Court.

All these came to an end following "The Debacle of 1979."[4] In the Constituent Assembly that debated the new Nigerian constitution which took effect in that year, the proposal for a *Federal* Sharia Court of Appeal was eliminated from the draft constitution after protracted and stormy debates spearheaded by Christian opposition to the

---
[3] Ostien, 2005.
[4] Ibid.

proposal. But what was at stake in that debate? Just a technical requirement of transferring constitutionally to the newly created states the powers and structures which earlier belonged to the Northern region.[5] Not only was this not done; on the basis of the provisions of the 1979 Constitution, the jurisdiction of the Sharia Courts of Appeal were further restricted, the seat of the *qadi*s on the Native Court Appellate Division of the High Courts was lost, finality and autonomy on issues of Islamic personal law were also lost – all setting the stage for the "unhappiness of the Muslims with the Nigerian Legal System."[6]

This was the background to the *shari'ah* "revolution" launched in Nigeria, in fulfilment of election promises by the Governor of Zamfara State, Ahmed Sani, who announced the implementation of comprehensive *shari'ah* legislation in the state in January, 2000, a step supported by Section 277(1) of the nation's constitution. This fact was noted by the author. The Zamfara example was soon followed by eleven other Northern states: Bauchi, Borno, Gombe, Jigawa, Kaduna, Kano, Katsina, Kebbi, Nasarawa, Sokoto and Yobe.

Professor Tayob has argued that the demands for *shari'ah* in Nigeria should be seen as part of the democratisation process, coming as it did after the end of the era of military dictatorship and the beginning of a democratisation process. One cannot but agree with this argument. But this does not fully explain the dynamics of the *shari'ah* "revolution" in Nigeria as we shall soon show

But while the implementation of a comprehensive *shari'ah* was spearheaded by Islamic activists, led by the governors who have used their political positions to advance the course of *shari'ah*, they have also turned to the constitution for justification.

There is this point about who the real advocates of *shari'ah* are. Are they really the politicians, Muslim youth groups, Muslim intellectuals and professionals, the imams or the Muslim masses? Definitely all Muslims are expected to be *shari'ah* advocates and activists. Acceptance of the *shari'ah* is part of the Islamic faith. And the governors no doubt appreciated and indeed exploited the political power of the *shari'ah*. However, we must register the role of prominent activist Muslim youth groups encouraged by some Islamic

---

[5] Ibid., 11.
[6] Ibid., 13.

scholars. The traditional imams were also enthusiastic about the prospects of the implementation of a comprehensive *shari'ah* and were quick in becoming active in the movement.

It is often argued that the agitation for *shari'ah* in the twelve Northern states that have adopted it was essentially a reaction to the loss of political power by the North following the election of a southern Christian president. Nothing could be further from the truth. In fact, both Christian and Muslim politicians have always exploited religious and other affiliations to advance their political interests. Both groups appropriate religious symbols for their political goals. Christian influences in the public sector, which have always been pronounced even when Muslims were presidents, have just been complemented by what Professor Tayob aptly called "a Muslim voice" and as Ostien correctly observed, the agitation for a more "respectable" position for *shari'ah* in the Nigerian legal system has been on for a very long time. The stormy debates over the *shari'ah* in the 1977-78 Constituent Assembly and the eventual tragedy of the 1979 Constitution for Muslims and the several other attempts made by Muslims to remedy the situation with every successive constitution-making process since then in 1988-89, 1995 and in 1999 would confirm the thesis of Professor Tayob, that the *shari'ah* revolution in Nigeria since 1999 only took advantage of the democratic environment. Besides, the 1999 constitution empowers the states to determine for themselves the jurisdiction of their Sharia Courts of Appeal.

Of course, there is no doubt that Nigerian Muslims, being over 50% of the population, are interested in having as much symbolic presence in the state as the Christians have. This was an idea, according to the author, which the late Islamic scholar Gumi pursued with vigour representing a third Islamic vision of society in addition to sufi and the judicial vision. Comprehensive implementation of the *shari'ah*, apart from its significant religious necessity for Muslims also provides opportunity for such symbolic presence.

In addition, the huge support which the *shari'ah* enjoys among the ordinary people is, apart from the religious requirements, the hope that with *shari'ah* would come an egalitarian society, a framework for addressing their abject poverty and oppression. This is why it is difficult to agree with Professor Tayob that the *shari'ah* would remain an instrument in the hands of the Muslim political elite or "a political tool in the hand of the patriarchal structure of the *shari'ah*-implementing Northern states." So far, the rigours of the *shari'ah* system and its demand for due process and the legal decisions made so far in Nigeria show that it is possible to achieve human rights in a modern sense following the *shari'ah* notwithstanding the fear that only the weak would be found guilty by the system because of corruption.

There is always this argument by some sections of the Nigerian society: that the introduction of a comprehensive *shari'ah* in some states makes Nigeria a potentially religious state as opposed to its secular nature; that it is an attempt to Islamise the nation. The truth is that the introduction of *shari'ah* in twelve out of thirty-six states does not make Nigeria an Islamic state, any more than having a Muslim president would make it an Islamic state. An Islamic state suggests a theocracy where religious and political powers are fused. This is not the case in Nigeria or in any of its states. The Judeo-Christian basis of the Nigerian legal system does not make Nigeria a "Christian state."

I, however, agree with the author that implementation of the *shari'ah* may be going beyond the judiciary. It is hoped that what the author termed "the pressure being put on Christian minorities in the affected states" would be lifted, following the true Islamic tradition of respect for the rights of non-Muslims.

GENERAL OBSERVATIONS

Generally, I would want to draw attention to some related issues that should concern us with regards to the campaign for *shari'ah* across Africa. These issues relate to the secularity of the African states, the issue of religious expansion and revival.

There are contradictions attending the notion of the secularity of African states, specifically, the three case studies. How really secular are Kenya, Nigeria and South Africa? The KNC demands for a clause in the Kenyan constitution intimating the role of God in creation. In Nigeria, both Christians and Muslims demand government involvement in their religious affairs, and the state obliges them. Sharp social stratification often leads to a new pattern of relationship towards religion with members of the society developing instrumental attitudes to religion.[7] Political leaders exploit it and the masses also apply it to advance their claims.

Thus, while today we can talk of secularity or the formal separation of religion and state globally, there are as already noted several points of contact between the two. Even in the US, the home of secularism, the US is still considered a Christian state! Secularism cannot resolve the competition between Muslims and Christians. In fact it is liberal democracy, which emerged from the ruins of Christendom, which was developed to handle competition between Catholics and Protestants.[8] Healthy democracy would reduce religious conflict in Nigeria as well.

Ali Mazrui has noted that outside Arab Africa, the central issue concerning Islam is not merely its revival – it is also the speed of its expansion.[9] Yet, there is a revival of religion globally in the wake of the end of the cold war and the end of ideological competition. It must be noted that colonialism helped the expansion of Christianity in Africa. It seems that this new era of democracy is also helping Islam across Africa, however, not so much for expansion but for revival.

Tayob quotes Justice Ambali who observed that "essentially, beyond the controversy the issue is actually that of *da'wah* for Muslims who support *shari'ah* and revival for the Christians who oppose it because they regard the successful application of *shari'ah* as growth of Islam at the expense of Christianity." Mazrui, for his part, had proposed that the campaign for *shari'ah* was for its revival, fuelled largely by economic disadvantage, oppression, and desperation.[10]

CONCLUSION

This is a very stimulating paper, written with a great deal of insight and on the basis of a wealth of literature. It draws attention to the different, but yet essentially similar approaches of Muslims in three different African states – South Africa, Kenya and Nigeria – to the promotion of Islam through demands for the *shari'ah*. Their

---

[7] Williams, 1997, 185.
[8] Ibid., 186.
[9] Mazrui, 1993, 248.
[10] Ibid., 261.

circumstances of democratic dispensation-post apartheid situation in South Africa, post-cold war climate in Kenya and post-military dictatorship in Nigeria are also similar. But while the efforts of the Muslims in these countries have no doubt advanced the interests of Islam, they cannot be said to be aimed at Islamising these countries or capable of changing the political status quo. Rather, the energetic and enthusiastic campaigns of the Muslims of these countries are reactions to the long period of oppression and denial of full religious rights to them and attempt to increase the symbolic presence of Islam in the state. The demands should also be seen as attempts at revival of Islam in those countries and this is not unique to Islam as Christianity is also undergoing a strong process of revival.

REFERENCES

Bakari, Mohammed, "The prospects for shari'a in East Africa", in: N. Alkali et al. (eds.), *Islam in Africa*, Ibadan: Spectrum Books Limited, 1993, 81-86.
Mazrui, Ali, "African Islam and comprehensive religion: between revivalism and expansion", in: N. Alkali et al. (eds.), *Islam in Africa*, Ibadan: Spectrum Books Limited, 1993, 247-265.
Ostien, Philip, "An opportunity missed by Nigeria's Christians: the *shari'a* debate of 1976-78 revisited", in: Benjamin Soares, ed., *Muslim-Christian Relations in Africa. Islam in Africa* series, volume 5. Leiden and Boston: Brill, forthcoming 2005.
Williams, Pat T., "New measures to ensure an effective separation of state and religion in Nigeria", in: Okafor F.U., (ed.), *New Strategies for Curbing Ethnic and Religious Conflicts in Nigeria*, Enugu: Fourth Dimension, 1997, 184-201.

II.

J. Isawa Elaigwu

Religion is a matter of primordial identity and means different things to different people. In some societies, it has taken ideological coloration to the extent that it provides a guide for faith, action and evaluation in private and public life. In others it guides only private life. For us, religion is a set of beliefs and practices based on faith, which are sacred and defy rational scrutiny. Therefore, it can quite easily trigger off emotional reactions. Religion makes the world more predictable, the vicissitudes of life more tolerable, and its complexities more understandable. It provides psychological relief and inspiration for the individual. At the social level, it provides a medium for fellowship and mutual support. Religion deals with the metaphysical world, which is expected to codify and guide our materialistic world.

DEMOCRACY

'Democracy' is a very controversial term. Even the Greek city-states which practised democracy in those old days, would be shocked to see the values attached to democracy today. However, there are certain principles of democracy which can be regarded as universal. The first is that in a democratic setting, authority (defined as the legitimate use of power) emanates from the people. The people are the repository of power, and they delegate this power to their representatives to use it to ensure the carrying on of their welfare and security. This delegated power from the people is called authority.

The second characteristic is the rule of law. A democratic polity must be based on law which is applicable to all and guarantees the security of all. It makes the system predictable. It makes it possible for the aggrieved to seek redress, instead of taking the law into his or her own hands. The third principle is legitimacy. This has two aspects – input and output. The input dimension presupposes that the government and/or the leader has the right to rule, based on the law guiding ascension to political power. The output aspect refers to the fact that it is not enough that you have the right to rule, but that you must rule rightly, given the mandate given to you by the people.

This leads us to the fourth point, the principle of choice. If you do not rule rightly, the people must have the right to change you through an established mechanism, and give a new mandate to someone else. Choice also refers to other forms of freedom, such as your freedom of worship, of thought, of movement, association, expression and others as permitted by law. There is no absolute freedom anywhere in the world. Your freedom stops where mine begins. Finally, there is the principle of accountability. Government and/or leaders must be accountable to the people for the mandate given to them to carry out certain activities on behalf of the people. Often, most societies have ways of establishing the principles of accountability in government business through a set of rules and regulations.

How these principles of democracy are implemented, would differ from one country to the other. The structures established for achieving these principles, and even their operation within a given country, may also differ. So democracy does not mean American or Western democracy. You may build over the years a democratic culture that is peculiarly Nigerian. For our purposes, we shall concentrate on the issues of choice and accountability as they affect our discussion of the *shari'ah*.

Professor Tayob uses two paradigms for the proper role of religion in pluralist democratic contexts – the civil religion model (as represented by Rousseau, Durkheim, and Bellah), and the public philosophy model (as represented by Habermas and Casanova). He skilfully applies both paradigms to the three cases he discusses – South Africa, Kenya and Nigeria. Unlike many Western and/or Western-educated scholars his use of the concept of pluralism shows great sensitivity to the peculiarity of the African setting. He uses the terms to refer to communalism, especially ethnic and religious dichotomy in society.

However, in his Kenya case these was no evidence of original proposition by Muslims. One saw evidence of Muslim reactions to the position of Christian churches. Perhaps, the author may want to have a second look at this. There might have been original positions held by Muslims, to which Christians might have reacted.

SHARI'AH IN THE DEMOCRATISATION PROCESS

Perhaps the process of democratisation provides a medium for the interplay of demands for participation and other rights on the one hand, and the challenges of faith in a political context, on the other. In South Africa, for example, there were demands for the recognition of Islamic law in matters of personal law. But this process for legislation was aimed at ensuring that justice was done, and that sections of Muslim society would be protected by law in the process of implementation. Thus the first challenge may be seen as that of the paradox of demands for recognition and rights. Not only was there a demand on the political system to recognise Islamic personal law, but also for legislation to protect rights of members of the Islamic community.

The second challenge, seems to be the crisis of class in the implementation of the *shari'ah* in a democratic process. The *shari'ah* aims at societal sanitisation from a religio-moral perspective. Unfortunately, there seems to be a class dimension in its implementation. So far, only the poor have suffered the pangs of *shari'ah* justice in Nigeria. There is hardly any evidence of members of the elite having their arms amputated for stealing like Jengebe or flogged for the consumption of alcohol.

Is it the case that members of the elite are less likely to run foul of the *shari'ah* or is it that they are more protected? Is this an equivalent of the Iranian revolution, in a way? The Iranian youths who fuelled the embers of revolution ended up being its first victims. Many of them were ruthlessly punished for wearing jeans and short skirts. The poor people have been the greatest proponents and supporters of the introduction of the *shari'ah*. In many cases, they put pressure on state governors, up to a point of *black or whitemail*, for the introduction of *shari'ah*. Now they seem to be the main victims. The elite seems untouchable by the law, and many of them do not seem to care about *zakat*, which the *shari'ah* requests them to carry out as an intra-class obligation. Candidly, this is a human problem, and it is found in all religions.

The third challenge is the challenge of gender and the *shari'ah*, the challenge of rights versus oppression. As Professor Tayob clearly showed, the South African case illustrates an example of gender pressure for legislation in order to protect the rights of women. In Nigeria, the cases of Safiya Husseini and Amina Lawal seem to show that the men have advantages over women when both violate *shari'ah* law. Is there any reason why, although the men who had affairs with these women are known, they are not or cannot be punished? If the *shari'ah* law of evidence works against dispensation of justice in the twenty-first century, is the challenge not one of adaptation? As an illustration, on January 25, 2004, the Government of Morocco adopted a landmark Family Law supporting women's equality and granting them new rights in marriage and divorce, among others. Can the implementation of *shari'ah* in Nigeria similarly respond to the challenges of change?

The fourth challenge is that of the *shari'ah* and the judiciary. So far, the Sharia Courts of Appeal have reversed death sentences imposed on women for the crime of adultery. What happens if similar judgments survive in the Sharia Courts of Appeal but are then reversed in the Federal Court of Appeal and Supreme Court, which have a more secular outlook? How would Muslims react to such judgements? Are there likely to be frictions between social and legal justice?

SHARI'AH AND THE POLITICS OF FEDERALISM

Let us see the context of the *shari'ah* in Nigeria. It is Nigeria's federal context that has made it possible for the implementation of criminal dimensions of the *shari'ah*. If Nigeria had been a unitary state, Zamfara State would not have had the autonomy or the powers to introduce criminal *shari'ah* that is, beyond constitutional provisions.

The politics of Nigeria's federation, after May 29, 1999, contributed to the emotional content of the introduction of criminal *shari'ah*. At the terminal period of transition from military to civilian rule in 1998-99, there were signs of resurgence of aggressive subnationalism which had been suppressed under the regime of General Abacha. After May 29, 1999 when the military handed over power to civilians, latent aggressive subnationalism exploded into violence. One effect of the over-centralisation of power by various military regimes was the emergence of strong centrifugal forces which felt disadvantaged in the system. Many subnational groups believed that if the Nigerian federation were not as centralised as it was, they would have had a fairer deal in the federation.

As an illustration, after May 1999, the O'dua People's Congress (OPC) declared its stand for the freedom of Yorubas to go it alone as an independent unit. It declared its desire to protect and defend Yoruba interests anywhere in Nigeria. The first eruption of violence was ignited in Shagamu between Hausa-Fulani settlers and OPC-backed groups. Many people were killed. There was retaliation in

Kano after dead bodies from Shagamu arrived for burial. OPC violence at Ketu and other places in Lagos, made President Obasanjo threaten to declare a state of emergency in Nigeria. If OPC activities were not properly curbed by President Obasanjo, then because of the logic of federal autonomy of Yorubas espoused by that group, how could the President deal with political manifestations of the desire for autonomy in other states?

On October 8, 1999, the Governor of Zamfara State, Alhaji Ahmed Sani, signed a bill establishing a new system of inferior *shari'ah* courts in Zamfara State, and another bill that constitutes the Sharia Penal Code; the bills took effect on January 27, 2000. Zamfara's new Sharia Penal Code adopted traditional criminal *shari'ah* in its entirety, with the exception of apostasy which was not criminalised. The adoption of what I call the "supreme *shari'ah*" by Zamfara State introduced a new factor in the politics of federalism. Until then, as explained above, state governments had operated *shari'ah* law as provided in the 1979, 1989 and 1999 constitutions, it was only applicable to civil proceedings involving Islamic personal law (such as inheritance, marriage and others). The supreme *shari'ah* expanded the parameters of *shari'ah* law to include criminal matters.

The initial reaction of the federal government was that the action of Zamfara State was unconstitutional. This view was clearly stated by President Obasanjo and his Attorney General, Dr. Akanu Agabi.[1] In response, the Governor of Zamfara, Alhaji Ahmed Sani, dared the federal government to go to court. Shortly after, additional Northern states declared supreme *shari'ah* in their states. Supreme *shari'ah* had spread to Sokoto, Kebbi, Kano and Niger States. Intergovernmental relations (both vertical and horizontal) became hostile. The Governor of Niger State also challenged the President – "The President of Nigeria has no final say on what is constitutional or not, only the court of law can determine what is constitutional."[2] President Obasanjo decided not to go to court but to seek a political solution. He had expressed the hope that the *shari'ah* debate would "soon fizzle out." But it did not.

---

[1] *The Source*, November 15, 1999, 18.
[2] Ibid., 19.

Christian groups protested and argued that the supreme *shari'ah* would affect them in many ways, even if they are not expected to be taken to *shari'ah* courts. They argued that closure of hotels and the ban on the sale of alcohol at beer parlours, would affect their economic life. In addition, they argued that their fundamental human rights, as enshrined in the constitution, were being eroded by the enactment of the supreme *shari'ah*. Some people also argued that *shari'ah* states should not benefit from Value Added Tax (VAT) from the sales of alcohol, since they were opposed to its sale.

For Muslims, Section 38 of the 1999 constitution protects the liberty of Muslims to worship according to their faith. In addition, Section 277 on the Sharia Court of Appeal allegedly protects the actions of Zamfara and the other *shari'ah* states.

In order to find a political solution to the *shari'ah* saga, President Obasanjo called a meeting of the National Council of States (NCS),[3] an intergovernmental forum which brings together former Heads of State, former Presidents of the Senate, current State Governors, the President of Federal Republic and his Vice. Even though the Vice-President, Alhaji Atiku Abubakar, had told the press that the NCS had agreed that every state which had adopted the supreme *shari'ah* should return to the status quo as at May 29, 1999, some state governors openly disagreed with him. A former Head of State, General Muhammadu Buhari, openly declared that the matter was not on the agenda before the NCS. Even the attempt at finding a temporary relief for the polity through an intergovernmental forum, had failed.

Rumours of the introduction of the supreme *shari'ah* in Kaduna State (which is multi-ethnic and multi-religious in nature) led to gross communal violence and the deaths of many Nigerians. The killing of Ibos and others in Kaduna State extracted reciprocal killings of Hausa-Fulani Muslims in Abia and Imo States. In fact, the governors of Abia, Imo, Enugu, Anambra, and Ebonyi States (of the Southeastern zone) called for a confederal Nigeria.[4] The governors were quickly backed by the Yoruba "Afenifere" leader, Chief

---

[3] *This Day*, March 3-4, 2002, 1.
[4] *Vanguard*, May 9, 2001, 1. See also *This Day*, July 19, 2001, 13. The Zamfara State Governor supported the call for confederation: *This Day*, July 12, 2001, 1.

Abraham Adesanya, who argued that there was hardly any difference between "true federation as demanded by Yorubas" and "confederacy which the Ibos are now demanding." In his usually blunt style, President Obasanjo described the call for a confederation as "highly mischievous and extremely unpatriotic."[5] Mischievous or not, the demand for confederation by the Southeast zone sent shivers down the political spine of the North, which then sent emissaries to the Southeast on reconciliation trips.

In essence, was the introduction of the supreme *shari'ah* just part of the politics of Nigerian federalism, or was it a genuine religious revival?

CONCLUSION

Yes, the demand for *shari'ah* in African democratisation processes provides *opportunities* and *pitfalls*. The question is how we maximise the opportunities and minimise the pitfalls. Candidly, in all these, we all need to build an ecumenical society in plural Nigeria. Values of accommodation, tolerance and participation must be imbibed and practised by all of us, in order to maximise the new opportunities that today and tomorrow may offer.

---

[5] *The Source*, April 3, 2000, 12.

Rethinking the Role of Religion in the Public Sphere: Local and Global Perspectives

Rosalind I. J. Hackett [1]

PREAMBLE

This essay represents my efforts as a scholar of comparative religion to situate the impetus for expanding *shari'ah* law in Nigeria in a broader, more global, perspective. That broader perspective is what I will call the resurgence of religion in the public sphere.[2] By this I understand the drive to claim recognition for, and the possibilities for implementation of, religious ideas, values, practices, and institutions in the governance of nation-states and the lives of their citizens. As has been well demonstrated for the Muslim world by Dale Eickelman and Jon Andersen,[3] the rise of modern media has been strategic in this connection – serving to transform the public realm into a marketplace of ideas, identities, values, and discourses. Coupled with the processes of democratisation, it means that religious authority and interpretation are now in many hands. The new discursive, performative, and participative public space is not confined to formal institutions recognised by state authorities. In order to illustrate and problematise these trends, I provide several current examples from various parts of the world. I pay particular attention to the American scene, since this is where I am based, and this is where the

---

[1] My thanks go to Bob Dowd, Predrag Klasnja, Rashied Omar and Charles Reynolds for their helpful comments and suggestions on this essay.
[2] By "public sphere" I understand a space open to all, rather than any Habermasian notion of it (Habermas, 1991). In fact, Birgit Meyer, one of the organizers of a conference in Amsterdam in December 2002 on "Religion, Media and the Public Sphere," summarizes the views of several participants that "Jürgen Habermas' rather normative and rationally inclined understanding of the public sphere is of little help in grasping the phenomenon of public religion . . ." Meyer, 2003, 126.
[3] Eickelman and Andersen, 1999.

significance of religion has assumed considerable prominence in public discourse in the post-September 11 context. My choice of topic was in part informed by recent visits to and/or participation in conferences on the changing role of religion in various national or regional contexts (India, Latin America, Europe). I am particularly interested in the way these public debates, often highly contentious, raise questions about religious and cultural difference, and the treatment of minorities in increasingly multi-religious and multi-cultural national contexts. While these are clearly local questions, they are increasingly framed in global terms by both actors and analysts. As already suggested, the modern media are instrumental in this regard, as we shall discuss below, so too are diasporic communities and international non-governmental organisations.

As several of the presenters demonstrated at the conference, these questions need to be treated from constitutional and international human rights perspectives. However, my focus is expressly less specific in that I want to show that the impetus for more public religion is a live issue in media, academic, political, religious, and social sectors across the globe. Debates and publications regarding the appropriate role of religion in both emergent and longstanding democracies increasingly shape political will and public policy. Consider, for example, the contentious debates in Europe at the present time over whether there should be any reference to God or to Europe's Christian heritage in the new European constitution. The Western paradigm of the secular state and privatised, individualised religion is now being openly challenged in post-colonial states, as well as on home turf by migrant populations and religious revivalism.[4]

As a concerned and hopefully conscientious academic, I believe that I have an essential role to play not just in providing knowledge, but also in analysing the interests and stakes at play in any given situation. The academic space allows me, in fact compels me, to ask critical reflective questions – in the present context on moves to accord religion more influence in public life – in a relatively unbiased way. (This resembles in part the work of the investigative journalist,

---

[4] See, e.g., Demerath, 2001.

but the latter may be more beholden to institutional control and market conventions.) Based upon my extensive experience in education and the media, I conclude by highlighting those areas which are instrumental in promoting harmonious coexistence between religious traditions in modern, pluralistic nation-states.

INTRODUCTION

Up until the early 1990s there was a clear disparity between the growing significance of religion on the world stage and the literature one could read on this score in either scholarly or popular publications. Historian Scott Appleby states candidly that "Western myopia on the subject of religious power has been astounding."[5] For a long time scholars predicted that as religions were assumed to be carriers of "tradition" they would enter into decline because of secularisation and privatisation. Because of these blinkers or blinders, scholars and observers missed the religious roots of the civil rights movement in the United States and misread the surge of the Iranian revolution.[6]

Then in 1993, Harvard professor of international relations Samuel Huntington published an article in the journal *Foreign Affairs* entitled "The Clash of Civilisations?"[7] This controversial article opened the floodgates for public debate on the significance of religion in international affairs. In it Huntington declared that "[t]he fault lines between civilisations will be the battle lines of the future." He argued that the world would be shaped in large measure by the interactions among seven or eight major civilizations, namely Western, Confucian, Japanese, Islamic, Hindu, Slavic-Orthodox, Latin American and possibly African. It was not just Huntington's oversimplified mapping of the contemporary world which provoked criticism, but the suggestion that the most important differentiating feature was religion, and that post-Cold War optimism would be shattered by dangerous and deep-rooted cultural conflict.[8] He also argued that

---

[5] Appleby, 2003, 231.
[6] Levine, 2000, 122.
[7] Huntington, 1993; see also Huntington's book on this subject, Huntington, 1996.
[8] See Kaplan, 2001.

democracy was only realisable within the context of church-state separation (or in more appropriate terminology – religion-state separation).

Prescient or not, Huntington's work stimulated a flood of long-overdue studies of the role of religion in international affairs. It sent diehard secular political scientists and social critics into a tailspin – if the flurry of publications in the last decade is any indication.[9] A landmark study was *Religion, The Missing Dimension of Statecraft*.[10] Religion plays a crucial role in many international conflicts, yet for the most part, diplomacy either ignores or misunderstands its role. The authors set out to restore this missing dimension to its rightful place in the conduct of international diplomacy. The book also offers the first systematic account of modern cases in which religious or spiritual factors have played a helpful role in preventing or resolving conflict and achieving non-violent change.

Another publication around the same time which helped focus attention on the growing importance of religion on the international scene was Jose Casanova's influential study, *Public Religions in the Modern World*.[11] This book reconsiders the relationship between religion and modernity, and argues that many religious traditions have been making their way, sometimes forcefully, out of the private sphere and into public life. This is occurring at an increasingly transnational level.[12] These processes are well captured by Hent de Vries: "the functions ascribed to modern subjectivity, to the political, the economy, the nation, the state, the public sphere, privacy, and so on have been radically transformed."[13] The mass mediated dimension of these developments has been well articulated by sociologist Manuel Castells who argues that we have passed from Giddens' era of "late modernity" into the age of the "network

---

[9] See Philpott, 2002 for a discussion of this, with comprehensive references. Of particular note is the special issue of *Millennium: Journal of International Studies* (29/3: 2000) on "Religion and International Relations."
[10] Johnston and Sampson, 1994.
[11] Casanova, 1994.
[12] Key works in this area are Robertson, 1992, Beyer, 1998, and Rudolph and Piscatori, 1997.
[13] De Vries, 2002, 19.

society."[14] This new form of society has been induced by the information technology revolution and the restructuring of capitalism. This has led, in his opinion, to a disjunction between the local and the global, and power and experience, for most individuals and social groups.[15] Consequently, he states, "[t]he search for meaning takes place then in the reconstruction of defensive identities around communal principles."[16] These new forms of "communal resistance" or "cultural communes" are at the base of the new primacy of identity politics in today's network society. He sees the resurgence of religious fundamentalisms as reflecting the contestations of the new global order.[17] These movements constitute a social barometer, given their reactive nature, aiming to construct "social and personal identity on the basis of images of the past and projecting them into a utopian future, to overcome unbearable present times."[18] For some it was more the turn of the millennium that occasioned rethinking about religion.[19]

As noted by a prominent commentator on contemporary religious affairs, Philip Jenkins,

> the twenty-first century will almost certainly be regarded by future historians as a century in which religion replaced ideology as the prime animating and destructive force in human affairs, guiding attitudes to political liberty and obligation, concepts of nationhood, and of course, conflicts and wars.[20]

Jenkins is alluding in part to the tragic events of September 11 and their aftermath. As a scholar of comparative religion, I can certainly

---

[14] Castells, 1997, ii, 10-11.
[15] Ibid., 11.
[16] Ibid.
[17] Peter van der Veer prefers to designate these movements as "religious nationalisms" since many of them "articulate discourse on the religious community with discourse on the nation." See van der Veer, 1997, 195.
[18] Ibid., 25. Odinkalu, 2003, 15, traces the "pathologies of suffering, conflict and systematic violations that Africa has suffered" back to colonial patterns of exclusion and ethnicisation. See also van der Veer, 1997.
[19] See Gifford et al., 2003.
[20] Jenkins, 2002.

confirm that the production of texts on Islam and on religion and violence more generally, as well as on peace and tolerance, has escalated exponentially. But I would also add that what September 11 brought home to many (I know this at least from talking to my own students and following the local and international news on a regular basis), is not only a stronger sense of the ambivalence of the sacred, as brought home to us by Scott Appleby in his book so entitled,[21] but also our global connectedness. Human rights scholar and advocate Abdullahi An-Na'im calls this "our shared vulnerability."[22]

FAITH-BASED DIPLOMACY

As an extension of the greater recognition of the role of religion on the international stage, one can note a number of new initiatives to extend the scope of faith-based organizations to the diplomatic realm. A number of recently published works realistically address the religious dimension of conflict transformation and peace-building.[23] A new book edited by Douglas Johnston, *Faith-Based Diplomacy: Trumping Realpolitik*,[24] gives shape to this emergent field. It reveals the change in thinking that is occurring among those who are international relations specialists:

> In some non-Western cultures, religion is a primary motivation for political action. Historically dismissed by Western policymakers as a divisive influence, religion in fact has significant potential for overcoming the obstacles that lead to paralysis and stalemate. The concept of incorporating religion as part of the solution to such problems is as simple as it is profound. It is long overdue.[25]

For instance, there is a chapter in Johnston's book by a Muslim scholar entitled "Conflict Resolution as a Normative Value in Islamic

---

[21] Appleby, 2000.
[22] An-Na'im, 1998.
[23] Docherty, 2001; Appleby, 2000; Gopin, 2000; Sampson and Lederach, 2000. Juergens-meyer, 2003 and Esposito, 2003 also address this dimension in their conclusions.
[24] Johnston, 2003.
[25] Ibid., jacket cover.

Law: Handling Disputes with Non-Muslims."[26] There is also a new journal, *Faith and International Affairs*, published by the Council on Faith and International Affairs located at the Institute for Global Engagement near Philadelphia. It not only encourages inter-faith dialogue and provides resources for those at the "nexus of faith and international affairs," but also encourages what it calls "holistic engagement in global issues." In a recent article in this journal, one can read about the rituals of prayer and fasting that led to a breakthrough in difficult peace negotiations in the Kashmir region.[27]

There is also the International Center for Religion and Democracy in Washington, DC that declares its mission to be:

> To facilitate increased understanding and collaboration between policymakers and diplomats on the one hand and religious leaders – both clergy and laity – on the other in resolving identity-based conflicts that exceed the reach of traditional diplomacy.

The Center's mission statement goes on:

> Regardless of one's spiritual persuasion, there are two compelling reasons why the Center's work is important: (1) the need for more effective preventive measures to minimise the occasions in which we have to send our sons and daughters in harm's way and (2) the need for a stable global environment to support continued economic growth that can benefit an expanding percentage of the world's population.
>
> By linking religious reconciliation with official diplomacy, the ICRD is creating a new synergy for peacemaking that serves both of these needs. It also provides a more fruitful approach for dealing with ethnic conflict, tribal warfare, and religious hostilities[28]

---

[26] El-Fadl, 2003.
[27] Cox and Philpott, 2003.
[28] www.icrd.org (accessed December 11, 2003).

The Program in Religion in Conflict and Peacebuilding at the Joan B. Kroc Institute for International Peace Studies also seeks to strengthen the potential for peacebuilding within religious traditions, in addition to exploring the complex roles of religion in contemporary conflicts.[29] Organisations with a specific focus on peace-building include the Tanenbaum Center for Interreligious Understanding's Program on Religion and Conflict Resolution and PeaceMakers International.[30]

BEST-SELLING RELIGION

Interestingly, while journalists and academic analysts have rushed to catch up with global religious resurgences, books promoting religion, more religion, or better religion are bestsellers in many parts of the world. The fact that these books now displace more academic works on the shelves of major US and UK bookstores is somewhat problematic from my vantage point as a scholar of religion. Books on religion or spirituality now feature regularly on the *New York Times* bestseller list. These can range from religious reflections and spiritual guides to modern interpretations of ancient sacred wisdom. One can also find histories and contemporary accounts of religious traditions, concepts, and holy places written for the general reader, such as those by popular British author Karen Armstrong, whose best-known works are *A History of God* and *The Battle for God*.[31]

Once President Bill Clinton started singing the praises of Yale law professor, Stephen Carter's works, such as *The Culture of Disbelief: How American Law and Politics Trivialize Religious Devotion*,[32] sales went up exponentially. Explaining how preserving a special role for religious communities can strengthen democracy, Carter criticises the trivialising of religious faith in contemporary American law and politics. In his more recent book, *God's Name in Vain: The Wrongs and Rights of Religion in Politics*,[33] Carter expresses his concerns about the

---

[29] kroc.nd.edu/research/religion.html (accessed March 6, 2004).
[30] www.tanenbaum.org (accessed March 6, 2004); www.peacemakers.net (accessed March 6, 2004).
[31] Armstrong, 1994 and 2000.
[32] Carter, 1994.
[33] Carter, 2000.

risks and limitations of political involvement for religious people and communities. In his words:

> We must never become a nation that propounds an official religion or suggests that some religions are more American than others. At the same time, one of the official religions we must never propound is the religion of secularism, the suggestion that there is something un-American about trying to live life in a way that puts God first. Quite the contrary: Preserving the ability of the faithful to put God first is precisely the purpose for which freedom of religion must exist.[34]

Carter worries about religious voices losing their prophetic edge by being co-opted by political forces, and about the anti-religious politics of the political elite. Without the independent religious conscience, he suggests, there might never have been the abolitionist movement, rights for industrial workers, or the civil rights movement.[35] In the book, he lays out what he considers to be the basis of "principled and prophetic religious activism."[36] Incidentally, Carter has been criticised for propagating a version of religion which is "self-evidently personalistic, moralistic, and experiential, and most definitely of the monotheistic variety," which sustains the misleading dichotomy of "church-state" and prevents people from seeing how values may be cultivated in the "secular" realm. [37] Another critic describes Carter's book as "a product of the very culture it purports to criticise," saying that it advances a view of religion as legitimate only when in service to democracy.[38]

Legal scholar John Witte sees the shift to more public religion in the US context as both inevitable and necessary. He notes that over the last fifteen years the US Supreme Court has abandoned much of

---

[34] Ibid., 4.
[35] Ibid. In a similar vein, Gifford, 1995 examines critically the contribution of the African churches in several countries to the processes of democratisation.
[36] Carter, 2000, 7.
[37] McCutcheon, 2001, 131.
[38] Craycraft, 1999, 156-157.

its earlier separationism.[39] The metaphorical "wall of separation between church and state" envisaged by Jefferson no longer looms large in the Court's opinions, and privatisation of religion is no longer the bargain that must be struck in order to attain religious freedom. According to Witte, there are two teachings which emanate from the recent cases. First, public religion must be as free as private religion, for religious groups, in his words, "provide leaven and leverage for the polity to improve." Second, the freedom of public religion sometimes requires the support of the state. This is because it is impossible for religious bodies to avoid contact with today's modern welfare state and all its ramifications in the educational, welfare, legal, social, and healthcare sectors.

Such developments in part explain the rise of what Dennis Hoover calls "an activist center in American public life."[40] This has manifested itself in two principal ways: first, a call by certain politicians and writers for religion to assume a more prominent role in public life, and second, advocacy of the "charitable choice" provision of the welfare reform law, whereby government support is provided for faith-based organisations to address social problems.[41] President George W. Bush has openly talked about the influence of his religious faith, particularly in the aftermath of September 11. This has occasioned numerous articles in leading news magazines and newspapers regarding the President's personal religious beliefs and practices.[42] While statistics show that the majority of Americans like their leader to be God-fearing, they are not so keen about public professions of faith. Some journalists have jumped on statements by politicians that there could be no morality without religion.[43]

Religion's influence in American politics is obvious in recent debates about school prayer, abortion, and homosexuality, as well as in the success of grassroots religious organisations in mobilising voters. Many liberal secularists decry this trend, rejecting any

---

[39] Witte, n.d.
[40] Hoover, 2000.
[41] See Silk, 1999.
[42] See, e.g., Lampman, 2003.
[43] See, e.g., the "Roundtable on Religion in Politics" *Tikkun* November 2000, www.tikkun.org/magazine/index.cfm/action/tikkun/issue/tik0011/article/001 111a.html (accessed April 22, 2004).

interaction between politics and religion. But in *Why I Am Not a Secularist*,[44] distinguished political theorist William E. Connolly argues that secularism, although admirable in its pursuit of freedom and diversity, too often undercuts these goals through its narrow and intolerant understandings of public reason. He believes that in dealing with controversial issues such as the death penalty, the right to die, and the war on drugs, secularism has failed to recognise the complexity of public views because it has excluded religious and theistic viewpoints. In doing so, he claims that it has ignored an opportunity to create public consensus. He argues further that the narrowness of the secularist vision has helped to increase support for the death penalty, which he himself opposes. As against the secularist vision, Connolly crafts a bold new model of public life that he believes more accurately reflects the diversity of voices and the needs of contemporary politics. He calls for a refashioning of secularism that would allow it to incorporate a wider variety of ethical views, and honour the desire of believers and nonbelievers alike to represent their faiths openly in the civic forum.[45]

For political philosopher Paul Weithman, any questions regarding the role religion may play in citizens' decision-making are essentially moral questions. This is because a society's commitment to liberal democracy entails certain moral and normative commitments for its citizens. Weithman has produced two well-argued books on this subject, *Religion and the Obligations of Citizenship* and an earlier, edited volume, *Religion and Contemporary Liberalism*.[46]. He identifies two main sets of questions that arise with regard to the proper role of religion in democratic politics. The first set asks how religion may affect political *outcomes* and how those outcomes square with the commitments of liberal democracy. For example, can state support for a religion, all religions, or for religion as such – as in the

---

[44] Connolly, 1999.
[45] It is worth noting that at the recent American Academy of Religion annual meeting in Atlanta (November 21-25, 2003), a panel on philosopher and ethicist Jeffrey Stout's new book, *Democracy and Tradition*, where leading public intellectuals debated a number of issues including the appropriate place for religion in a multicultural democratic context, drew a crowd of over 2000.
[46] Weithman, 2002 and 1997, respectively.

endorsement of religious codes of conduct – be consistent with liberal democracy? Weithman demonstrates how attention to political outcomes can illustrate and illuminate what he calls "puzzles" about liberal democracy.[47] For example, in the much debated case of whether prayer should be permitted in public schools, he shows how, if it is permitted because the majority favours it, then the liberty of the minority can be compromised in the name of a democratic commitment to majoritarianism. But if prayer is not permitted, he explains, it seems that the liberal commitment to freedom of religion (and the protection of minorities) can thwart measures the majority would like to enact. Weithman also explores the question of whether some citizens should be allowed to make ritual use of drugs which are generally proscribed. If so, then the commitment to the equal treatment of all before the law can, under some circumstances, cede to religious liberty. If not, he states, then it is rather that "religious liberty can be restricted in the name of treating all as equals before a law which the state has an interest in enforcing."[48]

The second set of questions highlighted by Weithman pertains to religious political *inputs*. This concerns the use of religious arguments in the political sphere either as a basis for voting, political preferences, or policy-making. As Weithman rightly notes, "liberal democratic commitments to religious toleration and church-state separation are sometimes thought to be incompatible with citizens' taking their religiously based political views as the basis of important political decisions."[49] He asks whether there is a difference between religious and political leaders and ordinary citizens, or between fora, in terms of the appropriateness of religious political inputs.

Weithman considers that these questions regarding the suitable role of religious convictions in the political sphere force us to think more critically and more deeply about the nature of citizenship. He argues that "citizens may offer exclusively religious arguments in public debate and that they may rely on religious reasons when they cast their votes."[50] Because voting and advocacy are collective

---

[47] Weithman, 2002, 2.
[48] Ibid.
[49] Ibid.
[50] Ibid., 3.

enterprises, they must be conducted responsibly and reasonably, in Weithman's view. The context is here significant. He notes that citizens in liberal democracies such as the United States are deeply divided on the nature and demands of citizenship. Sometimes these disagreements stem from the political activities of religious organisations. However, in those societies where the political role of such organisations is more valued this is less of an issue. Religious organisations may be instrumental in facilitating people's political participation and in developing their sense of citizenship. They may also generate debate regarding the conditions of participation and the goods that should be conferred by various levels of participation. Weithman underscores the need to distinguish between those who violate the obligations of citizenship and those whose politics we dislike. In other words, restrictions on religious political argument are sometimes based on assumptions about what religious citizens stand for, when in reality there may be considerable diversity of opinion. Departing somewhat from the almost exclusive reliance on conceptual argumentation in political philosophy, Weithman wisely employs empirical data and contextual differences to query presumptions, and to assess what he calls the "reasonability of deep disagreement."[51]

SECULARISM AND ITS DISCONTENTS

While some writers have sought ways to popularise religion for the Western consumer, or have tried to find cogent arguments for a greater public role for religion locally or globally, others approach these questions by addressing the tension between secularism and

---

[51] Ibid., 5. In this connection see also the work of Mark Chaves, e.g. Chaves, Stephens, and Galaskiewicz, 2004. On a lighter, more ironic note, there is no knowing where or what type of religion may appear in America's public sphere. Starting in December 2003, the figure of a guardian angel will be used in television, radio, print, outdoor and Internet advertisements and public service announcements directed to the US's 37 million Hispanics, to emphasize the importance of preparing for potential terrorist attacks. "Just like any good guardian angel, we want this one to be everywhere," Homeland Security Secretary Tom Ridge said in a speech to announce the start of the spiritually themed campaign. www.hispanicbusiness.com/news/newsbyid.asp?id=13960.

religion. Or, to be more specific, they see growing antagonism between the secularism and rights-based individualism of modern democratic states and the resurgence of religion with its communitarian emphasis. For example, the summer 2003 issue of the prestigious journal *Daedalus: Journal of the American Academy of Arts and Sciences* is devoted to the topic of secularism and religion. Several of the writers address the possibilities of religious pluralism and freedom, while others, such as renowned religion analyst Martin Marty, search for new paradigms, such as "religio-secular world", to represent these changing global dynamics.

One of the best scholarly takes on the contested place of religion in the public (local, national and international) sphere is anthropologist Talal Asad's latest book, *Formations of the Secular: Christianity, Islam, Modernity*.[52] In keeping with his understanding of modern anthropology, he explores this phenomenon in societies differently located in time and space. He shows how such "embedded concepts" as secularism and religion are supported or challenged by a variety of "sensibilities, attitudes, assumptions, and behaviors."[53] He is particularly interested in how secular discourse is perceived from the periphery of the modernisation process.

One of Asad's main arguments is that the modern idea of a secular society involves a distinctive relation between state law and personal morality, with the result that religion becomes a matter of (private) belief. However, translating into a legal right the individual's ability to express and practice his or her beliefs freely brings 'religion' back into the public domain.[54] These ideas developed in Western Europe in tandem with the formation of the modern state. In the final chapter of the book, on "Reconfigurations of Law and Ethics in Colonial Egypt," Asad probingly examines how the secular was thought about and translated in Egypt prior to involvement with modernity. He finds that the reconfigurations of law, religion and ethics in colonial Egypt created new social spaces in which 'secularism' could grow. One of his most important conclusions is that

---

[52] Asad, 2003.
[53] Ibid., 17.
[54] Ibid., 205f.

[a] secular state is not one characterized by religious indifference, or rational ethics – or political toleration. It is a complex arrangement of legal reasoning, moral practice and political authority. This arrangement is not the simple outcome of the struggle of secular reason against he despotism of religious authority.[55]

To get beyond the notion that religion and secularism are competing ideologies, it behoves us, Talad avers, to look at "what people do with and to ideas and practices,"[56] and why meanings and concepts change. He also argues that religion has always been involved in the world of power, and that "the categories of 'politics' and 'religion' turn out to implicate each other more profoundly than we thought."[57] In other words, modern state power is highly pervasive, and it seeks to regulate all aspects of individual and social life.[58]

Similarly nuanced analysis of the concept of the secular is also provided by historian Nikki Keddie, who emphasises the fact that the word 'secular' has had a far greater variety of meanings than current usage may suggest.[59] For centuries in Europe it referred to the change in clerical status whereby a monk became a secular priest. It was only in the nineteenth century that it began to refer to a doctrine of secularism, i.e. a belief that religious institutions and values should play no role in the affairs of the state. Keddie also provides a helpful comparison of the rise and fall of secular and religious politics in various parts of the world, noting the contextual factors which influence these trends. For example, Muslim countries have negative views of secularism because they associate it with autocratic rule and Western influence. By comparison, Islam as a force for mobilisation still seems relatively untainted. Yet, somewhat paradoxically, Keddie notes, the Islamic country where anti-clerical feelings run highest and secularist reforms are most successful is in present-day Iran.

Constant battles, as in South Asia – namely India and Sri Lanka – between religious nationalisms and secular movements serve to

---

[55] Ibid., 255.
[56] Ibid., 194.
[57] Ibid., 200.
[58] Ibid., 199.
[59] Keddie, 2003, 14f.

weaken support for secularism in a region, in Keddie's judgement.[60] So too does the imposition of secularist ideas from the top down, without ensuring support for them at the popular level or from religious leaders. Since Western political hegemony is less of an issue in India than it is in the Muslim world, there are many Indian intellectuals who defend secularism even if they may criticise its application.[61] In fact, Keddie states that contemporary India has probably produced the largest body of writing in the modern world debating the merits of secularism. With the controversial efforts of the present Indian government and the ruling party (BJP) to promote Hindu nationalism to the detriment of religious minorities,[62] a number of recent publications advocate the need to move beyond current understandings of secularism in order to effectively protect minority interests.[63]

So the very least that we can learn from the writings of scholars such as Asad and Keddie is the need to *historicise* and *contextualise* the concepts of secularism and religion. Seen in their many different historical contexts, these concepts are not always as unequivocal, or as polarised, as is commonly assumed.[64] Furthermore, secularisation has been in progress around the world for far longer, and its success has been far more partial, than is often known, not least because of the backlashes and counter-backlashes engendered by insensitive policies.

CHANGING PUBLIC SPHERES AND NEW CHALLENGES TO RELIGIOUS CO-EXISTENCE

In some parts of the world, such as Latin America, the concern is less about secularisation and the marginalisation of religion, but more about the rise of new religious groups competing for power, recognition and resources. Disestablishment of state religions, or dismantling of complicities between dominant religious groups and

---

[60] Ibid., 28. See also Tambiah, 1992; Gombrich and Obeyesekere, 1988; Juergensmeyer, 1993.
[61] See, e.g., Bhargava, 2000; Madan, 1998.
[62] Kishwar, 1998; Noorani, 2000.
[63] Chandokhe, 1999; Massey, 2003.
[64] See, e.g., An-Na'im, 2000.

state power, have changed the stakes of co-existence between religious communities. Against the backdrop of the forces of democratisation, mediatisation, and the global market, religious groups are compelled to justify their existence to state and consumers alike. These processes are clearly visible in many Latin American countries, where the powerful Roman Catholic Church now has to compete in the marketplace along with the burgeoning evangelical groups and indigenous revival movements. Political scientist Dan Levine, who has been conducting research on religion and politics in this region for many years, observes:

> Latin America is now approaching a state of pluralism (among Christian groups) for the first time in its history. This religious pluralism entails not only a multiplicity of voices speaking 'in the name of religion' but also a conflict for voice *within* specific groups. The spread of literacy and the access to mass media have diffused the tools of religious expertise into many hands.[65]

Works by local and international scholars reflect efforts to interpret this new pluralism. Some have even adopted a market model and talk about Latin America's new religious economy.[66] Levine offers a positive reading of the politicisation of religion in Latin America.

> A story that not long ago could be told with confidence about how Catholicism supported and reflected the established order became a story in which religion (Protestant as well as Catholic) has become a source of new ideas about how to organise society and politics, and how to lead the good life. It is no exaggeration to say that many of the region's most significant movements for change would have been unthinkable without religious participation and legitimation.[67]

---

[65] Levine, 2000, 135. The three presidential candidates in the December 2003 elections in Guatemala reflected this plurality: one was a Catholic, another an evangelical Protestant, and the third a priest of the Mayan indigenous religion.
[66] Chesnut, 2003; Gill, 1998.
[67] Levine, 2000, 123-124.

Levine also points out that the pluralisation of religious voices, and their growing activism and public presence, have immediate consequences for democracy. He states that "in a plural environment, it is to everyone's interest to maintain open civil society with guarantees of free speech and equal access to institutions and to public spaces."[68] This is especially important as these societies leave behind the dictatorships and religious monopolies which so characterised the Latin American scene up until the late 1980s. Levine points to the emergence of discourses on citizenship – that is, of the human and civil rights of the person – which have been helpful in modernising the state.

Efforts to accommodate religious and cultural diversity in transitional states and new democratic dispensations are naturally subject to extensive scrutiny. The new South Africa is a good case in point, with its explicit recognition of religious and cultural minorities and celebration of the country's diverse heritage after decades of neo-colonial repression. The key sites for negotiating the new South Africa have been the constitution,[69] religious broadcasting,[70] and religion education.[71] The new government has, for the most part, resisted efforts to continue to privilege South Africa's Christian majority (over 70% are Christians according to the most recent census).[72] Many of the religious leaders who fought for liberation from the brutal apartheid regime have become officials of the new government.[73]

Interestingly, many European counties have shown themselves to be regressive in terms of honouring the rights of minority religious groups in their territories. Alarmed at the growth of immigrant populations, particularly Muslims (there are now an estimated 4-5

---

[68] Ibid, 135.
[69] Van der Vyver, 1999.
[70] Hackett, 2004.
[71] Chidester, 1994; Gruchy, 1995; Steyn, 1999; Tayob and Weisse, 1998.
[72] encarta.msn.com/fact_631504863/South_Africa.html (accessed 6 March 2004).
[73] Hefner, 2000, emphasizes the importance of civil institutions' and public civility, as well as civilized state, in the democratization of Indonesia. Different religious groups were included in the broad base of civil society organizations that championed political and social reform.

million Muslims in France, for example),[74] some European governments have taken draconian measures to curb the activities of non-conventional and unpopular religious groups.[75] "Sects" are feared for their purported negative psychological and Americanising effects. In eastern Europe and Russia we find similar patterns of cultural preservation and animosity toward competing religious options.[76] The wearing of the Muslim veil in the workplace and schools has been hotly contested in France and Germany. French President Chirac has developed the idea that the veil or scarf is a sign of "aggressive proselytism" and has recently proposed controversial new legislation banning the wearing of religious symbols in public schools.[77]

The rise of religion in identity politics and the public debates about multiculturalism have given culture, and particularly cultural practice, a new prominence in national and international politics. Frequently the disputes over symbols, resources, recognition and access are resolved in the legal sphere.[78] Legal scholar Upendra Baxi explains that the right to difference is evidence of the deployment of the logics and paralogics of human rights by actors seeking "to subvert the 'monological' view of human rights through a pluri-universalistic praxis."[79] He emphasises that with the assertion of cultural and religious rights in modern democratic contexts,

> we are confronted by some of the most intractable problems of conflict of rights where self-chosen sedimentation of identity within a religious tradition is at odds with the

---

[74] Ewing, 2002; An-Na'im, 2000.
[75] See, especially, *Seminar on Freedom of Religion or Belief in the OSCE Region*, 2001; Richardson, 2004.
[76] This overt or covert denial of the rights of minority religions has been flagged by Human Rights Without Frontiers (Belgium), www.hrwf.net, as not being part of the test for being admitted into the European Union.
[77] www.reuters.com/newsArticle.jhtml?type=worldNews&storyID=4498057 (accessed March 6, 2004). For comparative analysis, see Gunn, 2004.
[78] Parekh, 2000; Barry, 2001. See, also, the forthcoming special issue of *Culture and Religion*, on Law and Human Rights, guest edited by Rosalind I. J. Hackett and Winni Sullivan.
[79] Baxi, 2002, 83.

universalistic mode of de-traditionalisation of the politics of difference, demanding gender equality and justice.[80]

The ongoing controversy, referred to above, over the possible inclusion of references to God or to Europe's Christian heritage in the new constitution of the European Union would be another pertinent example.[81]

What possibilities are there for new, more equitable conversations about religious difference and conceptions of the good life, asks respected and popular commentator, Bill Moyers?[82] Moyers wants to learn from difference but not be alienated by it, nor expect it to be glossed over by liberal common denominators.[83] Similarly, a team of renowned North American legal and cultural experts have recently published their extensive deliberations on how to balance communitarian demands (of which religious identity is a dimension) with the standards of modern liberal democracies.[84] Martha Nussbaum writes about these issues from the standpoint of women.[85]

CONCLUDING REMARKS

The eruption of religion into changing political landscapes the world over, as briefly adumbrated in the present essay, seems to indicate two important findings. First, the management of religious and cultural difference, and the treatment of minorities, has emerged as a key element of successful governance. Second, these issues necessitate public debate, with educational and media sites emerging as significant popular locations for this purpose – supplementing initiatives by political and religious leaders.

It is indeed heartening to learn that the awareness of heightened risks of religious conflict, or the threats to peace posed by extremist

---

[80] Ibid. See, also, Tahzib-Lie, 2000; Cook, 1994.
[81] www.csmonitor.com/2003/0410/p07s01-woeu.html (accessed March 6, 2004).
[82] Moyers, 2000.
[83] Cf. Jean Bethke Elshtain's rejection of "liberal monism" for postulating a "single voc-abulary of political discussion," Elshtain, 2003.
[84] Shweder, Minow, and Markus, 2002.
[85] Nussbaum, 2000; cf. Hackett, 2001.

religious groups, has engendered an upsurge in inter-religious dialogue in many parts of the world, and an increased attention to the significance of religious education and religious broadcasting. I would here cite the efforts of the South African government to have its religious programming reflect the new rainbow nation of post-apartheid South Africa.[86] Similarly, Professor Abdelfattah Amor, the Special Rapporteur of the Sub-Commission on Freedom of Religion and Belief of the United Nations Commission on Human Rights, has launched meetings and publications since 1995 to explore the role of school education in relation to religious tolerance and intolerance.[87]

However, we must be vigilant concerning the forces of deregulation and liberalisation that inevitably accompany democratisation and globalisation. While the new opportunities afforded religious individuals and communities to represent themselves and participate in the public sphere are undeniable, and indeed long overdue in many instances, they can equally lead to new forms of separationism and demonisation of religious others. The development of civil society values of tolerance, cooperation and civility can easily be subordinated to the logic of the market, or the pressures of religious and political fundamentalisms.[88] It therefore behoves us to play our humble parts, whether as religious or political leaders, educators, lawyers, media professionals, human rights activists, or simple laypersons, and whether as members of majoritarian or minoritarian groups, in ensuring that the call for more public expressions of religion is responded to in the most equitable way possible.

REFERENCES

An-Na'im, Abdullahi A, "Consciousness of vulnerability", in: *A Human Rights Message*, Ministry of Foreign Affairs, Government of Sweden (eds.), Stockholm: Government of Sweden, 1998, 16-19.

---

[86] See Hackett, 2004.
[87] www.unhchr.ch/huridocda/huridoca.nsf/0/DFDC01ED0062E4C8C1256D B1004EB2C8/$File/N0347258.doc?OpenElement (accessed March 6, 2004). See also Larsen and Plesner, 2002.
[88] See Appleby, Sivan, and Almond, 2003.

———, "Human rights and Islamic identity in France and Uzbekistan: mediation of the local and the global", *Human Rights Quarterly* 22, 2000, 906-41.

———, "Human rights, religion and secularism: does it have to be a choice?", Keynote Address, 18th Quinquennial World Congress of the International Association of the History of Religions, August 5-12, Durban, South Africa 2000.

Appleby, R. Scott, *The Ambivalence of the Sacred: Religion, violence, and reconciliation*, New York: Rowman and Littlefield, 2000.

———, "Retrieving the missing dimension of statecraft: religious faith in the service of peacebuilding", in: Douglas Johnston, (ed.), *Faith-Based Diplomacy: Trumping realpolitik*, New York: Oxford, 2003, 231-58.

Appleby, R. Scott, Emmanuel Sivan, and Gabriel Almond, *Strong Religion: The rise of fundamentalisms around the world*, Chicago: University of Chicago Press, 2003.

Armstrong, Karen, *A History of God: The 4,000 year quest of Judaism, Christianity and Islam*, New York: Ballantine Books, 1994.

———, *The Battle for God*, New York: Knopf, 2000.

Asad, Talal, *Formations of the Secular: Christianity, Islam, Modernity*, Stanford: Stanford University Press, 2003.

Barker, Eileen, "The opium wars of the new millennium: religion in Eastern Europe and the former Soviet Union", in: Mark Silk (ed.), *Religion on the International News Agenda*, Hartford, CT: The Leonard E. Greenberg Center for the Study of Religion in Public Life, 2000, 39-59.

———, "Why the cults? new religions and freedom of religion and belief", in: Tore Lindholm, W. Cole Durham and Bahia Tahzib-Lie (eds.), *Facilitating Freedom of Religion and Belief: Perspectives, impulses and recommendations from the Oslo Coalition*, Dordrecht: Kluwer (forthcoming 2004).

Barry, Brian, *Culture and Equality: An egalitarian critique of multiculturalism*, Cambridge, MA: Harvard University Press, 2001.

Baxi, Upendra, *The Future of Human Rights*, New York: Oxford University Press, 2002.

Beyer, Peter, "The modern emergence of religions and a global social system for religion", *International Sociology* 13, 1998, 151-72.

Bhargava, Rajeev (ed.), *Secularism and Its Critics*, New York: Oxford University Press, 2000.

Carter, Stephen L., *The Culture of Disbelief: How American law and politics trivialize religious devotion*, New York: Anchor Books, 1994.

———, *God's Name in Vain: The wrongs and rights of religion in politics*, New York: Basic Books, 2000.

Casanova, Jose, *Public Religions in the Modern World*, Chicago: University of Chicago Press, 1994.
Castells, Manuell, *The Information Age: Economy, society and culture*, Oxford: Blackwell, 1997. Vol. I: *The Rise of the Network Society*; Vol. II: *The Power of Identity*; Vol. III: *End of Millennium*.
Chandokhe, Neera, *Beyond Secularism: The rights of religious minorities*, Delhi: Oxford University Press, 1999.
Chaves, Mark, Laura Stephens, and Joseph Galaskiewicz, "Does government funding suppress nonprofits' political activities?" *American Sociological Review* 69, 2004.
Chesnut, R. Andrew, *Competitive Spirits: Latin America's new religious economy*, New York: Oxford University Press, 2003.
Chidester, David, Gordon Mitchell, A. Rashied Omar, and Isabel Apawo Phiri (eds.) *Religion in Public Education: Options for a new South Africa*, (2nd ed.), Cape Town: University of Cape Town, 1994.
Connolly, William E., *Why I Am Not A Secularist*, Minneapolis: University of Minnesota Press, 1999.
Cook, Rebecca (ed.), *Human Rights of Women: National and international perspectives*, Philadelphia: University of Pennsylvania Press, 1994.
Cox, Brian, and Daniel Philpott, "Faith-based diplomacy: an ancient idea newly emergent", *The Brandywine Review of Faith and International Affairs*, 1/2, 2003, 31-40.
Craycraft, Kenneth R., *The American Myth of Religious Freedom*, Dallas: Spence, 1999.
Demerath, N. J., *Crossing the Gods: World religions and worldly politics*, New Brunswick, NJ: Rutgers University Press, 2001.
De Vries, Hent, *Religion and Violence: Philosophical perspectives from Kant to Derrida*. Stanford, CA: Stanford University Press, 2002.
Docherty, Jayne Seminare, *Learning Lessons from Waco: When the parties bring their gods to the negotiation table*, Syracuse: Syracuse University Press, 2001.
Eickelman, Dale F. and Jon W. Anderson (eds.), *New Media in the Muslim World: The emerging public sphere*, Bloomington, IN: Indiana University Press, 1999.
Eickelman, Dale F., and Armando Salvatore, "The public sphere and Muslim identities", *European Journal of Sociology* 43, 2002, 92-115.
Elshtain, Jean Bethke, "Liberal monism", *Daedalus*, 132/3, 2003, 78-79.
Ewing, Katherine Pratt, "Legislating religious freedom: Muslim challenges to the relationship between church and state in Germany and France", in: Richard Shweder, Martha Minow, and Hazel Rose Markus (eds.), *Engaging Cultural Differences: The multicultural challenge in liberal democracies*, New York: Russell Sage Foundation, 2002, 63-80.

Gifford, Paul (ed.), *The Christian Churches and the Democratisation of Africa*, Leiden: E. J. Brill, 1995.
Gifford, Paul, David Archard, Trevor A. Hart, and Nigel Rapport (eds.), *2000 Years and Beyond: Faith, identity and the 'common era'*, New York: Routledge, 2003.
Gill, Anthony, *Rendering Unto Caesar: The Catholic Church and the state in Latin America*, Chicago: University of Chicago Press, 1998.
Gombrich, Richard, and G. Obeyesekere, *Buddhism Transformed: Religious change in Sri Lanka*, Princeton, NJ: Princeton University Press, 1988.
Gopin, Marc, *Between Eden and Armageddon: The future of world religions, violence, and peacemaking*, New York: Oxford University Press, 2000.
Gruchy, J. W. de and S. Martin (eds.), *Religion and the Reconstruction of Civil Society*, Pretoria: University of South Africa, 1995.
Gunn, T. Jeremy, "Under God but not the scarf: the founding myths of religious freedom in the United States and laïcité in France", *Journal of Church and State*, 46/1, 2004, 7-23.
Habermas, Jürgen, *The Structural Transformation of the Public Sphere: An inquiry into a category of bourgeois society* (reprint edition), Cambridge, MA: MIT Press, 1991.
Hackett, Rosalind I. J., "Conflicting rights: Martha Nussbaum's creative solution", *Soundings*, 83/3-4, 2001, 615-25.
———, "Mediated religion in South Africa: balancing air-time and rights claims", in: Birgit Meyer and Annelies Moors (eds.), *Media, Religion and the Public Sphere*, London: James Currey, (forthcoming 2004).
Hefner, Robert W., *Civil Islam: Muslims and democratisation in Indonesia*, Princeton, NJ: Princeton University Press, 2000.
Hoover, Dennis R., "Charitable choice and the new religious center", *Religion in the News* 3/1, 2000 http://www.trincoll.edu/depts/csrpl/RINVol3No1/charitable_choice_2000.htm (accessed April 22, 2004).
Huntington, Samuel, "The clash of civilizations?" *Foreign Affairs*, 72, 1993, 22-49.
———, *The Clash of Civilizations and the Remaking of World Order*, New York: Simon and Schuster, 1996.
Jenkins, Philip, *The Next Christendom: The coming of global Christianity*, New York: Oxford University Press, 2002.
———, "The next Christianity", *The Atlantic Monthly*, October 2002, http://www.theatlantic.com/issues/2002/10/jenkins.htm (accessed April 22, 2004).
Johnston, Douglas (ed.), *Faith-Based Diplomacy: Trumping realpolitik*, New York: Oxford University Press, 2003.
Johnston, Douglas and Cynthia Sampson (eds.), *Religion, The Missing Dimension of Statecraft*, New York: Oxford University Press, 1994.

Juergensmeyer, Mark, *The New Cold War? Religious nationalism confronts the secular state*, Berkeley and Los Angeles: University of California Press, 1993.

———, *Terror in the Mind of God: The global rise of religious violence*, Berkeley and Los Angeles: University of California Press, 2003.

Kaplan, Robert D., "Looking the world in the eye", *The Atlantic Monthly*, 288/5, 2001, 68-82 http://www.theatlantic.com/issues/2001/12/kaplan.htm.

Keddie, Nikki R., "Secularism and its discontents", *Daedalus*, 132/3, 2003, 14-30.

Kishwar, Madhu, *Religion at the Service of Nationalism and Other Essays*, Delhi: Oxford University Press, 1998.

Lampman, Jane, "New scrutiny of role of religion in Bush's policies," *The Christian Science Monitor*, March 17, 2003, 1.

Larsen, Lena, and Ingvild T. Plesner (eds.), *Teaching for Tolerance and Freedom of Religion or Belief*, Oslo: Norwegian Centre for Human Rights, 2002.

Levine, Daniel H., "The news about religion in Latin America", in: Mark Silk (ed.), *Religion on the International News Agenda*, Hartford, CT: The Leonard E. Greenberg Center for the Study of Religion in Public Life, 2000, 120-42.

Madan, T. N., *Modern Myths, Locked Minds*, Delhi: Oxford University Press, 1998.

Massey, James, *Minorities and Religious Freedom in a Democracy*, Delhi: Manohar/ Centre for Dalit/Subaltern Studies, 2003.

McCutcheon, Russell T., *Critics Not Caretakers: Redescribing the study of religion*, Albany, NY: State University of New York Press, 2001.

Meyer, Birgit, "Editorial", *Journal of Religion in Africa*, 33/2, 2003, 125-128.

Moyers, Bill, *Genesis and the Millennium: An essay on religious pluralism in the twenty-first century, including eight ecumenical responses*, Derek H. Davis (ed.), Waco, TX: J. M. Dawson Institute of Church-State Studies, 2000.

Noorani, A. G., *The RSS and the BJP*, New Delhi: LeftWord, 2001.

Nussbaum, Martha C., *Women and Human Development: The capabilities approach*, New York: Cambridge University Press, 2000.

Odinkalu, Chidi Anselm, "Back to the future: the imperative of prioritizing for the protection of human rights in Africa", *Journal of African Law*, 47/1, 2003, 1-37.

Parekh, Bhikhu, *Rethinking Multiculturalism: Cultural diversity and political theory*, Cambridge, MA: Harvard University Press, 2002.

Philpott, Daniel, "The challenge of September 11th to secularism in international relations", *World Politics*, 55, 2002, 66-95.

Richardson, James T., "Minority religions ("cults") and the law: comparisons of the United States, Europe and Australia", *University of Queensland Law Journal*, 18/2, 1995, 183-207.

Richardson, James T. (ed.), *Regulating Religion: Case studies from around the globe*, Dordrecht: Kluwer, 2004

Robertson, Roland, *Globalisation: Social theory and global culture*, London: Sage, 1992.

Rudolph, Susanne Hoeber and James Piscatori (eds.), *Transnational Religion and Fading States*, Boulder: Westview Press, 1997.

Sampson, Cynthia and John Paul Lederach (eds.), *From the Ground Up: Mennonite contributions to international peacebuilding*, New York: Oxford University Press, 2000.

Seminar on Freedom of Religion or Belief in the OSCE Region: Challenges to law and practice, The Hague: Ministry of Foreign Affairs, the Netherlands, 2001.

Shweder, Richard, Martha Minow and Hazel Markus (eds.), *Engaging Cultural Difference: The multicultural challenge to liberal democracies*, New York: Russell Sage, 2002.

Silk, Mark, "From the editor: a different kind of spiritual politics", *Religion in the News*, 2/2, 1999, http://www.trincoll.edu/depts/csrpl/RINVol2No/spiritualpolitics.htm.

Steyn, H. Christina, "The role of multi-religious education in the transformation of South African society", in: Thomas G. Walsh and Frank Kaufmann (eds.), *Religion and the Transformation of Southern Africa*, St. Paul, MN: Paragon House, 1999, 131-142.

Stout, Jeffrey, *Democracy and Tradition*, Princeton: Princeton University Press, 2003.

Tahzib-Lie, Bahia, "Applying a gender perspective in the area of the right to freedom of religion or belief", *Brigham Young University Law Review*, 2000, 967-88.

Tambiah, Stanley J., *Buddhism Betrayed? Religion, politics and violence in Sri Lanka*, Chicago: University of Chicago Press, 1992.

Tayob, Abdulkader and Wolfram Weisse (eds.), *Religion and Politics in South Africa*, New York: Waxmann Münster, 1998.

van der Veer, Peter, "The victim's tale: memory and forgetting in the story of violence", in: Hent de Vries and Samuel Weber (eds.), *Violence, Identity and Self-Determination*, Stanford: Stanford University Press, 1997, 186-200.

van der Vyver, Johann, "Constitutional perspectives of church-state relations in South Africa", *Brigham Young University Law Review*, 1999, 635-672.

Weithman, Paul (ed.), *Religion and Contemporary Liberalism*, Notre Dame, IN: University of Notre Dame Press, 1997.

———, *Religion and the Obligations of Citizenship*, New York: Cambridge University Press, 2002.

Witte, John, Jr., "The new freedom of public religion", editorial opinion, Center for the Interdisciplinary Study of Religion, Emory University. n.d.

Commentary

Muslih T. Yahya

My assignment here is not to summarise the lecture of Professor Hackett and I am not going to attempt to do that. Rather, I will try to highlight some of the salient points that she has made and on which I have comments and observations. This does not necessarily indicate agreement or disagreement with other points that I may not mention because I do not have comments on them.

SCHOLARSHIP AND BIAS

In the preamble to her presentation, Professor Hackett hints that as a scholar of religion and a concerned academic, she felt compelled "to ask critical reflective questions . . . on moves to accord religion more influence in public life, in a *relatively unbiased way.*" (The emphasis is mine.) This precisely is what she tries to do as she examines what seems to have informed the recent clamour for expanding *shari'ah* law in Nigeria, and the increasing wave of display of "Godliness" in the public sphere in other parts of the world.

I am impressed, not only because of the Professor's apparently careful choice of words in this subtle declaration, but also because we are in some kind of agreement. This approach to the study of religion agrees with the call I made a little over three years ago. This was in my contribution to the Round Table on the Interface Between Research and Dialogue especially in Africa, at the 18th Quinquennial Congress of the International Association for the History of Religions in Durban in August 2000.[1] This point is important because bias,

---

[1] Yahya, 2004.

tradition, and preconceived notions to a large extent affect the thinking of many writers and their attitude to the relationships between religion and state, and also between one belief system and another. This, I believe, is the reason why "diehard secular political scientists and social critics" want to ensure that religion in general or particular belief systems remain "the missing dimension in statecraft." As Professor Hackett observes, such writers are usually not willing to hear that there are "modern cases in which religion or spiritual factors have played helpful roles in preventing or resolving conflict and achieving non-violent change."

THE WEST AND THE SIGNIFICANCE OF RELIGION

In a keynote lecture delivered in London, Ali Mazrui argued that Western culture seems to have a homogenising effect on the rest of the world.[2] This, however, is only pretentious because there are other cultures, such as the Islamic culture, which also have strong bases and cannot be pushed aside or be brought to extinction. Nevertheless, and in Mazrui's words: "Western hegemony precipitated widespread homogenisation of values, styles and institutions."[3] Therefore, when this culture effectively pushed religion aside or away in the official conduct of public affairs, other non-Western attitudes to religion came to seem to many admirers of Western culture as unusual.

In this paper, Professor Hackett cites many recent books, journals and website publications to show that history has proven wrong the earlier expectations of the West on the significance of religion and predictions of Western scholars on its future. The titles of many of the books and articles[4] are enough to reflect the new thinking. Some of them are: *Faith-Based Diplomacy: An Ancient Idea Newly Emergent* (Cox and Philpot, 2003); *Religion, the Missing Dimension of Statecraft* (Johnston and Sampson 1994); and *2000 Years and Beyond: Faith, Identity and the 'Common Era'* (Gifford et al., 2003). Others like *The Clash of Civilizations* (Huntington, 1996) and *The News About Religion in Latin America* (Levine, 2000) also put up quite revealing arguments.

---

[2] Mazrui, 2000.
[3] Ibid.
[4] Complete bibliographical details are given in Hackett's list of references.

In other words, rather than "enter into decline because of secularisation and privatisation" as some Western scholars had predicted, religion is making greater incursions into the public sphere all over the world.

To my mind the reason for this is that the West had put too much emphasis on the material aspect of human existence and had ignored the spiritual aspect. What is strange about this is the fact that once upon a time, "Godlessness" used to be a major accusation some communities in Western Europe levelled against the Soviet Union. To many societies, morals and ethics matter, whether or not they are mentioned in the constitution, or are recognized in the judicial system. Secularism, however, leaves this to individual whims and caprices. Professor Hackett cites a legal scholar, John Witte, as seeing "the shift to more public religion in the US context as both inevitable and necessary." However, whether or not this new "public show" of religious tendencies is accompanied by practical involvement in the performance of religious rites and obligations is an entirely different issue. For instance, in many parts of Europe, culture and tradition grant recognition to Christianity or a specific denomination of it, either tacitly or openly. This not withstanding, most churches in those places are still virtually empty at times when they ought to be full.

SEPTEMBER 11 AND RELIGION

Hackett rightly observes that the events of September 11, 2001 made the significance of religion to assume "considerable prominence in public discourse" in the American scene. The context in which this happened is worth noting. I am not quite sure that the general public knows, as yet, the truth about September 11. Certainly, there are numerous non-religious causes of grievances, agitation, aggression, and international violence in various parts of the world today. Many publications are available now, which suggest that the planners and executors of the incident may be different from the ones the world is being told are the culprits. One such publication is the book *9/11: The Big Lie*.[5] The review of this book in the New York Times, quoted

---

[5] Meyssan, 2002.

on the book's cover, says that it "challenges the entire official version of the September 11 attacks." Similarly, the book *September 11: Before and Beyond*[6] argues that the truth about what really happened on September 11, 2001 goes beyond what is being portrayed presently: "The truth and answers to all the questions as to who the real oppressors and terrorists are does not lie in the present but are firmly rooted in history."[7] With alternative sources of information such as these, it is not likely that the real truth, if it were ever admitted, would connect the incident with religion in the sense that the American public, the European public and, indeed the whole world are presently made to believe. Indications are that the "super powers" have "the power" to cause things to happen the way they want them to. But whenever such things happen, whatever they (the super powers) tell the world are the causes, remain the causes, and whoever they say are the culprits remain the culprits. Again in the words of Professor Ali Mazrui, "the sins of the powerful acquire some of the prestige of power."[8] However, the curiosity about the significance of religion which September 11 has generated in the American and the European public may eventually be instrumental to bringing out, sooner or later, not only the real truth about the incident, but also the right attitude to religion.

THE DEBATE ON SECULARISM

One important point raised in this paper is how the definition, interpretation, or concept of secularism may determine the attitude to it. The paper dwells extensively on the views of the authors of two recent publications.[9] These are Talal Asad's book *Formations of the Secular: Christianity, Islam, Modernity* (2003) and Nikki R. Keddie's article "Secularism and its Discontents" (2003). I share, to a large extent, the fascination of the presenter with the two publications. She concludes on the basis of their arguments that there is "the need to historicise and contextualise the concepts of secularism and religion." I agree, especially for reasons I will mention shortly.

---

[6] Harun, 2002.
[7] Ibid., viii.
[8] Mazrui, 2000.
[9] Complete bibliographical details given in Hackett's list of references.

CONTEMPORARY CHALLENGES TO RELIGION

The paper observes "on a lighter, more ironic note" that "there is no knowing where religion or what type of religion may appear in America's public sphere." I think that our definition of religion should not be so loose and trivial that a new "religion" emerges every other day and will be part of what we are talking about when we discuss the role of religion in the public sphere. I believe that in order to attain its proper position in the public sphere and be given its due respect, religion itself needs to undergo some kind of "screening." This, to my mind, is because religion is too open to all sorts of manipulation and exploitation. This indeed, is one thing that those who are opposed to the involvement of religion in state affairs have against it, and this is where scholars of religion have a highly significant role to play.

Incidentally, religion can be its own instrument of screening. I believe that basically, religion has one long, continuous history and one purpose, from the time of the very first human being on earth to what we may want to regard as the end of the world. The cause and course of divergence, the implications of the ensuing plurality and the codes of interaction among the divergent belief systems should be part of the investigation. It should not be impossible for scholars of religion to help mankind to arrive at a kind of strategy to over-come the emergence of "religions" or religious practices of doubtful seriousness. Such strategies would help arrive at some global (not local) criteria with which "religious groups" would, in the words of the presenter of this paper, be "compelled to justify their existence to state and consumers alike." This, to my mind, is part of the "historicisation" and "contextualisation" of the concept of religion (along with secularism) that was recommended above, and with which I agreed.

THE ROLE OF THE CONSTITUTION, EDUCATION, AND THE MEDIA

One consistent argument in this paper is that, subject to constitutional provisions, education and the media have crucial roles to play in the dissemination of information on the place and role of religion in the public sphere. Impressed by the experience in South Africa, the presenter sees the constitution, religious broadcasting, and religious education as "key sites" for involving the various interest groups in the carving out of the role and status of religion in the public sphere.

My interpretation of this with regards to the constitution is that the designers of the constitution of a nation need to bear in mind the religious environment in the country. The point here is not necessarily that a "state religion" or even "state religions" are declared or identified. Rather, it is that religion be granted recognition, not only in the constitution itself, but also in such a way that the atmosphere is made conducive for the individual practice of religion. A person should not be forced or compelled to be involved in practices that are contrary to the injunctions of religion, simply because he is a public officer. The presenter cites Weithman (2002) as wondering if state support for religion as in the endorsement of religious codes of conduct would be consistent with liberal democracy. My answer is yes, if citizens of the country agree to it and so state in their constitution. This, to my mind, is because, liberal democracy should enable people to sit down together and fashion out their constitution and codes of conduct in such a way that they would take care of logical and contestable interests of all concerned.

While the role of the constitution may be straightforward if properly handled, that of religious broadcasting and religious education may not be that simple. The tendency, as is the experience in Nigeria, is for privately run educational institutions which throw their doors open to all, to influence the religious leaning of students who go through them, to the dissatisfaction of some parents of such students. Some public schools in places where a particular belief system is dominant also often take the liberty to be biased in favour of such a belief system. Similarly, electronic and print media houses are often found highly biased for or against particular belief systems.

CONCLUSION

The conclusion of the presenter is that the more visible presence of religion in the public sphere is a global phenomenon, which has unavoidably necessitated an overdue rethinking of the role of religion in this regard. She sees this rethinking as an essential ingredient of good governance anywhere in the world which requires the input of all stakeholders, with educational and media institutions having crucial roles to play. She warns, however, against the emergence of "new forms of separationism and demonisation of religious others."

Once again, I agree. I want to add, however, that while the dialogue between religion and state is essential, interfaith dialogue is crucial. The purpose of the latter is to foster interfaith and intercultural understanding, respect and harmony, and minimise, if not eradicate interfaith distrust and suspicion. I believe strongly that in this regard, international scholars of religion and the International Association for the History of Religions (IAHR) are "arbiters" who cannot afford to sit on the fence.

One obvious merit of this paper is its richness in what many people would see as "oven-fresh" information on new journal, book and website publications on the issue under discussion. This apparently comes from the presenter's wealth of personal experience and familiarity with very current sources that reflect a wide spectrum of ideas on the issue of religion and state at various levels of governance. Here, however, I try as much as possible to avoid the temptation to review those publications and comment on them, rather than commenting on the paper before us. All the same, these references are quite beneficial for follow-up "unbiased" researches on this issue.

REFERENCES

Harun, Abdulhakeem, *September 11: Before and beyond*, Nigeria: New Era Institute for Islamic Thought and Heritage (NEWITH), 2002.

Mazrui, Ali, "Pretender to universalism: western culture in a globalizing age", keynote address for the Royal Society of Art and the BBC, delivered in London, England on June 15, 2000, http://www.bbc.co.uk/worldservice/people/features/world_lectures/mazrui_lects.html (accessed 17 April 2004).

Meyssan, Thierry, *9/11: The big lie*, London: Carnot Publishing Ltd., 2002.

Yahya, Muslih T., "Christian-Muslim relations in Africa south of the Sahara: the interface between research and dialogue: a Muslim view", in: Klaus Hock (ed.), *The Interface between Research and Dialogue: Christian/Muslim relations in Africa*, Münster: Lit Verlag, 2004, 1-31.

The Enforcement of God's Law:
The *Shari'ah* in the Present World of Islam

Ruud Peters

1. INTRODUCTION

In the early nineteenth century, the *shari'ah* was the law of the land in the larger part of the Muslim world. This changed as a result of a process of Westernisation that set in during the second half of that century and affected the extent to which the *shari'ah* was applied by the courts and the way this was done. In this paper I want to examine to what extent the *shari'ah* nowadays plays a role in the national legal systems in the Muslim world. In the following, I will focus on the phenomenon of codification of the *shari'ah*. This is because this is a very recent phenomenon in Nigeria. Elsewhere, however, the first *shari'ah* codes were already introduced more than 130 years ago.

2. THE WESTERNISATION OF LEGAL SYSTEMS IN THE MUSLIM WORLD

In this section I'll briefly sketch the process of legal Westernisation in the Islamic world. I'll start with a description of the principal characteristics of the *shari'ah* and will then show how the process of Westernisation not only made parts of the *shari'ah* inoperative, but also affected the *shari'ah* itself as a result of codification.

2.1 The nature of the shari'ah

2.1.1 *The shari'ah as religious law*

Muslims regard the *shari'ah* as an expression of God's will. In this it is very different from modern Western law, which is seen as a purely human phenomenon, based either on conscious acts of the legislature or the judiciary, or on unconscious collective acts such as the gradual creation of customary law. The classical texts of Islamic jurisprudence define the *shari'ah* as: "The rules given by God to His servants as set forth by one of the prophets (may God bless them and grant them salvation)."[1] A swift glance at the tables of contents of the standard legal text books shows that they begin with purely religious topics like ritual prayer and fasting, before embarking on the discussion of the issues that are legal in the Western sense of the word, such as the contract of sale, legal capacity, succession, and criminal law. The *shari'ah* is therefore religious law, but this does not tell us very much. There are many different types of religious law. If we want to say something meaningful about the *shari'ah* as religious law, we must be more specific and define its religious character. This, I would argue, consists in two features: the fact that the basis of its validity is God's will, and the fact that the *shari'ah* also contains rules of a purely religious character.

In order to inform mankind of His commands, God, according to Muslim doctrine, has sent down revelations to successive prophets, the last of whom was Muhammad. To him the Qur'an was revealed. The contents of the Qur'an were supplemented by the Prophet's exemplary behaviour, the Sunnah, which, after his decease, was transmitted by generations of Muslims and, ultimately, compiled in the *hadith* collections. These are the divine sources of the *shari'ah* and, therefore, the foundation of its validity. This divine basis of the law may be compared with Kelsen's *Grundnorm*, the extra-legal norm explaining why laws are binding.[2]

A large part of the *shari'ah* is law as understood in the West. The rules of this domain of the *shari'ah* deal with the legal effects of certain acts or events and discuss the creation and extinction of rights and obligations between individuals and between the individual and the community. Here we find for instance the law of sale, of marriage, of tort, of procedure, laws that can be enforced by the *qadi* if the relevant facts can be established in court. However, the *shari'ah* is also envisioned as a set of norms constituting the code of behaviour of a

---

[1] Tahanawi, 1864, i, 759.
[2] On Kelsen, see Kelly, 1992, 384-8.

good Muslim, a guide to attain eternal bliss in Paradise. This representation of the *shari'ah* emphasises its religious character and focuses on the Hereafter, i.e. on whether, after one's death, one can expect to be rewarded or punished for certain acts. This is done by classifying them into five categories (obligatory, commendable, indifferent, reprehensible and forbidden) indicating their effects as far as reward and punishment are concerned. Performing an obligatory act results in reward, whereas neglecting it will be punished. Committing a forbidden act will entail punishment in the hereafter, and avoiding it will be rewarded. This applies not only to purely religious obligations, such as praying, fasting or dietary prescriptions, but also to legal ones, such as the obligation to pay one's debts. This part of the *shari'ah* falls outside the *qadi*'s competence. It is the exclusive domain of the mufti, the legal expert whose guidance is sought by individual Muslims in matters of the *shari'ah*, but whose opinions are not binding, unlike the sentences pronounced by *qadis*.

The following passage, taken from a seventeenth-century legal handbook that was popular in the Ottoman Empire, may help elucidate the double-sided character of the *shqri'ah*:

It is not reprehensible to lease out a house in the countryside (i.e. in a village) **if it will subsequently be used as a Zoroastrian temple, a church or a monk's cell, or if wine will be sold in it** . . . (at least according to the Imam [Abu Hanifa (d. 767)], because the lease confers the right to use the house and there is no sin in that. The sin is related to acts committed by the lessee of his own accord. That means that the relationship [between the landlord and the sin] is interrupted, just like in the case of the sale of a slave girl . . . to a person who wants to have anal intercourse with her, or the sale of a young slave to a homosexual . . .). **According to his companions** [al-Shaybani (d. 805) and Abu Yusuf (d. 798)] **it is indeed reprehensible** (to lease a house for such a use, because it promotes sin. The other three imams are of the same opinion . . .). **There is agreement [among the**

imams] **that such a lease is reprehensible in a village or a region inhabited mainly by Muslims.**[3]

Here the authors discuss an aspect of the law of lease. However, their concern in this passage is not whether or not under the given conditions such a contract is valid and binding, but whether a Muslim who concludes such a contract will be punished in the Hereafter because it is religiously reprehensible.

2.1.2 The shari'ah as jurists' law

A second feature of the *shari'ah* is that it is a jurists' law and that the jurists and not the state had the exclusive authority to formulate the rules of the *shari'ah*. They did so in a scholarly, academic debate, in which conflicting and often contradictory views were opposed and discussed. Actually, we must use a more precise terminology and distinguish between the *shari'ah* and the *fiqh*. If the *shari'ah* is God's law, the *fiqh* is the scholarly discipline aimed at formulating the prescriptions of the *shari'ah*, on the basis of the revealed texts and using various hermeneutic devices. What we find in the *fiqh* texts is the jurists' approximation to the divine law. Because of differences in understanding the texts and in the use of the hermeneutic tools, the *shari'ah* as laid down by the jurists in the *fiqh* is not uniform. From the beginning there were differences of opinion that resulted in the emergence of different schools of jurisprudence (*madhhab*, plur. *madhahib*), that ascribed their doctrines to and derived their names from famous jurists from the eighth and ninth centuries. Controversies not only existed between these schools, but also among the jurists of single schools, even on essential legal issues. The following passage, taken from the same Ottoman handbook quoted above, discusses the various opinions within the Hanafite school of jurisprudence on the question of whether a woman who is legally capable, may conclude her own marriage contract:

---

[3] Shaykhzade (d. 1667) and Ibrahim al-Halabi (d. 1549), 1884 (1301 H.), ii, 417. The passages in bold print are the translation of al-Halabi's elementary textbook; the remainder is Shaykhzade's commentary.

Marriage concluded by a free woman . . . of full legal capacity (irrespective of whether or not she is a virgin) **is valid** (even if such a marriage is concluded without the consent and presence of a matrimonial guardian. This is the authoritative opinion of Abu Hanifa [d. 767] and Abu Yusuf [d. 798]. This is so because she disposes of something to which she is exclusively entitled by being sound of mind and of age. For this reason she is entitled to dispose of her property and the principle here is that whoever may dispose of his property by his own right may conclude his own marriage and whoever may not [dispose of his property by his own right], may not [conclude his own marriage]. . . . According to the other *madhhab*s marriage cannot be concluded by a woman . . .). **However, the marriage guardian** (that is anyone of them as long as no one has given his consent) **is entitled to object [to such a marriage]** (that is he has the power to submit it to the judge for annulment. . . . The annulment is only effective by a judgement of the court since it is a matter of appreciation. Until such a judgement is pronounced the marriage is valid and the spouses inherit from one another if one of them should die before the judgement.). **If the husband is not her coequal (*kuf*)** (This is to avert damage and disgrace. If one of the matrimonial guardians has approved of the marriage, those who stand in the same or in a more distant degree [to her] cannot object anymore. This right [of objection] continues until she gives birth. . . . This rule can be found in most authoritative works. However, according to a less authoritative opinion this right of objection continues even after she has given birth to several children. . . .) **Hasan ibn Ziyad [d. 819] has reported from the Imam [Abu Hanifa] that it is not valid** (that is that such a marriage is not valid if she marries herself without a matrimonial guardian to a man who is not her coequal. Many of our scholars have adopted this rule since many cases are not submitted to judges.) **and Qadikhan [d. 1196] has issued fatwas according to this opinion.** (This opinion is more correct and cautious and therefore preferable for fatwas in our days because not every matrimonial guardian is proficient in litigation and not every judge is just. . . .) **According to Muhammad [al-Shaybani, d. 805] such a marriage is concluded conditionally** (i.e. subject to approval by the matrimonial guardian) **even if the husband is her coequal.** (If a marriage is contracted conditionally this means that before approval sexual intercourse is not allowed, that a repudiation is void and that they do not inherit from one another . . . .)[4]

Here we see that within the Hanafite school of jurisprudence there are three conflicting rules with regard to the marriage of a legally capable woman concluded on her own accord. According to one opinion she is fully entitled to do so, except that in case of a misalliance (*zawaj bi-ghayr kuf*) her agnatic male relatives may petition the *qadi* for an annulment. A second opinion holds that such a misalliance is per se invalid, whereas according to the third view all marriages concluded by legally capable women need the ratification of their marriage guardians.

This passage, which could be replaced by many other ones to illustrate the same point, is typical of the books on Islamic jurisprudence. They juxtapose different opinions on the same issue and it would appear that the legitimacy of dissent is one of the essential characteristics of the *fiqh*. There are several classical works of comparative *fiqh* in which the controversies are discussed and explained in terms of different interpretations of Qur'anic texts or Prophetic sayings, or the application of different hermeneutic tools.

As illustrated by this passage, *fiqh* texts do not resemble law codes. They contain scholarly discussions, and are therefore open, discursive, and contradictory. This discussion is the monopoly of the religious scholars, the *ulama*. Because of their religious training they have the prerogative of formulating the law on the basis of the revealed texts. Although in the early history of Islam this prerogative was contested by the rulers and state officials, the *ulama* ultimately emerged victorious.

---

[4] Ibid., i, 320-321.

2.2 Westernisation and codification of the law

During the nineteenth century, the Western powers brought large parts of the Islamic world under their sway. In some regions this resulted in conquest and colonial rule; in others, Western influence was exerted through economic pressure (many states in the Middle East were heavily in debt to Western powers), unequal trade relations, and gunboat diplomacy. In either case, legal change took place: in the colonies it was imposed, in various forms, by the colonial powers; in the semi-independent countries it was introduced by their own governments under Western pressure. Only in those regions where Western impact was minimal, such as on the Arabian Peninsula, did the *shari'ah* legal system persist without any restrictions. Northern Nigeria was a special case: there the form of indirect rule introduced by the British at the beginning of the twentieth century included the comprehensive preservation of Islamic justice, as long as it was not repugnant to British notions of natural justice, equity, and good conscience. This meant that the *shari'ah* was applied within boundaries set by British administrators and courts.

Westernising legal reform was nearly everywhere based on a concept of law that, until then, was unknown in the Islamic world: the notion of law as the expression of the will of the state, in the form of enacted codes. With the exception of Great Britain,[5] the colonial powers introduced, in the colonies they ruled, law codes based on those of the metropolis. In Muslim lands, only the law of personal status continued to be governed by the *shari'ah*, and even here the law courts applying the *shari'ah* were controlled by the colonial powers. In the parts of the Islamic world that were not or not yet colonised, legal Westernisation was a part of the modernisation of the state. This process was most in evidence in the Ottoman Empire and its dependencies like Egypt and Tunis. In other parts of the Islamic

---

[5] The common law tradition of Great Britain, based on custom and case law, caused the British to proceed differently from other colonial powers in legal matters. They preferred not to legislate but to apply the local law (including the *shari'ah*), but under the supervision of British administrators and courts that would regard as ineffective those laws that were repugnant to "natural justice, equity and good conscience." Only gradually did the British replace the local laws by enacted law.

world, such as Morocco and Iran, modernisation, including legal Westernisation, started much later. In the following I will focus on the Ottoman Empire, which can serve as an example for what happened in many other parts of the Islamic world.

The notion of the *shari'ah* as religious, divine law, monopolised by the *ulama*, would *prima facie* seem to be contradictory to and incompatible with the existence of state-enacted law. However, this was not the case, at least not in the Ottoman Empire. As from the fifteenth century the sultans began to enact regulations (*qanun*) dealing with land law and fiscal and criminal law. These regulations did not replace the *shari'ah* in the fields to which they applied; rather, they supplemented it where it was silent or did not give precise rules. This legislation was regarded as part of the Islamic legal order and not as being in conflict with the *shari'ah*. The enactment of these codes did not imply that the state had the monopoly of law-making, nor that state-enacted law was of a higher order that other types of law.

Codification, on the other hand, is based on an altogether different concept, for codification presupposes that the state enacts legislation that completely regulates a certain domain of the law, "covering the field" to the exclusion of all other types of law previously applicable in that field (unless the codification itself confers force of law on such other types, as is sometimes done in the case of custom). Codification therefore implies that only the state determines what law is and that state-enacted law is the highest form of law. This notion of codification has its origins in the European civil code tradition of the early nineteenth century.

In the Ottoman Empire codification began in the second half of the nineteenth century. During the era of reform (Tanzimat period, 1839-1876) the ideas on the relationship between the state and the law had begun to change. Tanzimat reform was very much administrative and legal reform, and legislation became one of its most important instruments. The first reform decree, the Gülhane Rescript (1839) emphasises the importance of legislation:

> In order to better administer the Sublime Empire (*Devlet-i Aliyye*) and the Well-Protected Dominions (*Memalik-i Mahruse*), it is deemed necessary and important to enact some new laws. The most important provisions of these

indispensable laws consist of more personal safety, of a better protection of honour, decency and property, of fixing the taxes and specifying the way of drafting the required soldiers and the period of their service.[6]

Codification was not only an instrument of reform, but also of centralisation and legal unification. Under the influence of Western, continental, constitutional notions, the Ottoman ruling elite became convinced of the necessity of codification of all domains of the law, so as to emphasise that the state should determine what the law of the land was. As a consequence, commercial (1850) and penal (1858) codes were introduced based on European models. Law cases in these fields were thenceforth heard by newly created courts and withdrawn from the competence of the *shari'ah* courts. In Egypt, this happened three decades later when, in 1883, the whole legal system, with the exception of personal status, was Westernised by the introduction of a new court system and French-oriented law codes.

However, it was also deemed necessary to modernise existing law, i.e. the *shari'ah* and customary law. Examples of the codification of traditional law are the Ottoman Penal Codes of 1840 and 1851 (abolished by the European type Ottoman Penal Code of 1858), the Land Law of 1858, the *Mecelle*, the Ottoman Civil Code based on Hanafite *fiqh* enacted between 1868 and 1876, and, finally, the Code of Family Law (*Hukuk-i 'Aile Kararnamesi*) of 1917. Behind this movement was the Western notion that traditional law, as found in the various books of *fiqh*, in administrative practices, and in custom, was "chaotic and inaccessible" and that "codification is civilisation." The need for codification was especially felt when new courts were established in which not all judges had a training in Islamic jurisprudence:

> Islamic jurisprudence, then, is an immense ocean and in order to find solutions for problems by bringing to its surface the pearls of the topics required [for solving the problems] needs an enormous skill and mastery. And especially for the Hanafite *madhhab*, there were, in subsequent generations, very

---

[6] Text in *Düstur*, 1865-66, i, 2-3.

many independent interpreters (*mujtahid*) and there emerged many controversies so that Hanafite jurisprudence, like Shafi'ite jurisprudence, has branched out and become diverse to the extent that it cannot anymore be examined carefully. Therefore it is tremendously difficult to distinguish the correct opinion among the various views and to apply it to the cases. . . . Therefore, if a book on legal transactions (*mu`amalat*) were to be composed that is easy to consult being free from controversies and containing only the preferred opinions, than everybody could read it easily and apply it to his transactions.[7]

During the same period there emerged also semi-official codifications, i.e. private compilations of the rules of the *shari'ah* in some fields, arranged in sections like law codes and presenting these rules in a conveniently arranged fashion so that they could be used as easy reference tools for legal practitioners. In Egypt Muhammad Qadri Pasha (d. 1889), former minister of justice, composed compilations on family law, the law of property, and contracts and *waqf* law, which were published between 1875 and 1890.[8] These compilations had a semi-official status in those fields of law that continued to be governed by the *shari'ah* after the reforms of 1883, when French civil, commercial, criminal and procedural law was adopted. In the Ottoman Empire, `Ömer Hilmi, a former president of the Court of Cassation, composed an authoritative compilation of the law of homicide and personal injury, a part of criminal law that was still enforced by the *shari'ah* courts.[9] The French, ruling North Africa, commissioned Marcel Morand, a French specialist in Islamic law, to compile a code of the Malikite doctrine of personal status.[10]

If one compares the *fiqh* texts on a certain legal issue with the codified provisions, the differences are striking. As I said before, the *fiqh* doctrine is jurists' law and the *fiqh* texts are discursive and include various, often conflicting opinions on the issue. They are open texts in the sense that they do not offer final solutions. Provisions of a law

---

[7] From the explanatory memorandum of the first book of the Mecelle (1868), quoted in Kaşıkçı, 1997, 75-6.
[8] Qadri Pasha, 1909[a], 1893, and 1909[b].
[9] Hilmi, 1881-1882.
[10] See Schacht, 1964, 98.

code, on the other hand, must be authoritative, clear and unequivocal. In a law code there is no room for contradictory opinions or argumentation and its provisions must be definitive and final. Therefore, choices have to be made when codifying the *shari'ah*. This will become clear when we compare the codified provisions of the Hanafite doctrine regarding the marriage of a legally capable woman with the *fiqh* text on the same subject quoted above.

Muhammad Qadri's compilation (ca.1875):

If [a free and legally capable woman] concludes a marriage with someone who is socially her inferior (*ghayr kuf'*) without her agnatic guardian's express consent before the marriage, then that marriage is per se invalid and the guardian's consent given after the conclusion of the marriage is of no avail. If she has no agnatic guardian and marries herself to a person who is socially her inferior or if her guardian has consented to her marriage with a socially inferior man, then the marriage is valid.[11]

The Ottoman Code of Family Law (1917):

If a woman of full age marries herself without informing her matrimonial guardian and without having obtained his consent, then the matter must be examined. If she has married herself to a person who is socially her equal, then the marriage is binding even if the bride price is less than her proper bride price. However, if she has married herself to someone who is socially her inferior, then the guardian can have recourse to the judge for rescission of the marriage.[12]

Both these code sections contain clear and unequivocal legal rules. The dissenting opinions that existed in the *fiqh* text quoted previously have been excised, in order to produce one authoritative, final statement of the law. But, if we read the two code sections carefully, it will be evident that the authors of these texts have made different choices. Muhammad Qadri Pasha followed the more

---

[11] Qadri Pasha, 1909[a], Section 52.
[12] *Huquq-i `A'ile Qararnamesi* (1917), Section 47.

conservative view, attributed to Abu Hanifa by Hasan ibn Ziyad, which was the prevailing view in the Ottoman Empire. The Ottoman legislator of 1917, however, followed another authoritative Hanafite opinion, also ascribed to Abu Hanifa, that was more favourable to women. These two texts clearly illustrate the effects of codification: the transformation from a scholarly discourse in which different and opposing opinions are juxtaposed, to an authoritative, definitive statement of the law, purged of all alternative views. But this is not the only effect. The adoption of the Western concept of the law code also means the adoption of the Western concept of law. As a result, the religious norms are also eliminated from the *shari'ah* codes. Codified *shari'ah*, then, is no more that an impoverished, reduced version of the rich *fiqh* doctrine.

When states during the second half of the nineteenth century assumed the power to define the *shari'ah*, the role of the *ulama* did not end completely. Their co-operation was essential in order to legitimise the state-enacted *shari'ah* codes. But more importantly, they were needed for their expertise. This explains the pivotal role of men like Ahmed Cevdet (1822-1895) in legal reforms. Trained as religious scholars and having an open eye for reform, they staffed the committees that prepared the codifications of the *shari'ah*. The necessary participation of the *ulama* limited in practice the freedom of the state in codifying the *shari'ah*. They had the power to refuse to participate if the state should enact laws that they would regard as repugnant to the *shari'ah*. Such a step would greatly undermine the legitimacy of codifications of the *shari'ah*.

3. THE PRESENT SITUATION

In the course of the twentieth century the Westernisation of the legal systems in the Islamic world continued, by the adoption of Western substantive and adjective laws and Western notions of law. However, in most national legal systems, the *shari'ah* still has a role to play. These roles vary and we can classify these legal systems in four types according to the position of the *shari'ah* in them.

▶ The completely secularised legal systems, from which the *shari'ah* has been removed.

▶ The legal systems that are dominated by the *shari'ah*, in the sense that the *shari'ah* is the supreme law of the land and that state legislation can only take place in areas where the *shari'ah* is silent or not unequivocal.
▶ The legal systems in which *shari'ah* is applied in some domains, but within a Western constitutional and administrative framework. This is the most common type. Usually the domain left to the *shari'ah* is the field of personal status (family law, law of succession) and the law of *waqf*, although in Northern Nigeria, other private transactions may also be governed by the *shari'ah* at the election of the parties. However, nearly everywhere, the law in these fields has been codified.[13] In its uncodified form, *shari'ah* rules are enforced only in Northern Nigeria and Egypt. In Nigeria there was, before 2000, no codification of the *shari'ah* at all; in Egypt, family law and the law of succession have been only partially codified and uncodified *shari'ah* is applied on all issues for which there is no enacted law.
▶ Finally there are those legal systems that have been re-Islamised. They developed out of systems of the previous type, after Islamist regimes came to power. This re-Islamisation was implemented by introducing Islamic law codes in many fields, noticeably in that of criminal law. This type of legal system exists in Iran, Sudan, and, to some extent, in Libya. Outside the Middle-East we find it in Pakistan and in twelve Northern, predominantly Muslim states of the Nigerian federation.[14]

3.1 The Completely Secularised Legal Systems

The most prominent example of a completely secularised legal system exists in Turkey, as a result of the radical Westernisation policies of Atatürk, which resulted in drastic law reform in the 1920s. If *shari'ah* still plays a role, it is at the informal level. For a long time, rural Turks would regulate their family life and inheritance according to the *shari'ah* without recourse to the state law. Since Islamic

---

[13] For the modernization of the law of personal status, see Ebert, 1996 and Beck-Peccoz, 1990.
[14] For the Islamisation of criminal law, see Peters, 1994; on Nigeria in particular see Peters, 2003.

marriages and births within those marriages were often not registered, this compelled the state, on several occasions, to issue regularisation laws.

3.2 The Completely Islamic legal systems

In those geographical regions that were not of interest to the West, or where the interest did not emerge until very late in the twentieth century, the *shari'ah* remained the law of the land. This is the case in Yemen and in Saudi Arabia.[15] In Yemen most of the *shari'ah*-based laws have by now been codified. This is not the case in Saudi Arabia, which has the purest form of a traditional Islamic legal system in the world: the *shari'ah* is applied by the courts by having recourse to the classical Hanbalite texts and no codification of *shari'ah* law has been undertaken. Only in those fields where the *shari'ah* is silent, such as with regard to company law or traffic law, has the state issued regulations, which, as a rule, are not enforced by the *shari'ah* courts, but by special councils or commissions. The only *shari'ah* rules that have been codified are the fiscal decrees on the *zakat* tax (Royal decree 17/2/28i/8634 of 29 Safar 1370 (7 April 1951).

3.3 *Shari'ah* application within the framework of westernised legal systems

In the majority of Muslim countries, the legal systems have been Westernised by the introduction of Western type law codes, a Western type constitution and a Western type judiciary. The domain of personal status, however, continues to be governed by the *shari'ah*, but within a Westernised legal order and usually in a codified form. In some countries, such as Egypt (since 1956), the *shari'ah*, to the extent it is operative, is applied by the regular judiciary (the national courts). In other countries the *shari'ah* is applied by special *shari'ah* courts, in many cases functioning side by side with Christian ecclesiastical and Jewish courts in matters of personal status.

---

[15] On Saudi Arabia, see Vogel, 2000.

The most conspicuous change in this domain was the codification of the law of personal status (see Appendix One). This was prompted by various motives:

- ▶ The wish to create greater legal security
  - ◆ by removing ambiguities in the legal doctrine and thus facilitating the application of the *shari'ah* by the courts, and
  - ◆ by creating greater clarity about the civil status of persons (marriage, divorce, filiation), by introducing obligatory registration.
- ▶ The wish to introduce reforms of the substantive law (such as: minimum age for marriage, abolition of forced marriages, restriction of polygamy, introducing more grounds for obtaining divorce by women) with the aim of strengthening the rights of women.

In order to confer greater legitimacy on the reforms in the substantive law, the legislators took care to remain within the orbit of the *shari'ah*. This was achieved by using the following expedients:

- ▶ Using adjective or penal law to realise a certain objective, without changing the substantive law of the *shari'ah*. E.g. making child marriages punishable offences for the parents of the minor spouse and for the other spouse, if adult; or forbidding marriage registrars to register marriages in case one of the spouses has not reached a certain age and at the same time introducing the rule that marriages can only be proven by marriage documents issued by an official registrar. Another example is that in some countries polygamous marriages may only be registered after the court has been satisfied that the husband has a lawful reason for such a marriage and is financially able to support all wives.
- ▶ By selecting those opinions from the various schools of jurisprudence that are most conducive to the aims of the legislator. This was used in Hanafite countries when they introduced the Malikite grounds for divorce with the aim of extending the possibilities for women to end their marriages; and in Malikite countries, when they introduced the Hanafite rule that legally capable women always must give their consent to a marriage, and cannot be forced into a marriage by their fathers or grandfathers.

▶ By using *ijtihad*, i.e. a new interpretation of the relevant texts of the Qur'an and *hadith*. This was done, for example, when the Tunisian government, in 1956, abolished polygamy. The legislators argued that Q 4:3[16] in combination with 4:129[17] actually implied a ban on polygamy.

In some countries of this group the constitution stipulates that the principles of the *shari'ah* are the main source of legislation. Such provisions were inserted into several constitutions by ruling elites to take the wind out of the sails of the Islamist opposition. So far little comparative research has been done on the effect of these provisions. In Egypt, which has one of them (Section 2 of the Egyptian constitution as amended in 1979), its effect is very limited. On the one hand, the Supreme Constitutional Court has interpreted Section 2 to mean that legislation enacted after 1979 which is in conflict with *shari'ah* principles is unconstitutional. But in applying Section 2, the Court has measured challenged legislation only against those rare injunctions of the *shari'ah* that are based on clear, unambiguous and unchangeable texts of the Qur'an and Sunnah that are not subject to interpretation. The result is that no legislation challenged under Section 2 has yet been overturned.

3.4 Re-Islamised legal systems

Since the 1970s the legal systems of a number of Islamic countries have been re-Islamised, by replacing Western type law codes by new ones based on the *shari'ah*. (For a survey of the recent *shari'ah* legislation, see Appendix Two.) This took place in various political contexts:

▶ after an Islamic revolution, such as in Iran (1979)

---

[16] "And if ye fear that ye will not deal fairly by the orphans, marry of the women, who seem good to you, two or three or four; and if ye fear that ye cannot do justice (to so many) then one (only) or (the captives) that your right hands possess. Thus it is more likely that ye will not do injustice."

[17] "Ye will not be able to deal equally between (your) wives, however much ye wish (to do so). But turn not altogether away (from one), leaving her as in suspense. If ye do good and keep from evil, lo! Allah is ever Forgiving, Merciful."

- after an coup d'état, for which Islam was used as a legitimisation (Pakistan, 1979)
- after a policy change of a sitting regime (Libya, 1972-3, Sudan, 1985)
- after popular pressure resulting in legislation passed by democratically elected legislative organs (twelve states of Northern Nigeria, from 2000 onwards)

When Islamist movements gained strength in the Muslim world, the prevailing Westernised legal systems came under attack. The Islamists wanted to establish an Islamic state and the main characteristic of an Islamic state was, for them, the enforcement of the *shari'ah* in all domains, including, of course, criminal law. In their view, full application of the *shari'ah* had come to an end when the Western colonial powers invaded the Muslim world and imposed Western laws. The introduction of the *shari'ah* became the rallying cry of many of the religiously inspired political movements. The idea of going back to the cultural roots and of imposing Islamic norms on society was appealing to large segments of the population that were opposed to the increasing Western political and cultural influence.

In 1972 Mu ammar al-Gaddafi surprised the world by announcing that he had re-introduced the *shari'ah* provisions on theft and robbery, making these offences punishable by amputation. Observers of the Arab and Muslim world were puzzled, since this return to Islamic criminal law did not fit in the prevailing modernisation theories that were based on the assumption of a continuous and unstoppable spread of secularisation. Most of these observers regarded Islamic criminal law as something of the past, enforced only in backward countries like Saudi Arabia, where, they believed, it would in due course disappear under the influence of modernity. Nobody expected that Gaddafi had inaugurated a trend and that from the 1970s more Muslim countries would adopt Islamic penal codes.

The re-introduction of Islamic criminal law is surrounded by a powerful ideological discourse, that was shaped by the propagandists of Islamism but has its roots in deeply felt religious convictions and emotions. The crucial element is that Muslims, in order to be good Muslims, must live in an Islamic state, a state which implements the *shari'ah*. It is not sufficient that such a state gives Muslims the choice whether or not they follow the *shari'ah*; it must actually impose the *shari'ah* on them, by implementing Islamic criminal law. Preaching and admonition do not suffice and a big stick is needed to change behaviour in an Islamic direction. Islamic criminal law is a tool to impose an Islamic moral order on society, by imposing rigorous rules, especially in the fields of sexual morality, the consumption of alcohol and drugs, and blasphemy and un-Islamic utterances.

The establishment of an Islamic state is presented as a religious duty for all Muslims and as an endeavour that may bring Paradise within their reach. And there is another felicitous prospect connected with it: that of a pious and virtuous community on earth that enjoys God's favour and is actively aided by Him to overcome poverty and humiliation. Such a community will be prosperous and strong. The re-introduction of Islamic criminal law is, in this perspective, a step towards salvation in the Hereafter as well as salvation in this life and, therefore, much more than merely a technical reform of penal law. The notions that are connected with it may make the project of enforcing Islamic criminal law attractive to both the ruling elite and to large parts of the Muslim population.

For the elite, the re-Islamisation of criminal law may have two sorts of advantages – ideological and practical. One ideological advantage is that it confers an Islamic legitimacy. Islamist regimes that have come to power as a result of a revolution or *coup d'état* need to demonstrate immediately that they make a start with the construction of a real Islamic state by implementing Islamic criminal law. Other regimes, that have already been in power for some time, have introduced Islamic criminal law merely as a political expedient to enhance their legitimacy and take the wind out of the sails of the Islamist opposition. Egypt is a case in point, although in the end Islamic criminal law was not implemented. Between 1976 and 1982 enormous efforts were made by various parliamentary committees set up to draft Islamic legislation, including an Islamic criminal code. This was done in order to demonstrate the Islamic character of the state as a reaction to the ideological attacks of the Islamist opposition. However, the fickle political nature of the process became clear a few years later. When in the early 1980s, after the assassination of President Sadat, the political climate changed and the government decided to take a firm stand against radical Islamist groups, these proposals were officially consigned to the dustbin.[18]

A second ideological motive for a regime to adopt Islamic criminal law is that, in doing so, it makes a clearly anti-Western statement. Islamic criminal law is one of those parts of the *shari'ah* that are most at variance with Western law and Western legal notions, much more so than e.g. the private or commercial law of the *shari'ah*. In implementing Islamic criminal law, there is a clear emphasis on the fixed punishments, because here the contradictions between Islamic criminal law and Western-type penal law are glaring. The fixed punishments, or *hudud*, which go directly back to the Qur'an and Sunnah, are very much at variance with the modern accepted system of legal punishment, both in the Islamic world and in the West. Islamic criminal law, then, and especially the law of *hudud*, has a highly symbolic value and its introduction is regarded by many Muslims as the litmus test for a real Islamisation of the legal system.

There are also two practical aspects that make the implementation of Islamic criminal law an attractive option for political elites in the Muslim world. The first one is that it provides an effective instrument of control and repression. The enactment of Islamic criminal legislation has been a pretext for the introduction, on a large scale, of corporal punishment, especially flogging, not only for *hadd* crimes, but also for offences that have nothing to do with Islamic criminal law *stricto sensu*. The Nimeiri regime in the Sudan, for instance, introduced flogging as a possible punishment for all offences mentioned in the Penal Code. Corporal punishment, especially when administered in public, is an effective instrument of repression. This is not only true with regard to those who are directly subjected to it, but even more so for society as a whole. The spectacle of public executions, amputations and floggings symbolises the supreme power of the regime and the futility of resistance against it.

The second reason why adopting Islamic criminal law might be attractive for a regime is that the way homicide is tried under Islamic criminal law is closer to the sense of justice of large parts of the population in the Islamic world. As we have seen, legal proceedings for homicide are based on private rather than state prosecution. The

---

[18] See Peters, 1988, 231-253.

victim's heirs control the litigation in the sense that they are parties to the trial, the prosecution depends on their wills, and they can agree to an extrajudicial settlement. This is different from their position under the Western-inspired codes, where the victim's heirs are not admitted as parties to the trial and are, in the best case, relegated to the position of witnesses, without a say in the proceedings. The doctrine of Islamic criminal law is attractive in societies where private justice or revenge prevails, because it combines the idea of private prosecution with orderly judicial proceedings.

When Islamic criminal law was introduced in the various re-Islamising countries, it did not meet with much opposition among the Muslim population; on the contrary, in most countries it was supported by large groups in Muslim society. This is due to the powerful ideological discourse surrounding it, which holds promises for the "ordinary people." In the first place, there is the religious aspect, the idea that by implementing Islamic criminal law the community complies with God's wishes and will be rewarded. But on a practical level, Islamic criminal law also holds promises of eliminating crime and corruption as a result of its deterrence and its swift justice. Those who are apprehensive about rising crime rates and corruption, will welcome Islamic criminal law as a panacea for the cure of social evils and the restoration of a virtuous society. Its advocates argue that Islamic criminal law offers effective tools to fight crime because it allows the application of severe and painful punishments consisting in whipping, amputation and stoning to death. This is an often-used argument in favour of Islamic criminal law. The amputation of the hand of one thief, it is repeatedly asserted, will deter many others from violating the property of others. The advocates always contend that the crime rate in countries like Saudi Arabia, where fixed punishments are carried out, is much lower than elsewhere.

A further advantage mentioned in support of the introduction of Islamic criminal legislation is the fact that trials can be short and justice can be implemented quickly. Khomeini expressed this notion as follows:

> Islamic justice is based on simplicity and ease. It settles all criminal and civil complaints and in the most convenient,

elementary, and expeditious way possible. All that is required is for an Islamic judge, with pen and inkwell and two or three enforcers, to go into a town, come to his verdict in any kind of case, and have it immediately carried out.[19]

These words show a desire not only for quick justice, but also for a simple and transparent procedure. With disapproval, attention is drawn to the slowness of justice under Western law, where trials can drag on for many years. Such statements express a longing among many groups in Muslim societies for a less complicated and orderly society, where good deeds are immediately rewarded and evil deeds punished right away. It has already been noticed that there are great similarities between the positive self-image of the Iranian clerics who administer justice, and the heroic sheriff that we know from Wild West pictures who single-handedly, with only his gun, restores law and order in a little town where crime is rife.[20]

A striking aspect of the way Islamic criminal law is implemented is that it is effectuated through state legislation. Islamic jurisprudence, the *fiqh*, is, as we have seen, essentially a legal doctrine formulated by scholars and not by the state. *Fiqh* is jurists' law. Judges applying the *fiqh* have to consult the scholarly works of jurisprudence and to select with regard to the case they must adjudicate, the most authoritative from several, often conflicting opinions with a bearing on the issue. The regimes that reintroduce Islamic criminal law in the form of penal codes claim that they are returning to the situation that prevailed before the West began to exert its influence in the Islamic world. This, of course, is illusory. Going back to the pre-colonial past would have meant introducing Islamic criminal law not by legislating it, but by referring the judges to the classical works on *fiqh*. Although this was done in two exceptional cases,[21] introducing Islamic criminal

---

[19] Quoted in Newman, 1982, 561.
[20] Ibid.
[21] In Afghanistan and the United Arab Emirates. When the Taliban came to power in Afghanistan they began to apply Islamic criminal law on the basis of the classical doctrine and did not codify Islamic criminal law. In the UAE, Islamic criminal law was introduced in 1987, when the Federal Penal Code laid down that *hadd* offences, homicide, and wounding, would henceforth be tried by the *shari'ah* courts according to the *shari'ah*. See al-Muhairi, 1996, 350-71.

law by statute law has been the rule. This is a consequence of modern, Western ideas on the relationship between state and law that became current in the Islamic world, as we have seen in section 2.2. This means that, in spite of the ideology of returning to the *shari'ah*, it is the state that determines which laws the courts must enforce. By instructing the courts to have recourse to state legislation and not to the classical body of *fiqh*, the *ulama* are relegated to the second level. The result of the reintroduction of Islamic criminal law, in most countries, is that something new is created, a hybrid form of criminal law consisting of Islamic substantive rules in a Western garb and embedded in a Western type adjective law, with Western type courts and Western institutions like the state prosecutor.

4. CONCLUSIONS

As a result of the codification of the *shari'ah*, the *ulama* lost their time-honoured position as the exclusive guardians of the law. This affected their status in society, which had already been impaired as their economic resources, especially employment opportunities, had declined. Traditionally, the *ulama* had the monopoly not only of religious functions connected with the mosques, but also of education and the administration of justice. Because of this monopoly, they enjoyed a high status in society. However, all this began to change as from the end of the nineteenth century. Because of the creation of new types of schools for the training of military officers, civil servants, doctors, and engineers, the *ulama* lost the monopoly of education. At the same time, their intellectual authority was challenged by some of these new professionals and by those who had come into contact with the intellectual debates in the West. This erosion of their intellectual status went hand in hand with a gradual decline of the economic foundations of their livelihood. Whereas originally all judges and teachers were from the *ulama* class, now, after the introduction of new types of schools and the Westernisation of the legal system, they had to compete for these employments with graduates of other schools. The *ulama*'s intellectual leadership was no longer unconditionally accepted. They were fiercely attacked by Islamist intellectuals, who did not unquestioningly accept the traditional interpretations of the revealed texts propagated by the *ulama*. Although most Islamist intellectuals had not had a traditional religious education, they regarded themselves as competent in this field on the strength of their knowledge of the Qur'an and *hadith*, which they often understood in new ways.

This has enormously affected the discourse on the *shari'ah*, both the codified and the uncodified parts. For, as we have seen, codified *shari'ah* is only a section of the entire body of *shari'ah* doctrine. Not subject to codification are the purely ritual, religious and ethical provisions of the *shari'ah*, dealing e.g. with ritual prayer (*salat*), pilgrimage (*hajj*) and dietary prescriptions, and those rules that have a legal character but are not implemented, such as, in most countries, *shari'ah* private law (especially the provisions on interest), criminal, and constitutional law. The rules of the *shari'ah* that were not enforced by the judiciary, were traditionally within the competence of the muftis, who belonged to the *ulama* class and had a traditional religious training. They were the religious authorities who would counsel believers on specific questions of the *shari'ah*. Although there were controversies and disagreements among them, their authority was not fundamentally challenged. This, however, has changed now. Many of the issues that used to belong exclusively to the domain of the muftis have now become subject to public debates, in which intellectuals without a traditional religious training also participate. During the twentieth century, intellectuals without a religious training increasingly put their imprint on the religious debates and started to question accepted religious dogmas. Initially, these were intellectuals who, under the influence of Western ideas, became critical of what they saw as backward religious views and practices that would block "progress." However, during the last decades other types of believers have become more prominent in these debates. There is a growing group of pious Muslims who argue that the traditional doctrine of the *shari'ah*, as expounded by the *ulama*, has deviated from the pure teachings of the Qur'an and Sunnah and who want to get back to these pure teachings as guidelines for their daily lives.

These developments have resulted in a situation in which defining the *shari'ah* is not any more the exclusive competence of the *ulama*, but has become a public concern. As to codified *shari'ah*, the debate is directly connected with national politics. Depending on the extent to which a state has adopted democratic procedures of legislation, the *shari'ah* codes are discussed in parliament and the media. Although the traditional *ulama* still may play a role in the preparation and the "marketing" of these codes, the ultimate decision is with the politicians. Codification of the *shari'ah*, as well as the question of which parts of the national legal system must be immediately based on the *shari'ah*, have therefore become prominent and important political issues.

Since the *ulama* have lost their intellectual monopoly, the legally unenforced sections of the *shari'ah* are also publicly debated. Although this debate is less political than the discussions on the codified *shari'ah*, it certainly has political aspects. Islamic symbols and doctrines are connected with political positions and are used to legitimise political points of view. Whether or not all existing views can be fully expressed depends, naturally, on the extent to which the media are free from government interference and censorship. There are many instances where certain religious views are not permitted to be expressed, because of their political associations.

What does all this mean for the *shari'ah* in contemporary Muslim society? The most important development has been that the authority of the *ulama* has been challenged and has declined. There are now also Muslims without a religious training who can have their say about *shari'ah* issues. Those parts of the *shari'ah* that have been codified and are part of the national legal systems are now brought under control of the state instead of being controlled by the *ulama*. This means that they have become political and, if the structures of the state permit it, even democratised. Concerning the other aspects of the *shari'ah*, here, too, the *ulama* have lost control, although not as drastically as in the purely legal domain. The issues of the *shari'ah* that fall outside the scope of codified law, are now debated by all kinds of Muslim intellectuals, with and without a formal religious training. These debates have not only been politicised, as I showed before, but also, at least potentially, democratised. However, to what extent this may lead to a real democratisation depends on whether these debates are free from political constraints that block freedom of expression.

5. APPENDIX ONE: CODES AND LEGISLATION ON PERSONAL STATUS

1917 Ottoman Code of Family Law
1920-2000: series of Egyptian codes
1939 Dissolution of Muslims Marriages Act (India)
1951 Jordanian Code of Personal Status, replaced in 1976 by a new code
1953 Syrian Code of Personal Status, amended in 1975
1956 Tunisian Code of Personal Status, amended in 1993
1958 Moroccan Code of Personal Status, amended in 1993
1959 Iraqi Code of Personal Status
1961 Muslim Family Laws (Pakistan)
1967 Protection of the Family Law (Iran), amended in 1975; abolished in 1979 during the Iranian Islamic Revolution
1974 South-Yemeni Family Code (abolished in 1992 after the unification) 1975 Somalian Family Code (almost identical to the South-Yemeni one)
1977 Afghanistan Marriage Law
1982 Algerian Code of Personal Status
1984 Libyan Marriage Law
1984 Kuwaiti Code of Personal Status
1991 Sudan Code of Personal Status
1992 Yemeni Code of Personal Status

6. APPENDIX TWO: CODES OF RE-ISLAMISATION

6.1 Criminal law

Libya

Law 148 of 11 October 1972 on theft and robbery, (Fr. tr. : Rycx, Jean-François (tr.), "Loi no 148 de l'année 1392 H correspondant à l'année 1972 C précisant les peines fixées par la Charia pour le vol et le brigandage," *Annuaire de l'Afrique du Nord* 11 (1972), pp. 763-768

Law 70 of 20 October 1973 on illegal sexual intercourse (amended by Law 10/1428). See YIMEL 5 (1998-9), 289

Law 52 of 16 September 1974 on unfounded accusation of fornication

Law 89 of 20 November 1974 on the drinking of alcoholic beverages

Law 6/1994 on homicide and wounding (Eng. tr. in YIMEL 1 (1994), 543-4

Pakistan

Offences Against Property (Enforcement of Hudood) Ordinance, 1979
Offences of Zina (Enforcement of Hudood) Ordinance, 1979
Offences of Qazf (Enforcement of Hadd) Ordinance, 1979
Prohibition (Enforcement of Hadd) Ordinance, 1979
Execution of the Punishment of Whipping Ordinance, 1979
Texts in: Government of Pakistan, *New Islamic Laws: Enforcement of Hudood Ordinance 1979*. Lahore: Lahore Law Times Publications, n.d. 87 pp.
Qisas and Diyat Ordinance, 1990
Text in R. Mehdi, *The Islamization of the Law in Pakistan*, Richmond, UK: Curzon Press, 1990, 298-320.

Iran

Qanun-i qisas ve hudud ve muqarrarat an, 25 Aug. 1982 *Ruznama-yi Rasmi*, No. 10972, d.d. 26-10 1982
Persian text and English tr. in S. Naqvi (tr.), "Hudud and Qisas Act of Iran," *Islamic Studies*, 24, 1985, 521-556, and 25, 1986, 107-50 (includes Persian text); English tr. in Government of Iran en Kia, Masouduzzafar Samimi (tr.), *Law of Hodoud and Qasas [Punishment and Retribution] and Provisions Thereof*. Tehran: Pars Associates, 1983. iv, 59 pp
Qanun-i diyat of 15-12 1982. *Ruznama-yi Rasmi* No. 11.030, dd 8-1, 1983
Qanun-i Ta'zirat of 9-8 1983. *Ruznama-yi Rasmi* No. 11.278, dd 14-11-83.
This law was roughly identical with the pre-revolutionary penal code.
In 1991 the laws on qisas, hudud, diyat and the general provisions were incorporated into one penal code, to which, in 1996, a new chapter in ta'zir was added. See Tellenbach (1996) and YIMEL 3 (1996), 342-351
German tr. of all Iranian Criminal Codes by S. Tellenbach, *Strafgesetze der Islamischen Republik Iran*, Berlin: W. de Gruyter, 1996.

Nigeria

Twelve Northern states have introduced Islamic criminal legislation. See R. Peters, *Islamic Criminal law in Nigeria*, Ibadan: Spectrum Books, 2003

Sudan
Sudanese Criminal Code of 8 September 1983, replaced by the Criminal Code of 1991 (Law 8 of 1991)

Yemen
Yemeni Criminal Code of 1994 (Law 12 of 1994)

6.2 Tax law

Libya
Law 89 of 1971 regarding the zakat

Pakistan
Ordinance XVIII of 1980 (Zakat and Ushr Ordinance)

Sudan
Zakat and Tax Law 1984 (Provisional order 3 of 1984); replaced by the Zakat Law of 1406 H. (Law 72 of 1986); replaced by the Zakat law of 1990

6.3 Ban on Riba (interest)

Pakistan
Banking and Financial Services Ordinance and Banking Tribunal Ordinance (1984). These ordinances banned interest-based transactions by banks, with the exception of transactions with parties abroad.

Iran
In Iran interest-based transactions have also been prohibited.

REFERENCES

al-Muhairi, B.S.B.A., "The Islamisation of laws in the UAE: the case of the penal code", *Arab Law Quarterly* 11/iv, 1996, 350-71.

Beck-Peccoz, Roberta Aluffi, *La modernizzazione del diritto di famiglia nei paesi arabi*, Università di Torino, Memorie dell'Istituto Giuridico, III, 35, Milano: Giuffrè, 1990.

Düstur, (official collection of Ottoman legislation enacted between 1839 and 1865), 2nd ed., 4 vols., Istanbul: Matba-yi Amira, 1865-1866.

Ebert, Hans-Georg, *Das Personalstatut arabischer Länder: Problemfelder, Methoden, Perspektiven: Ein Beitrag zum Diskurs über Theorie*, Leipziger Beiträge zur Orientforschung, 7, Frankfurt a.M. etc.: Peter Lang, 1996.

Government of Pakistan, *New Islamic Laws: Enforcement of Hudood Ordinance 1979*, Lahore: Lahore Law Times Publications, n.d.

Hilmi, Ömer, *Mi'yar-i Adalet*, Istanbul: Bosnawi Haji Müharrem Matba'asi, 1881-1882.

Huquq-i `A'ile Qararnamesi, Istanbul: Kitabhane-yi Sudi, 1917.

Kaşıkçı, Osman, *Islam ve Osmanlı hukukunda Mecelle: hazırlanışı, hükümlerinin tahlili, tadil ve tamamlama çalışmalar*, Istanbul: Osmanlı Araşrmalı Vakfı, 1997.

Kelly, J.M., *A Short History of Western Legal Theory*, Oxford: Oxford University Press, 1992.

Mehdi, R., *The Islamization of the Law in Pakistan*, Richmond, UK: Curzon Press, 1990.

Newman, Graeme, "Khomeini and criminal justice: notes on crime and culture", *Journal of Criminal Law and Criminology*, 73, 1982, pp. 561-81.

Peters, Ruud, "Divine law or man-made law? Egypt and the application of the *shari'ah*", *Arab Law Quarterly* 3, 1988, 231-253.

———, "The Islamization of criminal law: a comparative analysis", *Welt des Islams* 34/ii, 1994, 246-274.

———, *Islamic Criminal Law in Nigeria*, Ibadan: Spectrum Books Limited, 2003.

Qadri Pasha, Muhammad, *Qanun al-`adl wa-l-insaf li-l-qada' `ala mushkilat al-awqaf*, (repr.) Al-Qahira: Al-Matba`a al-Ahliyya, 1893.

———, *Al-Ahkam al-shar`iyya fi al-ahwal al-shakhsiyya*, 2nd ed., Cairo: Matba`at al-Sa`ada, 1909[a].

———, *Murshid al-hayran ila ma`rifat ahwal al-insan fi l-mu`amalat al-shar`iyya*, 3rd ed., Cairo: Al-Matba`a al-Amiriyya, 1909[b].

Schacht, Joseph, *An Introduction to Islamic Law*, Oxford: Clarendon Press, 1964.

Shaykhzade and Ibrahim al-Halabi, *Majma` al-anhur fi sharh Multaqa al-Abhur*, 2 vols., Istanbul: 1884 (1301 AH).

Tahanawi, Muhammad `Ali b. `Ali, *Kitab kashshaf istilahat al-funun*, repr. of Calcutta, 1864 ed., 2 vols., Istanbul: Kahraman Yayinlari, 1984.

Tellenbach, S., *Strafgesetze der islamischen Republik Iran*, Berlin: W. de Gruyter, 1996.

Vogel, Frank E., *Islamic Law and Legal System: Studies of Saudi Arabia*, Studies in Islamic Law and Society, Leiden etc.: E.J. Brill, 2000.

Commentary

I.

Joseph Kenny, O.P.

When Muslims demand to be governed by *shari'ah*, their intention is clear and simple: they want to be governed by God's law as revealed in the Qur'an and the *hadith*. Who could object to that? We can only applaud it.

Yet when it comes to the implementation of *shari'ah*, the matter becomes very complicated. Ruud Peter's paper shows us some of these complications. I will point to some of them and add other considerations:

THE MEANING OF *SHARI'AH*

- There is frequent confusion between *fiqh* and *shari'ah*. *Fiqh* is a human interpretation of *shari'ah*. It enjoys human, not divine authority. A sign of this is the abundance of *ikhtilaf* among and within the different *madhahib*s, stemming from different approaches to the four *usul al-fiqh*. But there are no *usul al-shari'ah*, since *shari'ah* is itself the *asl*, the heavenly word of God which has no discrepancy within itself. *Fiqh* only approximates, reflects, interprets and applies *shari'ah*, always remaining on the human level.

- In spite of this, the majority of *shari'ah* proponents take the *fiqh* positions that have prevailed for some centuries in certain areas as representing divine law. This may be because the standard Maliki *fiqh* texts in West Africa: the *Risala* of Ibn-abi-Zayd al-Qayrawani[1] and the *Mukhtasar* of Ibn-Khalil, unlike the *fiqh* works Peters cites, do not present different opinions on a question, but take a single definite stand on every matter. They thus carry the aura of an incontestable orthodox expression of divine *shari'ah*.

---

[1] See Kenny, 1992.

- A number of Muslim reformers challenge the authority of traditional *fiqh*. They argue that traditional *fiqh* masters have not only overstepped their bounds by claiming divine authority for their opinions, but also that the legal rulings of the Qur'an itself must be understood in their historical context and not universalised to cover all circumstances for all time.[2] They decry the zealous self-assurance of some Islamists who insist that their understanding of Islam is pure orthodoxy and any other way of thinking is wrong. These have no sense of historical criticism, or any sociological and anthropological perspective on how Muslim opinion and *fiqh* are conditioned by political, economic and other historical currents.

- In view of the tremendous variety of interpretations of *shari'ah* and the chaos that would result if it were left to the discretion of rulers, judges and an oligarchy of *ulama* to choose which interpretations to follow, codification has become inevitable. This is what has been done in Zamfara and the other *shari'ah* states. Codification does not necessarily mean that the State assumes supreme authority and pushes God out of the picture. Most codes drawn up for Muslim areas, even the criticised 1960 criminal code for Northern Nigeria, are *shari'ah*-inspired. It should be hoped that the *ijtihad* required for codification will give serious consideration not only to the latitude of classical *fiqh*, but also to the contextual intent of Qur'anic laws and the general *maslahah* of society.

BEWARE OF GOVERNMENT

- Almost all places throughout Islamic history where *shari'ah* has been the law of the land in the form of one or another *fiqh* school, the cry of pious Muslims has been that the governments were not righteous and did not in fact follow *shari'ah*, but were worldly and oppressive. And they condemn the court *ulama* who

---

[2] For some contemporary authors thinking in this vein, see Arkoun 1995, Talbi 1985, Ashmawi 1994, and Abu-Zayd 1995.

are yes-men to the powers that be. During the recent Taliban experiment with *shari'ah*, Muslims cried out again against their rigid anti-worldliness and oppression. Has there ever been a place where true *shari'ah* has been implemented? Some answer: "In the time of the Prophet and the *khulafa' ar-rashidun*," but others dispute even that.

- Any government that ensures security, order, justice, opportunity, development, welfare and religious freedom for the citizens is conforming to *shari'ah*, just as it is conforming to the Gospel. That is quite distinct from formal government enforcement of *shari'ah*. What are the problems with government *shari'ah*?

- First, it amounts to the government coercing Muslims to practise their faith, or to conform to government Islam. Are Muslims so uncommitted and lax that they need coercion? I do not think so.

- Secondly, although the *shari'ah* states officially restrict *shari'ah* enforcement to Muslims, full *shari'ah*, in the form of *fiqh*, (which many aspire to) includes many provisions that affect the rights of non-Muslims as well.[3] In claiming that *shari'ah* does not affect Christians, the Northern states have opted for a truncated *shari'ah*. Do they really mean to truncate it? In practice, Christians are stopped from selling alcoholic drinks even among themselves. Churches have been destroyed, such as St. Dominic's Church, Dashi (where years back I used to celebrate Mass), knocked down at the order of Governor Sani, and Christians are not given equal opportunity and see themselves as second-class citizens.

- Thirdly, Islamic history in many ways corroborates Christian history in showing that government sponsorship and control of religion are the kiss of death. As independent unestablished churches are more vigorous than established ones, so also we find Muslim communities and Islamic organisations thriving in places where the government assures them liberty of practice and nothing more, whereas state-sponsored organisations have greater incidence of corruption and scandals. Why let politicians take charge of your religion, when it is glaring that they have a

---

[3]This is documented in Kenny, 1999; see also Kenny, 1984, 1986, 1989, 1996, and "Nigeria Chronicle", www.nig op.org/kenny/Nigeria.

different, worldly agenda, and only manipulate religion to suit their personal advantage?
- Ibadan and Lagos have initiated *shari'ah* courts administered by the Muslim community themselves, without bringing in the government. I have always encouraged Muslims to set up such courts and congratulated them when they did so. These resemble the canon law courts which the Catholic Church runs for its internal affairs, although their scope is wider. These courts are not empowered to order stoning or amputation, but nothing prevents them from settling disputes with provision for *diyah* and other forms of compensation. The government should give legal recognition to some of these courts' enactments, as it does to marriages conducted by the churches.

FINAL POINT

Much of the discourse about *shari'ah* has to do with image making. It is not so much about the truth of what Islam stands for, but about how it is publicly perceived. *Shari'ah* commonly appears as the symbol of an Islam eager to parade its dominance, to grab and hold the organs of government and exclude others. Nigerian proponents of *shari'ah* seem to feel no need to package it in a way that will attract outside support, unlike Muslims in Europe and America who use the most professional advertising methods to present their religion in a way that meets and captures the public mind.[4] Why try to persuade when you are in a position to impose yourself? The result is only apprehension on the Christian side.

Apart from this negative image, anyone with his eyes open can also observe an Islam that fights for justice, combats corruption, promotes development and welcomes the cooperation of others. This can only attract people and win their support. In another paper I document an encouraging trend in this direction in Nigeria.[5]

---

[4] A good example of professional "packaging" of Islam is the *Newsletter* of the International Institute for the Study of Islam in the Modern World (ISIM). Cf. www.isim.nl.
[5] Kenny, 2004.

REFERENCES

Abu-Zayd, Nasr Hamid, *At-tafkir fi zaman at-takfir*, Cairo, 1995.

Arkoun, Muhammad, *Min faisal at-tafarruqa ila fasl al-maqal: ma huwa al-fikr al-islami al-mu'asir*, Beirut: Dar as-Saqi, 1995.

Ashmawy, Muhammad Sa'id, *Islam and the political order*, Washington, D.C.: Council for Research in Values and Philosophy, 1994.

Kenny, Joseph, "Sharia in Nigeria", *Bulletin on Islam and Christian-Muslim Relations in Africa* 4/1, 1984, 1-21. French version: "La Shari'a au Nigeria: aperçu historique", *Bulletin – L'Islam et les relations islamo-chrétiennes en Afrique* 4/1, 1986, 1-22.

——————, "The shari'a question in Nigeria: a historical survey", in: E. Ikenga Metuh (ed.), *The Gods in Retreat: Continuity and change in African religion*, Enugu: Fourth Dimension Publishers, 1986, 245-256.

——————, "Shari'a: implications for the church in West Africa", *Christianity and Islam in Dialogue*, Cape Coast: Association of Episcopal Conferences of Anglophone West Africa, 1987, 30-37.

——————, *The Risala of Ibn-abi-Zayd al-Qayrawani, an annotated translation*, Minna: Islamic Education Trust, 1992.

——————, "Shari'a and Christianity in Nigeria: Islam and a 'secular' state", *Journal of Religion in Africa*, 26/4, 1996, 338-364.

——————, *Views on Muslim-Christian Relations*, Lagos: Dominican Publications, 1999.

——————, "Interreligious dialogue in Nigeria: personal reminiscences of forty years", forthcoming in: Anthony Akinwale, O.P. (ed.), *All that they had to live on: Essays in honour of Archbishop Onaiyekan and Msgr. John Aniagwu*. Ibadan: The Michael J. Dempsey Center for Religious and Social Research (Dominican Institute), 2004.

——————, "Nigeria Chronicle," http://nig.op.org/kenny/nigeria.

Talbi, Muhammad, "Religious liberty: a Muslim perspective," *Islamochristiana*, 11, 1985, 99-113.

II.

Auwalu Hamisu Yadudu

I had the opportunity of reading this paper in advance and was privileged to make an extempore comment on it during the conference. These are my considered observations on the paper.

This is a paper in which the author, Professor Peters, who has shown keen academic interest in the ongoing efforts by some twelve states in Nigeria to implement the *shari'ah* and has even published on the subject matter, gives a worldwide, albeit historical, perspective to the enforcement of this law in the aptly coined topic of his paper. From a restatement of some of the classical principles of the *shari'ah*, he moves to a discussion of the forces and factors which have impacted, over the years, on the changing nature of this law, showing how its codification and re-enactment into positive law are taking place and what consequences have flowed from these developments.

As a worldwide survey, the essay is instructive. However, to the extent it seeks to pass off as a commentary on the ongoing efforts to implement the *shari'ah* in Nigeria, broadly understood for the purpose of this essay as its fresh adoption as a co-partner with the English common law and the extension of its jurisdiction to regulate criminal matters, the essay has not grasped nor fully accounted for or explained certain unique Nigerian phenomena associated with this undertaking. For a better appreciation of what is taking place in Nigeria in the realm of "the enforcement of God's law" one must situate things in context. In particular one must understand:

1. that it was intense public agitation and struggle which forced the unwilling Governors of many of the twelve implementing states to champion or join the bandwagon of the implementation process;
2. that the *shari'ah* is being implemented not by military decrees or fiat but within the context of and constrained by democratic and legislative processes and in response to popular demand and/or agitation;
3. that the implementation has been anchored on constitutional legitimacy and is subject to its constraints;
4. that the *shari'ah* is applied within the English common law tradition which accords primacy of place to judicial precedent for any authoritative pronouncement on the law which, in turn, thrives on a hierarchical relation of courts;
5. that sufficient time has not elapsed from the first gale of the adoption of *shari'ah*, which commenced late in 1999, to the

present, to lead to the emergence of any discernible trend or pattern;
6. that the *shari'ah* is being implemented within the concrete setting of a federal polity by some of the federating units and not by the Nigerian State or national government, with all the attendant consequences of diversity in the content and methods of incorporating the codes by the various implementing states.

Having said this, I wish to make some remarks about certain conclusions reached or general observations made by the author in the paper under review as follows:

The consequences, which have occurred in some jurisdictions where the *shari'ah* was codified, as pointed out by the author, to wit: ". . . its religious norms . . . eliminated . . . codified *shari'ah* becoming no more than an impoverished, reduced version of the rich *fiqh* doctrine . . ." may or may not occur in Nigeria. On the one hand, this is because most of the penal legislations which have codified the *shari'ah* have, in addition, retained the other sources and mechanisms for the extra-judicial development of its doctrines. On the other hand, the laws have also retained other sources of the *shari'ah* as fountains from which to draw guidance for its interpretation, application and further development. In other words, although *shari'ah* norms, regulating for instance theft, have been codified in positive legislation, those called upon to apply the new codes are not kept in the dark as to the source where the norms emanate from and are thus urged to be guided by the vast, even if conflicting, repository of knowledge to be found in *fiqh* treatises.

The author, in Section 3.4 of his paper, has summarised what I have characterised as the many routes to the adoption of the *shari'ah*, placing Nigeria among nations such as Iran, Sudan and Pakistan, which have re-Islamised their legal systems with the adoption of various Islamic codes. Although there appear to be some similarities in the content of some of the codes adopted by the countries referred to by the author and the Nigerian states, such a conclusion ignores the important contexts highlighted above and risks misrepresenting the true Nigerian situation.

Owing to the fact that the implementation of the *shari'ah* has been carried out in the concrete federal setting in Nigeria, it will be a misnomer to represent the situation as if there exists a uniform, seamless penal code for all the implementing states. On the contrary, it may not be far off the point to state that there are as many varied codes as the number of these states. Judicial practice in the multiple and diverse state jurisdictions, absent any authoritative pronouncement by the superior courts, is bound to add to divergence in content as well as introduce further discrepancies in the meaning and interpretation of the provisions.

I have found quite a few comparisons which the author has made as rather misplaced and some statements as over-generalisations. I now turn my attention to these matters.

To compare an Iranian judge, even in the tumultuous and chaotic wake of the revolution, as behaving like the heroic but lawless sheriff during the frontier days of the wild, wild West may, in the eyes of many Muslims, amount to an irreverent attitude towards what they believe to be their sacred law or, in the least, a misplaced analogy. One clear difference between the two is that the sheriff appeals to the gun to settle issues whereas the judge, however much you may disagree with him, relies upon the law first and offers a reasoned basis of his decision before condemning the convict to his deserved sentence.

Moreover, statements and assertions by the author, especially where these are hedged and admitted to be lacking in empirical bases, such as the assertion that the *shari'ah* implementation is politically motivated or ". . . that *shari'ah* criminal law is attractive in societies where private justice or revenge prevails . . ." are unsubstantiated over-generalisations and uncalled-for. What is more, they ignore the unique Nigerian setting wherein many of the suppositions of the author do not, in my view, obtain. For instance, although the victims of a murdered relation in Kano State may demand for *diyah*, the decision whether or not to prosecute the accused person does not lie with them.

The assertion that "the *shari'ah* is nowadays not applied by using the classical books of *fiqh* but via legislation" gives an incorrect account of the situation which obtains in Nigeria. In Nigeria, the vast majority of civil relations of Muslims are indeed regulated by the *shari'ah* as embodied in classical *fiqh* books of the Maliki School. Even the various penal codes enacted by the implementing states have imbedded in their provisions a reference to and mandated reliance on these books. Certainly the implementation of the *shari'ah* in Nigeria has not yet led to the loss by the *ulama* of "their time-honoured position as the exclusive guardians of the law." On the contrary, it has, arguably, enhanced it.

As far as Nigeria is concerned, it is, in my view, too early for the author to arrive at the sort of sweeping conclusions he has reached to wit: "the most important development [resulting from the codification of the *shari'ah*] has been that the authority of the *ulama* has been challenged and has declined. . . ." The enforcement of God's law has recommenced in Nigeria only recently. The outcome, while the situation remains fluid and unique, will, in the long and short-term, be determined by the interplay of the forces released by the agitators, the positive or negative reactions from the Western world, and what happens especially in the appellate superior courts when issues are litigated.

Nigeria's 'State Religion' Question in Comparative Perspective

W. Cole Durham, Jr.

INTRODUCTION

The aim of this paper is to provide a comparative perspective on Section 10 of the Nigerian constitution. The language of this provision is deceptively simple: "The Government of the Federation or of a State shall not adopt any religion as State Religion." This "no state religion" clause appears in the context of a modern constitution, which also includes a general provision affirming freedom of religion:

> Every person shall be entitled to freedom of thought, conscience and religion, including freedom to change his religion or belief, and freedom (either alone or in community with others, and in public or in private) to manifest and propagate his religion or belief in worship, teaching, practice and observance.[1]

This provision tracks the language of the religious freedom provision of the Universal Declaration of Human Rights in all essential respects, except that it affirms the right not only to "manifest" but also to "propagate" one's religion or belief, thereby underscoring the right to engage in religious persuasion and witnessing or sharing one's beliefs.[2] The 1999 Nigerian constitution also includes an array of

---

[1] Nigerian Const., Section 38(1)
[2] Universal Declaration of Human Rights, art. 18, U.N. General Assembly Resolution 217A(III) of December 10, 1948. This article provides: "Everyone has the right to freedom of thought, conscience and religion; this right includes freedom to change his religion or belief, and freedom, either alone or in community with others and in public or private, to manifest his religion or belief in teaching, practice, worship and observance." For useful analysis of issues relating to missionary work, *see* Stahnke, 1999 and 2004.

other provisions characteristic of modern democratic societies, including provisions affirming rights to dignity,[3] freedom of expression,[4] freedom of assembly and association,[5] equal treatment,[6] and so forth.[7] It is important to mention this entire complex of rights, together with the related limitations provisions,[8] because it is generally impossible to have a full understanding of the way that freedom of religion norms operate in a particular country without understanding the interrelationships, overlaps, patterns of modelling and reinforcement, and the general interactions of this entire set of rights and their limitations.

Nigeria's religious freedom provisions follow general patterns of international and constitutional law that have become entrenched in legal systems around the world in the last half-century. By the time that international human rights were being codified in the aftermath of World War II, freedom of religion or belief emerged as an axiomatic feature, memorialised in Article 18 of the Universal

---

[3] Nigerian Const., Section 34.
[4] Ibid., Section 39.
[5] Ibid., Section 40.
[6] Ibid., Sections 15-19.
[7] Fundamental rights are addressed in Chapter 4 of the Nigerian constitution, encompassing Sections 33-46.
[8] Limitation provisions in the Nigerian constitution are consolidated in Article 45, which reads as follows: "(1) Nothing in sections 37, 38, 39, 40 and 41 of this Constitution shall invalidate any law that is reasonably justifiable in a democratic society—(a) in the interest of defence, public safety, public order, public morality or public health; or (b) for the purpose of protecting the rights and freedom or other persons. (2) An act of the National Assembly shall not be invalidated by reason only that it provides for the taking, during periods of emergency, of measures that derogate from the provisions of section 33 or 35 of this Constitution; but no such measures shall be taken in pursuance of any such act during any period of emergency save to the extent that those measures are reasonably justifiable for the purpose of dealing with the situation that exists during that period of emergency: Provided that nothing in this section shall authorise any derogation from the provisions of section 33 of this Constitution, except in respect of death resulting from acts of war or authorise any derogation from the provisions of section 36(8) of this Constitution. (3) In this section, a 'period of emergency' means any period during which there is in force a Proclamation of a state of emergency declared by the President in exercise of the powers conferred on him under section 305 of this Constitution."

Declaration of Human Rights,[9] Article 18 of the International Covenant on Civil and Political Rights (ICCPR),[10] and in a variety of other international instruments.[11] Most modern constitutions have provisions affirming the right to freedom of religion or belief. It is recognised in the overwhelming majority of the world's constitutions,[12] including virtually every European constitution and

---

[9] G.A. Res. 217 (A(III), December 10, 1948, U.N. Doc. A/810, at 71 (1948)).
[10] G.A. Res. 2200A, U.N. GAOR, 21st Sess., Supp. no. 16, at 52, 55, U.N. Doc A/6316 (1966), 999 U.N.T.S. 171 (1976) (Art. 18).
[11] *American Declaration of the Rights and Duties of Man*, art. III, O.A.S. res. XXX, adopted by the Ninth International Conference of American States, Bogotá (1948): *Novena Conferencia Internacional Americana, 6 Actas y Documentos* (1953), 297-302. See also *United Nations Declaration on the Elimination of All Forms of Intolerance and of Discrimination Based on Religion or Belief*, adopted 18 Jan. 1982, G.A. Res. 55, 36 U.N. GAOR Supp. (No. 51), U.N. Doc. A/RES/36/55 (1982).
[12] *See, e.g.*, Afghanistan Const. art. 40 (pre-2004 constitution); Albania Const. art. 24; Algeria Const. art. 36; Andorra Const. art. 11; Angola Const. art. 45; Antigua and Barbuda Const. art. 11; Argentina Const. §14, §20; Armenia Const. art. 23; Australia Const. Act §116; Austria Const. art. 7; Azerbaijan Const. art. 48; Bahamas Const. arts. 15 cl. 2, 22; Bahrain Const. art. 22; Bangladesh Const. arts. 39, 41; Barbados Const. art. 19; Belarus Const. art. 31; Belgium Const. art. 19; Belize Const. arts. 3 cl. 2, 11; Benin Const. art. 23, Bolivia Const. art. 182; Bosnia and Herzegovina Const. art. II cl. 3g; Brazil Const. art. 5; Bulgaria Const. art. 37; Burkina Faso Const. art. 7; Burundi Const. art. 27; Cambodia Const. art. 43; Cameroon Const. pmbl., art. 86; Canada Const. Act. § 2a; Cape Verde Const. arts. 27 cl. 2, 45, 48; Chile Const. art. 19 cl. 6; People's Republic of China Const. art. 36; Republic of China Const. art. 13; Colombia Const. arts. 18, 19; Congo Const. Art. 26; Democratic Republic of Congo Art. 25; Cook Islands Const. arts. 64 cl. 1d; Costa Rica Const. art. 75; Croatia Const. art. 40; Cuba Const. art. 8; Cyprus Const. art. 18; Czech Republic Const. art. 10 (provision incorporating international human rights treaties); Denmark Const. ch 7; Dijbouti Const. art. 11; Dominica Const. art. 9; Dominican Republic Const. art. 8 cl. 8; Ecuador Const. art. 23 cl. 11; Egypt Const. art. 46; El Salvador Const. art. 25; Eritrea Const. art. 19; Estonia Const. arts. 40, 41; Ethiopia Const. art. 27; Fiji Const. art. 35; Finland Const. §11; France Const. art. 1; Gabon Const. art. 1; Georgia Const. art. 9, 19; Germany Basic Law arts. 4, 7, 12a, 140, 141; Ghana Const. art. 21 cl. 1; Greece Const. art. 13; Grenada Const. Order art. 9; Guatemala Const. art. 36; Guinea Const. art. 7; Guyana Const. art. 145; Haiti Const. art. 30; Honduras Const. art. 77; Hong Kong Basic Law art. 32; Hong Kong Bill of Rights art. 15; Hungary Const. Art. 60; Iceland Const. art. 73; India Const. art. 25; Indonesia Const. art. 29, amend. 2; Iraq Const. art. 25; Ireland Const. art. 44; Italy Const. art. 19; Jamaica Const. art. 21 cl. 1; Japan Const. art.

the constitution of every independent country in the Western Hemisphere. Nigeria's constitutional provisions are thus part of a grand legal tradition.

In construing the "no state religion" clause, the Nigerian Supreme Court has recognized that the experience of other constitutional traditions may provide persuasive authority that can help with the interpretive task:

20; Jordan Const. art. 14; Kazakhstan Const. art. 22; Kenya Const. art. 78; Kiribati Const. Art. 11; North Korea Const. art. 68; South Korea Const. arts. 19, 20; Kuwait Const. art. 35; Kyrgyzstan Const. art. 16; Latvia Const. art. 99; Lebanon Const. art. 9; Liberia Const. art. 14; Libya Const. art. 2; Liechtenstein Const. art. 37; Lithuania art. 26; Luxembourg Const. art. 19; Macedonia Const. art. 10; Madagascar Const. art. 10; Malawi Const. art. 33; Malaysia Const. art. 11; Mali Const. art. 4; Malta Const. §32b, §40; Marshall Islands Const. art. II, §1; Mauritania Const. art. 10 cl. 1; Mauritius Const. para. 2; Mexico Const. art. 25; Micronesia Const. art. IV, §2; Moldova Const. art. 31 cl. 2; Monaco Const. art. 23; Mongolia Const. arts. 16 cl. 15, 35 cl. 8; Morocco Const. art. 6; Mozambique Const. art. 78; Namibia Const. art. 21; Nauru Const. art. 11; Nepal Const. art. 19; Netherlands Const. arts. 6, 23 cl. 3; New Zealand Bill of Rights Act §13; Nicaragua Const. art. 29; Nigeria Const. art. 38; Northern Mariana Islands Const. §2; Norway Const. art. 2; Oman Basic Law art. 28; Pakistan Const. art. 20; Panama Const. art. 35; Paraguay Const. art. 24; Peru Const. art. 2 cl. 3; Philippines Const. §5; Poland Const. art. 53; Portugal Const. art. 41; Puerto Rico Const. art. 22, §3; Qatar Const. art. 50; Romania Const. art. 29; Russia Const. art. 28; Rwanda Const. art. 18; St. Kitts and Nevis Const. art. 11; St. Lucia Const. art. 9; St. Vincent Const. art. 9; American Samoa Const. §1; Western Samoa Const. Art. 11; Senegal Const. art. 19; Serbia and Montenegro Const. art. 43; Seychelles Const. art. 21; Sierra Leone Const. art. 24; Singapore Const. art. 15; Slovakia Const. art. 24; Slovenia Const. art. 41; Solomon Islands Const. art. 11; Somaliland Const. art. 5; South Africa Const. arts. 15, 31, 185; Spain Const. art. 16; Sri Lanka Const. art. 15; Suriname Const. art. 18; Swaziland Const. art. 24; Sweden Instrument of Government ch. 2 art. 1 cl. 6; Switzerland Const. art. 15; Syria Const. art. 35; Taiwan Const. art. 13; Tajikistan Const. art. 26; Thailand Const. §38,Tibet Const. art. 10; Tonga Const. art. 5; Trinidad and Tobago Const. §4h; Tunisia Const. art. 5; Turkey Const. art. 24; Turkmenistan Const. art. 11; Tuvalu Const. arts. 23, 29; Ukraine Const. art. 35; Uruguay Const. art. 5; US Const. amend. 1; Uzbekistan Const. art. 31; Vanuatu Const. art. 5 cl. 1f; Venezuela Const. art. 57; Vietnam Const. art. 70; Zambia Const. preamble, art. 19; Zimbabwe Const. art. 19. The texts of the foregoing constitutions and the cited provisions can be found at <http://confinder.richmond.edu> or at <http://www.religlaw.org>.

> It has long been [a] cardinal principle of our constitutional law that on account of the unique character and diversity of our Constitution, the courts should always endeavour to find solutions to constitutional questions within the Constitution through its interpretation, but the courts may seek guidance as persuasive authorities from the decisions of the courts of other common law jurisdictions on the interpretation and construction of the provisions of their Constitutions which are *in pari materia* with the relevant provisions of our Constitution.[13]

The Supreme Court refers expressly to the relevance of "persuasive authorities from . . . other common law jurisdictions" that deal with similar issues. Other common law jurisdictions use similar interpretive techniques, so presumably authorities from these jurisdictions are more likely to understand the key texts in a way that will be sufficiently similar to be relevant. In fact, it is not just common law jurisdictions that wrestle with such problems, but virtually every contemporary legal system. Analogies from non-common law jurisdictions may be slightly more remote, but can still help give us relevant perspective on the issues at stake.

Accordingly, in what follows, I will draw on materials without regard to whether they come from common law, civilian, or other legal traditions. In doing so, my effort is not to advocate any particular view of how the Nigerian "no state religion" clause should be interpreted. That must ultimately be left to Nigerians. I believe, as apparently did the framers of the Nigerian constitution, that there are certain principles that have come to be recognized by the nations of the world as having universal validity. Freedom of religion or belief is one such principle,[14] and constitutions and laws should be construed

---

[13] *Ogugu v. State* [1998] 1 HRLRA 167, 189 (Sup. Ct. Nigeria, decided 14 Oct. 1994) (per Bello, C.J.N.).

[14] A sign of its universality is that the right to freedom of religion or belief has been broadly recognised along with other key human rights as having acquired the status of customary international law. See, e.g., Alston, 1983, 69 (arguing that the Universal Declaration is customary law); Bilder, 1978, 8 (same); Davis, 2002, 230 (arguing that the 1981 Declaration is customary law); Henkin, 1990, 19 (arguing that the Universal Declaration is customary law); Humphrey, 1989,

in ways that respect this fundamental principle, recognizing that although it is universal, it can and should be implemented in diverse ways in different cultural and historical settings. My aim is to help portray the range of options, in light of the experience of other nations. In the end, however, Nigerians must determine which of these options (or which synthesis drawn from them) best comports with a sound interpretation of the Nigerian constitution. In the words of Nigerian justices:

> [I]t is always of great help to know the line of thinking jurisprudentially in other countries' courts with constitutional provisions resembling our own; nonetheless our Constitution must always remain a creature of its own circumstance and must always be interpreted in its own location and meaning.[15]

> [I]t is in the end the wording of the [Nigerian] Constitution itself that is to be interpreted and applied, and this wording can never be overridden by the extraneous principles of other constitutions which are not explicitly incorporated in the formulae that have been chosen as the frame of this Constitution.[16]

Comparative constitutional analysis can expand horizons, but in itself, it has no intrinsic authority, except to the extent it yields insights that are genuinely persuasive to those charged with interpreting their own legal system – to the judges and other officials responsible for interpreting constitutional norms, and to the people (the individuals

---

155 (same); Humphrey, 1976, 529 (same); Lillich, 1984, 116 (same); Robertson, 1989, 96 (same); Sohn, 1977, 133 (same); Tahzib, 1996, 184-185 (arguing that the 1981 Declaration is customary law); Thornberry, 1991, 237-238 (arguing that the Universal Declaration is customary law); Waldcock, 1965, 15 (same). See also Hurst, 1995/1996, 317-352 (summarising statements of constituents of several states and international bodies as well as influential authors holding that the Universal Declaration of Human Rights is customary law).
[15] *Ogugu v. State* at 211 (per Belgore, J.S.C.).
[16] *Adegbenro v. Akintola and Aderemi* (1962), 1 All N.L.R. 454, 479 (per Viscount Radcliffe in his judgment for the Privy Council), quoted in *Attorney-General Bendel State v. Attorney-General of the Federation* (1981), 10 S.C. 1, 3 NCLR 1, 1981 NSCC 314, 331 (per Fatai-Williams, C.J.N.).

and the communities) who ultimately judge the judges, constitute the constitution, and choose their own freedom by deciding how they will rule and be ruled.

THE RANGE OF INTERPRETIVE OPTIONS

The "no state religion" clause has parallels in many constitutions around the world,[17] although it is clearly not the only type of provision guaranteeing freedom of religion. It is the commitment to

---

[17] Parallel provisions are of three types: (1) those, like Nigeria's, banning any state religion (or state church) or the "establishment" of any religion or church; (2) those mandating the "separation" of religion (or church) and state; and (3) those declaring the state to be "secular" or, in French, "laïque". Some constitutions include two or even all three of these types of provisions, often in the same article. **Type 1**: Australia Const. art. 116; Belarus Const. art. 16 cl. 1; Ethiopia Const. art. 11 cl. 2; Germany Basic Law art. 140, incorporating Weimar Const. art. 137 cl. 1; Ghana Const. art. 56; Ireland Const. art. 44 cl. 2 (no "endowment" of any religion); Liberia Const. art. 14; Lithuania Const. art. 43 cl. 7; Nigeria Const. art. 10; Russia Const. art. 14 cl. 1; South Korea Const. art. 20 cl. 2; Spain Const. art. 16 cl. 3; Uganda Const. art. 7; United States Const. Amendment I. **Type 2**: Azerbaijan Const. art. 18 cl. 1; Bulgaria Const. art. 13 cl. 2; Cameroon Const. Preamble ¶ 5 cl. 14 ("neutrality and independence of the State"); Croatia Const. art. 41 cl. 1; Ethiopia Const. art. 11 cl. 3; Kyrgystan Const. art. art. 8 cl. 3; Hungary Const. art. 60 cl. 3; Liberia Const. art. 14; Mexico Const. art. 130; Peru Const. art. 50 ("independent and autonomous" systems); Philippines Const. art. II cl. 6; Poland Const. art. 82 cl. 2; Portugal Const. art. 41 cl. 4; Slovenia Const. art. 7 cl. 1; South Korea Const. art. 20 cl. 2; Russia Const. art. 14 cl. 2; Japan Const. art. 20 clauses 1 and 3 ("No religious organization shall receive any privileges from the State, nor exercise any political authority"; "The State and its organs shall refrain from religious education or any other religious activity"). **Type 3**: Angola Const. art. 8, cl. 1, Azerbaijan Const. art. 7 cl. 1; Cameroon Const. Preamble ¶ 5 cl. 14; Congo-Brazzaville Const. art. 178, cl. 5; Ethiopia Const. art. 11 cl. 1; France Const. art. 1; India Const. Preamble cl. 1; Ivory Coast Const. art. 2, Kazakhstan Const. art. 1, Kyrgystan Const. art. 1; Madagascar art. 1 cl. 1; Mali Const. Preamble, cl. 2; Mozambique Const. art. 9 cl. 1; Namibia Const. art. 1 cl. 1; Russia Const. art. 14 cl. 1; Senegal Const. art. 1; Tajikistan Const. art. 1; Turkey Const. art. 2; Turkmenistan Const. art. 1. **Cf.** Czech Republic Charter of Human Rights and Freedoms art. 2(1) ("The State ... must not be tied either to an exclusive ideology or to a particular religion"); Slovak Republic Const. art. 1 ("The Slovak Republic . . . is not bound by any ideology or religion").

freedom of religion or belief that constitutes a universal right – not necessarily the institutional means of protecting it. In that respect, separation of religion and the state is merely one of many approaches to structuring the institutions of state, religion and society that may be consistent with actualising the right. Some forms of separation of religion and state have been highly protective of religious freedom, but some forms have been extremely hostile. Both the United States of America and the former Soviet Union had constitutional provisions calling for separation of church and state; both provisions were applied in practice; but the results were radically different. Similarly, the degree of religious freedom can vary widely among regimes that have state religions, as is evident when one thinks of the contrast between Iran on the one hand and the United Kingdom, Norway, and Finland on the other. The institutional configuration of state and religion play a significant role in determining the vitality of religious life and the actualisation of religious freedom. But this structure is not an end in itself: it is a means to protecting the values ultimately protected by freedom of religion and belief.

In order to help situate the Nigerian "no state religion" clause among other possible constitutional configurations of religion and state, it will be helpful to line up the array of possible configurations along a continuum, extending from absolute identification of religion with the state at one end to negative identification (i.e., harsh persecution and repression) at the other. As the examples I gave a moment ago make clear, however, there appears to be no straight line correlation between this "degree of identification" gradient on the one hand and the degree of religious liberty in a society. Indeed, the two ends of the continuum both seem to line up with lack of religious freedom, whereas the intermediate positions seem to support it. As the diagram in Figure 1 (p. 153) suggests, it is possible to map the correlation between institutional configurations and religious freedom if one conceives the identification gradient as a curve, with the top corresponding to higher degrees of religious freedom, and the bottom corresponding to lower degrees.[18] In what follows, I describe the various types of religion-state relations depicted in Figure 1 and what

---

[18] The analysis suggested by Figure 1 is a reformulated version of the identification gradient first worked out in Durham, 1996.

they imply for the parameters of interpretation of Nigeria's "no state religion" clause. I should stress at the outset that I regard these as ideal types in the sense that actual regimes are always more complex, and the various configurations tend to blend into each other.

Theocracy. The strongest imaginable identification of the state and religion occurs in theocracy. In this form of regime, there is a total fusion of religion and the state. Religious institutions are state institutions and vice versa. Religious law is the law of the state. In the contemporary setting, Iran may approach this type of arrangement, though there are some signs of liberalisation. There is a tendency to think that the unity of religion and the state (and law) was more typical of ancient historical societies, and that the progressive trend has been toward increasing separation,[19] though it is not clear that this picture really holds up when one looks closely at the older societies.[20]

Established Religion. This is the type of regime in which the state officially identifies a particular religion as the religion of the state. A state with an established religion is a confessional state. There is a somewhat sharper separation of religious and state institutions than in a theocracy. The state has become distinct enough from religion that it can specify a particular religion and set of religious institutions as "its" religion. This is the type of state that was typical in the Reformation period in European history, when the prince determined the religion of his realm (*cuius regio, eius religio*[21]). Originally, established churches tended to be quite exclusive and monopolistic, with painful consequences for adherents of other faiths. Over time, however, the tendency in Europe has been for states with established churches (such as the United Kingdom, Norway, Denmark and Finland) to become much more tolerant and equalitarian. This helps to explain why one thinks of these latter countries as having high degrees of religious freedom, despite their established churches. Incidentally, one might assume that at least for the preferred religion in a strong positive identification regime, there

---

[19] Maine, 1891.
[20] Diamond, 1971. See also Durham and Dushku, 1993, 427-429.
[21] Literally, "whose the region (or realm), his the religion."

Comparative Perspectives on Religion and the State

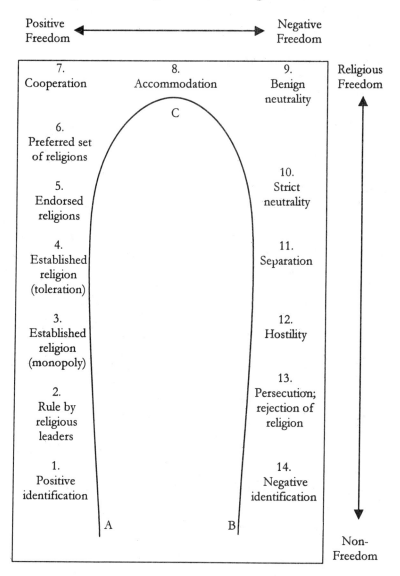

Figure 1: Comparative Perspectives on Religion and the State

would be a high degree of freedom. But in fact, established religions tend to be captured by their states, and while the citizens adhering to an established church are unlikely to suffer persecution, the autonomy of the religious institution suffers, as does the range and depth of religious choice in society. Considerations such as these led the Swedish state church to seek (and obtain) disestablishment in 2000.[22]

Endorsed Religion. In many countries, constitutions recognise the special role that a particular religion has played in the history of a country, but then go on to affirm that other religious faiths are entitled to freedom of religion or belief and non-discrimination. This pattern is discernible in many Roman Catholic countries, especially since Vatican II (although the trend was already underway in Latin American countries earlier). The special recognition may be spelled out in religious association laws or may be evident in other ways. Thus, the 1997 Russian Law on Freedom of Conscience and Religious Associations recognised the special status of the Russian Orthodox Church in its preamble.[23] Similarly, the recently adopted Bulgarian Religious Denominations Act gives special recognition to the Bulgarian Orthodox Church.[24]

Preferred Set of Religions. There has been some tendency in recent years to give favoured status to a preferred set of religions. This is often in effect something like giving endorsed status to a small number of religions in a country. One form this takes is a preference for "traditional religions," even though this is inconsistent with principles of equal treatment and non-discrimination, and is contrary to international norms.[25] Another form is that leaders are so conscious of the major groups, that smaller groups are simply forgotten. Thus Albanians tend to speak of the "three religions" (Muslims, Orthodox believers, and Catholics), even though numerous

---

[22] For background on this development, see Stegeby, 1999.

[23] Law on the Freedom of Conscience and Religious Associations, No. 125-FZ (1997).

[24] Religious Denominations Act, (2002), art. 10 [Bulgaria], available at www.religlaw.org.

[25] Human Rights Committee General Comment 22 (1993) on ICCPR article 18, 20 July 1993, 48th session, U.N. Doc. CCPR/C/21/Rev.1/Add.4 (1993), reprinted in U.N. Doc. HRI/GEN/1/Rev.1 at 35 (1994), para. 2 ("Article 18 is not limited in its application to traditional religions").

Protestant denominations have been in the country for decades. Much the same can be said about Bosnia, though there the count would be "four religions" because of the presence of a small Jewish community. All too often, this is the practical consequence of "cooperation" schemes. Despite the fact that the intent in such arrangements is to remain neutral, actual state cooperation tends to be limited to major religious groups.

Cooperation. In cooperation regimes, the state is constitutionally committed to neutrality among religious communities, but is willing to "cooperate" in a variety of ways with religion. Germany is the classic example of this type of system, with its willingness to assist religious denominations by gathering "church tax," providing religious education in public schools, and making a variety of other benefits available. In Italy, Spain and several other countries with substantial Catholic presence (including Germany), cooperation is often managed through agreements modelled on the system of entering into concordats with the Holy See, but now available to a larger number of denominations.[26] In Italy, agreements have been worked out with a number of denominations, but the total is less than ten. Spain has taken a different approach. While the relationship with the Catholic Church is with a single denomination, the other three agreements that have been entered into are with federations of religious communities: Protestants, Muslims, and Jews. This has been convenient as an administrative matter, while allowing the state to deal fairly effectively with a large number of diverse religious groups. The theory of the agreement system is that it is an appropriate institutional move as a country moves from having an established church into a more neutral and equalitarian mode. Instead of lowering the previously established church to the level of other groups, the idea is to bring other groups up to the level of the established church. The difficulty is that this never quite happens in reality. Moreover, there is a tendency of some of the smaller groups to get left out. This is obvious in Italy, but even in Spain, the various federations have not proven infinitely elastic.[27] For the groups that

---

[26] De la Hera, 1998 ; Ferrari, 1995.
[27] The system has shown considerable flexibility, however. Orthodox believers are affiliated with the Protestant federation, and the Muslim federation, at least

are left out – typically a tiny minority of the total population – there is seldom political will to extend additional agreements to them. The cooperation system is very attractive in its support for various aspects of religious life. The complexity it induces is the need for fairly fancy footwork (not always successful) in reconciling cooperation with equal treatment.

Accommodation. As my chart no doubt suggests, "accommodation" is the approach I tend to prefer, though I recognise that due to a variety of cultural and historical factors, what is optimal in one country may differ from what is optimal in another. Like cooperation, accommodation is committed to neutrality, but in part because of the equality problems that direct subsidies tend to entail, accommodation abstains from direct subsidy of religion. Indirect benefits such as tax exempt status are allowed. At the heart of the accommodation model lies a willingness to grant exemptions from otherwise generally applicable laws, in the absence of compelling state interests not achievable through by less burdensome or more narrowly tailored means. Examples of accommodation would be exemptions from conscription for conscientious objectors, accommodation of days of rest, and many other distinctive religious practices. This was a major interpretation of the United States model until the United States Supreme Court decided *Employment Division v. Smith*,[28] which held that neutral and general laws always override religious freedom claims. From my perspective, and that of the United States Congress,[29] this is an impoverished understanding of the meaning of freedom of religion or belief, and one that puts formal equality above substantive equality.

---

thus far, has remained intact, despite the non-hierarchical structure of Islam and the range of different beliefs.

[28] 494 US 872 (1990).

[29] The United States Congress passed the Religious Freedom Restoration Act of 1993, 42 U.S.C. §§ 2000bb et seq. (1994), in an effort to restore the "compelling state interest/least restrictive alternative" test that had required strict scrutiny of laws that imposed substantial burdens on the free exercise of religion. However, the Supreme Court struck down this legislation, at least insofar as it applies to legislation or other official action at the state level. *City of Boerne v. Flores*, 521 U.S. 507 (1997).

Separation. The United States is often thought of as the archetypal separationist model. In fact, the US constitution does not use the term 'separation,' but instead provides that "Congress shall make no law respecting an establishment of religion . . . ."[30] Ironically, this language originally meant that the federal government should not interfere with churches established by the states.[31] But over the ensuing 200 years (and taking into account the adoption of the 14th Amendment, which has been interpreted to apply many federal constitutional protections against state action), the US Establishment Clause has come to be interpreted to mean the exact opposite: that states may not engage in any activity remotely tending towards establishing religion. The result is that the clause has long been open to a very separationist interpretation – going back to the time when Thomas Jefferson originally spoke of a "wall of separation between church and state." A number of communist constitutions dating back to the Stalinist era did expressly talk in terms of "separation" of church and state, but this had a very different meaning than in the US. The communist view of separation was that religion should not be present anywhere that state influence extended. But since the totalitarian state was virtually all-encompassing, religion was driven into an ever-shrinking and ever-more-marginalised private sector. As noted earlier, a substantial number of other countries have adopted a separationist approach, either by proscribing a state religion, by calling for separation of church and state, or by declaring that the state is to be secular.[32]

Neutrality. In many ways, one can understand virtually the entire set of arrangements from cooperation through separation as being fundamentally about "neutrality," in the sense of impartial and equal treatment. In fact, the regimes in this sector of the identification gradient shade into one another. Accommodation is a kind of benign neutrality that is committed to substantive equal treatment and to making exceptions to accommodate religious needs where this is necessary. Cooperation is committed to neutrality, but it could be viewed as a "positive freedom" version of accommodation.

---

[30] US Const., amend. I.
[31] Smith, 1995.
[32] See note 17 above.

That is, it contributes to the actualisation of substantive rights, making accommodations but also providing affirmative subsidies and support. Separation is also concerned with neutrality, but takes the opposite stand from cooperation on providing affirmative support to religion.

It is useful to notice that the different types of regimes tend to correlate with varying conceptions of neutrality and equality. Thus, **separation** could be understood as neutrality by abstention or state inaction. The state remains impartial to all by remaining separate from all. **Strict neutrality** (formal equality) insists that the state simply should not make classifications on the basis of religion; the state should be blind to religious considerations. This is the neutrality of the impartial umpire. **Benign neutrality** is essentially formal equality with a reminder that when all other things are equal, there is no need to be hostile to religion. **Accommodation** is neutrality as substantive equality. Accommodation recognizes that treating people in ways that ignore valid and distinctive religious requirements can work substantive injustice. **Cooperation** also believes in neutrality and impartiality, but senses no objection to affirmatively aiding religion, so long as the aid is distributed equally, or at least so long as any differences in allocations can be justified by objective (non-religious) factors.

Associated with the differing conceptions of neutrality and equality are differing conceptions of freedom. **Separation** takes an absence-of-power perspective, and assumes that religious freedom will be maximised by imposing structural limits on the extent to which the state may intrude into the domain of religion. In effect, it constructs a buffer zone between the realm of the state and the sphere of religious rights. **Strict neutrality** is associated with laissez faire freedom. Law defines the boundaries of the playing field, and assures that it is level; religion must operate within that playing field, and it gets no special favours. **Accommodation** assumes that religious freedom rights are sufficiently strong to carve out exemptions from otherwise general and neutral laws (or other state action). It asserts the priority of liberty over equality, at least in certain sufficiently compelling cases. Finally, **cooperation** reflects a positive conception of freedom, according to which the state should not only avoid intermeddling in religious affairs, but should also contribute affirmatively to the actualisation of the conditions of freedom.

Hostility. It is surprisingly easy for normal neutrality and separation to slide into hostility toward religion. One of the premier current examples concerns the French commitment to *laïcité* or secularism. The idea is closely tied to the ideals of the Enlightenment and French republicanism, but by making the exclusion of religion from the public square an end in itself instead of a means to protecting freedom, the idea seems to be losing its moorings. The result is the recent French legislation banning Islamic headscarves from French schools.[33] This transforms what is supposedly an ideal of neutrality and equal treatment into an engine of discrimination against those Muslim girls who conscientiously believe they should wear headscarves.

IMPLICATIONS FOR NIGERIA'S "NO STATE RELIGION" CLAUSE

When Section 10 of Nigeria's constitution proclaims that "The Government of the Federation or of a State shall not adopt any religion as State Religion," what it most transparently rules out is a state theocracy or established church (even a tolerant established church). At the other end of the identity gradient, the fundamental right to freedom of religion or belief, as embodied in Section 38(1) rules out strong forms of negative identification such as persecution and hostility. Further, preferred or endorsed religions are arguably ruled out by Section 15(2), which provides, "national integration shall be actively encouraged, whilst discrimination on the grounds of place of origin, sex, religion, status, ethnic or linguistic association or ties shall be prohibited."

The question, then, is where does Nigeria's "no state religion" clause require its system of religion and state to fit in the remaining range between cooperation and separation? In this regard, it may be helpful to compare analogous provisions from three other constitutions. First, consider article 14 of the new Russian constitution:

---

[33] www.legifrance.gouv.fr/WAspad/UnTexteDeJorf?numjo=MENX0400001L (visited April 20, 2004).

constitutions. First, consider article 14 of the new Russian constitution:

1. The Russian Federation shall be a secular state. No religion may be instituted as state-sponsored or mandatory religion.
2. Religious associations shall be separated from the state, and shall be equal before the law.

In contrast to the Russian constitution, there is no provision in the Nigerian constitution specifying that Nigeria is to be a "secular" state. To the contrary, Section 15(1) of the latter provides, "The motto of the Federal Republic of Nigeria shall be Unity and Faith, Peace and Progress." Nigeria does not have a strong tradition of secularism akin to *laïcité* in France, or Kemalist secularism in Turkey. Nor is there a strong pronouncement that "[r]eligious associations shall be *separated* from the state," although the emphasis on equality in Nigeria might welcome the obligation that all religious associations "shall be equal before the law." In short, what the contrast with the Russian provisions brings out is that Nigeria's "no state religion" clause does not appear to call for a strict separationist and surely not for a hostile secularist system. That suggests that an interpretation falling in the range between cooperation and benign neutrality is probably the most plausible interpretation.

The second constitutional provision to consider is that of the United States. As noted above, the key phrase provides that "Congress shall make no law respecting an establishment of religion . . . ."[34] This provision is even closer to Nigeria's Section 10 than might at first be thought, because it has been interpreted over the years to mean that both federal and state governments are barred from engaging in conduct "respecting an establishment of religion." The key difference is that whereas the Nigerian clause provides that government "shall not adopt any religion as State Religion," the United States constitution forbids federal or state action "respecting" or "having regard to" an establishment of religion. This is a much broader prohibition. Professor Philip Ostien, writing with J.D.

---

[34] US Const., amend. I.

Gamaliel, has made an excellent case for the relevance of the United States provisions as persuasive authority for Nigeria, but has ultimately concluded that precisely because "'respecting an establishment of religion' . . . sweeps far more broadly than the language of Section 10, . . . [this] decisively sets the two provisions apart."[35]

This conclusion seems sound. Moreover, it is significant to note that over the past few years, the United States Supreme Court has been softening its interpretation of the Establishment Clause to allow greater flexibility for legislative initiatives to exercise at least benign neutrality, if not accommodation or cooperation.[36] Three aspects of the Court's decisions are worth emphasizing. First, the Court has held that granting religious groups equal access to public facilities does not violate the Establishment Clause.[37] For example, although it remains impermissible for a public school to initiate or facilitate public prayer, Bible readings, and the like,[38] where a public school allows other extracurricular clubs, it cannot ban a religious club that holds prayers or reads the Bible.[39] Second, in a very significant line of cases dealing with financial aid to education,[40] the Court has reversed earlier presumptions that any aid going to primary and secondary schools impermissibly advances religion. Instead, it has reasoned that such aid only has the effect of advancing religion if it (1) results in governmental indoctrination, (2) defines its recipients by reference to

---

[35] Ostien and Gamaliel, 2002, 24.
[36] The series of cases beginning with *Employment Division v. Smith*, 494 U.S. 872 (1990), clearly reduced the range for accommodation through *judicial* creation of exemptions from general laws under the Free Exercise Clause, but this did not foreclose legislative exemptions under either Free Exercise or Establishment Clause analysis. In this sense, *Smith* and its progeny can be understood as narrowing judicial power and deferring to legislative power, consistent with broader trends in United States Supreme Court jurisprudence.
[37] *Board of Educ. of the Westside Community Schools (Dist. 66) v. Mergens*, 496 U.S. 226 (1990).
[38] *Engel v. Vitale*, 370 U.S. 421 (1962); *School Dist. of Abington Township v. Schempp*, 374 U.S. 203 (1963).
[39] *Good News Club v. Milford Central School*, 533 U.S. 98, 113-14 (2001) (religious speech cannot be excluded from limited public forum).
[40] *Mitchell v. Helms*, 530 U.S. 793 (2000); *Agostini v. Felton*, 521 U.S. 203 (1997).

religion, or (3) creates an excessive entanglement.[41] Finding that various carefully structured aid programs benefiting parochial schools in economically depressed areas did not violate this test, the Court sustained the aid programs in question. Third, a critical factor in the Court's analysis has been whether government action or individual choice steered government aid to an arguably religious institution. Thus, where a handicapped student otherwise eligible for aid decided to attend a religious rather than a secular institution, and there was no indication that the government funding itself influenced the choice, the Court concluded there was no Establishment Clause violation.[42]

Implicit in these cases is a recognition that as state institutions grow more pervasive, strict interpretation of Establishment Clause precedents along separationist lines may have the unintended effect of consigning religion to an ever narrower private sector, and may actually discriminate against religion in comparison with other groups and entities routinely eligible for state assistance. Accordingly, a more flexible interpretation of the Establishment Clause is needed to avoid such discrimination and to recognise the realities of state involvement in the support of many aspects of modern life. Adequate protection for the fundamental aims of protecting religious freedom is assured if it is clear that individual choice rather than state action is guiding the decisions involved. Since Nigeria is in many ways more committed to the "social state" than the United States, the same concerns argue for similar openness to accommodation and/or cooperation in Nigeria.

The third constitution deserving mention is that of the Federal Republic of Germany. The fundamental rights enunciated in the German Basic Law adopted in 1949 contain a "religious freedom" provision,[43] but not a direct analogue to Section 10 of the Nigerian constitution or the United States Establishment Clause. However, the church-state provisions of the Weimar constitution, incorporated in the German Basic Law by article 140 thereof, do have an analogous provision. Specifically, Article 136 of the Weimar constitution provides "there shall not be a state church." Unlike the US constitution, this provision has never been interpreted expansively

---

[41] *Agostini v. Felton*, 521 U.S. at 233-34.
[42] *Witters v. Washington Dept. of Servs. for Blind*, 474 U.S. 481, 489 (1986).
[43] Basic Law, art. 4.

to cover anything that might *tend* toward creating a state church; it has been understood more narrowly as a ban on actually creating an official state church. The language is very close to that of Nigeria's "no state religion" clause. My contention would be that the Nigerian provision should probably be given a similar reading. (Indeed, strict constructionists would argue that even the United States Establishment Clause should have been interpreted in the same way, as merely a ban on the creation of an official state church or of excessive governmental involvement in such a church.) Like Germany, Nigeria is a modern social state in which it would be inappropriate to abandon state neutrality, but rigid refusal to cooperate with religious institutions could in effect discriminate against them and could also undermine the productive role they can play in a pluralistic society.

Ultimately, as stated at the outset, the interpretation of Nigeria's "no state religion" clause will need to lie with Nigerian courts, taking into account the unique history, culture and general setting of Nigerian constitutional law. However, if my comparative argument is correct, this interpretation ought to fall somewhere in the range between cooperation and benign neutrality. There is nothing in the Nigerian constitution calling for the harsh separationism of French or Turkish secularism. And there is much to commend the recent trend in the United States and the long-settled pattern in Germany of positive cooperation of the state with religion, while maintaining a commitment to neutrality among religions and the protection of voluntary choice and conscience for the individual.

CONCLUSION: POSSIBLE IMPLICATIONS FOR THE *SHARI'AH* DEBATE

Not being an expert on *shari'ah* and its role in modern states, I hesitate to venture into this field at all. But by way of conclusion, let me mention a few considerations that may bear on the debate about adoption of *shari'ah* by some of Nigeria's states. I realise that these suggestions may not necessarily square neatly with traditional understandings of *shari'ah*, but with Nigeria's common law tradition, it may be possible for practices implementing some of the underlying principles to evolve.

In the first place, as I have mentioned in connection with respect to the US system, and could easily document with respect to Germany, it is vital that any configuration of religion and the state must respect individual conscience. It is true in Germany that the state cooperates with religious communities in gathering church tax, but this is worth examining more closely. Under German law, the major churches (and many smaller ones) are "corporations of public law," having among other things authority to levy taxes. The German state enters into agreements with the churches to collect taxes for the churches, but it is the taxing power of the churches that lies behind the church tax – not the power of the state. The state is merely serving as a helper, since it can collect the church taxes as part of its own tax collection system much more efficiently than the churches could. The churches pay the state a percentage of the collections – approximately 4.5% – for this service. Significantly, anyone who objects to this exaction is free to leave the church levying the tax, and when he or she does so, the tax liability ends. The important point to see is that while the religious institution has considerable power, it cannot assert this power to coerce contributions from non-members, or against individuals who do not choose to remain subject to the church levies. This may suggest useful analogies for thinking about how a state could cooperate in recognising *shari'ah* for those who are believers, or who still identify themselves sufficiently with Islam to submit themselves to it. But individuals should be free to opt out if they so desire, remaining subject, of course, to the general laws of the state.

Second, it is worth thinking about an extremely important line of cases emerging from the jurisprudence of the European Court of Human Rights in Strasbourg. These cases are based on interpretation of Article 9 of the European Convention, which closely parallels Section 38(1) of the Nigerian constitution. The cases involved situations where countries sought to appoint "official muftis" and to refuse recognition to religious leaders chosen by Muslim sub-communities. The appointment or recognition of "official" Muslim leaders was a standard technique for dealing with Islam in the former socialist bloc, and remains a factor in Russia and Central Asia today. Without going into detail, these cases made it very clear that it is a violation of Article 9 and of the state neutrality presupposed thereby for a state to refuse to recognize the religious leaders chosen by a particular group. Where matters in which the state has a clear interest are involved, the state has some latitude in determining whom it will entrust with such functions, but the state cannot refuse recognition to a particular religious leader if he is the leader preferred by a religious group, even if this results in fissure of the religious community. State power cannot be used to coerce a unified denomination.[44] A parallel line of cases insisting on the autonomy of religious organizations with respect to their religious law is deeply entrenched in the United States.[45] Here the message seems to be that to the extent that Nigerian states seek to follow *shari'ah*, they need to respect the fact that different religious subcommunities may have different interpretations of religious law, and neutral state institutions should stay out of second-guessing such religious disputes.

A final point: the fact that secular law coincides with religious law is not itself a ground for invalidating it. Key features of virtually every secular legal system can be traced back historically to religious roots. Moreover, even controversial current provisions may be argued for on the basis of religious beliefs without undermining the constitutionality of resulting legislation. For example, the United States Supreme Court has rejected arguments that abortion legislation would violate the Establishment Clause merely because it was supported by religious groups on the basis of their religious beliefs.[46] The right to be treated equally in matters of religion does not mean that the state will have the same beliefs as everyone in society; this is manifestly impossible. Surely state choices will invariably coincide with the beliefs of some and not others. The mere coincidence is not the problem. What is critical is that people are left free in matters of conscience, and that when conscientious beliefs are manifested in

---

[44] *Hasan and Chaush v. Bulgaria* (ECtHR, Application No. 30985/96, Decision of Oct. 26, 2000); *Serif v. Greece* (ECtHR, App. No. 38178/97, Decision of Dec. 14, 1997); *see also Metropolitan Church of Bessarabia v. Moldova* (ECtHR, Dec. 13, 2001, App. No. 45701/99).
[45] *Serbian E. Orthodox Diocese v. Milivojevich*, 426 U.S. 696 (1976); *Presbyterian Church v. Mary Elizabeth Blue Hull Mem'l Presbyterian Church*, 393 U.S. 440 (1969); *Kedroff v. Saint Nicholas Cathedral*, 344 U.S. 94 (1952); *Gonzalez v. Roman Catholic Archbishop*, 280 U.S. 1 (1929); *Watson v. Jones*, 80 U.S. (13 Wall.) 679 (1871).
[46] *Harris v. McRae*, 448 U.S. 297 (1980).

behaviour, the behaviour should only be limited as prescribed by laws genuinely necessary to further vital state interests, as recognised in all the key international instruments.[47]

Precisely how all the issues involved in the *shari'ah* debate should be resolved is clearly beyond my competence; resolving them peacefully and to the general satisfaction will be one of the great challenges for Nigerian society in the years ahead. It is very clear, however, that Nigeria has found impressive answers to such questions in the past, and the new solutions it is now developing will no doubt be profoundly helpful in working out the proper place of Islam in the modern global setting.

REFERENCES

Alston, Philip, "The Universal Declaration at 35: western and passé or alive and universal?", *The Review of the International Commission of Jurists*, 31, 1983, 60-70.

Bilder, Richard "The status of international human rights law: an overview", in: James Tuttle (ed.), *International Human Rights Law and Practice*, Chicago: American Bar Association, 1978, 1-14.

Davis, Derek, "The evolution of religious freedom as a universal human right: examining the role of the 1981 United Nations Declaration on the Elimination of all Forms of Intolerance and of Discrimination Based on Religion or Belief", *Brigham Young University Law Review*, 2002, 217-236.

De la Hera, Alberto, "Relations with religious minorities: the Spanish model", *Brigham Young University Law Review*, 1998, 387-400.

Diamond, A.S., *Primitive Law Past and Present*, London: Methuen & Co., 1971.

Durham, W. Cole, Jr., "Perspectives on religious liberty: a comparative framework", in: Johan D. van der Vyver and John Witte, Jr., (eds.), *Religious Human Rights in Global Perspective: Legal perspectives*, The Hague/Boston/London: Martinus Nijhoff Publishers, 1996, 1-44.

Durham, W. Cole, Jr., and Alexander Dushku, "Traditionalism, secularism, and the transformative dimensions of religious institutions", *Brigham Young University Law Review*, 1993, 421-460.

Ferrari, Silvio, "The emerging pattern of church and state in Western Europe: the Italian model", *Brigham Young University Law Review*, 1995, 421-437.

---

[47] ICCPR, art. 18(3); ECHR, art. 9(2); ACHR, art. 12(3).

Hannum, Hurst "The status of the Universal Declaration of Human Rights in national and international law", *Georgia Journal of International and Comparative Law* 25, 1995/1996, 287-397.
Henkin, Louis, *The Age of Rights*, New York: Columbia University Press, 1990.
Humphrey, John, *No Distant Millennium: The international law of human rights*, Paris: UNESCO, 1989.
_____, "The international bill of rights: scope and implementation", *William and Mary Law Review* 17, 1976, 527-541.
Lillich, Richard B., "Civil Rights", in: *Human Rights in International Law: Legal and policy issues*, Theodor Meron (ed.), Oxford: Clarendon Press, 1984, 115-170.
Lindholm, Tore, W. Cole Durham, Jr., and Bahia G. Tahzib-Lie (eds.), *Facilitating Freedom of Religion or Belief: A deskbook*, Leiden: Brill Academic Publishers (forthcoming 2004).
Ostien, P. and J.D. Gamaliel, "The law of separation of religion and state in the United States: a model for Nigeria?", in S.O.O. Amali et al. (eds.), *Religion in the United States*, Ibadan: American Studies Association of Nigeria, 2002, 14-32.
Robertson, A.H. and J. G. Merrills, *Human Rights in the World*, 3d ed., Manchester: Manchester University Press, 1989.
Smith, Steven D., *Foreordained Failure: The quest for a constitutional principle of religious freedom*, New York: Oxford University Press, 1995.
Sohn, Louis B. "The human rights law of the Charter", *Texas International Law Journal* 12, 1977, 129-140.
Stahnke, Tad, "Proselytism and the freedom to change religion in international human rights law", *Brigham Young University Law Review*, 1999, 251-350.
_____, "The right to engage in religious persuasion", in Tore Lindholm, W. Cole Durham, Jr., and Bahia G. Tahzib-Lie (eds.), *Facilitating Freedom of Religion or Belief: A deskbook*, Leiden: Brill Academic Publishers (forthcoming 2004).
Stegeby, E. Kenneth, "An analysis of the impending disestablishment of the Church of Sweden", *Brigham Young University Law Review*, 1999, 703-767.
Tahzib-Lie, Bahia G., *Freedom of Religion or Belief: Ensuring effective international legal protection*, Boston: Martinus Nijhoff, 1996
Thornberry, Patrick, *International Law and the Rights of Minorities*, Oxford: Clarendon Press, 1991.
Waldock, Humphrey, "Human rights in contemporary international law and the significance of the European Convention", *The European Convention of Human Rights* (British Institute of International & Comparative Law), Series No. 5, 1965, 1-23.

Commentary

I.

Musa A.B. Gaiya

Professor Durham's paper gives us Western models of state/religion relationship. He acknowledges his limited knowledge of the Nigerian situation and leaves it to the Nigerians to fill in the gap. I see my task here as that of complementing Durham's. My comments therefore will not be on those Western models, which Professor Durham has ably handled. I will dwell instead on the implication for the Nigerian state/religion relationship of Section 10 of the Nigerian constitution and the issue of human rights as they are set forth in the Nigerian constitution.

SECTION 10 OF NIGERIA'S CONSTITUTION

Section 10 of the Nigerian constitution says, "The government of the Federation or of a State shall not adopt any religion as State Religion." This is supposed to define, in part, the relationship between the state and religion. It must be stated, as Professor Durham has also argued, that this does not make Nigeria a secular state, whether in the way the term is understood in France, Turkey or in the United Sates of America. There are constant government interventions in religious matters in Nigeria that would not warrant the designation of Nigeria as a secular state. Indeed the intention of the formulators of the Section 10 of the Nigerian constitution was, I imagine, that the state would be "impartial" and give "equal treatment," using Professor Durham's words, to all religions. Thus government at different levels support religious institutions with public funds, for example the building of mosques and churches in state houses. The idea of impartiality and equal treatment of all religions is hardly practised, however, since not all religions are accorded the same privileges in Nigeria. And we think the action of the *shari'ah* states in Northern Nigeria further erodes this neutrality, since revivalist Muslims believe "a state cannot be religiously neutral."¹ But by and large, and using Professor Durham's "continuum" of religion-state relationships, Nigeria can be placed between "benign neutrality" and "cooperation."

So the pertinent question that has agitated the minds of Nigerians, for which answers are not readily available, is whether the extension of the scope of the *shari'ah* as the government of Zamfara and other states in Northern Nigeria did, is tantamount to adopting Islam as the state religion? Now this question can be answered glibly by saying "Yes" or "No." A definitive interpretation must be left to the Supreme Court of Nigeria. Be that as it may, the actions of these governments are based on certain historical antecedents. When the British took over Northern Nigeria in 1903, they first of all dismantled the Caliphate, then reduced the scope of the *shari'ah* – the Islamic law operating then – by removing aspects of it that looked "repugnant to natural justice and humanity."² The changes by the British, according the former Chief Justice of Nigeria, Hon. Mohammed Bello, were:

1. death by hanging for offences of homicide and adultery [replaced] beheading and stoning to death respectively under *shari'ah*;
2. imprisonment as punishment for theft instead of amputation of hand under *shari'ah*; and
3. payment of *diyah* in lieu of capital punishment was abolished.³

According to Philip Ostien, this was further eroded in what he calls "the Settlement of 1960."⁴

The Northern Nigeria government under the Sardauna of Sokoto, Sir Ahmadu Bello, and with supervision of the British colonial authorities, in an attempt to bring unity and cohesion, formulated and enacted a hybridised penal law to take care of the interests of Muslims, Christians and Traditionalists, the last two called "the minorities." The Sardauna felt this was necessary because there were increasing fears by non-Muslims in Northern Nigeria of Muslim

---

[1] Westerlund, 1992, 84.
[2] Kumo, 2001, 168.
[3] Bello, 2001, 8-9.
[4] Ostien, 2005.

domination.⁵ These fears continued to be expressed by non-Muslims during the constitutional debates in Nigeria which led up to independence. The arrangement of 1960, in which Ostien feels Muslims made "great concessions,"⁶ seemed to have worked until Muslims felt the need to extend the scope of the *shari'ah* courts beyond the state level, and demanded in 1979 the creation of a separate Federal Sharia Court of Appeal to hear cases springing from the state *shari'ah* courts. What was decided at the end of the debates in 1979, to my mind, was best for the country. The Federal Court of Appeal was to have a section within it manned by Muslim jurists to hear cases from the state Sharia Courts of Appeal. This was a neat compromise.

However, Muslims were not satisfied with the arrangement hence the action taken in 1999 – an attempt to restore the *shari'ah* to its Caliphate (pre-colonial) status. Indeed, Philip Ostien has argued that because Christians opposed the Muslims' demand in 1979, they created discontent in the minds of Muslims to make them take the action they took in 1999, by re-examining the "delegation clause" in Section 277 subsection 1 of the constitution, which was a reproduction of what was in the 1979 constitution, Section 242, subsection 1 (see below). One wonders why Muslims in Nigeria had to wait for twenty years to discover the opportunity offered by the 1979 constitution for the extension of the jurisdiction of the *shari'ah* in the states *ad lib.*! What a golden privilege they had at that time, with a constitution, which, according to Ostien, Christians cavalierly orchestrated. Thus, Ostien's argument that if Christians did not oppose Muslims' demand in 1979, Muslims would have no reason to extend the scope of the *shari'ah* as was done in 1999,⁷ is simply begging the question. He seems to be saying, what Muslims could not achieve in 1979 through the front door because of Christian opposition, they got in 1999 through the back door in spite of Christian opposition. Thus, Ostien blamed the development in 1999 on Christians' intolerance.

---

⁵ See Okpu, 1977. This is an interpretation of the *Report of the Commission Appointed to Enquire into the Fears of Minorities and the Means of Allaying them* [the Willink Commission], 1958.
⁶ Ostien, 2005.
⁷ See ibid., 17.

Closely related to the above question, is an equally valid question, which the courts must decide, that is, whether the "delegation clause" can be given rigid interpretation such as the *shari'ah* states have done. The section in question can be found in the 1979 constitution (Section 242(1)), 1989 constitution (Section 261(1)), and 1999 constitution (section 277(1)) and which states:

> The Sharia Court of Appeal of a State shall, *in addition to such other jurisdiction as may be conferred upon it by the law of the State*, exercise such appellate and supervisory jurisdiction in civil proceedings involving questions of Islamic personal law which the court is competent to decide in accordance with the provisions of section (2) of this section.

Could what was intended by "other jurisdiction," in a layman's understanding, be an area of jurisdiction within the "Islamic personal law" which was not included in the constitution?

I personally think that the *shari'ah* phenomenon may fizzle out in practice, although it may continue to exist on paper alone. *Shari'ah* is a religious law carrying with it all the emotions religion evokes. Muslims may continue to look back to actions of these *shari'ah* governors with nostalgia, beside the number of people that are now on the payroll of government because of the *shari'ah* implementation who will not want to lose their jobs.[8] As such, the Supreme Court's interpretation should serve as a basis for constitutional review. As Africans whose tradition provides means of communal settlement of problems, we should be able to discuss this problem in our legislative houses with the view to arriving at a workable arrangement. These matters can be negotiated if approached with sincerity of purpose. I personally learnt from Americans not only the spirit of tolerance but that religion can be negotiated. The idea of the American "melting pot" is a myth although an ideal,[9] particularly in some states, such as Utah, where there is apparent religious tension but the tension does

---

[8] *Shari'ah* has created jobs for the jobless due to the number of structures established in these states, for example, the *Hisbah*, Sharia Anti-corruption Bureau, Sharia Monitoring and Implementation Directorate, Zakat Commission, etc.
[9] See Hutchison, 2003, 170-195.

not end in conflict. American know how "to live and let live" when it comes to matters of religion.

THE MATTER OF FREEDOM OF RELIGION

I think neither the Universal Declaration of Human Rights (UDHR) as contained in Article 18, formulated in 1948 nor Article 18 of the International Covenant on Civil and Political Rights (ICCPR) are sacrosanct. The Universal Declaration of Human Rights in particular was forged by the then superpowers when Nigeria, for example, was yet to achieve its independence. Thus Britain must have signed such a document on Nigeria's behalf. I wonder how such document would have "universal validity," as Durham puts it, when Muslims have their own declaration of human rights. Muslims consider the UDHR not only secular but individualistic and contrary to Islam's understanding of religion in society. Islam holds that an individual's rights are those bestowed on him/her by the community, the Muslim *ummah*. The *World of Islam* explains the Islamic understanding of human rights this way:

> The rights of the individual come second to the greater good of the *Ummah* . . . . Islamic thinking then is far more concerned with the group, the family, community and society. Humans exist within an established social structure and it is difficult for a traditional Muslim to mentally pluck an individual out of that structure and ascribe rights to him or her which might conflict with those of the community to which they belong.[10]

This Islamic understanding of human rights may help us to understand why Islam does not allow an individual to "abandon one [religion] and adopt another religion."[11] Besides the above, the secular nature of the UDHR is seen in making religion a personal matter which is the basis of Western privatisation of religion. But in Africa religion is never a private matter. As John Mbiti has said,

---

[10] *The World of Islam*, 2000, Section 15 of the "Survey of Islam".
[11] Appleby, 2003, 219.

religion "permeates into" every department of the African's life.¹² Because of this, the African does not make a distinction between the sacred and the secular or between the "religious and the non-religious [and] between the spiritual and the material areas of life."¹³ Mbiti goes on to write that:

> [w]herever the African is, there is his religion: he carries it to the fields where he is sowing seeds or harvesting a new crop; he takes it with him to the beer party or to attend a funeral ceremony; and if he is educated, he takes religion with him to the examination room at school or university; if he is a politician he takes it to the house of parliament.¹⁴

This is why it is not out of place for an African soccer team to take some time off, particularly before a match, to pray. This why R Scott Appleby observes that:

> The Universal Declaration of Human Rights and subsequent conventions impose post-Enlightenment ways of knowing and Western cultural assumptions and ideologies, opponents charge, which are no more universally binding than any other culturally determined set of principles.¹⁵

Thus in spite of these disparities African and Islamic states were made to sign these international charters and some, like Nigeria, adopted them into their constitutions without much reflection with the view of adapting them to suit their peculiar, as Durham puts it, "cultural and historical settings."

REFERENCES

Appleby, R. Scott, "Religions, human rights and social change", in: Gerrie ter Haar and James J. Busuttil (eds.), *The Freedom To Do God's Will:*

---

¹² Mbiti, 1970, 1.
¹³ Ibid., 2.
¹⁴ Ibid.
¹⁵ Appleby, 2003, 205.

Religious fundamentalism and social change, London: Routledge, 2003, 197-229.

Bello, Mohammed, "Keynote address", in: A.M. Yakubu, A.M. Kani, and M.I. Junaid (eds.), *Understanding Shari'a in Nigeria*, Ibadan: Spectrum Books Limited, 2001, 7-14.

Hutchison, William R., *Religious Pluralism in America: The contentious history of a founding ideal*, New Haven: Yale University Press, 2003.

Kumo, Suleiman, "Shari'a and the Nigerian constitution: issues and perspectives", in: A.M. Yakubu, A.M. Kani, and M.I. Junaid (eds.), *Understanding Shari'a in Nigeria*, Ibadan: Spectrum Books Limited, 2001 168-175.

Mbiti, John S., *African Religions and Philosophy*, New York: Anchor Books, 1970.

Okpu, Ugbana, *Ethnic Minority Problems in Nigerian Politics: 1960-1965*, Stockholm: Almqvist & Wilksell International, 1977.

Ostien, Philip, "An opportunity missed by Nigeria's Christians: the *shari'a* debate of 1976-78 revisited", in: Benjamin Soares, ed., *Muslim-Christian Relations in Africa. Islam in Africa* series, volume 5. Leiden and Boston: Brill, forthcoming 2005.

Report of the Commission Appointed to Enquire into the Fears of Minorities and the Means of Allaying them (the Willink Commission), London: Her Majesty's Stationary Office, 1958.

Westerlund, David, "Secularism, civil religion, or Islam? Islamic revivalism and the national question in Nigeria", in: Austin Metumara Ahanotu, *Religion, State and Society in Contemporary Africa*, New York: Peter Lang, 1992, 71-101.

The World of Islam (compact disk), Colorado Springs: Global Mapping International, 2000.

II.

Ibrahim Na'iya Sada

In line with the generally accepted practice in international and constitutional law, the Nigeria constitution of 1999 provided for "no state religion" and "the freedom of religion" clauses under Sections 10 and 38 respectively. Section 10, which provides that "The Government of the Federation or of a State shall not adopt any religion as State Religion," is generally construed as laying down the principle of the separation of state and religion. The whole issue of separation of state and religion is skewed in favour of the Western Christian tradition which has no equivalent in the Islamic tradition or historical experience. In Islam there is nothing like what Jefferson calls a "wall of separation between church and state." In fact, according to most Muslim scholars, religion needs the state to thrive while the state needs religion to survive.

In the mental climate of the modern world, it has become almost axiomatic among many Western educated people that religion ought not to interfere with political life. While the principle of "secularism" is automatically identified with "progress," every suggestion to consider politics and socio-economic planning under religion is dismissed out of hand as reactionary.

The principle of separation of state and religion in the United States means that government must not foster an "excessive entanglement with religion." This includes among other things the prohibition of (a) the use of religious symbols by municipalities, (b) teaching of religion in public schools, (c) prayer and other religious exercise in public schools.

The position in the United States when compared with Nigeria, can be seen to be radically different. This is so especially when we read Section 10 of the 1999 constitution in conjunction with Sections 38, 247, 275–279, and 288 which are talking of a variety of subjects ranging from teaching of religion in public schools, establishment and jurisdiction of Sharia Courts of Appeal for states, to the composition of the Court of Appeal and the Supreme Court. The provisions of these sections of Nigeria's constitution clearly show entanglement of government with religion or with institutions that are religiously based. To this extent this is a clear departure from the position in the United States constitution.[1]

The concept, definition and role of government under the two systems, i.e. Western and Islamic, are also different. While the two may agree that government is an organ that is set up to work for the welfare of the people, they differ on the role religion is to play and the permissible scope of its involvement in government. To Muslims

---

[1] For a fuller discussion of these points see Ostien and Gamaliel, 2002, 24-28.

in their understanding of Islam, the most important role and duty of government is, as summarised by Sheikh Usman Dan Fodio, "protecting the spiritual well-being of the people."[2]

The extent or limit of religious liberty may also depend on the definition and scope of religion according to the world view under which you are looking at the issue. If you define religion to mean a body of rituals private to individuals, you are likely to restrict and see religion as a private affair with little or no role in public affairs. If you define religion to mean "a way of life" covering the entire gamut of people's thoughts and actions, you are likely to give a wider role to religion in public life. Islam is defined and understood by Muslims in this wider sense. The application of *shari'ah* in some of the Northern states of Nigeria is seen by Muslims as a natural consequence of the exercise of their religious freedom. It will be interesting to speculate on what may be the reaction of the government of the United States if any community within that country were to insist on having all aspects of their lives, political, economic, social, and spiritual, dictated in line with their religious beliefs. Muslims understand Islam to be not only a way of life but a civilisation with its distinct world view.

The implementation of *shari'ah* is not understood by Muslims as a declaration of a "state religion" by the implementing states. It is not necessary to have an Islamic state before implementing *shari'ah*, rather it is the *shari'ah* and the extent of internalisation of Islamic values in the society that determines its Islamicity. The Islamic state is neither a theocracy nor a democracy. In fact there is no common or agreed postulation of the Islamic state, al-Mawardi, Ibn Taimiyyah, al-Ghazali, Ibn Khaldun and the rest, all have different ideas of the nature and structure of an Islamic state. However, they all agree that such a state can take any form or shape as long as the *shari'ah* principles relating to government are being implemented.

Islamic law is generally held to be a "believers' law," in the sense that its application is limited to believers in the message of Islam. This can be seen even in the application of the Sharia Penal Codes that have recently been enacted in some of the states in Northern Nigeria. These codes specifically exempt non-Muslims from their jurisdiction, despite the fact that many non-Muslims are living in the

---

[2] Dan Fodio, 1960, 563.

states in which the codes have been adopted. This is contrary to the general norm of criminal law according to which the same penal code applies to all people living within the same territory. In the application of *shari'ah*, this exemption of non-Muslims from the application of the Sharia Penal Codes is seen as a very generous concession to those of them who chose to stay among the Muslims as a minority.

Muslims find it difficult to understand the reasons behind the massive interest of the West in *shari'ah* implementation, considering the West's open hostility and aversion to Islam and the Muslims especially after the 9/11 incident. Be that as it may there is the view widely held among Muslims that Western civilisation despite its claim to being the champion of human rights, liberty, and freedom is the most intolerant civilization ever evolved in the history of humanity. It is not willing to stand side by side with another world view. All of humanity must accept its standards as the supposedly most superior and civilised. The world's Muslims, of course, beg to differ.

REFERENCES

Dan Fodio, Sheikh Usman, *Kitab al-Farq*, edited and translated by M. Hiskett, *Bulletin of the School for Oriental and African Studies*, XXIII/3, 1960, 558-79.

Ostien, P. and J.D. Gamaliel, "The law of separation of religion and state in the United States: a model for Nigeria?", in S.O.O. Amali et al. (eds.), *Religion in the United States*, Ibadan: American Studies Association of Nigeria, 2002, 14-32.

Freedom of Religion and Its Limitations: Judicial Standards for Deciding Particular Cases to Maintain the State's Secular Role in Protecting Society's Religious Commitments

John C. Reitz[1]

INTRODUCTION

The Santeria religion developed in the nineteenth century among the slaves in Cuba who had come from Yoruba lands in what is now Nigeria. It is a fusion of traditional Yoruba and Roman Catholic practices and beliefs that has come to be called "the way of the saints," or Santeria, because a key aspect of the religion is devotion to spirits, called *orishas*, who are represented by symbols of the Catholic saints. One of the principal ways the follower of Santeria shows his or her devotion to and establishes a relationship with an *orisha* is through animal sacrifice. The sacrificial animals may include chickens, pigeons, doves, ducks, guinea pigs, goats, sheep, and turtles. Santeria was practised chiefly in secret in Cuba because of widespread persecution. It was brought to the United States by exiles from the Cuban revolution, and by the early 1990s there were estimated to be at least 50,000 practitioners in South Florida.[2] It proved to be equally controversial in the United States.

In the late 1980s, the City of Hialeah in Florida learned that the Church of Lukumi Babalu Aye, Inc., a not-for-profit corporation organised under Florida law, was planning to build a house of

---

[1] The author acknowledges the generous support of the Iowa Law School Foundation, the developmental leave program at the University of Iowa, and the strong support of Dean N. William Hines. The Obermann Center for Advanced Studies at the University of Iowa provided a congenial workplace for much of the research and writing. The author also gratefully acknowledges the help provided by his research assistant Steffen Rupp on this paper.

[2] Noonan & Gaffney, 2001, 536-37.

worship to practise the Santeria religion in Hialeah. Horrified by the prospect of animal sacrifice, the city council reacted by adopting a series of ordinances to outlaw the sacrifice of animals in Hialeah. The Church of Lukumi Babalu Aye and its adherents invoked their right to the "free exercise" of religion under the First and Fourteenth Amendments of the U.S. constitution,[3] and the resultant litigation eventually came to the U.S. Supreme Court.[4]

The great American scholar of law and religion Judge (and formerly Professor) John T. Noonan has trenchantly portrayed the high stakes raised by this kind of conflict between religious freedom and the state's regulatory power. Quoting the Father of the First Amendment, James Madison, who termed private conscience "a great Barrier," Noonan observes that for the believer, the duty to obey religious dictates takes precedence over the commitment to obey state authority and civil society, and accordingly, the state must respect conscience by exempting it from political authority if it is to avoid "making itself a tyrant and the citizen a slave."[5] I see this point as a question of legitimacy. How can the state enjoy the support it needs from its citizens if it does not respect each person's separate search for meaning and values in life, whether that search ends in religion or in a secular rejection of religion?

But can any state so respect "the great Barrier" that it insulates religious practice entirely from state regulation? Noonan says, "No,"

---

[3] The First Amendment provides in relevant part: "Congress shall make no law respecting an establishment of religion, nor prohibiting the free exercise thereof." The First Amendment is a restriction only on the federal government. But the Fourteenth Amendment applies to the states and provides, in relevant part, that "[n]o State shall make or enforce any law which shall abridge the privileges or immunities of citizens of the United States; nor shall any State deprive any person of life, liberty, or property, without due process of law; nor deny to any person within its jurisdiction the equal protection of the laws." Starting with *Cantwell v. Connecticut*, 310 U.S. 296 (1940), the Supreme Court has held that the religious freedoms of the First Amendment are incorporated in the protections of the Fourteenth and so apply against the states.
[4] *Church of Lukumi Babalu Aye, Inc. v. City of Hialeah*, 508 U.S. 520 (1993).
[5] Noonan, 1996, 596 (quoting James Madison, "To the Honorable the General Assembly of the Commonwealth of Virginia: A Memorial and Remonstrance," in William T. Hutchinson and William M.E. Rachal, (eds.), *Madison Papers* 8:298 (1962)).

for three compelling reasons: (1) there are certain tasks, like collecting taxes and providing for military defence, that a state must perform if it is to be a state, and these state duties must therefore take precedence over claims of conscience; (2) states under constitutionalism and the rule of law "must operate by laws of general character" and "exceptions for religious rights endanger this generality"; and (3) "the State, through its organs such as the judiciary, must determine what is religion. The last word in theology must be the State's, for if the State does not see the rights being exercised as religious, the State will not be bound by any barrier safeguarding religious observance."[6]

As a result, Noonan says, we have an Hegelian antinomy: "rights to religious freedom founded on conscience beyond the authority of the State, set off against powers of the State that it cannot surrender without ceasing to exist."[7] The courts that are called to arbitrate these conflicts are thus faced with "tragic choices." In each case, either they curtail the power of the state in ways that may ultimately threaten its political integrity or they permit the state to breach the "great Barrier" in ways that threaten to enslave individuals by causing them to act against their conscience and thus against their very nature.[8] At the end of the day, as Noonan indicates, where law seeks to govern this conflict, the courts will set some limits to freedom of religious practice. The state will dominate, at least to some extent, and the extent to which the courts of a given country permit it to do so defines the boundaries of religious freedom for that country. But the intellectual pressure on the courts deciding these issues is intense because of the significance of the conflict and its "tragic" nature. As a consequence, the precise legal boundaries are inherently unstable.

The issues are also highly political and polarising. Since the disputes are about belief, people are reluctant to compromise. The polarisation may create huge rifts in society, as when several large religions have opposing views on an issue; or it may generate very substantial consensus, as in Hialeah, where the dominant, traditional U.S. Christian groups were as horrified by animal sacrifice as the

---

[6] Ibid.
[7] Ibid., 600.
[8] Ibid., 595.

unchurched. In either case, because of the primacy of religious belief and action to our individual identities and because most religious doctrine is meant to influence, not just belief, but also action, religious views will have an impact on politics. It is all too understandable that many groups seek to use the power of the state to implement their particular visions of the good life. The political saliency of these issues thus adds to the instability of the law.

How do courts decide these explosive, highly political conflicts between conscience and state power? This paper will examine how several different national courts (the Canadian and U.S. Supreme Courts and the German Constitutional Court), and the international court of one well-known human rights regime (the European Convention on Human Rights (ECHR)), have applied the guarantees for freedom of religion, which it is their duty to uphold, to resolve some of the chief issues involving religious freedom.

The courts whose decisions we will consider are all Western courts supported by strong traditions of democracy and the rule of law. But despite their significant commonalities, these courts do not resolve all conflicts over religious exercise in the same way. In view of the nature of these conflicts, as I have just argued, that is hardly surprising. Moreover, as a result of its unique history, each legal order has a somewhat different relationship between religion and the state. To some extent, these differing relationships may be expressed in the differing wording of the relevant constitutional phrases, but not necessarily and not entirely. At any rate, the different national experiences create different starting points for the courts with respect to many of these conflicts. The issue of conscientious objection to service in the military offers one simple example. Reflecting the misuse of state power under the Nazis and the strong aversion to war following in the wake of World Wars I and II, the German Basic Law (the German constitution) provides explicitly that "no one may be compelled against his conscience to render military service involving the use of arms."[9] But the U.S. constitution is silent on the matter, and while the U.S. Congress has provided statutory exemptions for certain types of conscientious objectors, the U.S. Supreme Court has

---

[9] Basic Law, Article 4(3). The provision adds, "Details shall be regulated by a federal law."

refused to interpret the First Amendment to create a constitutional right to exemption from military service for those who object to it on religious grounds.[10] To some extent, then, the German and U.S. courts approach some religious freedom issues with different law to apply. Even where they start with similar legal principles, the severity of the conflict between individual conscience and state power may lead different courts to different results. For all these reasons, Judge Noonan has cautioned that there can be "no single universal formula for reconciling religious rights and State authority."[11] The following discussion will use major cases in the selected jurisdictions in an effort to understand the reasons for some of the most important differences in the way the different courts have approached these issues.

At the same time, the cases we will examine also show some profound commonalities. The most important commonalities have to do with the insistence of the courts on the neutrality of the state in matters of religion. The courts may differ on what exactly neutrality means in concrete cases, but they share the basic idea that the state must be sufficiently non-religious – i.e. neutral as among all religions – so that individuals may be religious according to their dictates. This idea represents an important meaning of the terms so much criticised and misunderstood around the world today, "secularism" and the "secular state." The model of *state* secularism presented here does not mean that *society* is necessarily also secular. The U.S. provides a good example: despite (or perhaps because of) its quite rigid regime of religion-state separation, there is widespread agreement on the vital role that religion plays in U.S. society.[12] But religion is not a negligible force in any of the legal regimes surveyed in this paper. Rather, this model of the secular state insists that the state remain secular in order to protect society's religious commitments. In illuminating these commonalities, the paper will thus provide insight into the way a secular state can protect religions in society.

---

[10] *Gillette v. United States*, 410 U.S. 437 (1971) (no constitutional right to exemption for person who objects only to some wars on the basis of religion, but not to all wars, as required by statutory exemption).
[11] Ibid., 600.
[12] Monsma & Soper, 1997, 17.

This study is a comparative one designed to help enrich the discussion in Nigeria by describing the practice of courts in parts of the world about which I have some modest knowledge. I do not attempt to say how these ideas ought to be applied in Nigeria, about which I regrettably have too little knowledge. I have, however, limited the study to constitutional regimes that do not recognize a formal establishment of any religion. While it is true that all constitutional regimes have some de facto establishment of the dominant forms of religion in their societies and while even a formal, de jure establishment of religion does not necessarily prevent a state from aspiring to state neutrality in religious matters, nevertheless, formal establishment qualifies neutrality in important ways and thus complicates the issue of state neutrality.[13] Such complications are, however, not relevant to Nigeria because Nigeria also does not formally establish any religion and in fact, like the United States, has an anti-establishment clause in its constitution.[14]

The following description tries to make the cases analysed accessible to non-lawyers, but I hope that the comparative parallels and critical thinking about these cases will also be of interest to lawyers. In view of the huge number of cases on religious freedom decided in even the limited number of jurisdictions considered in this study, the paper necessarily proceeds somewhat impressionistically by discussing selected cases. The paper pursues the analysis of differences and commonalities in five parts. Part I examines the case of intentional discrimination against particular religions, looking chiefly at cases from the United States and Canada, including the one involving Santeria. Part II takes up the difficult question of the standards to be applied in adjudicating conflicts between religious

---

[13] Durham, 1996 (arguing that the degree of religious freedom in a country does not correlate with the degree of establishment of a church and that some countries with established religions may nevertheless provide substantial protection for the practice of other religions); Monsma & Soper, 1997, 121-54 (describing the substantial freedom of religion in England, despite the status of the Church of England as the state church, though concluding that church establishment "does undermine, to some degree, the basic goal of governmental neutrality on matters of religion" (148)).
[14] Section 10 of the Nigerian Constitution states: "The Government of the Federation or of a State shall not adopt any religion as State Religion."

practices and non-discriminatory statutes of general applicability, the issue on which there is the most significant difference among the courts surveyed here. This section discusses leading decisions by all of the courts on which this study focuses. Part III uses German Constitutional Court decisions about prayer, crucifixes, and headscarves in school to illustrate further the particular German standard of review, a technique of balancing constitutional rights in order to create a practical concordance of rights. Part IV assesses the chief differences this selection of cases reveals and focuses especially on the arguments for and against the various standards of review employed by the courts and the reasons that might account for the differences. Part V argues that, despite the differences, all these constitutional regimes manifest a common commitment to a secular state in order to protect religious freedom.

I. FREE EXERCISE CASES INVOLVING INTENTIONAL DISCRIMINATION

A. The United States: Regulations Against Animal Sacrifice

We start with two relatively easy cases of intentional discrimination. In the case I mentioned at the outset, in which adherents of Santeria wished to establish a church in Florida, the Hialeah City Council obviously understood that a rule simply banning Santeria would be an unconstitutional discrimination against that religion because it would single out one religious group for differential treatment solely on the grounds of religion.[15] So the City Council adopted a series of ordinances that by their terms applied equally to all religions. The ordinances forbade animal sacrifice and defined 'sacrifice' as "to unnecessarily kill, torment, torture, or mutilate an animal in a public or private ritual or ceremony not for the primary purpose of food consumption."[16] If all that the freedom of religion required were that government operate by regulations which on their face appear neutral

---

[15] "[A] law targeting religious beliefs as such is never permissible . . . ." *Church of Lukumi Babalu Aye, Inc. v. City of Hialeah*, 508 U.S. 520, 532 (1993) (citing *McDaniel v. Paty*, 435 U.S. 618 (1978)).

[16] *Church of Lukumi Babalu Aye, Inc. v. City of Hialeah*, 508 U.S. 520, 527 (1993).

and generally applicable, then there could be no free exercise objection to Hialeah's regulations. Meaningful protection of free exercise, however, obviously has to look beyond the facial neutrality of challenged governmental regulations. The fact that Episcopalians, Presbyterians, Roman Catholics, and all other Christian and Jewish groups in Hialeah were equally subject to the ban on animal sacrifice is not enough to show that the law is neutral because the regulations particularly burdened the exercise of one specific religion, Santeria, which was the only one in Hialeah then intending to engage in animal sacrifice. The United States Supreme Court started its analysis with the statement that "[f]acial neutrality is not determinative."[17]

But what should count then as proof of discrimination against a religion? Whenever a facially neutral statute impinges more burdensomely on one particular religion than on others, the disadvantaged religion is going to feel discriminated against. The mere fact of disproportionate impact cannot definitively establish discrimination because different religions require such different actions from their adherents. Disproportionate impacts certainly might indicate discrimination, but forbidding all regulation that creates a disproportionate, negative impact on a particular religion might curtail state regulatory power too much.

The City advanced a number of non-discriminatory, secular goals that its ordinances were designed to serve: (1) to eliminate health risks both to participants in animal sacrifice and to the general public, (2) to eliminate emotional injury to children who witness animal sacrifice; (3) to prevent cruel and unnecessary killing of animals, and (4) to prevent slaughter of animals outside of areas zoned for slaughterhouses.[18] There also was considerable evidence that the members of the Hialeah City Council did intend to discriminate against Santeria in passing the challenged ordinances, but only two Justices thought that such evidence should be taken into account.[19] Nevertheless, the majority of the Supreme Court agreed in this case

---

[17] Ibid., 534.
[18] The federal district court in the case had held that all of these interests support the ordinances and that they were "compelling state interests." Ibid., 530.
[19] Only Justice Stevens joined Part II A 2 of Justice Kennedy's opinion, which as to all other parts, was the opinion for the Court.

that the Hialeah ordinances were in fact discriminatory, despite their facial neutrality and despite their obvious secular purposes.[20]

The majority based its approach on a metaphor Justice Harlan had first used in a 1970 case, in which he wrote, "The Court must survey meticulously the circumstances of governmental categories to eliminate, as it were, religious gerrymanders."[21] 'Gerrymander' is the term used for a voting district of such improbable shape that the political party in control of the process of redrawing the electoral districts has obviously manipulated the process to achieve certain political results. Harlan's point was that facially neutral statutes must be examined carefully to see whether they are in effect drawn so as to prohibit or burden particular religious practices. The majority so found in *Church of Babalu Lukumi Aye*:

> The net result of the gerrymander is that few if any killings of animals are prohibited other than Santeria sacrifice, which is proscribed because it occurs during a ritual or ceremony and its primary purpose is to make an offering to the *orishas*, not food consumption. Indeed, careful drafting ensured that, although Santeria sacrifice is prohibited, killings that are no more necessary or humane in almost all other circumstances are unpunished.[22]

In fact, the majority noted, kosher slaughter, which is often criticised as cruel because it involves killing an animal without any prior anaesthetisation, was also exempted from the killings prohibited by the ordinances. Consequently, the Court invalidated the ordinances just as if they had facially discriminated against Santeria.[23] The

---

[20] Three justices, Souter, Blackman, and O'Connor, refused to join the portions of the opinion for the Court which found a discriminatory purpose based on the terms of the statute itself. However, nothing about their concurring opinions suggest that they disagreed with the majority's finding of discriminatory intent. They concurred separately just to make clear their opposition to applying the standard from *Employment Division v. Smith*, discussed in Section II.A., below.
[21] *Walz v. Tax Comm'n of New York City*, 397 U.S. 664, 696 (1970).
[22] *Church of Babalu Lukumi Aye*, 508 U.S. at 536 (five justices).
[23] A slightly stronger majority also found the ordinances, for the same reasons, not to be rules of general applicability. Under the general rule of the *Smith* case,

"gerrymander" analysis is an important tool to prevent government from deviously suppressing specific religions under the cover of facially neutral laws. It provides the best way of showing improper legislative intent if the court is disinclined, as it often is, to examine or depend on legislative history.[24] Another important aspect of this case is the liberal approach the justices took to the question of whether religious freedoms extend to such non-traditional, unusual religious practices as Santeria's animal sacrifice. The Court stated:

> The city does not argue that Santeria is not a "religion" within the meaning of the First Amendment. Nor could it. Although the practice of animal sacrifice may seem abhorrent to some, "religious beliefs need not be acceptable, logical, consistent, or comprehensible to others in order to merit First Amendment protection." . . . Given the historical association between animal sacrifice and religious worship, petitioners' assertion that animal sacrifice is an integral part of their religion "cannot be deemed bizarre or incredible."[25]

The issue should be whether the religious claimant has a sincere belief that behaviour conflicting with state regulation is required of him by his religion, not whether the religious belief in question is somehow within acceptable boundaries.[26] An oft-quoted line is, "The law knows no heresy, and is committed to the support of no dogma, the establishment of no sect."[27]

---

discussed in Section II.A., below, and in Appendix I, in order to burden free exercise rights by rules that are not of general applicability, the state must demonstrate "compelling" interests or "interests of the highest order," a very high standard. 508 U.S. at 546 (Part III of the opinion, supported by 6 justices).
[24] See Section I.B., below, for the Canadian Supreme Court's decisions on intentional discrimination.
[25] 508 U.S. at 531 (citations omitted).
[26] See *Frazee v. Illinois Department of Unemployment Security*, 489 U.S. 829, 834 (1989) (concerning a claim that religious beliefs prevented the claimant from working on Sunday).
[27] *Watson v. Jones*, 80 U.S. (13 Wall.) 679, 728 (1871).

A case which shows by negative example how problematic it can be for a court to make judgments about religious doctrine in the context of free exercise claims is *Zaheeruddin v. State*,[28] a decision of the Supreme Court of Pakistan. The case involved a challenge to an ordinance forbidding Ahmadis from using the symbols of Islam and claiming to be Muslim. The Ahmadis are an offshoot of Islam but they are regarded by most Muslims as heretical because of their belief that a certain person after the time of the Prophet Muhammad was also a prophet. As a result, they have been the target of considerable persecution in Pakistan. In *Zaheeruddin*, the Court upheld the ordinance:

> The Court acknowledged that religious freedom is not confined to religious beliefs, but rather extends to "essential and integral" religious practices. It claimed, however, that the appellants [the Ahmadis challenging the ordinance] had not explained how the prohibited epithets and public rituals were an essential part of their religion.[29]

By limiting religious freedom to "essential and integral" religious practices, the Pakistan Supreme Court opened a door to the substantial limitation of religious freedom, and any rule leaving it open to the courts to determine what types of religious practice qualify to be protected could have a similar effect.

The German Constitutional Court used similar language which indicated that it might reserve to itself the power to restrict freedom of religion to those religious ideas and practices it deemed acceptable. In rejecting a free exercise claim by a prisoner to whom parole was denied because he tried to persuade fellow inmates to give up their Christian faith by offering them tobacco, the Court stated, "One who violates limitations erected by the Basic Law's general order of values cannot claim freedom of belief. The Basic Law does not protect every manifestation of belief but only those historically developed among civilised people on the basis of certain fundamental moral

---

[28] 26 S.C.M.R. (S.Ct.) 1718 (1993) (Pak.) (described in detail in Mahmud, 2003).
[29] Mahmud, 2003, 47-50.

opinions."[30] However, the Court backed away from that statement in subsequent cases, holding, for example, in a case sustaining an evangelical pastor's right not to take the oath required of witnesses in court:

> A distinctive characteristic of a state which has proclaimed human dignity to be its highest constitutional value and which guarantees the inalienable freedom of religion and conscience unrestricted by statute is that it permits even outsiders and sects to develop their personalities in keeping with their subjective convictions, free of harassment. [This freedom is granted them] so long as they do not contradict other values of constitutional rank and their behaviour does not palpably encroach upon the community or the fundamental rights of others. [31]

The Court noted that the dissident pastor's refusal to take the oath found some support in the Bible and "is espoused by a school of newer theology," but it also stated that "[t]he state may not evaluate its citizens' religious convictions or characterise these beliefs as right or wrong."[32]

Of course, the courts must be convinced of the sincerity of the religious liberty claimant, but the test of sincerity must not be deformed into a test of what religious beliefs and practices are "acceptable." Nor, as Judge Noonan has told us, can the courts avoid making a determination of whether the asserted religious claims are in fact "religious."[33] But the courts must be prepared to respect and

---

[30] Kommers, 1997, 452 (translating portions of the *Tobacco Atheist Case*, 12 BVerfGE 1, 4-5 (1960)).
[31] Ibid., 454 (translating portions of the *Religious Oath Case*, 33 BVerfGE 23 (1972)). In reaction, the legislature amended the statute to offer an alternative equivalent to an oath ("eine eidesgleiche Bekräftigung").
[32] Ibid., 455.
[33] See, e.g., *Wisconsin v. Yoder*, 406 U.S. 205 (1972) (concluding that the Amish determination to live separate from modern society was grounded in their religious beliefs and was not just a personal, secular rejection of modern life like Thoreau's choice to isolate himself at Walden Pond); also the German Constitutional Court's decision in the *Religious Oath Case*, translated in relevant part in Kommers, 1997, 453-58.

tolerate dissident religious views so much that they can soberly consider that there are constitutional protections for a person's religious ideas even though they seem absurd and in fact affront the majority's ideas – and the judge's own ideas – of what counts as a reasonable religious idea.[34] In particular, the courts must avoid any inquiry into the truth or falsity of religious ideas.[35]

B. Canada: Sabbath-keeping Laws

As already mentioned, cases of explicit state attempts to ban particular religious practices hardly ever arise in constitutional orders that guarantee freedom of religion because such attempts would so clearly be unconstitutional. But one recurrent free exercise problem involves the situation in which the state establishes general regulations which in some way reflect or facilitate the religious practices of the majority. Quite naturally, in view of the dominant role Christianity has played in Western history, the whole calendar in the Western world has tended to reflect the Christian calendar, from the division of years into "B.C." and "A.D.," to the major holidays around Christmas and the choice of a "weekend" with the main

---

[34] Cf. Dorsen, et al., 2003, 925-27 (summarizing Italian Supreme Court decision on Scientology, Cass., sez. Sesta Penale, Registro Gen. n.116835/97 (Oct. 8, 1997) (case summary by Cesnur at <www.cesnur.org>)). The Italian Supreme court rejected a theistic definition of "religion" and found that Scientology is a religion, even if some of its methods of proselytisation may be subject to prosecution for fraud. Accord, *Hernandez v. Commissioner of Internal Revenue*, 490 U.S. 680 (1989) (Scientology a religion). As of the late 1990s, German authorities were still refusing to recognize Scientology as a religion in a struggle that had become quite bitter on both sides. Noonan & Gaffney, 2001, 569-70; Monsma & Soper, 1997, 170-71.

[35] *U.S. v. Ballard*, 322 U.S. 78 (1944). For a contrasting negative example, see Justice von Schlabrendorff's dissenting opinion in the *Religious Oath Case*, translated in part in Kommers, 1997, 456-58. Justice von Schlabrendorff took issue with the majority's statement that there was some support in the Bible for the pastor's refusal to take an oath. With references to Thomas Aquinas and Martin Luther, Justice von Schlabrendorff refuted the pastor's claim that the Sermon on the Mount justified his refusal to take an oath and concluded, "A citizen who, according to his own statement, ascribes to the Christian belief and makes an obvious misinterpretation has no claim to the protection of [freedom of religion in] Article 4 of the Basic Law . . . ." Ibid., 457.

business closings on Sunday, the sabbath day for most Christians. In like manner, predominantly Muslim states have tended to shape the calendar to reflect the practices of Islam. To what extent is a secular Western state free to require business closings on Sunday? The state may argue that such a law simply accommodates the majority practice of religion, but other religions, including some Christian groups, observing a different sabbath day, may respond that such a rule violates their right to free exercise if it does not also provide accommodations for their practices.

In 1970, the Canadian federal government adopted a statute entitled "Lord Day's Act," which prohibited gainful employment or commercial activity on Sunday. The Act contained no exception for persons who chose to observe a different sabbath or day of rest, but it did provide that some types of jobs were exempt from the closing requirement, and persons who had to work on Sunday for an employer operating in conformity with those exemptions had to be given a different day off. The Calgary police charged Big M Drug Mart with selling groceries on Sunday in violation of the Act, and Big M defended by challenging the Act as a violation of the "freedom of conscience and religion" protected in the Canadian Charter of Rights and Freedoms.[36] The action resulted in the leading case on freedom of religion in Canada,[37] *R. v. Big M Drug Mart, Ltd.*[38] In this case the Canadian Supreme Court invalidated the Lord's Day Act because it found that it

> works a form of coercion inimical to the spirit of the *Charter* and the dignity of all non-Christians. In proclaiming the standards of the Christian faith, the Act creates a climate hostile to, and gives the appearance of discrimination against, non-Christian Canadians. It takes religious values rooted in Christian morality and, using the force of the state, translates

---

[36] Article 2 of the Canadian Charter provides: "Everyone has the following fundamental freedoms: a) freedom of conscience and religion; b) freedom of thought, belief, opinion and expression, including freedom of the press and other media of communication; c) freedom of peaceful assembly; and d) freedom of association."
[37] Hogg, 1997, 39-4.
[38] [1985] 1 S.C.R. 295.

them into a positive law binding on believers and non-believers alike.[39]

In the United States, in addition to this type of free exercise argument on the basis of intentional discrimination, one could also raise an argument based on the Establishment Clause of the First Amendment to the effect that this kind of statute effectively establishes the majority forms of Christianity, which observe the sabbath on Sunday, over those forms of Christianity and non-Christian religions which recognise a different sabbath. The Canadian Charter does not contain a clause expressly forbidding the establishment of an official church, but the Canadian Court had no trouble distilling from the general freedom of religion the principle that the state is not free to discriminate against the practice of some religions by seeking to compel everyone to follow the practice of any particular religion, a position that would certainly be endorsed by U.S. decisions under the Establishment Clause.[40]

The chief argument against the holding in *Big M* was that, while the Lord's Day Act undoubtedly was originally enacted for the religious purpose of enforcing the Christian sabbath, in more recent times the effect of the Act had come to be the secular one of providing a common day of rest to everyone, whether or not Christian. Thus in effect, one could argue that the law had come to have a secular purpose. The U.S. Supreme Court accepted this argument and sustained similar Sunday closing laws in several cases in the early 1960s.[41] The Supreme Court of Canada ruled that a similar provincial law had a non-discriminatory, secular purpose in a later

---

[39] [1985] 1 C.S.R. at 337.
[40] See, e.g., *Lee v. Weisman*, 505 U.S. 577 (1992) (prayer at public school graduation exercises forbidden by Establishment Clause of the First Amendment).
[41] *McGowan v. Maryland*, 366 U.S. 420. 445 (1961) (rejecting Establishment Clause claim and holding that "Sunday Closing Laws ... have become part and parcel of this great governmental concern wholly apart from their original purposes or connotations"); *Braunfeld v. Brown*, 366 U.S. 599 (1961) (rejecting free exercise claim).

case, *R. v. Edward's Books*.[42] However, in *Edward's Books*, the evidence showed that the statute had from the start been conceived of as serving the secular purpose of providing a common day of rest, as reflected in its title, "Retail Business Holidays Act." In *Big M*, by contrast, the federal "Lord's Day Act" announced its religious purpose in its title, and had been found by numerous court decisions to have a religious purpose. Indeed, under Canada's peculiar form of federalism, the Act would not have been within the federal Parliament's legislative powers to enact criminal law if it had not had the purpose of safeguarding public morality by compelling religious observance.[43] So the Canadian Supreme Court was prevented by the details of Canadian federalism from accepting in *Big M* the common secular rationale for Sunday closing laws.

The argument that laws patently establishing the majority's sabbath as the mandatory day of rest serve the secular purpose of coordinating a general day of rest may smack of self-interested rationalisation. There is some truth, however, to the view that the Sunday rest day has come to have an entirely secular function for many people. But surely the better position is that of Justice Stewart, who would have struck down a Sunday closing law which made no exception for those who celebrated a different sabbath day.[44] In the United States, the law came a step closer to this position in *Sherbert v. Verner*,[45] holding that before a state may deny someone unemployment compensation on the ground that she refused to work on her non-Sunday sabbath, the employer must have offered the employee an accommodation by allowing her time off on her sabbath. However, under Sunday closing statutes that make no

---

[42] [1986] 2 S.C.R. 713. The statute in question provided for an exemption for businesses having no more than seven employees and less than a certain amount of retail space and which were closed on Saturday. One of the defendants was a kosher delicatessen, but it failed to qualify for the statutory exemption because it had too many employees.
[43] [1985] 1 S.C.R. at 354-55 ("Were its purpose not religious but rather the secular goal of enforcing a uniform day of rest from labour, the Act would come under s. 92(13), property and civil rights in the province and, hence, fall under provincial rather than federal competence....")
[44] *Braunfeld v. Brown*, 366 U.S. 599, 616 (1961) (Stewart, J., dissenting).
[45] 374 U.S. 398 (1963). For further discussion of this case, see Appendix I.

accommodation for observance of alternative sabbaths, entrepreneurs who observe the sabbath on days other than Sunday are still put to the Hobson's choice of keeping their business open on their own sabbath or forgoing an extra day's profit in order to observe their own sabbath and obey the Sunday closing law.

II. THE STANDARD OF REVIEW FOR NONDISCRIMINATORY LAWS OF GENERAL APPLICATION

Having disposed of the relatively easy case of intentional discrimination, we come to the nub of the problem in the whole realm of free exercise: what should the standard be by which the courts decide whether or not to approve regulations of general application which are not the product of discriminatory intent but are in fact designed to serve valid, non-discriminatory state interests without any "religious gerrymander"?

Let us consider this problem using the facts of *Employment Division v. Smith*.[46] Two members of the Native American Church, which incorporates certain Native American religious practices, were fired from their jobs with a private organisation providing drug rehabilitation services in the State of Oregon because they had ingested peyote in religious services within the Church. Especially because they were in the business of helping rehabilitate drug users, their use of a proscribed drug was regarded as "work-related misconduct," and they were therefore denied unemployment compensation by the State of Oregon. Peyote is a hallucinogenic drug and its use is generally proscribed by both federal and state law. Adherents of the Native American Church believe that the peyote plant embodies their deity and that eating it is an act of worship and communion. Federal drug law and the drug laws of 23 other states at that time made an exception for the sacramental use of peyote, but the Oregon statute did not, and the Oregon Supreme Court had ruled that it would not read such an exception into the statute. In these circumstances, is the state's denial of unemployment compensation an impermissible restriction on the free exercise of religion? No one contended that Oregon's general law proscribing use of peyote was

---

[46] 494 U.S. 872 (1990).

the result of a "religious gerrymander." In fact all states and the federal government had similar laws. Peyote was recognised as a dangerous drug, and both the federal and state governments had an obvious interest in proscribing its use and preventing traffic in the drug. Does the Free Exercise Clause in effect require Oregon to recognize a religious exemption to its law forbidding the use of peyote? What standard of review should the court apply in reviewing a statute that fails to grant a religious exemption?

The decisions of the courts described in this paper show that there are two or three main types of standards in use today with respect to free exercise claims brought to challenge statutes of general application, that is, statutes which do not distinguish expressly on the grounds of religion and are not the product of religious gerrymanders. (1) In the United States, we find "minimum scrutiny," which means no further review under principles of freedom of religion once the statute in question has been found to be non-discriminatory. Statutory distinctions are also subject to general regulation by the Equal Protection Clause of the Fourteenth Amendment,[47] so equal protection review may be thought of as providing a base level of review, on which religious freedom review builds. In the absence of "suspect classifications" like race or religion, equal protection review has tended to uphold challenged economic or social welfare regulation as long as it can be shown to be *rationally related* to any *legitimate* state interest. This standard is thus understood as a minimal standard of review that rarely justifies invalidating challenged legislation.[48] "Minimum scrutiny" refers to this minimal, baseline

---

[47] The Fourteenth Amendment provides in relevant part: "nor shall any State . . . deny to any person within its jurisdiction the equal protection of the laws." By its terms, the Fourteenth Amendment does not apply to the federal government, but the U.S. Supreme Court has interpreted the Fifth Amendment's guarantee of due process, which applies to the federal government, to include the same protections. See *Bolling v. Sharpe*, 347 U.S. 497 (1954). See generally Nowak & Rotunda, 2000, 633-34.

[48] Nowak & Rotunda, 2000, 639, 644-60 (arguing on the basis of recent decisions that the Supreme Court may be moving to converting the minimal scrutiny under the rationality test to a slightly more demanding test of reasonableness, but noting that the Court's majority has disavowed any change in standard for review of economic and social welfare legislation which does not involve a fundamental constitutional right or a suspect classification).

standard of equal protection review. (2) In the United States, we also find another level of religious freedom review called "strict scrutiny" because it adds to review for non-discrimination the requirement that the reviewing court invalidate the challenged law unless it is *narrowly tailored* to achieve a *compelling* state interest. Strict scrutiny is also applied in equal protection cases, to review laws which involve fundamental constitutional rights or "suspect classifications" like race, religion, or national origin, which have historically been used for invidious discriminatory purposes.[49] In cases covered by strict scrutiny under either the Free Exercise Clause of the First Amendment or under the Equal Protection Clause, the courts subject the challenged government regulation to a high standard of scrutiny. (3) The ECHR uses a standard of review that inquires into whether an infringement on free exercise is "prescribed by law" and "necessary in a democratic state." I argue below that this standard is really a form of "strict scrutiny" or a somewhat less demanding standard we might call "intermediate scrutiny."[50] The Canadian Charter for the Protection of Rights and Freedoms uses a very similar standard. The German Constitutional Court tends to use a balancing approach, which looks at all the interests involved, both state interests and potentially competing individual interests, and seeks to find a way to balance them all without sacrificing any completely. This approach is also, I argue, a form either of strict or intermediate scrutiny.

A. Minimum and Strict Scrutiny in the United States

The United States Supreme Court took its earliest approach to this issue by making a sharp distinction between religious belief and religiously motivated action. The Free Exercise Clause, the Court held, protects belief only, not action. The Court announced this reading of the Free Exercise Clause in the 1879 case of *Reynolds v.*

---

[49] Ibid., 639-40.

[50] The U.S. Supreme Court has developed an intermediate standard of review in equal protection cases, especially those involving gender classifications and illegitimacy classifications. "Under the intermediate standard of review, the Justices will not uphold a classification unless they find that the classification has a 'substantial relationship' to an 'important' government interest." Nowak & Rotunda, 2000, 641.

United States,[51] a case that took place against the backdrop of rather savage persecution of the Mormons in the nineteenth century and their sometimes violent response. In *Reynolds*, the Court upheld the bigamy conviction of a leading Mormon. Under the *Reynolds* approach, the state could not tell a person what their religious beliefs should be, but the state could regulate action, even action thought to be required by one's religion, as the Mormons then regarded polygamy to be.[52] It is hard to square this distinction with the language of the First Amendment, which by the term "free exercise" of religion suggests that it covers more than mere belief, but the distinction had been made by Jefferson shortly after the adoption of the First Amendment.[53]

By the middle of the twentieth century, the *Reynolds* approach had been soundly repudiated in favour of the "strict scrutiny" standard to be discussed next.[54] But in 1990, in the *Smith* case itself, a narrow majority of five justices resuscitated *Reynolds*. Oregon's drug law was a neutral law of general application which regulated conduct, not belief, Justice Scalia wrote for the Court, so there was no requirement for the state to make an exception for sacramental use. According to Justice Scalia, the state cannot regulate religious action solely because it is religious action or because of the religious beliefs that the action represents. He gives as examples of prohibited regulation a statute banning the casting of statutes to be used for worship or the bowing down before a golden calf. But those kinds of regulations discriminate expressly on religious grounds because they use religiously defined categories. Regulations of general applicability burden religious exercise only "incidentally" if they do not use

---

[51] 98 U.S. 145 (1879).
[52] Noonan & Gaffney, 2000, 288 (at that time Mormons "exalted [polygamy] as the highest form of marriage").
[53] 98 U.S. at 164 (describing Jefferson's address to the Danbury Baptist Association).
[54] See, e.g., *Cantwell v. Connecticut*, 310 U.S.296, 303 (1940) (protecting religious proselytisation on public streets and stating, "Thus the [First] Amendment embraces two concepts – freedom to believe and freedom to act. The first is absolute but, in the nature of things, the second cannot be"); *Wisconsin v. Yoder*, 406 U.S. 205, 241(1972) (Douglas, J., dissenting in part) ("[t]he Court rightly rejects the notion that actions, even though religiously grounded, are always outside the protection of the Free Exercise Clause of the First Amendment").

religious categories and are not the product of attempts to discriminate against any religion or religious belief. Expressly citing *Reynolds*, Scalia's opinion holds that the Free Exercise Clause does not impose any barrier to generally applicable, non-discriminatory regulations, even if they impose such incidental burdens. Religious belief is thus protected by the Free Exercise Clause, as well as by the general protections for free speech in the First Amendment, but religiously motivated action is not protected any more than non-religious action from non-discriminatory, generally applicable government regulation. In 1993 in *Church of Lukumi Babalu Aye*, a majority of six justices reaffirmed the basic *Smith* minimum scrutiny standard, but held it inapplicable, as we have discussed, on the grounds that the ordinances in question in that case were not neutral, but the result of intentional discrimination against Santeria. As explained above, the result of the *Smith* case is to remit religious exercise in cases involving generally applicable, non-discriminatory regulation to the same minimum standard of review that the Equal Protection Clause imposes.

In between *Reynolds* and *Smith*, the U.S. Supreme Court had seemed to settle on the "compelling state interest" test as the appropriate standard for judging statutes of general applicability challenged by free exercise claims. The Court applied the test, for example, in the case of *Sherbert v. Verner*[55] in 1963 to hold that the state could not withhold unemployment compensation from a member of the Seventh-day Adventist Church who was fired from her job for refusing to work on Saturday, the sabbath day of her faith. Having found that the policy of refusing to pay unemployment compensation to workers who are discharged because of religious scruples against working on a particular day constituted an infringement of the free exercise right, the Court stated, "We must next consider whether some compelling state interest enforced in the eligibility provisions of the [state's] statute justifies the substantial infringement of [the Seventh-day Adventist's] First Amendment right."[56] The Court held that no such interest could be shown in that case.

---

[55] 374 U.S. 398 (1963).
[56] 374 U.S. at 406.

If we apply the strict scrutiny standard to the facts of *Smith*, the peyote case, the religious claimant does not automatically win, but strict scrutiny obviously makes it more difficult for the state to prevail. Application of the "compelling state interest" test has quite often resulted in court decisions striking down the state regulation. As the Court said in *Church of Lukumi Babalu Aye*, "A law that targets religious conduct for distinctive treatment or advances legitimate governmental interests only against conduct with a religious motivation will survive strict scrutiny only in rare cases."[57] The three dissenting justices in *Smith* thought that Oregon could not show a compelling interest in refusing to make an exception for sacramental use of peyote, especially in light of Oregon's long history of non-prosecution of religious violators of the ban on use of peyote, but Justice O'Connor concurred in the judgment against the religious claimants on the grounds that Oregon did have a compelling interest in banning use of the drug and suppressing trade in it. Had the "compelling state interest" test been applied to the ban on Mormon polygamy at issue in *Reynolds*, it seems likely that the Court would have found the bigamy statutes to serve compelling state interests, but it is, of course, impossible to be sure.

In the wake of *Smith*, minimum scrutiny applies today in the United States to some free exercise claims and strict scrutiny applies to others. The Court's decisions in this area have created a complex and somewhat unclear rule that incorporates both standards but assigns them to different cases. The problem has been complicated even more by several congressional attempts to overrule or limit *Smith*, and the waters have been muddied even more by the fact that the Supreme Court has invalidated one of those attempts at least in part on constitutional grounds. Since the goal in this section is to understand how these different standards of review are applied by the courts, the precise details of current U.S. doctrine need not detain us here, but the interested reader can find them in Appendix I. For present purposes, suffice it to say that the application of minimum scrutiny to free exercise claims has been highly controversial in the United States.

---

[57] 508 U.S. at 546.

B. Limits "Necessary to a Democratic Society": The European Convention, the Canadian Charter, and the Regulation of Proselytisation

The 1950 European Convention for the Protection of Human Rights and Fundamental Freedoms (ECHR) uses a standard similar to strict scrutiny. Article 9 states:

> 1. Everyone has the right to freedom of thought, conscience, and religion; this right includes freedom to change his religion or belief and freedom, either alone or in community with others and in public or private, to manifest his religion or belief, in worship, teaching, practice and observance.
> 2. Freedom to manifest one's religion or beliefs shall be subject only to such limitations as are prescribed by law and are necessary to a democratic society in the interests of public safety, for the protection of public order, health or morals, or for the protection of the rights and freedoms of others.

Similarly, the Canadian Charter of Rights and Freedoms guarantees freedom of religion in Section 2, but provides for general limitations on Charter rights in Section 1, which states that the Charter guarantees rights and freedoms "subject only to such reasonable limits prescribed by law as can be demonstrably justified in a free and democratic society."[58]

To see what kind of standard of review the courts deduce from this type of guarantee of religious freedom, we will examine two decisions by the European Court of Human Rights (ECtHR) involving extensive interpretation of Article 9 of the ECHR. The first, *Kokkinakis v. Greece*,[59] involved a Jehovah's Witness who had been imprisoned several times for violating Greek law which criminalised "proselytism." A criminal statute defined proselytism as

---

[58] Although it is not relevant to the analysis in this paper, it should be noted that Section 33 also provides for express legislative override of Charter rights and freedoms.

[59] 260 Eur. Ct. H.R. (ser. A) (1993), reprinted in 17 E.H.R.R. 397 (1993).

any direct or indirect attempt to intrude on the religious beliefs or a person of a different religious persuasion (*eterodoxos*), with the aim of undermining those beliefs, either by any kind of inducement or promise of an inducement or moral support or material assistance, or by fraudulent means or by taking advantage of his inexperience, trust, need, low intellect or naïvety.[60]

Kokkinakis was charged with having violated this law because he and his wife visited the wife of a cantor in the Greek Orthodox Church in her home, and Kokkinakis tried for ten to fifteen minutes to persuade her to convert to the faith of Jehovah's Witnesses. According to the Greek courts, while he was in the cantor's wife's home, Kokkinakis read from Scripture, interpreted it in light of the teachings of Jehovah's Witnesses, spoke of their pacifist views, and offered her books about their faith, including one containing professions of faith by various Jehovah's Witnesses. The Crete Court of Appeal found that he had "importunately tried, directly and indirectly, to undermine her religious beliefs."[61]

By a six-to-three decision, the ECtHR ruled that by his conviction Greece violated Mr. Kokkinakis's religious freedom. The ECtHR had no trouble finding that the criminal sanctions interfered with his freedom "to manifest his religion or belief." The Court stated, "Bearing witness in words and deeds is bound up with the existence of religious convictions."[62] The chief issue in the case was under Section 2 of Article 9, the so-called "limitations" clause, which required Greece, in order to defend the conviction, to show that the criminal sanction was (1) prescribed by law, (2) directed at one or more of the legitimate aims set out in the limitations clause, and (3) necessary in a democratic society for achieving them. The Court found that the criminal law in this case was not so vague as to justify a finding that the limitation was not imposed by "law."[63] Without much discussion, the Court accepted that the aim of the statute was that of protecting the religious beliefs and dignity of other people,

---

[60] 260 Eur. Ct. H.R. at 12 (¶ 16).
[61] Ibid., 8, 9 (¶¶ 7, 10).
[62] Ibid., 17 (¶ 31).
[63] Ibid., 19-20 (¶¶ 40-41).

including the Orthodox majority. Such a purpose seems to fit the catalogue of acceptable purposes in Section 2 of Article 9, which includes "protection of the rights and freedoms of others."[64]

But the Court ruled against Greece on the third prong of the test. While the Court noted that it has consistently shown deference to the Contracting States subject to the ECHR, something which the Court expresses as granting them a "margin of appreciation," it held that its task was

> to determine whether the measures taken at national level were justified in principle and proportionate. In order to rule on this latter point, the Court must weigh the requirements of the protection of the rights and liberties of others against the conduct of which the applicant stood accused.[65]

The Court recognised a distinction between "bearing Christian witness and improper proselytism."[66] The majority of the Court thought that the Greek criminal law in effect attempted to follow this distinction, but the Court found that the Greek courts in this case had not. In particular, "the Greek courts established the applicant's liability by merely reproducing the wording of [the criminal statute] and did not sufficiently specify in what way the accused had attempted to convince his neighbour by improper means. None of the facts they set out warrants that finding."[67] Therefore, the Court ruled, "it has not been shown that the applicant's conviction was justified in the circumstances of the case by a pressing social need. The contested measure therefore does not appear to have been proportionate to the legitimate aim pursued or, consequently, "necessary in a democratic society . . . for the protection of the rights and freedoms of others.'"[68]

One could argue with the way the Court applied the standard of review. Judge Pettiti argued in his partly concurring opinion that the Greek legislation itself was facially invalid under Article 9 of the

---

[64] Ibid., 20 (¶ 44).
[65] Ibid., 21 (¶ 47).
[66] Ibid., (¶ 48).
[67] Ibid., (¶ 49).
[68] Ibid.

ECHR because it allowed conviction for "proselytism that is not respectable."[69] According to Judge Pettiti, "[f]reedom of religion and conscience certainly entails accepting proselytism, even where it is 'not respectable'."[70] In his concurring opinion,[71] Judge Martens took the view that Article 9 should be interpreted to forbid absolutely making it a criminal offence to attempt to induce someone to change his religion.[72] But the majority decision at least protects the applicant from a conviction for merely professing his belief and trying to persuade someone of another religion to convert. It cannot be permissible for the state to criminalise that kind of activity, or even to provide civil remedies against such activity if freedom of religion is to have any meaning.

In 1996, the ECtHR decided *Manoussakis v. Greece*,[73] another quite similar freedom of religion case under Article 9, in much the same way. Again the case involved Greek efforts to restrict proselytism. Another Jehovah's Witness was convicted of operating a place of worship without obtaining the prior authorisation of the Minister of Education and Religious Affairs, as required by Greek law. Under the statute, the Minister was supposed to consult with authorities of the Greek Orthodox Church before issuing or withholding his authorisation. The ECtHR reversed the conviction, finding that it violated Article 9. It applied the same standard it had used in *Kokkinakis*, basing its holding on a finding that the infringement on Manoussakis' free exercise right was not "necessary in a democratic society" because of the "far-reaching interference by the political, administrative and ecclesiastical authorities with the exercise of religious freedom." The court noted that the formal provisions of the law conferred wide discretion on local officials to deny authorisations discriminatorily and in fact the state had "tended to use the possibilities afforded by the above-mentioned provisions to impose rigid, or indeed prohibitive, conditions on practice of religious beliefs

---

[69] Ibid., 25 (Pettiti, J., concurring in part).
[70] Ibid., 26.
[71] Judge Martens styles his opinion a "partly dissenting" one, but since he supports the ruling of the majority for other reasons, his would be regarded under U.S. usage as a concurring opinion, and I have used that terminology.
[72] Ibid., 37 (¶ 13) (Martens, J., concurring).
[73] 1996-IV Eur. Ct. H.R. Rep. Judgments & Dec. 1346 (1996).

by certain non-Orthodox movements, in particular Jehovah's Witnesses."[74]

This aspect of the decision is very similar to an exception to minimum scrutiny the *Smith* case made for situations in which officials are given over-broad discretion to create individualised exemptions to a regulatory burden.[75] It also agrees with the holding in *Cantwell v. Connecticut* that "to condition the solicitation of aid for the perpetuation of religious views or systems upon a licence, the grant of which rests in the exercise of a determination by state authority as to what is a religious cause, is to lay a forbidden burden upon the exercise of liberty protected by the Constitution."[76] It should also be noted that in the course of its opinion the ECtHR firmly held that the free exercise right under the ECHR "excludes any discretion on the part of the State to determine whether religious beliefs or the means used to express such beliefs are legitimate," thus agreeing with the similar statements already mentioned by the U.S. and German courts.

There is not time and space to deal here with all the ramifications of the problem of proselytism. However, we should note that proselytism does sometimes involve abuses with which states may legitimately concern themselves. Some of these abuses can best be regulated, not by defining new crimes specifically involving proselytism, but by applying already-existing laws that apply to the abusive behaviour itself. For example, there was some suggestion in *Kokkinakis* that the defendant hid from the cantor's wife his proselytising purpose until after he had gained entrance to her home – although it appears that he did nothing more devious than appearing at her front door saying he was bearing "good news" and persisting until he gained admittance.[77] If he had truly engaged in fraud in order to gain admittance – for example, by masquerading as a police officer – it seems that the state should be able to sanction that behaviour in some way, including perhaps using the criminal law. The

---

[74] Ibid., 1365. For a more recent case basically following *Kokkinakis*, see *Larissis and Others v. Greece*, 27 EHRR 329 (1999) (ECtHR 1998-I, No. 65, February 24, 1998), discussed in Nowak & Vospernik, 2001, 15-16.
[75] 494 U.S. at 882-84; for further discussion of case, see Appendix I.
[76] 310 U.S. 296, 307 (1940).
[77] 260 Eur. Ct. H.R. at 31 (Valticos, J., dissenting).

state should certainly be able to sanction a proselytiser who tries to convert at the point of a sword or the muzzle of a gun. But, as Judge Martens' concurrence argues, the state should regulate the fraud or misuse of force directly. The fact that the fraud or misuse of force is linked to proselytism should not affect the definition of the wrong or the sanction at all. "Brainwashing" of converts should be a criminal act if it corresponds to a regular criminal offence, such as assault, battery, or false imprisonment, but not because it is linked to proselytism.

Beyond that point, however, there may be further concerns that might justify some state regulation of proselytism, at least on behalf of some weak and poorly protected groups. Makau Wa Mutua has lamented the great harm that the evangelising religions, Christianity and Islam, have done to indigenous African cultures and suggested that a right to evangelise may need to be tempered in order to permit the preservation of what indigenous culture is left.[78] In *Wisconsin v. Yoder*[79] the U.S. Supreme Court held that freedom of religion requires the State of Wisconsin to exempt Old Order Amish children from compulsory education after the eighth grade so that the Amish might insulate and preserve their culture from the dominant secular culture. The great solicitude the U.S. Supreme Court shows for the Old Order Amish indicates a concern somewhat similar to Wa Mutua's. Obviously, the attempt by Greece to insulate Orthodox Christianity, the religion that is followed by the vast majority of its citizens, raises much more serious "establishment" issues than would a case in which the state tries to shelter a weak minority. But even majority religions might in certain circumstances be so weak as to warrant protection. Harold Berman has given a sympathetic account of the argument by the Russian Orthodox Patriarchate to be allowed at least for some time to shield ethnic Russians from foreign evangelists, on the grounds that the Orthodox Church in Russia, with which historically the identity of ethnic Russians has been bound up, is actually quite weak because of the history of suppression of the Church by Communism, and also on the grounds of the tumultuous political, economic, and spiritual changes that the society is currently

---

[78] Wa Mutua, 1996.
[79] 406 U.S. 205 (1972).

undergoing.⁸⁰ Berman does not clearly endorse this argument himself, but his pleading for understanding the position constitutes considerable advocacy. Islamic groups might want to raise similar arguments to restrict Christian missionaries from evangelising in an unrestricted manner in the Middle East – or perhaps even in Northern Nigeria. I am not clear that all these majority groups should necessarily be protected in this way, but I think the issue is worthy of more discussion.

For present purposes, our main concern is to compare the way the ECHR and Canadian standards compare to the other standards of review. The Canadian standard, based on the similar wording in the "limitations clause" of Section 1 of the Canadian Charter (guaranteeing the Charter freedoms "subject only to such reasonable limits prescribed by law as can be demonstrably justified in a free and democratic society"), is very similar, but perhaps a bit more elaborate, involving (1) a determination of whether there is an infringement of a Charter right, (2) whether the infringement was prescribed by law, and (3) whether the infringement is within reasonable limits demonstrably justified in a free and democratic society. Satisfying the last requirement, involves establishing the following four points:

1. Sufficiently important objective: The law must pursue an objective that is sufficiently important to justify limiting a Charter right.
2. Rational connection: The law must be rationally connected to the objective.
3. Least drastic means: The law must impair the right no more than is necessary to accomplish the objective.
4. Proportionate effect: The law must not have a disproportionately severe effect on the persons to whom it applies.⁸¹

---

⁸⁰ Berman, 1996.
⁸¹ Hogg, 2002, 35-16 to 35-17. The Canadian Supreme Court applied the Charter's standard in *Big M*, but the discussion of that case, see Section I.B., above, focused on the point about discrimination instead of the standard of review. A year after *Big M*, the Canadian Supreme Court elaborated the standard of review for all cases involving the "limitations clause" of Section 1 of

Nearly all the decided cases have turned on step 3, the least drastic means test. I think it is clear that both the Canadian and the ECHR standards of review are basically variants of strict scrutiny. Neither of these standards uses the term "compelling state interest," but unlike *Smith*'s minimum scrutiny standard, these standards do not permit all limitations on free exercise as long as they are the product of non-discriminatory law of general application. The phrase "limitations justified in a free and democratic society" seems to require a comparative law exercise free of balancing. If that were true, I would be concerned that the standard might set the bar for infringement too low. All courts surveyed here have on occasion approved of various forms of accommodation for the majority religion that arguably has resulted in coercion of the minority religions. At the end of the day, however, the courts applying this kind of standard are not concerned with comparative law but with making a judgment about how important the asserted state interests for infringing the free exercise right are. The catalogue of interests recognized in Section 2 of Article 9 of the ECHR as justifying infringement of religious freedom – public safety, public order, health, or morals, or the rights and freedoms of third parties – are most likely to qualify under the compelling state interest test in the United States. The "least restrictive means" test in U.S. strict scrutiny corresponds quite literally to the "least drastic means" or "minimal impairment" standard in the Canadian court's test, and both seem covered by the "proportionality" analysis applied by the ECtHR. It should also be noted that the ECtHR's decision in *Kokkinakis* uses a form of balancing of competing interests that seems somewhat similar to the German balancing test to be described next.

C. Balancing in Germany: Accommodations for Religious Objections to Blood Transfusions

In the *Blood Transfusion Case*,[82] the German Federal Constitutional Court had to decide whether the husband of a woman who died for

---

the Charter in R. v. *Oakes*, [1986] 1 S.C.R. 103. Professor Hogg's summary of the standard of review is based on the test applied in *Oakes*.
[82] Kommers, 1997, 449-52 (translating in part 32 BVerfGE 98 (1971)).

lack of a blood transfusion in the course of giving birth could be convicted under a statute criminalising failure to render assistance. The wife had refused to consent to a transfusion on religious grounds and the husband, who shared her religious views, did not try to persuade her to consent. His failure was alleged to be a violation of the criminal statute imposing a general duty to render assistance if possible, but the Court held that:

> Criminal punishment, no matter what the sentence, is an inappropriate sanction for this constellation of facts under any goal of the criminal justice system (retribution, prevention, rehabilitation of the offender). The duty of all public authority to respect serious religious convictions, . . . must lead to a relaxation of criminal laws when an actual conflict between a generally accepted legal duty and a dictate of faith results in a spiritual crisis for the offender that, in view of the punishment labelling him a criminal, would represent an excessive social reaction violative of his human dignity.[83]

In other words, the Court weighed the severity of the infringement on religious freedom against the state's interests in criminalising such conduct, and in this case found that the state interests were not significant enough to justify the imposition of a criminal sanction.[84] Like strict scrutiny and the somewhat similar ECHR and Canadian Charter standards, balancing places some limit on the individual right

---

[83] Ibid., 451.
[84] In upholding the right of the Old Order Amish to exempt their children past the eighth grade from state compulsory schooling laws that extend through the twelfth grade, the U.S. Supreme Court held that "a State's interest in universal education, however highly we rank it, is not totally free from a balancing process when it impinges on fundamental rights and interests, such as those specifically protected by the Free Exercise Clause of the First Amendment, and the traditional interest of parents with respect to the religious upbringing of their children . . . ." *Wisconsin v. Yoder*, 406 U.S. 205, 214 (1972). In the United States, however, this version of balancing has been abandoned for the strict scrutiny, which is sometimes referred to as "balancing" because it implicitly asks the court to weigh the state interest against the individual freedom to see if it is sufficiently "compelling."

of religious exercise. It suggests an inquiry into the significance or "weight" of both the asserted state interest and the individual one though rhetorically it does not sound as demanding for the state interest as strict scrutiny.

U.S. courts would give similar protection to an individual who on religious grounds refuses a blood transfusion for himself that doctors believe to be medically necessary.[85] But what distinguishes the German decision is that it required a religious accommodation in the criminal law in a situation where the violation affected the health of another person. U.S. courts have routinely upheld the power of the state to force a pregnant mother to undergo medical procedures to save her or her foetus[86] and they have upheld the prosecution of parents who on religious grounds failed to obtain medical treatment for their minor children who died as a result.[87] The Canadian Supreme Court has similarly upheld the power of the state to order medical care for a child over the religious objections of the parents.[88]

The German Constitutional Court's use of balancing might seem remarkable in light of the fairly absolute language in Article 4 of the German Basic Law guaranteeing the right of religious exercise. The point is often made that it "contains no reservation clause that would allow the regulation of religion by law. It therefore imposes an absolute ban on any law regulating religious belief. Equally absolute is the ban on any direct regulation of the free exercise of religion."[89] Nevertheless, according to Donald Kommers, a leading U.S. scholar of German constitutional law, German law provides that where free exercise conflicts with the general peace and safety of the community, "the job of the courts is to balance the interests of the individual and society. If in the context of a particular case the individual's claim can

---

[85] See, e.g., *Aste v. Brooks*, 205 N.E.2d 435 (Ill. 1965) (court-ordered transfusion against religious beliefs of adult with no minor children constituted a violation of free exercise).
[86] See Noonan & Gaffney, 2001, 554-55 (discussing cases).
[87] See ibid. at 555-57 (discussing cases; some states have enacted accommodations).
[88] *B. v. Children's Aid Society of Metropolitan Toronto*, [1995] 1 S.C.R. 315.
[89] Kommers, 1997, 448-49.

be sustained without significantly burdening the good order of the community, the claim should usually be upheld."[90]

The balancing approach might seem to invite the court to weigh the importance, not only of the state interests in regulation, but also of the individual interest in the religious practice at issue. If it did, it would be objectionable on the same grounds as the *Zaheeruddin* case in Pakistan, discussed in Section I.A., supra, in which the Pakistan Supreme Court decided what was "essential and integral" to the religion at issue. The German Constitutional Court seems to have avoided this pitfall through its broad definition of the scope of belief and action protected by Article 4 of the German Basic Law. Rather than making the sharp dichotomy between belief and action which we have seen the U.S. Supreme Court employ in *Reynolds*, the German Constitutional Court held in the *Blood Transfusion Case* that freedom of religion

> encompasses not only the internal freedom to believe or not to believe but also the external freedom to manifest, profess, and propagate one's belief. This includes the right of the individual to orient his conduct on the teachings of his religion and to act according to his internal convictions. Freedom of belief protects not only convictions based on imperative principles of faith; it also encompasses religious convictions which, while not requiring an exclusively religious response to a concrete situation, nevertheless view this response as the best and most appropriate means to deal with the situation in keeping with this belief. Otherwise the fundamental right of freedom of religion could not develop fully.[91]

By taking such a broad view of the right, the Court did not make the mistake of considering how important to the husband's overall religious views the religious scruples against blood transfusions were. Rather, the Court accorded great respect to these views. It held:

---

[90] Ibid., 449.
[91] Ibid., 450.

One cannot reproach the complainant for not trying to convince his wife to give up their shared convictions [that taking a blood transfusion would violate their faith]. He was bound to her by their common conviction that prayer was the "better way." His behaviour, and that of his wife, was a profession of their shared faith. It was supported by mutual respect for each other's opinions in a question concerning life and death, and by the faith that this opinion was right. In this type of case, criminal law cannot require two people with the same beliefs to influence one another so as to convince themselves of the danger of their religious decision.[92]

Balancing is thus similar to strict scrutiny in that it does not merely uphold state regulation as long as it is neutral and not intentionally discriminatory. Balancing seems rhetorically less demanding of the state interest than strict scrutiny, but the result in the case of religious scruples against blood transfusions seems more protective of religious freedom in Germany than in the United States – arguably too much so since it failed to protect the interest of the unborn child. We will take up further examples of German balancing in the next section.

III. STATE ACCOMMODATION FOR FREE EXERCISE RIGHTS OF THE MAJORITY: PRAYER, CRUCIFIXES, AND HEADSCARVES IN THE PUBLIC SCHOOLS

The Canadian Supreme Court case of *Big M* and the ECtHR cases of *Kokkinakis* and *Manoussakis* have already introduced us to the special problems that accompany the attempt of governments to accommodate religious practice, especially that of the majority. There is always the question whether the accommodation of one religion's practice effectively limits the practice of other religions. Closely related to that question, there is, in U.S. terms – also relevant to Nigeria's constitution – the problem of "establishment": does the

---

[92] Ibid., 451.

accommodation associate the state so closely with the accommodated religion that it effectively has been "established" by the state?

Let us consider these problems further by looking at a series of German Constitutional Court decisions and their analogues, principally in the United States, that involve religion in the public schools. This comparison will highlight the very different roles the German and U.S. constitutions envision for the state to play in protecting religious freedom.

The German *School Prayer Case*[93] of 1979 arose out of two diametrically opposite complaints. One parent claimed that the administrative prohibition of prayer in the interdenominational (Christian) school his children attended violated his free exercise rights, which he alleged to include a right to determine the care and education – including religious education – of his children; another parent challenged the practice of "voluntary" prayers in the interdenominational school his children attended as a violation of his same rights. The administrative prohibition in the first school was in response to complaints from parents like the second complainant, who objected to school prayers, even on a voluntary basis. The German Constitutional Court dealt with both complaints in the same case and ruled that prayer in public schools was constitutional as long as it was truly voluntary. A key aspect of its opinion is the following passage:

> If the state permits school prayer in interdenominational state schools, then it does nothing more than exercise its right to establish a school system pursuant to Article 7(1) of the Basic Law, so that pupils who wish to do so may acknowledge their religious beliefs, even if only in the limited form of a universal and transdenominational appeal to God....
>
> To be sure, the state must balance this affirmative freedom to worship as expressed by permitting school prayer with the negative freedom of confession of other parents and pupils opposed to school prayer. Basically, [schools] may

---

[93] Ibid., 461-66 (translating in part 52 BVerfGE 223 (1979)).

achieve this balance by guaranteeing that participation be voluntary for pupils and teachers. . . .[94]

The Court found the arrangements in this case to be voluntary for several reasons: the prayers were spoken only at the beginning or end of class for a short period, so a student could simply avoid being in the classroom at that time or the student could remain in the classroom but not take part in the prayer. The Court recognised that such behaviour would mark the child as different. The Court even conceded that "[t]his distinction could be unbearable for the person concerned if it should place him in the role of an outsider and serve to discriminate against him as opposed to the rest of the class. Indeed, the pupil in a classroom is in a different, much more difficult position than an adult who publicly discloses his dissenting conviction by not participating in certain events."[95] Yet despite this sensitivity to the particular vulnerabilities of schoolchildren, the German Constitutional Court concluded that there was no danger of coercion in this situation.

The Court took a very different view of the issue of coercion, however, in the *Classroom Crucifix II Case*[96] in 1995. In that case it invalidated a Bavarian law which required display of a crucifix in every elementary school classroom. The Court ruled that if any student objected to the display, it would have to be removed. The Court was clear that the cross was a religious symbol. Some people had argued that the cross could be seen, not as a religious symbol, but in view of the deep historical connection between Christianity and Europe, as a cultural symbol.[97] To do so, would, the Court said, be "a profanation contrary to the self-understanding of Christians and the Christian church."[98] The Bavarian statute violated the state's duty to be neutral on matters of religion because the presence of the cross

---

[94] Ibid., 464-65.
[95] Ibid., 465.
[96] Ibid., 472-82 (translating in part 93 BVerfGE 1 (1995)).
[97] Similar arguments were raised recently in defense of an Italian statute requiring display of the cross in all public schools, which a local judge in Ofena found to be inconsistent with the Italian constitution's guarantee that all religions are "equally free before the law." Bruni, 2003, A4.
[98] Kommers, 1997, 475.

"constitutes a deeply moving appeal; it underscores the faith commitment it symbolises ...This is particularly true with young and impressionable people who are still learning to develop their critical capacities and principles of right conduct."[99]

One could argue that the German Constitutional Court got these two cases exactly wrong. Does it not appear that a crucifix on the wall exercises much less coercion over a young person than a prayer led by the teacher in the classroom at the beginning or end of class? One can ignore a cross on the wall by simply looking away, but a child who wishes to dissent from school-room prayer has to do something much more public, either by leaving the room or by remaining silent while others pray.

The comparison with comparable U.S. cases also suggests questions about the German decisions. In *Stone v. Graham*,[100] the U.S. Supreme Court invalidated a Kentucky statute similar to the Bavarian statute in the *Crucifix Case*. The Kentucky statute required the posting of a copy of the Ten Commandments in every public classroom in the state. The Court simply held that the Act "has no secular legislative purpose." Thus the *Crucifix Case* is quite understandable from an American perspective. The German *School Prayer Case*, however, contrasts sharply with United States Supreme Court rulings on school-sponsored prayer, which it has uniformly disapproved.[101] In *Lee v. Weisman*,[102] the Justice Kennedy's opinion for the Court indicated that the pressure on a student who wishes not to participate

---

[99] Ibid. 0
[100] 449 U.S. 39 (1980).
[101] See, e.g., *Engel v. Vitale*, 370 U.S. 421 (1962); *Abington School District v. Schempf*, 374 U.S. 203 (1963); *Wallace v. Jaffree*, 472 U.S. 38 (1985); *Lee v. Weisman*, 505 U.S. 577 (1992). The Court did, however, uphold the constitutionality of a federal statute requiring public secondary schools which receive federal financial assistance to give to student religious groups the same access to school meeting facilities as given to any other student groups, *Board of Educ. of the Westside Community Schools*, see n. 37 above, thus facilitating student-initiated, student-led voluntary prayer in schools.

In Canada, the Ontario Court of Appeal has similarly disapproved regulations requiring prayer in public schools. *Canada Civil Liberties Ass'n v. Ontario*, (1990) 71 O.R. (2d) 341 (C.A.); *Zylberberg v. Sudbury Board of Education*, (1988) 65 O.R. (2d) 641 (C.A.). See generally, Hogg, 2002, 39-9.
[102] 505 U.S. 577 (1992).

in a school-led prayer "though subtle and indirect, can be as real as any overt compulsion. ...[F]or the dissenter of high school age, who has a reasonable perception that she is being forced by the State to pray in a manner her conscience will not allow, the injury is no less real."[103]

Is it possible that the two German cases illustrate the process of development in German law? The *School Prayer Case* came first and in that case, the Court showed itself somewhat sensitive to the pressures that school prayer put on students. Was it at that time not yet convinced that this kind of pressure was really serious? Or was it simply not yet willing to brave the enormous public outcry that tends to accompany court decisions invalidating broadly popular accommodations to the religious practice of the majority? In any event, the *Crucifix Case* is the later of the two cases and might be read to cast some doubt on whether the judgment about coercion in the *School Prayer Case* would be sustained today. In fact, the *Crucifix Case* was greeted with extraordinary levels of public outrage in Germany, so much so that Justice Dieter Grimm took the highly unusual step of publishing a major statement in one of Germany's leading newspapers, the *Frankfurter Allgemeine Zeitung*, "argu[ing] for the rule of law and call[ing] for obedience to the Court's decision, even by those who strongly disagree with it."[104]

The cases also demonstrate deep differences between the German and U.S. constitutional texts insofar as they deal with religion in public schools. One must start, certainly, with Article 7(3) of the German Basic Law, which provides:

> Religious instruction shall form part of the ordinary curriculum in state and municipal schools, except in secular schools. Without prejudice to the state's right of supervision, religious instruction shall be given in accordance with the tenets of the religious communities. No teacher may be obliged against his will to give religious instruction.

Thus, unlike the United States, whose constitution makes no mention of religion in public schools, but much more like Nigeria, whose

---

[103] Ibid., 593.
[104] Monsma & Soper, 1997, 182. See also Kommers, 1997, 482-84.

constitution does,[105] Germany is constituted as a legal order whose constitution explicitly provides for religious, that is non-secular, state schools as well as secular schools, and for religious instruction in all the state schools except the so-called "secular" ones. The Constitutional Court had already upheld state "interdenom-inational" – that is, Christian – schools in the 1975 *Interdenominational School Case*.[106]

Today, most state schools in Germany are either interdenominational or confessional, and they provide religious instruction, but the student and his or her parents can choose what type to take and the content of the courses is controlled, not by the state schools, but by the religious authorities of the principal confessions. This system illustrates the "cooperative" relationship that is said to exist between the German state and the chief religions.[107] In 1948, the United States Supreme Court found this kind of cooperation to constitute a violation of the Establishment Clause under the then prevalent test requiring strict separation of church and state.[108] Today the dominant value in U.S. Establishment Clause jurisprudence has arguably shifted to neutrality.[109] Religion is not so categorically excluded from the public schools, but the state must be scrupulously neutral, and neutrality is interpreted to mean avoiding discrimination for or against any religion.[110]

---

[105] Section 38(2) of the Nigerian Constitution presupposes that religious instruction will be provided and religious ceremonies and observances will be conducted in public schools because it implicitly sanctions such practices, subject only to the following limitation: "No one attending any place of education shall be required to receive religious instruction or to take part in or attend any religious ceremony or observance if such instruction, ceremony, or observance relates to a religion other than his own, or a religion not approved by his parent or guardian." As quoted and discussed in Ostien & Gamaliel, 2002.
[106] Kommers, 1997, 467-70 (translating in part 41 BVerfGE 29 (1975)).
[107] Monsma & Soper, 1997, 176-180.
[108] *McCollum v. Board of Education*, 333 U.S. 203 (1948) (invalidating released time system for religious instruction in public schools by private groups).
[109] Gedicks, 2003, 18.
[110] See, e.g., *Agostini v. Felton*, 521 U.S. 203, 234(1997) (holding that "a federally funded program providing supplemental, remedial instruction to disadvantaged children on a neutral basis is not invalid under the Establishment Clause when

In Germany, the state must also be "neutral," but that word can mean in certain circumstances cooperation with religion.[111] The dissenting opinion of Justices Seidl, Söllner, and Haas in the *Crucifix Case* makes this point most clearly by stating:

> The state has a constitutional mandate to remain neutral in religious and ideological matters. But the principle of neutrality must not be construed as indifference toward such matters. The church-state articles of the Weimar Constitution, which have been incorporated into Article 140 of the Basic Law, envision neutrality in the sense of cooperation between the state, churches, and religious communities. These articles [may even require the state] to support churches and religious communities.[112]

The German version of neutrality reflects the German political economy, which imposes on the state substantial duties to promote the general welfare. As the majority opinion in the *Crucifix Case* says:

> Article 4(1) does not simply command the state to refrain from interfering in the faith commitments of individuals or religious communities. It also obliges the state to secure for them a realm of freedom in which they can realise their personalities within an ideological and religious context. The state is thus committed to protect the individual from attacks

---

such instruction is given on the premises of sectarian schools by government employees pursuant to a program containing safeguards such as those present here"). By "safeguards," the Court referred to its finding that the program "does not run afoul of any of the three primary criteria we currently use to evaluate whether government aid has the effect of advancing religion: it does not result in governmental indoctrination; define its recipients by reference to religion; or create an excessive entanglement." Ibid. Invoking the other Establishment Clause test employed in recent Supreme Court decisions, the Court added that "this carefully constrained program also cannot reasonably be viewed as an endorsement of religion." Ibid.

[111] Kommers, 1997, 466 (citing unpublished paper by Cole Durham).
[112] Ibid., 480.

or obstructions by adherents of different belief or competing religious groups.[113]

The provision for religious instruction in the schools in Article 7(3) of the Basic Law is one concrete example of this broader concept of the activist state that takes responsibility for securing the basic welfare of the people. This kind of political economy does not reject the market but, by contrast with that of the United States, tends to rely to a greater extent on state intervention to assure that the benefits of the market are well distributed. For that reason, we can call it a more "state-centred" political economy. By contrast, the U.S. political economy, which tends to be quite ambivalent about state regulation even though it uses a considerable amount, is much more "market-centred" and more suspicious of state intervention in the market through ownership and management of the means of production, regulation, or subventions as a response to social problems.[114] The situation in the United States is a long way from the "cooperative" relationship in Germany, and the U.S. constitution does not provide the kind of specific authorisation for a partnership between religion and law that the German Basic Law does.

The German decisions on prayer and crucifixes also illustrate in greater detail than we have heretofore discussed the German method of balancing. It is deeply engrained in German constitutional law that the courts are to construe the Basic Law on the theory that it, like the great codes of private law, represents a "unified structure of principles and values."[115] Consequently, "constitutionally protected legal values must be harmonised with one another in the event of their conflict" in a form of "practical concordance (*praktische Konkordanz*)" so that neither eliminates the other, but all are preserved "in a creative tension."[116] In the *School Prayer Case*, the Court engaged

---

[113] Ibid., 473-74. The opinion continues, however, "Article 4(1) . . . grants neither to the individual nor to religious communities the right to have their faith commitments supported by the state," and the opinion then stresses a concept of neutrality that is closer to the U.S. model of non-discrimination. Ibid., 474.
[114] See generally Reitz, 2002; Reitz, 2001; Reitz, 1999.
[115] Kommers, 1991, 851.
[116] Ibid.

in a form of balancing and "practical construction" of rights, holding that "[t]he state's mandate to establish a school system is autonomous and stands on the same footing as parents' right to control the education and upbringing of their children; neither has an absolute priority over the other."[117] The Court expressly relied in the *School Prayer Case* on its 1975 decision in the *Interdenominational School Case*, characterising the latter as holding that "the incorporation of Christian references is not absolutely forbidden when establishing public schools, even though a minority of parents may not desire religious instruction for their children and may have no choice but to send their children to the school in question."[118] But, the Court said in the *School Prayer Case*, its 1975 decision upholding state-supported religious schools was subject to a very important condition necessary to give proper effect to the free exercise rights of dissenting students and parents:

> the school may not be a missionary school and may not demand commitment to articles of Christian faith. [State] schools also must be open to other ideological and religious ideas and values. They may not limit their educational goals to those belonging to a Christian denomination except in religion classes, which no one can be forced to attend.[119]

The *Interdenominational School Case* thus created a delicate balance. Religion and the state can cooperate with regard to education, but the practical concordance the Court has made of the various competing rights requires assuring that space is created for the autonomy of dissenters in the interdenominational schools as well as for the realisation by the adherents of the majority religion of their right to express their religion. As a result of that case, dissenters have to be "tough" enough to attend a school where there will be religious instruction with which they disagree. They will not be required to attend it, but the state will also not necessarily provide them with religious instruction of their own liking. In the *School Prayer Case*, the

---

[117] Kommers, 1997, 462-63.
[118] Ibid., 463. The case the Court cited is the *Interdenominational School Case*, 41 BVerfGE 29 (1975), translated in part in Kommers, 1997, 467-70.
[119] Ibid., 463.

Court was seeking to extend this practical concordance without completely denying either the interest of the state to fulfil its duty to enable majority students to express their religion or the interest of the dissenting students in not being subjected to too great a pressure.

The *Crucifix Case* could be interpreted as an attempt to preserve that delicate balance. As the Court said in that case,

> Inasmuch as schools heed the Constitution, leaving room for religious instruction, school prayer, and other religious events, all of these activities must be conducted on a voluntary basis and the school must ensure that students who do not wish to participate in these activities are excused from them and suffer no discrimination because of their decision not to participate. The situation is different with respect to the display of the cross. Students who do not share the same faith are unable to remove themselves from its presence and message. Finally, it would be incompatible with the principle of practical concordance to suppress completely the feelings of people of different beliefs in order to enable the pupils of Christian belief not only to have religious instruction and voluntary prayer in the public schools, but also to learn under the symbol of their faith even when instructed in secular subjects.[120]

In other words, placing a crucifix in every classroom is just too much; it upsets the delicate balance. Under this understanding of the German decisions, the *Crucifix Case* does not cast doubt on the decision in the *School Prayer Case*. They are both parts of an ongoing attempt to work out the "practical concordance" of the competing constitutional values and interests.

The most recent German Constitutional Court case involving religion in the schools concerned the wearing of a headscarf by a Muslim teacher. The case further illustrates the balancing method and the high value that German law places on the philosophical and religious neutrality of the state. The Baden-Württemberg administration had rejected a Muslim applicant's request to be

---

[120] Ibid., 478.

certified as a public school teacher because of her insistence on wearing a headscarf in accordance with her Islamic faith. In its decision in the *Headscarf Case*,[121] the German Constitutional Court held, with three of the eight justices in the chamber dissenting, that the state could not infringe her freedom of religion in this way without the authority of a statute. The Court applied the "so-called *Wesentlichkeitstheorie*, that states that essential matters, e.g., matters that are relevant for the exercise of a fundamental right by a citizen, are to be regulated by a legislative act."[122] Because Baden-Württemberg had no statute forbidding teachers to wear a headscarf in public schools, the Court ruled that this particular person could not be denied a teaching position on this ground.

The opinion, however, emphasises the freedom that state legislatures have to enact a statute forbidding teachers in the public schools from wearing all exterior signs of religious devotion. The Court recognises that such a rule would constitute an infringement of the teachers' freedom of religion.[123] Nevertheless, such a legislative ban could be justified, the Court holds, because the wearing of external signs of religious devotion could conflict with three other constitutionally protected values: (1) the state's duty to provide a philosophically and religiously neutral education, (2) the parents' right to determine the education of their children, and (3) the religious freedom of the school children. The state legislatures have to balance all of these competing interests, but the Court contemplates that not all German states will necessarily come to the same solution because in striking the balance, each legislature may take into account the different school traditions, the confessional composition of the

---

[121] BVerfG, 2 BvR 1436/02, 24.9.03, available at <http://www.bverfg.de>, paraphrased or quoted in part and discussed in Mahlmann, 2003, 1099.
[122] Mahlmann, 2003, 1105.
[123] The Court held that it did not matter that there was controversy over whether and to what extent the wearing of a veil or headscarf was in fact required by the rules of the Muslim faith. The key point was that a credible claim could be made based on behaviour and appearances that in the self-understanding of various Muslim religious communities women were supposed to wear a head covering when in public. 2 BvR 1436/02 Rnr. [Marginal Number] 40 (Part B. II. 4(a)).

people, and the greater or lesser strength of the role that religion has played among its people.

In any event, the opinion strongly suggests that a state statute prohibiting all teachers in public schools from wearing signs of religious devotion could be sustained as constitutional. The Court cites with approval the similar *Dahlab*[124] decision by the ECtHR in which that court found no conflict with the ECHR when a Swiss public school dismissed an experienced Muslim teacher for wearing a headscarf. That action, the ECtHR held, was within the "margin of appreciation" granted to states under the freedom of religion article in the ECHR. Furthermore, the German Constitutional Court's opinion emphasises the high value attached to the state's duty to remain neutral, especially in matters pertaining to the schools. While a state legislature could view the growing cultural and religious pluralism in Germany as an opportunity to accept greater religious expression in the public schools in order to encourage tolerance, the Court also holds that the legislature could take quite the opposite view: it could view the growing pluralism as a good reason to strengthen the duty of the state to be neutral in the educational field by restricting teachers' freedom to wear external expressions of their religious devotion, thus insulating the students from religious influence by the teachers in order to avoid conflicts with students, parents, or other teachers.[125]

The *Headscarf Case* thus openly invites the German states to pass legislation barring the wearing of Muslim headscarves by teachers in the public schools. The only limitation is the very significant one that all religions must receive equal treatment. The legislation must apparently therefore also forbid the wearing of Christian or Jewish symbols in order to comply with this ruling. The ruling has unleashed a vigorous debate in Germany. "There are some states, apparently the majority, indicating that they have the intention to interdict the wearing of head scarves in German public schools. Some participants in the discussion demand the consequent interdiction of any religious symbols in schools, others want exceptions for Christian symbols."[126]

---

[124] *Dahlab v. Switzerland*, Judgment of 15 February 2001, Appl. Nr. 42393/98, available at <http://hudoc.echr.int>.
[125] 2 BvR 1436/02, Rnr. 65.
[126] Mahlmann, 2003, 1109.

It is difficult to reconcile the *Headscarf Case* with the *School Prayer Case*. If it is permissible for a teacher to start or conclude class with a "voluntary" prayer, an act which will certainly put some degree of pressure on the students to participate, why is it not even more acceptable for a teacher to wear a sign of his or her adherence to a given religion, an act which by itself puts far less pressure, if it puts any at all, on the students to join the religion in question? The answer I suggested above in relation to the *Crucifix Case* is that the balancing may not be so much about coercion as about maintaining a balance among all the competing rights so that none are completely eliminated. However, the *Headscarf Case* invites the state legislatures to eliminate the teacher's right to exercise her religion entirely to the extent it requires the wearing of specific clothing even though granting a Muslim the right to wear visible signs of her religion would hardly change the balance struck by the previous cases, which were only about Christian symbols and activities. Moreover, in all these cases, the German Constitutional Court has said that the state has a duty to offer state-sponsored but non-coercive education with regard to matters of philosophy and religion. The requirement to avoid coercion is at the root of the idea and cannot be disregarded.

Therefore, if the *Headscarf Case* is right – if the state is permitted to view a teacher's wearing of religiously expressive clothing or jewellery as violative of the school's neutrality – it would seem to follow that a teacher's institution of "voluntary" prayer is even more violative of that neutrality, and the *School Prayer Case* is therefore now wrong and would have to be decided differently today. I thus interpret the *Headscarf Case* as a move in the direction of the French model of "laicism," a banning of all manifestations of religion from the public sphere, including public schools.[127] This decision does not go as far as recent French legislation banning the wearing by students in public schools of headscarves and other "ostentatious" symbols of religion.[128] The German case does not require the German states to

---

[127] Troper, 2000; Robert, 2003.
[128] The French law passed in early 2004 prohibits the wearing in public schools of "signs and dress by which students show conspicuously their religious affiliation." The French text of the law is available on the internet at http://ameli.senat.fr/publication_pl/2003-2004/209.html. Even before passage

forbid all teachers in public schools to wear religious clothing or symbols; it only authorises them to do so. Moreover, the German case does not discuss the students' rights to wear symbols of religious devotion. Although U.S. officials,[129] among other foreign representatives,[130] saw fit to lecture France publicly on its policy, in fact, U.S. courts have tended to uphold schools when they have enforced generally applicable bans on the wearing of religious symbols by refusing to let Muslim or Sikh teachers or students attend school wearing the headscarf. The relatively greater decentralisation of U.S. public education systems insures a greater diversity of policy in this regard than in France. But even in the U.S., the courts have tended to accept the argument that there is a strong public interest in having religiously neutral public schools that justifies infringing teachers' and students' free exercise and free speech claims through rules forbidding the wearing of religiously devotional clothing or jewellery. The argument has, however, not yet been examined by the U.S. Supreme Court.[131]

---

of the new law concerning students, French law already prohibited teachers from wearing religious symbols. Troper, 2000, 1267.

[129] Marquis, 2003, A8.

[130] "Anglican Leader," 2003, A 21 (quoting the Archbishop of Canterbury).

[131] The only Supreme Court decision on free exercise claims involving clothing is *Goldman v. Weinberger*, 475 U.S. 503 (1986), in which the Court upheld the Air Force's refusal to let a Jewish Air Force captain wear a yarmulke, but the military setting is obviously quite distinct from that of public schools. In *Cooper v. Eugene School District No. 4J*, 723 P.2d 298 (Ore. 1986), the Oregon Supreme Court upheld a state statute forbidding teachers to wear religious dress against a challenge by a convert to the Sikh faith who believed she should teach in a white turban and white clothes. *See also United States v. Board of Education for the School District of Philadelphia*, 911 F.2d 882, 894 (3d Cir. 1990) (upholding application of Pennsylvania's Garb Statute prohibiting the wearing of religious attire in public schools to forbid a female Muslim teacher from teaching while wearing a headscarf; statute upheld as just and constitutional means to prevent "a significant threat to . . . religious neutrality"). *But see Nichol v. ARIN Intermediate Unit 28*, 268 F. Supp. 2d 536 (W.D. Pa. 2003) (Garb Statute unconstitutional limitation on free speech and free exercise of religion to extent applied to prevent wearing of small items of jewelry expressing religious devotion like a Christian cross as long as not disruptive).

IV. THE MOST IMPORTANT DIFFERENCES IN CONSTITUTIONAL ADJUDICATION OF ISSUES OF RELIGIOUS FREEDOM, ESPECIALLY THE QUESTION OF MINIMAL SCRUTINY VERSUS STRICT SCRUTINY OR BALANCING

In the previous section we explored the very different conceptions of the proper role of religious instruction and observance in state schools. That discussion makes clear that different constitutional orders are founded on expectations for the relationship between the state and religion that are different in some important ways. It is precisely these differences that argue against any easy transference of rules from one system to another. To some extent, these differing expectations are reflected in different constitutional clauses. In addition to the issue of religious instruction in public schools, the issue of conscientious objection to military service, discussed at the outset of this paper, furnishes another example. But even without express differences in the respective constitutions, the foregoing discussion has shown that different constitutional regimes have come to different conclusions about such issues as the permissible limits on religious proselytism, religious opposition to blood transfusions for dependents, and school prayer in public schools. And these are just some of the specific differences one can find if one examines all the different religious freedom issues litigated in these particular constitutional regimes.

The most systematic difference among these issues concerns the standard of review to be applied to the state interests when there is a conflict between generally applicable state regulation and the dictates of religion. The most important contrast is between minimum scrutiny and all the other standards. Only the United States has adopted minimum scrutiny though, as explained in Appendix I, it is currently unclear how extensively it applies and when strict scrutiny applies instead. The standards used in the other countries and under the ECHR all ask the courts to make some judgment about the nature and significance of the state interests purportedly served by the challenged law. Minimum scrutiny alone does not add anything to the relatively low standard of rationality review which applies under equal protection to non-suspect classifications and which is not very demanding at all concerning the significance of the state's asserted interest in regulating. By contrast, to the extent that the courts use strict scrutiny or any other standard that requires them to scrutinize the weight of the state's interests, the courts employ a significant process of judicial review. If they use *Smith*'s minimum scrutiny, they provide virtually no review after checking for signs of discriminatory intent.

So the most important question concerns the arguments for *Smith*'s standard of minimum scrutiny. The standard has proven controversial in the United States. On the negative side, one must admit that a rule that essentially allows the state to regulate religiously inspired action as long as it does so without discriminatory intent significantly limits the guarantee of religious freedom, as a matter of constitutional law, since the essence of much of religious belief is to require or encourage adherents to engage in specific behaviour. Their behaviour is thus likely to bump up against the regulatory power of the state, often in ways that are not the product of obviously intentional discrimination on the state's part. Under the *Smith* test, the regulations will generally prevail over the religiously inspired activity because the standard of review is so low. Justice Scalia's opinion for the Court in *Smith* closes by remitting religious exercise interests to the political process. The legislature, Scalia suggests, may still protect religious exercise by making religious accommodations in statutes of general applicability.[132] But there are two problems with his argument. First, accommodations may, in U.S. terms, constitute establishment if they are not required by the Free Exercise Clause.[133] Second and more tellingly, the whole point of constitutional protection of fundamental freedoms is to protect them from the normal political process. For the Court to remit them back to the political process seems like an abdication of judicial responsibility.

---

[132] 494 U.S. 872 at 889.
[133] In *Thomas v. Review Board*, 450 U.S. 707, 720 (1981), Justice Rehnquist, in dissent, raised the possibility that accommodation of free exercise claims might in some cases result in establishment. However, the Court has not adopted that position squarely, and in *Locke v. Davey*, 540 U.S. ___,124 S. Ct. 1307 (2004), held that there is sufficient "play in the joints" between the Establishment and Free Exercise Clauses to allow a state to exclude from a general scholarship program for higher education those students who are pursuing training as clergy.

But the principal alternative standard of review in the United States, strict scrutiny, exacerbates the anti-majoritarian aspect of judicial review through its implied bias against governmental regulation. Under strict scrutiny, the courts are directed to sustain regulation against a free exercise claim only if the state can show a compelling interest which the regulations pursue in a way calculated to produce the least infringement on the right necessary to achieve the compelling interest. This standard thus creates a most intrusive form of judicial review. In *Smith*, Justice Scalia raises the spectre of chaos for all governmental regulatory programs if they all have to meet strict scrutiny challenges with respect to all the varied religious practices in the country.[134] For advocates of limited judicial review, like Justice Scalia, the author of *Smith*, minimum scrutiny is attractive as a way of reducing the intrusion of the courts into the democratic process. Because judicial review is not explicitly provided for in the United States constitution, as it is in most of the more modern constitutions of countries which have a form of judicial review of the constitutionality of legislative and executive action, there is a persistent strain in U.S. constitutional law in which U.S. courts show themselves to be particularly susceptible to doubts about how far to push doctrines of judicial review.[135] Doctrines limiting judicial review are arguably prudent self-restrictions by the judges designed to show respect for democratic principles, the simplest understanding of which gives primacy to the legislature. Perhaps this is the way we should understand Scalia's statement at the end of his opinion in *Smith* suggesting that religious exercise interests should seek their protection in the normal political processes.

But there is another factor that underlies the choice between minimum and strict scrutiny. Under minimum scrutiny, as we have said, once the court is convinced that the challenged regulation is not intended to discriminate against the religion of those challenging it, the court usually upholds the regulation. The Free Exercise Clause is thus interpreted to be nothing more than a guarantee that the state

---

[134] 494 U.S. 872 at 888 ("we cannot afford the luxury of deeming presumptively invalid, as applied to the religious objector, every regulation of conduct that does not protect an interest of the highest order.")
[135] Even as there is another strain that exercises judicial review quite uninhibitedly.

will not intentionally discriminate against any religion. It is essentially a footnote to the Equal Protection Clause and has the function simply to ensure that explicit religious classifications (and their covert "religious gerrymanders") will be treated as suspect classifications subject to strict scrutiny. By contrast, applying strict scrutiny to all cases in which neutral state regulation infringes religious freedom institutes through the "compelling state interest" test a different concept of the Free Exercise Clause, one that sees it, as Justice O'Connor has written, as "an affirmative guarantee of the right to participate in religious practices and conduct without impermissible government interference, even when such conduct conflicts with a neutral, generally applicable law."[136] This vision of the free exercise right sees the state as bearing, not just the obligation not to discriminate, but also the duty to accommodate religious practice within its regulatory function to the extent it can without prejudicing its vital interests. On the current U.S. Supreme Court, only Justice O'Connor seems to be a spokesperson for this point of view,[137] but we can see that all the other legal systems surveyed here in effect subscribe to that view by employing some form of strict or intermediate review or balancing.

It may be understandable why Justice O'Connor's vision of the Free Exercise Clause is not so well accepted in the United States. In general, as the discussion about political economy in the context of religion in public schools showed,[138] conceptions of the state that impose on it duties to act affirmatively to promote welfare are not favoured in the United States. It is true that the duty to make accommodations by granting exemptions from generally applicable regulations could be characterised as a passive duty to abstain from acting, quite different in principle from state duties to promote welfare that tend to be disfavoured in the United States, but the boundary between active and passive duties is not perhaps so clear.

---

[136] *City of Boerne v. Flores*, 521 U.S. 507, 545 (1997) (O'Connor, J., dissenting).
[137] See the concurring opinion she joined in *Church of Lukumi Babalu Aye* and her dissenting opinion in *City of Boerne v. Flores*, 521 U.S. 507 (1997), disavowing the *Smith* standard. The separate dissenting opinions by Justices Souter and Breyer in *Boerne* indicate that they want the issue of the *Smith* standard reargued but they do not indicate which way they would decide the issue.
[138] See Section III, above, at notes 113-15.

In the case of complex regulations and the great plurality of religious groups in the United States, the obligation to make accommodations for bona fide religious practices adds a layer of complexity – and hence, cost – to the drafting and administration of laws and regulations. Most importantly, the obligation to make accommodations casts the state in the role of looking out for religious practice, a notion quite out of step with the basic umpireal concept of the state in a market-centred political economy.

Perhaps the discussion of these points in the United States has been unduly prejudiced by the extreme rhetoric of strict scrutiny. If it were not thought of as a standard that state regulation could but rarely pass, it would at least not appear to invite the courts to make as great an intrusion into the realm of politics. Nor would it impose on the state as substantial a duty to accommodate. There are quite a number of substantial state interests that ought to justify infringing on religious practice. The catalogue in the ECHR seems like a reasonable list: interests of public safety, protection of public order, health, or morals, or protection of the rights and freedoms of others.[139] To ensure that the state could protect those interests, I would favour softening the standard of review from strict to intermediate. I do not favour the minimum scrutiny of *Smith* because I do not believe that free exercise should be reduced entirely to the principle of non-discrimination. Moreover, I do believe strongly that courts have an important role to play in protecting human rights, especially minority rights.

The German method of using a balancing approach to create a practical concordance of conflicting constitutional rights is the most distinct approach. It does not seem as rhetorically extreme as U.S. strict scrutiny, yet it has resulted in decisions favouring free exercise claims that have not been protected in the United States, as in the *Blood Transfusion Case* and in the *School Prayer Case*. How can we explain how and why Germany has come to use this standard of review?

Practical concordance has the advantage that by inviting the court to take into consideration all of the interests, the test seems to empower the court to come to a more nuanced analysis. None of the

---

[139] ECHR Art. 9(2).

conflicting interests are left out; all are given sympathetic consideration. Nevertheless, in the end, the dissident parents and students in the *School Prayer Case* lost, and one wonders whether they really felt better that the German Constitutional Court had seemed to understand that having to leave or stand silent during classroom prayers put the school child in a pressured situation.

Moreover, it is precisely all the nuance of the German approach that makes a common law lawyer nervous. The German form of balancing seems especially unstructured. It seems especially susceptible to the criticism that it magnifies the power of the courts. At its core, balancing confers on the courts wide discretion because it is never clear how the different interests formally included in the balance are to be weighed against each other. How can one rationally critique the balance struck by a court between matters of individual conscience and state interests in regulation? The two factors in the balance are fundamentally incommensurate. The "compelling state interest" test and all other forms of strict or intermediate scrutiny also require some balancing by asking the court to weigh the state's interest to see if it is strong enough – or proportional – to justify infringing an important individual interest.

This objection to a general balancing methodology, however, undoubtedly has greater weight in the United States, where judicial review is not anchored in a clause of the constitution, than it does in Germany, where it is. U.S. courts always have to be concerned about extending their self-created powers of judicial review too far. Moreover, the common law background of U.S. courts inclines them to the view that positive, written law, even if it is a constitution, imposes limits on courts and does not provide merely a set of principles with which the courts are to begin the analogic search for solutions to specific cases. But in Germany, centuries of legal science and experiences with codification at least since the nineteenth century have created a judicial style that tends to accept broad principles written into code provisions as delegations of considerable power to develop the general principles in ways that are guided by the generalising tendencies of legal science.[140] Constitutions include of

---

[140] See generally Dawson, 1968. Also consider, for example, the extensive law governing automobile accidents which the French courts fashioned from the

necessity some of the broadest principles and they call forth the most creative judicial efforts. U.S. lawyers, however, have often shown a tendency in interpreting the constitution to wear the blinders of "original intent," precisely in order to inject a degree of discipline against too much judicial creativity. German constitutional lawyers have tended to prefer teleological reasoning, and the German Constitutional Court has not hesitated to develop the written constitution in a quite forthright manner. Thus, the balancing method of creating a practical concordance of interests, while going quite a bit beyond acceptable balancing tests in U.S. legal practice, fits German legal culture quite well.

There is one more explanation to consider for the different standards of review, and in order to discuss it, we must first consider again the issue of state neutrality in religious matters. I will argue in the next and last section that all of these constitutional regimes agree in placing high value on state neutrality. But the foregoing discussion has made clear that there are at least three models of state neutrality on the subject of religion, and they differ in the degree to which they create a risk that state action will place some pressure in favour of or against some religions.

The first is the model of "passive neutrality," which is created by the minimum scrutiny standard of the U.S. Supreme Court's decision in *Smith*. Under this model, the state may not intentionally and openly discriminate against any religions but it is also not required to accommodate religious practice in any way. The state must simply act without regard to religion. State action that complies with this mandate cannot apply pressure for or against any religion.

The second model we might label "neutrality with some accommodation." It is the model created by judicial review standards using intermediate or strict levels of scrutiny, as in Canada or in the United States to the extent that *Smith* does not apply. The state is not permitted to discriminate openly or intentionally for or against any religions, but by invalidating state regulation which infringes on the

---

five basic tort provisions of the French Civil Code, Schlesinger, et al., 1998, 616, 618-25, or the extensive law on the revalorization of contracts the German courts derived from Section 242 of the BGB on good faith to deal with the severe inflation Germany experienced between the World Wars, von Mehren & Gordley, 1977, 1066-99.

freedom of some religions unless the state regulation can pass relatively strict tests, the standard in effect creates a judicially enforceable duty for the state to accommodate religious practice unless it has particularly weighty interests and narrowly tailors its regulation to accomplish those interests. The very act of accommodation creates some risk that state power may be seen as favouring the accommodated religions, but this is, of course, tempered by the requirement that the state in fact not discriminate against any religion, even in making accommodations.

The third model that emerges from this study we might label "neutrality with greater accommodation." This model is exemplified by countries like Germany (and possibly Nigeria), which provide in their constitutions for certain greater accommodations between the exercise of state power and religious freedom, such as the provision of religious instruction in public schools. As we have seen, the German model for this kind of more accommodationist neutrality sees the state as having a duty that goes beyond mere accommodation to an active role in securing religious freedom for each religious group. The German model of neutrality with greater accommodation could be argued to create greater risks of state coercion. To the extent that state structures like public schools can be used to teach religion from particular sectarian points of view, there is greater potential that state power will be perceived as endorsing those sectarian points of view, or at least endorsing religion against non-religion.

From this standpoint, one can see that the standard of minimum scrutiny, which creates the passive form of state neutrality, also most strongly eliminates the potential for state action to exercise any degree of coercion or pressure for or against any religion. In that sense, proponents of the minimum scrutiny standard of *Smith* may argue that minimum scrutiny best protects religious freedom by most completely removing the state as a source of pressure in religious matters. But it does so by insisting on a fairly absolute separation of church and state and by minimising the role that religion can play in the public sphere.[141] The intense conflict over the standard of review

---

[141] See, e.g., *Catholic Charities of Sacramento, Inc. v. Superior Court of Sacramento County*, 32 Cal. 4th 527, 2004 Cal. LEXIS 1667 (2004) (upholding application to

in the United States demonstrates that even in that country there is currently considerable controversy over whether such an extreme form of separatism is acceptable to society. The other models represent attempts to find less extreme forms of separation that may better represent society's preference in those countries for religion to play a larger role in the public sphere. It should be noted, however, that all three of these models are models of state neutrality. Whether the more accommodationist forms of neutrality must necessarily entail greater risks of coercion, state endorsement, or other forms of pressure in favour of the dominant religion is open to debate. As long as the state grants accommodations to all religions and invites all religions to play the same roles in the public sphere that it grants to

---

Catholic charity of state statute requiring employer who offers prescription drug benefits in its employees' health plans to include coverage for prescription contraceptives). The charity wanted to offer its employees insurance coverage generally for prescription drugs, but using contraception devices or drugs violates Catholic teaching. The charity in the case did not qualify for the statutory exemption for religious employers. Among other reasons, the charity did not employ or serve Catholics primarily, and was organised, not to inculcate religious teachings, but to serve the poor and vulnerable generally with social services. These characteristics of the charity made it more attractive as a partner for the government-funded provision of social services because they minimised the danger that government funds might be used to support proselytism. However, since the state statute concerning prescription contraceptives was a generally applicable regulation, the California Supreme Court applied minimum scrutiny according to the *Smith* decision of the U.S. Supreme Court to uphold application of the statute to the charity. Thus the very characteristics that made this religiously affiliated charity an attractive partner for government-funded provision of welfare services turns out to subject it to state regulation that forced it to violate its religious beliefs. By failing to require the state to accommodate religious belief when state regulatory interests are not so strong, the *Smith* standard in effect limits the role religious charities can play in the provision of government-funded welfare. The case raises the possibility that religious charities may have to choose either to tie themselves more closely to the proselytising or devotional work of their sponsoring religions, in which case they may disqualify themselves from receiving government funds to support their work, or give up their religious scruples insofar as they conflict with government regulations in order to qualify to receive state support for their charitable work. Steinfels, 2004, A12. The *Smith* standard thus contributes to preventing the kind of extensive partnerships between religions and the state that one finds in Germany. Monsma & Soper, 1997, 184-89.

any one religion, it is hard to see how the more accommodationist forms of neutrality necessarily compromise the neutrality principle, at least in constitutional regimes like the ones under study in this paper; none of which provide for any formal establishment of any religion. However, what does appear to be true is that the more accommodationist regimes, like the German one, may as a practical matter disadvantage the smaller or newer religions or the ones, like Islam, which are not centrally organized, because they are less likely to be able to interact with the state to take advantage of the opportunities the state holds out to all religions to play a role in the public sphere.[142]

Thus, as is so often the case in comparative law, differences in judicial approach to a specific issue, such as that of the standard of review in religious freedom cases, reflect major differences in legal traditions, especially with regard to such basic values as political economy; the relative positions of judge, legislator, and scholar; and the preferred relationship between the state and religion.

V. THE MOST IMPORTANT COMMONALITIES IN CONSTITUTIONAL ADJUDICATION OF RELIGIOUS FREEDOM: THE MEANING OF THE "SECULAR STATE"

The foregoing discussion has also revealed a surprising degree of consensus among the legal regimes surveyed with respect to issues of religious freedom. Many specific issues are decided the same way under these different constitutional regimes. For example, the ECtHR, the U.S. Supreme Court, and the German Constitutional Court are all on record upholding public school rules prohibiting

---

[142] Monsma & Soper, 1997, 169-70, 172-73, 180, 186-87 (reporting that Muslim groups have had difficulties participating in the German state's willingness to allow churches to collect financial support from members through the so-called "church tax," a sum religious members may voluntarily add to their income tax, because Muslim groups are not centrally organised with a group that can negotiate authoritatively with the state; for similar reasons, Muslim groups have not been able to organise religious instruction in many public schools or participate in state-funded charitable activities to the extent that the Catholic and Evangelical Churches have).

teachers from wearing the headscarf for religious reasons. The ECtHR and the U.S. Supreme Court have both protected the right to propagate one's faith peacefully although the U.S. cases probably provide stronger protection. Even the different wording of constitutional provisions turns out not necessarily to be important. Despite the reference to limits "necessary to a democratic society" in the Canadian Charter and the ECHR, language which is not found at all in U.S. or German statements of the standard of judicial review for infringements of religious freedom, the Canadian Supreme Court and the ECtHR have not had any trouble interpreting that phrase to imply a mode of analysis which, I have argued, provides a close functional equivalent to strict scrutiny in U.S. law and to German balancing.

The most significant commonalities, however, have to do with the state's duty to remain neutral among the religions in society. All of the constitutional regimes surveyed here agree on this principle and on three subprinciples derived from it. The first is that the state may not intentionally discriminate against any religion or religions, whether openly by regulation that categorises by religion or covertly by generally applicable regulation that amounts to a "religious gerrymander" or special discrimination against specific religions. Whatever else freedom of religion does, it protects people against intentional discrimination on the basis of religion. Certainly this is the core meaning of the "neutrality" in both Germany and the United States. Clearly both the Canadian Supreme Court in *Big M* and the ECtHR in *Kokkinakis*, and even more in *Manoussakis*, were concerned about the strong hint in those cases of intentional discrimination. Open, intentional discrimination against specific religions is thus the simplest case and is clearly prohibited by the guarantee of religious freedom.

While I cited chiefly the U.S. case of *Church of Lukumi Babalu Aye* for the concern about covert discrimination, I think it apparent that examples of covert discrimination would not likely withstand the stricter standards of review in the other jurisdictions surveyed here. A "religious gerrymander" would, for example, seem unlikely to qualify as "proportional" and "the least restrictive alternative" for achieving a permissible state purpose. The special test for "religious gerrymanders" is especially important in the United States because a majority of the Supreme Court has rejected strict scrutiny. The Court would arguably not have needed that analysis if it had applied strict scrutiny in the *Lukumi* case. It is interesting, however, to note that the U.S. Supreme Court's decision in *Smith* recognizes that one important way in which intentional discrimination might be hidden is through a law which grants administrative officials particularly broad discretion with regard to the granting of licences or exemptions from regulatory burdens.[143] The *Manoussakis* decision of the ECtHR makes exactly the same point.

The second subprinciple of state neutrality is that the courts should avoid making judgments about religious matters. For that reason, the courts do not make judgments about how important to a person's faith a given practice that conflicts with general regulation is, nor whether there is adequate authority within the individual's faith tradition for the views the individual now claims to bring her into conflict with state regulation. To do so would involve the courts unnecessarily and dangerously in religious matters. More importantly, it would open the door for courts to restrict religious freedom very substantially, as we saw happening in the case of *Zaheeruddin* from Pakistan. For that reason, the only test imposed on the religious freedom claimant, even under the German balancing standard of review, is the test of good faith. If the court is convinced that the claimant sincerely believes that his religious faith requires him to act in a manner inconsistent with state regulation or, as the German Constitutional Court said in the *Blood Transfusion Case*, he views that response "as the best and most appropriate means to deal with the situation in keeping with [his] belief,"[144] the claimant has passed all the scrutiny the court will direct to his side of the balance.

The third neutrality subprinciple, about which there is strong consensus, is that the state must not apply coercion in matters of religion. Despite the three different models of state neutrality outlined in the preceding section, the cases discussed in this paper show that a major concern of the courts is to prevent state power from being used coercively, even in countries that interpret state neutrality in the most accommodationist ways. In Germany, for example, the Constitutional Court has shown a great concern in its

---

[143] 494 U.S. at 884. See also Appendix I.
[144] Kommers, 1997, 450.

decisions about religion in the state schools to prevent coercion. While I have criticized its decision in the *School Prayer Case* as being insufficiently sensitive to the coercive effect of "voluntary" prayer in the public schools, its subsequent decisions in the *Crucifix Case* and especially in the *Headscarf Case* show its concern to prevent the public schools from being used to subject school children and adolescents to the pressure of religious proselytism unless they voluntarily submit to it and their parents do not object. Thus, the German Constitutional Court has interpreted the accommodationist rules of its constitution to prevent coercion.

These three dictates of state neutrality – (1) the state should not discriminate against religion either openly by using religion as a category for regulation or covertly by "religious gerrymanders"; (2) the courts should avoid making judgments about religious matters and in particular should require of religious beliefs assertedly infringed by challenged state regulation only that the beliefs be in fact religious and that they be asserted in good faith; and (3) state power should not be used to coerce or put pressure on individuals for or against any religion – are the bedrock of the freedom of religion. They represent a collective judgment that in order to protect religious freedom for each individual, the state itself must not be part of any religion. Under the more accommodationist models of state neutrality, the state may be involved with religion to some extent, but only to the extent that it invites all religions to be involved with it on the same basis and does not discriminate against or for any religion. In this sense, all of these constitutional regimes are interpreted by their respective courts as regimes in which the state itself must remain secular, that is non-religious, in order to protect the right of individuals and groups within society to exercise their religion freely.

APPENDIX

THE SCOPE OF APPLICATION OF "MINIMUM SCRUTINY" TO FREE EXERCISE CLAIMS IN THE UNITED STATES TODAY

The U.S. Supreme Court's general rejection of the compelling state interest test for free exercise claims in *Employment Division v.*

Smith[145] has led to a rather complex legal situation in the United States for several reasons. First, the majority in *Smith* itself recognised several exceptions to its general standard of minimum scrutiny. Second, *Church of Lukumi Babalu Aye v. City of Hialeah*[146] laid an important gloss on the *Smith* standard, and finally, Congress has tried, with varying success, to overturn the effect of *Smith* in a number of ways.

The majority opinion in *Smith* recognises two situations in which free exercise claims would still be subject to strict scrutiny. First, by the terms of the majority opinion in *Smith*, minimum scrutiny applies only to free exercise claims standing alone; it does not apply to a free exercise claim that also involves other constitutional rights to which strict scrutiny applies, like freedom of speech and of the press (which would, for example, be involved in the case of religious proselytising on public streets) or the privacy right of parents (to provide sectarian education for their children, for example).[147] It is of course clear in such a situation that one cannot really say that strict scrutiny is being applied at all to the free exercise claim. Strict scrutiny applies in those cases because there is also a free speech right or a parental privacy right.

The other exception mentioned in *Smith* concerns free exercise claims against a law which vests an administrative official with discretion to make an "individualised assessment" of claims to exemption from the burden of the law.[148] The exception was crafted in order to distinguish the facts of *Smith* from those of *Sherbert v. Verner*,[149] which applied strict scrutiny to the denial of unemployment benefits. In both cases, a statutory board was authorised to grant unemployment benefits as long as the employee had not been discharged "for cause." The *Smith* majority reasoned that in *Verner*, the statutory board had relatively unbounded discretion to decide whether the employee's refusal to work on his own sabbath could

---

[145] 494 U.S. 872 (1990).
[146] 508 U.S. 520 (1993).
[147] 494 U.S. at 881-82.
[148] 494 U.S. at 884 ("where the State has in place a system of individualized exemptions, it may not refuse to extend that system to cases of 'religious hardship' without compelling reason").
[149] 374 U.S. 398 (1963).

constitute a valid reason for denying the benefits because no criminal law prohibited the observance of a sabbath on a day other than Sunday, but in *Smith* the state statute criminalizing the use of peyote took that discretion away with respect to considering whether peyote use constituted "cause" for discharge. The majority opinion in *Smith* is somewhat unclear about whether or not this exception is a special rule for unemployment cases.[150] Is it in effect a way of saying that *Verner* is limited to its facts, a conventional ploy in the United States to get around inconvenient precedent without having to overrule those cases explicitly? Or is it an exception which has the potential to apply, not only to unemployment compensation cases, but to other similar cases, as well?[151] The Supreme Court has not yet had an opportunity to further define the scope of this exception, but there is clearly a basis for concern that religious uses, especially by minority religions, will be discriminated against in other similar situations where officials have general discretion unbounded by clear standards or rules to grant exemptions, as is the case, for instance in zoning exemptions.[152] At least in such cases, it may make sense to apply strict scrutiny in order to ferret out covert discrimination.

The second source of exceptions to *Smith*'s general standard of minimal scrutiny is the gloss that *Church of Lukumi* adds. Minimum scrutiny does not apply to a free exercise claims against a law which is not truly neutral and of general applicability, but is in fact a type of disguised discrimination. Even if the law is formally neutral and phrased in general terms, it is not really neutral if it can be shown in

---

[150] Justice Scalia's opinion for the Court indicates some doubt about whether the Court would be "inclined to breathe into *Sherbert* some life beyond the unemployment compensation field, . . ." 494 U.S. at 884.

[151] Justice Scalia's opinion for the Court also characterized the principle in *Verner* as follows in a way that suggests it could have broader application: "where the State has in place a system of individualized exemptions, it may not refuse to extend that system to cases of "religious hardship" without compelling reason." 494 U.S. at 884. When the Court subsequently reaffirmed the *Smith* ruling in *City of Boerne v. Flores*, 521 U.S. 507 (1997), it simply repeated that language. 521 U.S. at 514.

[152] Gedicks, 2003, 34-36 (arguing that this exception fits well with the Supreme Court's doctrine relating to "standardless licensing" of expression under the Speech Clause of the First Amendment, as well as with *Yick Wo v. Hopkins*, 118 U.S. 356 (1886)).

fact to constitute a "religious gerrymander." In such cases, the Court applies strict scrutiny.

Finally, Congress has tried in several ways to nullify the effect of *Smith* through legislation. The most ambitious attempt was the Religious Freedom Restoration Act (RFRA) of 1993,[153] which purported to overrule *Smith* by providing that governmental restrictions on the exercise of religion may be justified only if it is shown that they are the "least restrictive means" of furthering a "compelling state interest."[154] In *City of Boerne v. Flores*, the Supreme Court held that statute constitutionally invalid as applied to state governments. Vis-à-vis state governments, Congress claimed the power to enact RFRA on the basis of Section 5 of the Fourteenth Amendment, Congress' so-called "enforcement power" to guarantee implementation of the substantive rights of due process and equal treatment granted against the state governments by the Fourteenth Amendment.[155] The Supreme Court has long held the religious freedoms of the First Amendment to be incorporated in the guarantees of the Fourteenth Amendment.[156] However, the enforcement power of Section 5, the Supreme Court held in *City of Boerne*, could not be stretched so far as to include the power to change the meaning of the constitutional guarantees.[157] The opinion also contains separation of powers argumentation suggesting that it is inappropriate for Congress to overrule the courts in this way.[158] If

---

[153] 42 U.S.C. §§ 2000bb-2000bb-4 (1993). This act was passed with an astonishing level of support. Only three Senators voted against it; it passed the House unanimously. Noonan & Gaffney, 2001, 496.
[154] 42 U.S.C. § 2000bb-1(b) (1993).
[155] Section 5 states: "The Congress shall have power to enforce, by appropriate legislation, the provisions of this article."
[156] At least since *Cantwell v. Connecticut*, 310 U.S. 296 (1940).
[157] "Legislation which alters the meaning of the Free Exercise Clause cannot be said to enforcing the Clause. Congress does not enforce a constitutional right by changing what the right is. It has been given the power 'to enforce,' not the power to determine what constitutes a constitutional violation." 521 U.S. at 519.
[158] See 521 U.S. at 535-36: "Our national experience teaches that the Constitution is preserved best when each part of the government respects both the Constitution and the proper actions and determinations of the other branches. When the Court has interpreted the Constitution, it has acted within the province of the Judicial Branch, which embraces the duty to say what the law is.

that argument is taken seriously, it means that the application of RFRA to federal government restrictions on free exercise is also unconstitutional, as a number of commentators have argued, but so far the federal appellate courts that have considered the matter have upheld RFRA as it applies to the federal government and the Supreme Court has not yet ruled.[159] So for the time being at least, we have to entertain the possibility that RFRA has succeeded in overturning the precedential value of *Smith* for the federal government.

A year after enacting RFRA, Congress also responded to *Smith* by enacting the American Indian Religious Freedom Act,[160] which overrules the specific result in *Smith* by providing an exemption from all federal and state drug laws for bona fide religious use of peyote by Native Americans. This act, however, does not purport to change the standard of review.[161] In 2000, Congress responded to the decision in *Boerne* by passing the Religious Land Use and Institutionalised Persons Act (RLUIPA),[162] which is grounded, not on the enforcement clause of the Fourteenth Amendment, but on Congress' spending power and its power under the Interstate Commerce Clause. Accordingly, RLUIPA seeks to reinstate the compelling state interest test in all cases of state or federal governmental restrictions on religious land use or religious practices of persons in prisons or nursing homes, but only if such persons are under programs that either receive federal money or are part of interstate commerce. As in

---

Marbury v. Madison, [5 U.S. (1 Cranch) 137 (1803)]. When the political branches of the Government act against the background of a judicial interpretation of the Constitution already issued, it must be understood that in later cases and controversies the Court will treat its precedents with the respect due them under settled principles, including *stare decisis*, and contrary expectations must be disappointed. RFRA was designed to control cases and controversies, such as the one before us; but as the provisions of the federal statute here are beyond Congressional authority, it is this Court's precedent, not RFRA, which must control."

[159] Gedicks, 2003, 6-7.
[160] 42 U.S.C. § 1996a (1994).
[161] It should also be noted that shortly after the decision in *Smith*, Oregon enacted a special exemption for Native American sacramental use of peyote. Or. Rev. Stat. § 475.992(5) (1993). See generally Noonan & Gaffney, 2001, 496.
[162] 42 U.S.C. §§ 2000cc to 2000cc-5 (2000).

the case of the application of RFRA to federal government infringements of free exercise, it is arguable that the separation of powers language in *Boerne* implies that this attempt to overturn *Smith*'s choice of the standard of review is also unconstitutional, but the only federal appellate court to consider the matter so far has upheld the statute and the few federal district courts are split.[163]

As a result, the scope of application of *Smith*'s minimum scrutiny test is at least complex and currently still quite contested. Minimum scrutiny may apply to all free exercise claims except for the two exceptions noted in the opinion for (1) free exercise claims joined to another constitutional claim, like free speech, parents' privacy rights, or equal protection claims by suspect classes who have been the victims of a history of discrimination, which have enjoyed the special protection of strict scrutiny and (2) free exercise claims involving standardless official discretion to make individualized determinations. However, by reason of RFRA, strict scrutiny may still apply to all cases of infringement on free exercise by the federal government. It may also apply to both federal and state government infringements on religious use of land or religious practice by certain individuals in either prisons or nursing homes by reason of RLUIPA.

REFERENCES

"Anglican leader chides France for moves to bar head scarves," *New York Times*, December 26, 2003, A21.

Berman, Harold J., "Religious rights in Russia at a time of tumultuous transition: a historical theory", in: Johan D. van der Vyver & John Witte, Jr. (eds.), *Religious Human Rights in Global Perspective: Legal perspectives*, The Hague: Martinus Nijhoff, 1996, 285-304.

Bruni, Frank, "On display in Italy: classroom crosses, and a raw nerve", *New York Times*, October 30, 2003, A4.

Dawson, John P., *The Oracles of the Law*, Ann Arbor, MI: University of Michigan Law School, 1968.

Dorsen, Norman; Rosenfeld, Michel, Sajó; András; & Boer, Susanne, *Comparative Constitutionalism: Cases and materials*, St. Paul, MN: West Group, 2003.

---

[163] Gedicks, 2003, 7 (citing *Mayweathers v. Newland*, 314 F.3d 1062 (9th Cir. 2002) and four federal district court cases).

Durham, W. Cole, "Perspectives on religious liberty: a comparative framework", in: Johan D. van der Vyver & John Witte, Jr. (eds.), *Religious Human Rights in Global Perspective: Legal perspectives*, The Hague: Martinus Nijhoff, 1996, 1-44.

Gedicks, Frederick Mark, "Legal limitations on freedom of religion in the United States", draft dated October 5, 2003, paper presented at Fourth Meeting of the European-American Law and Religion Consortium, Budapest, Hungary, December 4-7, 2003 (copy on file with author; cited with permission).

Hogg, Peter W., *Constitutional Law of Canada*, Scarborough, Ontario: Thompson/Carswell, 4th looseleaf edition, 1997 (updated by 2002—Release 1).

Kommers, Donald P., "German constitutionalism: a prolegomenon", *Emory Law Journal*, 40, 1991, 837-873.

_____, *The Constitutional Jurisprudence of the Federal Republic of Germany*, Durham, NC: Duke University Press, 2d ed. 1997.

Mahlmann, Matthias, "Religious tolerance, pluralist society and the neutrality of the state: the Federal Constitutional Court's decision in the Headscarf Case", *German Law Journal*, 4/11, November 1, 2003, 1099-1116, available at www.germanlawjournal.com/print.php?id=331.

Mahmud, Tayyab, "Freedom of religion and religious minorities in Pakistan: a study of judicial practice", *Fordham International Law Journal*, 19, 1995, 40-100.

Marquis, Christopher, "U.S. chides France on effort to bar religious garb in schools", *New York Times*, December 19, 2003, A8.

Monsma, Stephen V. & Soper, J. Christopher. *The Challenge of Pluralism*, Lanham, MD: Rowman & Littlefield, 1997.

Noonan, John T., Jr. & Gaffney, Edward M., Jr. *Religious Freedom: History, cases and other materials on the interaction of religion and government*, New York: Foundation Press, 2001.

Noonan, John T., Jr. "The tensions and the ideals", in: Johan D. van der Vyver & John Witte, Jr. (eds.), *Religious Human Rights in Global Perspective: Legal perspectives*, The Hague: Martinus Nijhoff, 1996, 593-605.

Nowak, John E. & Rotunda, Ronald D., *Constitutional Law*, St. Paul, MN: West, 6th ed. 2000.

Nowak, Manfred & Vospernik, Tanja, "Permissible restrictions on freedom of religion or belief", in: Tore Lindholm, W. Cole Durham, Jr., & Bahai G. Tahzib-Lie (eds.), *Facilitating Freedom of Religion or Belief: A deskbook*, Kluwer-Law International, forthcoming 2004 (copy on file with author).

Ostien, P. & Gamaliel, J.D., "The law of separation of religion and state in the United States: a model for Nigeria?" in: S.O.O. Amali et al. (eds.),

Religion in the United States, Ibadan: American Studies Association of Nigeria, 2002, 14-32.

Reitz, John C., "Political economy and abstract review in Germany, France and the United States", in: Sally J. Kenney, William Reisinger, & John C. Reitz (eds.), *Constitutional Dialogues in Comparative Perspective*, New York, NY: St. Martin's Press, 1999, 62-88.

_____, "Political economy as a major architectural principle of public law", *Tulane Law Review*, 75, 2001, 1121-1157.

_____, "Doubts about convergence: political economy as an impediment to globalization", *Transnational Law & Contemporary Problems*, 12, 2002, 139-160.

Robert, Jacques, "Religious liberty and French secularism", *Brigham Young University Law Review*, 2003, 637-660.

Schlesinger, Ruldolf B., Baade, Hans W., Herzog, Peter E., & Wise, Edward M., *Comparative Law*, New York: Foundation Press, 6th ed., 1998.

Steinfels, Peter, "Beliefs: religious groups have long had a role in providing social services. Does a new California law threaten it?" *New York Times*, March 13, 2004, A12.

Troper, Michel, "Religion and constitutional rights: French secularism, or laïcité", *Cardozo Law Review*, 21, 2000, 1267-1284.

von Mehren, Arthur Taylor & Gordley, James Russell, *The Civil Law System*, Boston, MA: Little, Brown & Co., 2d ed., 1977.

Wa Mutua, Makau, "Limitations on religious rights: problematizing religious freedom in the African context", in: Johan D. van der Vyver & John Witte, Jr. (eds.), *Religious Human Rights in Global Perspective: Legal perspectives*, The Hague: Martinus Nijhoff, 1996, 417-440.

Commentary

Jamila M. Nasir

Ethnic and religious matters have historically been extreme issues. Governments all over the world are obliged to handle these issues with utmost care lest they are brought down prematurely. Ethnicity and religion have had pre-eminence in many conflicts around the world. Nigeria has not escaped the troubles associated with ethnicity and religion. The Civil War of 1967-70, the political crisis of June 12, 1993, and the numerous outbreaks of ethnic/communal and religious violence in Nigeria are instances of how such differences have troubled us. Any discussion on these issues is viewed with suspicion and is always perceived as a divisive discourse especially when the actors are not animated even to a small degree by democratic or human rights ideals. Emotions and sentiments then become commonplace. The proceedings of the 1977-1978 Constituent Assembly almost came to a standstill when some members walked out of the debates on whether a Federal Sharia Court of Appeal would be provided for in Nigeria's constitution. During the political bureau proceedings in 1986, the debate on religion generated a great deal of heat especially between Christians and Muslims.

Nigeria has tried various formulas to settle these twin issues: the creation of more states and local governments, division of the country into zones, establishment of a federal character commission, establishment of an advisory council on religious affairs, issues of rotational presidency, the creation of chiefdoms amongst others. Despite constitutional provisions on ethnic and religious rights, cries of marginalisation or injustice remain loud from many quarters. The procedures for enforcement of such rights, from my research, have never been utilized to the fullest except for two cases,[1] which in the end were both decided on technicalities, the courts declining to make definite pronouncements on the scope and extent of these rights.

Professor Reitz's paper on "Freedom of Religion and its Limitations: Judicial Standards for Deciding Particular Cases" has demonstrated how various jurisdictions have dealt with freedom of religion and its limitations by discussing court decisions to show how states in those jurisdictions have tried to meet and satisfy the ideals of the people on freedom of religion. The situation in Nigeria presents a good comparison.

RIGHT TO FREEDOM OF RELIGION

Section 38 of the 1999 constitution of the Federal Republic of Nigeria provides for the freedom of thought, conscience and religion. In positive terms it provides that every person has a right to hold and practice any religious belief. Section 8 of the African Charter on Human and Peoples Rights, Cap 10 Laws of the Federation of

---

[1] Discussed in Plang, 1988.

Nigeria, further provides for the protection of this right. The right is to be exercised by all persons throughout the country, Nigerians and non-Nigerians alike, either individually or collectively and in public or private to propagate their religion or belief in worship, teaching, practice and observance. The constitution allows any person to change his/her religion or belief at any time. Further, a religious community or denomination is allowed to provide religious instruction for its pupils in any place of education maintained wholly by it.

The Freedom of Association and Assembly provided for in Section 40 of the constitution also facilitates the enjoyment of this right as it allows a person to associate with her adherents to propagate their religion. Section 49 of the constitution also protects a person's right to hold an independent religious belief by prohibiting any discrimination against him by any government or agency simply because he holds such a belief. Section 15 of the constitution further prohibits discrimination on ground of religion. A breach of the freedom of religion may thus also involve a breach of the freedom of association and assembly and freedom against discrimination.

Our penal laws also protect religious freedom by prescribing punishment for acts inimical to religious freedom. For instance, Sections 210-213 of the Northern Nigerian Penal Code, still in force in all Northern states, prescribe as punishment a maximum sentence of two years imprisonment, or fine, or both, for insulting or inciting contempt of a religious creed, injuring or defiling a place of worship, disturbing a religious assembly, or committing trespass on a place of worship. The Regulation of Religious Preaching Edicts of the various states also prescribe punishment for similar offences.

RESTRICTIONS TO THE RIGHTS

Ethnic and religious rights are not absolute. Even under a democratic setting, the enabling provisions in the constitution provide for exceptions to the enjoyment of these rights. First, while every person is allowed to choose any religion, in respect of religious instruction, Section 38(3) of the constitution provides that persons who are under the care of their parents are subject to their parents' religious instructions and guidance. Any religious ceremony, observance or practice must be one approved by the parents. This section must, however, be read in conjunction with Section 35(1)(d) of the constitution in order to identify the category of persons affected. It provides that persons that have not attained the age of 18 years may be deprived of their personal liberty for the purpose of their education or welfare. This category of persons therefore would have no choice as per religious instructions except as dictated by their parents. Secondly, freedom of religion does not extend to formation of secret cults or societies in the name of religion, see Section 38 sub-section (4). This sub-section, as it appeared in the 1979 constitution, came for interpretation and application before the Supreme Court in the Rosicrucian case.[2] The Supreme Court held that the doctrines and practices of the appellants made them a "Secret and Satanic Society" within the meaning of the sub-section, and therefore subject to banning.

Section 45 of the constitution further restricts religious rights by providing that nothing in Section 38 (freedom of religion) shall invalidate any law that is reasonably justifiable in a democratic society in the interest of defence, public safety, public order, public morality or public health or for the purpose of protecting the rights and freedom of other persons. Sections 210–213 of the Penal Code and the Regulation of Religious Preaching Edicts of some states, referred to above, may fall within this exception. But whether these laws are reasonably justifiable in a democratic society is a matter of interpretation for the courts and not for the executive or legislative arm of government. In my research, I have, however, not come across a court ruling regarding this provision as far as religious rights are concerned. The general rule, however, is that the court should construe strictly any law that restricts the exercise of fundamental rights so as to give a wide and liberal interpretation to fundamental rights in order not to defeat the intent and purpose of the rights in general. The question to occupy the attention of the court is whether a democratic society (in any part of the world) can impose such restriction in the interest of order, morality, health etc.

---

[2] *Registered Trustees of the Rosicrucian Order, Amorc (Nigeria) vs. Henry O. Awoniyi & 3 Ors (1994)* 7 NWLR Pt 35 P.154.

In respect of freedom against discrimination on grounds of religion, ethnic background or place of origin, it would appear the prohibition does not apply where the discrimination is applied equally to all the ethnic and religious groups. The constitution only prohibits discrimination against a person on ground of ethnic group, place of origin, and religion where persons of other ethnic groups, place of origin and religion are not subjected to the same treatment.

Secondly, the prohibition against discrimination does not extend to the appointment of persons to any office under the state, or as a member of the armed forces of the federation, or a member of the Nigerian police force, or to an office in the service of a body corporate established directly by any law in force in Nigeria. This section is a corollary to Section 14 of the constitution, which speaks of federal character. There the constitution provides that the composition of the government and its agencies, and the conduct of their affairs, shall be in such manner as to reflect Nigeria's federal character, the diversity of the people and the need to prevent domination by one ethnic or sectional group. In other words, while every citizen should be treated equally on merit in respect of appointments to certain bodies, selective criteria can be adopted in order to give a fair representation to each group within the system even though it may be discriminatory to one group or the other.

However, while Section 14 is wide and encompasses every aspect of national life, any restriction pursuant to Section 42(3) must be backed by law and not mere administrative or executive action. Secondly, it does not extend to private organisations but only to offices of the state, armed forces, police and statutory organisations mentioned in the section.

The stories of Islam and Christianity in Nigeria differ significantly in terms of the historical and cultural experiences of Nigerians with them. When both religions arrived, they sought to assert themselves by dislodging the traditional religions of the communities with which they interacted by offering their people new gods as a basis of moral legitimation. This was one of the areas of intense, even of unequal conflict. It has been argued that the attitudes of the missionaries of these religions sowed the seeds for their subsequent politicisation in Nigeria. Their quest for converts and subsequent expansion created various forms of internal problems for some communities where relationships had been largely non-conflictual. Apart from the tensions created by conversions among families, many communities used these conversions to assert their hegemony over and strangeness from neighbouring communities. Today, there are two dominant religious groups in Nigeria, Muslims and Christians. Almost the entire gamut of social, political and economic relations revolve around these two identity formations.

In practice, however, any restriction of the freedom of religion which does not fall within the constitutional exceptions is a breach of the right guaranteed. It is conceded that no nation in the world is perfect in the implementation of its human rights provisions. But this fact should not in itself be used as an open invitation and licence to flagrantly violate the rights of citizens. We cannot hide the fact that there are violations in Nigeria of the rights to freedom of religion and freedom from discrimination on ethnic and religious grounds. The commonest and most glaring examples are disruption of religious assemblies or worship by individuals, groups, or government agencies. There are also instances that are not as glaring as the above. An instance today is where educational institutions owned by religious organisations are threatened with closure if they do not give religious instructions other than or in addition to their own.

However, from the constitutional provision, except where the institutions receive subventions from the government with a condition that they must provide an all-round religious instruction, or both the government and the religious denomination jointly own the institution, it is a breach of the freedom of religion to force them to give religious instruction other than theirs.

The constitution has provided enforcement mechanisms. The problem of enforcement of these rights is not different from the problems associated with the enforcement of other rights. These include inaccessibility to courts, disobedience of court orders, ignorance etc. The other complex problem is how to identify the perpetrator of the act and how to enforce the right against such persons. Even where the perpetrator is identified the religious groups and organisations have failed to utilize these provisions and have instead resorted to self-help or retaliation, which in most cases have led to bloody confrontations as we have so very often witnessed in Nigeria.

As I pointed out earlier there is a dearth of judicial decisions on these issues in Nigeria since most solutions proffered by government, when we are faced with problems, stem from the executive and legislative branches, under Section 45 of the constitution, rather than from efforts of individuals to enforce their rights in court.

REFERENCES

Plang, Danladi, *Constitutional Protection of Ethnic and Religious Rights in Nigeria*, Kaduna: Human Rights Monitor Publications, 1988.

The West and the Rest: Reflections on the Intercultural Dialogue about *Shari'ah*

Sanusi Lamido Sanusi

INTRODUCTION

The title of this paper in itself raises questions of definition in view of the contemporary prominence of post-modernist paradigms in philosophical discourse. Reflections are by nature philosophical, and indeed one can say all philosophy *is* reflection (although admittedly Lenin, and following him Althusser, would dispute this[1]). The title thus suggests a certain detachment by the reflecting subject, an attempt to present an objective and panoramic overview of the various points of view in the dialogue about *shari'ah*. Detachment and objectivity are indeed ideal states to which all participants and observers should aspire, since the critical reflection they facilitate is, in my view, a necessary condition of any fruitful dialogue.

We must, however, avoid the tendency to presume the complete realisation of these ideal states in the participants in any dialogue. Even the most detached and objective reflections are necessarily accompanied by subjective evaluations. They are thus never completely free of value-judgments and partisanship, and cannot make objectivating truth-claims, in the sense of their being the product of an overarching consciousness, detached from embodiment in concrete history. As an active participant in the dialogue about *shari'ah*, and in my position as a Muslim from Northern Nigeria, which is the site of discourse, my reflections are conditioned by the determinants of my own understanding, including my theoretical presuppositions and ontologies that play a key role in the interpretive process. To pretend to any form of universalisation of the local, totalisation of the partial, eternalisation of the historical,

---

[1] See Althusser, 1971, 11-43. More on this point later.

or objectivisation of the subjective would be counter-intuitive to the project of criticism. I make no such pretentious claims.

Having started with this disclaimer, it is nonetheless correct to say that reflecting on a debate, and presenting and evaluating opposing arguments as objectively as possible, will remain the best path to arriving at mutually acceptable solutions to social crises. Without recognition of the existence of plural possibilities and convictions the opportunities offered by dialogue are missed, and we will continue to fail in our quest for reciprocal and inter-subjective understanding. Students of philosophical hermeneutics place emphasis on the critical importance of dialogue to the formation of communities of interpretation, even though they differ on the question of the objectivity of dialogue and the legitimacy of a consensus that may be based on communication between unequal subjects. This debate, within the hermeneutical tradition, is well-known to students of Gadamer (and his interpreters like Grondin[2] and Warnke[3]), and Habermas (and again interpreters like MacCarthy[4]). I will not go further into the details of this debate here other than refer to it as a way of indicating the theoretical context for this paper.

A second point relates to the definition of terms such as '*shari'ah*' and 'the West'. By '*shari'ah*' I do not mean Islamic law or the Islamic religion as such. I refer instead to the totality of discourse in contemporary Muslim Northern Nigeria, which includes a substantial element that represents, or at least presents itself as, some form of Islamic revivalism. This discourse includes the declaration of *shari'ah* by a number of state governments and the various real and cosmetic signifiers of the dimensions of this declaration, such as the new legislation, judicial and political pronouncements, amputations, sentences to death by stoning (yet to be carried out), the emergence of *hisbah* corps or religious police, new dress codes for men and women, the question of the place of women in public space etc. In other words, the term refers in large part to a specific, culturally- and historically-conditioned interpretation of the meaning of *shari'ah*, and the projection of that interpretation in the repackaging of the self-

---

[2] See for example Grondin 2003[b], 1994 (especially 106-123), and 2003[a] (especially Chs. 13-15).
[3] Warnke, 1987.
[4] McCarthy, 1978, especially Ch. 5.

identity of Northern Nigerian Muslims. But it is also a discourse dominated by Nigerian politicians, traditional rulers, and religious scholars, in an environment filled with poverty and illiteracy, reputed for corruption and parasitism, and integral to an articulate mode of production that has succumbed to the de-industrialising, predatory forces of globalisation.

It is therefore a discourse that is not simply Islamic. The "Muslimness" of the majority of the people of Northern Nigeria cannot be divorced and studied separately from the exploitative tendencies of the region's elite and the impoverishment of its poor, nor from the alienation of its women and the abuse of its children. Any consensus that seems to emerge from the discourse about *shari'ah* among the North's Muslims must, therefore, be assessed against the background of the totality of the discursive formation – the structure of power relations, the control of and impediments to free inter-subjective communication, the instruments of domination and alienation, the level of literacy, awareness and enlightenment of the populace, and the general tendency of power to appropriate knowledge and monopolise the right to definition of truth to the detriment of subaltern discourses. In summary, the conclusions we may draw from the popular support given to the *shari'ah* project in Northern Nigeria must take cognisance of the sustained *massification* of the population, that is to say the intensive and deliberate process of qualitative levelling for the purpose of quantitative maximisation.

The reference to "the West" is no less problematic. In general the term refers to Western Europe and North America, although in the context of a "clash of civilisations" where Islam is concerned, the West may well include other nations like Russia and the emergent Christian fundamentalist states of Eastern Europe. The term is problematic because the West does not speak with one voice, and any claims that it is in its entirety opposed to Islam or *shari'ah*, may be stereotypic on the level of claims like "all Muslims are fundamentalists" or "all Islamists are terrorists." However, although the West may show some fragmentation on wider issues like Iraq or Afghanistan or the Arab-Israeli question, it is I think fair to say that a certain consensus seems to exist among Westerners against the *shari'ah* as discourse, and against what is generally represented as the spread of fanaticism in Northern Nigeria. The criticism has generally been on the basis of shared Western conceptions of human rights and liberties. I will therefore use the concept in reference to the opposition voices from Europe and America, in the form of governments and non-governmental organisations, which have stridently condemned the implementation of *shari'ah* in the name of dogmatic adherence to a Western conception of universal rights and political values such as separation of religion from state.

I conclude this preliminary discussion by making a final point on the title. In its apparent construction it presumes a dialogue – a discussion between *two* parties – between the West and Northern Nigerian Muslims (a dialogue which has sometimes degenerated into total hysteria and often seems a dialogue of the deaf). But so construed, the title obscures a third, important party to the discussion, the Muslim critics of the discourse, a group that seems to hang somewhere between the Muslim world and the West. Portrayed by Muslim opponents as agents of the West because of the confluence of positions on certain pertinent questions on *shari'ah*, this group in turn is suspicious of Western powers and critical of the West's strategic approach to the Muslim world. However, no discussion of the intercultural dialogue about *shari'ah* is complete without an analysis of the views of this third group – the Western-educated Muslims.

This paper will, therefore, adopt a tripodal taxonomy: I will reflect first on the position of progressive Muslim critics of the discourse, followed by the Western criticism and finally the defence of the Northern religious establishment. I hope in this way to clarify the nature of the "hermeneutics of suspicion" underpinning ideology critique, the philosophical weaknesses of Western criticism, and some justifiable concerns of traditional Islam.

THE CRITICAL PROJECT

The defining element of Muslim criticism is that it engages the discourse on two planes: ideological and philosophical. At the level of ideology, it holds that the discourse exhibits tendencies of political violence toward the weaker segments of society. Slicing through the opacity of religious jargon and propaganda, social critics highlight the reality that the poor and the women seem to be on the receiving end of harsh punishments, and that the intensification of the process of religious revival is accompanied by a deepening of contradictions in the social formation. This is for example reflected in the restriction of the role of women in public space, the strengthening of patriarchal discourses, apparent double standards in legal sanctions imposed on crimes of the rich (like embezzlement of public funds) and crimes of the poor (like theft of goats), and an excessive focus on punishments after the fact as opposed to such more proactive initiatives as increased transparency in the management of public funds, the elimination of official corruption, and the provision of social services to the poor like shelter, education, and health care. In short, critical theorists insist that no transformation has meaning unless it leads to meaningful and concrete changes in the material living conditions of the masses of the population. In the absence of this, all appearances of change are cosmetic. Even the financial benefits accruing to some religious scholars from government largesse (and the new opportunities for earning income given to unemployed youth who join the religious police), may represent no more than co-option of elements of the religious establishment by politicians. One recalls Frantz Fanon's coinage of the term "selective hibernation" in reference to "decolonisation" by flag independence, where nothing changed in reality apart from the assumption to office of a few native (i.e. black) politicians in place of (white) colonial officers.[5]

On the level of philosophy, the critical project challenges the objectivistic claims of traditional epistemology, by insisting on the relativity and historical specificity of certain interpretations of Muslim law, which are presented as immutable by the ascendant discourse. A fundamental premise of traditional Muslim thought is that the interpretation by early scholars of the Divine law is objective. It is said that the scholar is able to free himself from his own desire (*hawa*) and prejudiced opinion (*ra'y*). His rulings are thus free from coloration by such considerations as his sex, class, race, and even the history through which he lives. This argument is not unique to Muslim scholarship. Similar claims have been made in respect of Biblical scholarship by objectivistic hermeneuticists like Emilio Betti,

---

[5] Fanon, 1968, especially. Ch. 1: "Concerning Violence".

who insist on preserving the autonomy of the object of interpretation and its distinct alterity from the interpreting subject.[6]

The problem with this claim lies in its obvious self-negation. We can only concede that the jurist is objective by assuming that he is able to purify his own consciousness from the impurities of embodiment. By making "individual self-consciousness the locus and arbiter of truth . . . objectivity as an ideal derives from a highly subjectivist epistemology."[7] The implication of this critical challenge is that the religious claims of the *shari'ah* discourse are compromised. Historicisation leads to contextualisation, such that the rejection of interpretations considered valid in a given historical context is not to be equated with a rejection of religion, or of God's eternal law.

In its criticism of certain elements of *shari'ah* in Northern Nigeria, the radical wing of the Muslim intelligentsia keeps stressing the essentially Islamic nature of its project. Muslim feminists like Ayesha Imam have stressed that their struggle for women's rights has been based on arguments drawn from Muslim texts, particularly the Qur'an, the Sunnah, and some interpretations of earlier scholars in areas of dispute. They have also argued that modernist interpretations of Qur'anic verses have been adopted by Muslim nations like Tunisia and Egypt, and that these new interpretations are actually more in keeping with the Islamic ideals of freedom and equality.[8] The South African Muslim feminist, Sa'diyya Shaykh, to quote another example, writes that "the primary incentive for some feminist Muslim scholarship is the reality that there is a dissonance between the ideals of Islam which are premised on an ontology of radical human equality and the fact that in varying social contexts women experience injustice in the name of religion."[9]

The thesis is brilliant, but in my opinion it rests on shaky philosophical grounds. The assertion that women are victims of "injustice," and that this is contrary to the Islamic ideal, takes as given not only a preconception of what constitutes gender "justice," but also the claim that this preconception is in fact the Islamic ideal, premised, as it were, on the posited "ontology of radical human

---

[6] See for example Weinsheimer, 1991, 11.
[7] Ibid., 13.
[8] See Imam, 2002.
[9] Shaykh, 2003, 156.

equality." In fact, I would argue, the concept of justice and equality that is held by progressive Muslims originates in a tradition of Western scholarship since the Enlightenment, and the interpretations conferred on Islam represent a hermeneutical process of finding meanings in the Qur'an and the *hadith* that are consistent with the presuppositions of the Western-trained intellect. As noted by Lyotard, the whole project of modernity revolves around the globalisation of a European idea, the idea of emancipation. This idea appears in many forms in European thought: as emancipation from original sin through love (the Christian version); or as emancipation from ignorance and servitude through knowledge and egalitarianism (the *Aufklärung* or Kantian version); the realisation of the universal Idea through the dialectic of the concrete (Hegel); emancipation from exploitation and alienation through socialisation of work (Marx); and the bourgeois narrative of emancipation from poverty through techno-industrial development.[10]

The egalitarian ontology posited by Shaykh is therefore a *pre*-text grounded in Western rationalist philosophy, used to produce a new interpretation of the Muslim *text*. The weakness of the critical claim is that while it correctly insists on the subjectivity and relativity of interpretations of Islam in traditional society, it uncritically pretends, itself, to an objective apperception of the Islamic ideal. In fact, the perception of progressive Muslims of this Islamic ideal is itself mediated by philosophical and theoretical presuppositions imbibed from Western education, and as such is no less subjective and relative than the interpretations of the traditionalists.[11]

The point I would like to make is the following. The debate between modern criticism and traditional Islam is not to be seen as one between absolute right and absolute wrong. The argument is not about which interpretation of Islam is more consistent with a metaphysical Islamic "ideal"; it is rather about which conceptualisation of this ideal is more in line with the aspirations of Muslims living in our modern world. In adopting a defensive attitude, progressive Muslims make untenable claims of unsubstantiated authenticity for their ontology of equality. This

---

[10] Lyotard, 1993, 24-25, quoted in Serequeberhan, 1998, p. 67
[11] I have illustrated this point in Sanusi, 2001.

defensiveness is, in my view, completely unnecessary. The Muslim of today is in dialogue with a tradition inherited from the past, and it is natural that the process leads to tension whose resolution will lie not, as some fear, in a negation of received tradition, but in a synthesis of itself with its negation. The dialogue, ultimately, takes place between two conflicting ontologies, each incorporating its own standards of truth and justification. As noted by Gadamer, "it is precisely in confronting other beliefs and other presuppositions that we can both see the inadequacies of our own and transcend them."[12]

Critical scholarship therefore represents an ideology of liberation and emancipation (by exposing and challenging moments of domination in the manifestation of religion) as well as a hermeneutics of suspicion that refuses to accept the objectivity of historically-conditioned interpretation. Indeed it is in the nature of critical thought that it considers the distinction I make between philosophy and ideology as somewhat superficial. Althusser for instance argues, following Marx and Lenin, that philosophy is but an intervention into theory and, specifically, the intervention of class struggle and partisanship into theory. As noted by Jameson, such interventions are "always polemical and situation specific," and "every idea ... appears as the idea of someone, as the ideological projection of that idea from an identifiable (political) position."[13]

This fiercely ideological character of critical thought, reflected in the over-determination of the political moment in concepts and ideas, accounts in my view for the controversial character of its interventions.[14] There is a tendency to question the motives of all actors in authority, and to view all pronouncements and actions through the prism of unequal socio-economic relations and antagonistic class positions. After Michel Foucault and Edward Said,[15] few serious persons would question the dominant role of power in the production of knowledge. However, critical theory makes excessive claims in its demonization of all power, and in its reduction of the motives of all domination to the control of the mode

---

[12] Warnke, 1987, 172.
[13] Jameson, 1971, viii.
[14] For a criticism of Althusser, see for example Thompson, 1978.
[15] Especially Said's *Orientalism* (1978), which was an application of Foucault's post-structuralist thesis on the role of power in the production of knowledge.

of production. Central to the argument of (post-structuralist) criticism is the ultimately determining character of the economic instance. Sometimes this criticism seems unfair to Muslims, especially since the objective norms of Muslim jurisprudence are, on the face of things, opposed to all forms of materialism, exploitation, repression, arrogance and wickedness. Power is, at least in theory, to be exercised with benevolence, generosity, compassion and humility. In Islam, political office and power are supposed to be a tool for service to God and humanity, not for personal aggrandisement and economic corruption.

In a sense, however, Muslim critics fail to recognise the real intellectual problem they face. In reality, many Muslims who are steeped in tradition do not accept the egalitarian conceptions of Western society on, for example, gender issues, and they sincerely consider the manifestations of inequality denounced by ideology critique to be divinely ordained. "Justice," in Muslim ethical theory, is defined as "placing everything in its appropriate place" (*wadh'u kulli shay'in fi makanihi*). In traditional Muslim thought, or at least in its most prevalent readings, a slave is not the equal of a free-born, a woman is not equal to a man and a non-Muslim is not equal to a Muslim, even though clear guidelines are given for compassionate treatment of women and slaves, and the protection of certain non-Muslims (who pay a special poll-tax, the *jizya*).[16] Justice therefore does not mean that *self* must be treated as equal to *other*, without reference to status, gender or class. From the early days of the Islamic polity, this topic was integral to the debate between the *Kharijites*, on the one hand, and the *Sunnites* and *Shiites* against whom they waged war. Whereas the former group held up certain Qur'anic verses and prophetic *hadith*s as evidence of the absolute equality of human beings without regard to sex, race or other secondary characteristics except the fear of God, their opponents justified their exclusivist politics by interpreting those same verses and *hadith*s in terms of all humankind's equality before God on the Day of Judgment.[17] Since Islam came to be dominated by *Sunnites* and *Shiites*, social hierarchy here on

---

[16] See Sanusi, 1998.
[17] For more on the democratic credentials of the Kharijites, see Hasan,(1991), especially I: 316-318.

Earth became a Divinely-ordained state of affairs and every Muslim was expected to accept his allotted place with gratitude to God.[18] In this, the Muslim tradition is no different from most other pre-modern systems of thought. The Stoics, for instance, had similar conceptions of justice, as can be gleaned from, say, the *Meditations* of Marcus Aurelius.[19]

This is not to say, as Gadamer would suggest, that the egalitarian and emancipatory consensus of modern critical theory represents some ideologically neutral agreement on the objective and absolute truth. On the contrary, it is a consensus forged on the terms of the dominant elements of the Western discourse of modern times. But its very existence as an unquestioned consensus – in the West – complicates the task of criticism, which can easily fail to recognise the fact noted by Axel Honneth, that critical theory ultimately depends upon a *pre-theoretical* interest in the emancipation it seeks to articulate.[20] This is again the point made above about the egalitarian ontology posited by Sa'diyya Shaykh. There can be no objective and articulate class-*position* without a subjective and instinctive class-*consciousness*, forged from the contradictions of modern life. It is through "violations of identity claims acquired through socialization" that subjects experience the "constriction of . . . their moral expectations." Unless those who are alienated feel a sense of shame, anger, and indignation in response to these violations, the critical project is destined to failure.

WESTERN OBJECTIONS

The criticism of *shari'ah* from Western governments, diplomats and NGOs has been in general less articulate than that of progressive Muslims. The Western response to *shari'ah* has been near hysterical, characterised by widespread condemnation in the name of human rights of what the West terms "cruel and dehumanising," even

---

[18] As for the inferiority of the non-Muslim to the Muslim, this was, a fortiori, taken for granted and justified in many apologetic works. Two good examples are Ibn Taimiyyah, *Iqtidha' as-Sirat al-Mustaqim Mukhalafah Ashab al-Jahim* and Ibn Qayyim, *Ahkam Ahl al-Dhimmah*.
[19] Hays, 2002, especially xxviii-xxix.
[20] See Honneth, 1999, 320, 329-30.

"barbaric" punishments. The West speaks to Islam from a position of arrogance, demanding not a dialogue but capitulation to its values. I will in this section discuss why, in my view, the West has so far only succeeded in alienating Nigerian Muslims.

The first problem with Western criticism of *shari'ah*, in my view, is that it fails to take into account the wider global context of the perceived confrontation between the West and the Muslim world. The dominance of the US as the sole remaining superpower, and its ideologically-inspired promotion of the processes of globalisation have led to a perception among Muslims that every criticism of the Muslim world from the West is, in fact, American-inspired. The truth, to be blunt, is that Muslims detest America. This has not, contrary to what the Bush government would have us believe, always been the case. It also has nothing to do with Muslims hating "American values" of "freedom and liberty," another characteristically disingenuous claim made by the US administration. Muslims detest America because they believe America detests Islam and Muslims. I have elsewhere given instances of how the statements and actions of senior members of the Bush administration have only served to give the present US government the stamp of a Christian fundamentalist regime on a messianic crusade against Muslim lands.[21]

The Nigerian Muslim does not believe that the condemnation of the stoning verdicts on Safiya Husseini and Amina Lawal was inspired by humanitarian considerations. Muslims note the number of Afghan citizens bombed and killed by US troops. They follow news of mass graves discovered in Afghanistan and believe there is a calculated attempt to cover up Western complicity in mass murder. They believe the West instigated Saddam Hussein to start a long war with Iran that led to the loss of millions of Muslim lives. They have watched Iraqi children die, first under Western imposed sanctions and then under bombs from Western planes and shells from Western tanks. They have seen Israel occupy Muslim land, create in Palestine a 21st century reincarnation of the Jewish ghettos of Europe, and kill Palestinian men, women, and children with impunity. The US continues to veto UN resolutions that aim merely to condemn the excesses of the Zionist regime. It seems not even a slap on the wrist is permissible.

---

[21] See Sanusi, 2003[b].

This is the manner in which Muslims read current affairs. It is immaterial if the West accepts this perception as a fair or balanced one because ultimately it is what the Muslims themselves believe that determines their response to Western criticism. Consequently, Muslims view criticism as merely one more opportunity taken to open a new flank in the battle against Islam. The use of adjectives like "barbaric" or "inhumane" in describing the punishments of the Muslim code are considered value-judgments reflecting a certain element of cultural arrogance and unacceptable claims of superiority.[22] In general, the West demands from other cultures unconditional acceptance of its concepts and values, showing little respect for their desire to protect their own cultural integrity. This makes dialogue difficult, if not impossible.

This last point was addressed by Jürgen Habermas in an interview with Eduardo Mendieta[23] with such clarity that it bears quotation:

> Let's take the example of human rights. Notwithstanding their European origins, human rights now compose the universal language in which global commercial relationships come under normative regulation. In Asia, Africa, and South America, they also constitute the only language in which the opponents and victims of murderous regimes and civil wars can raise their voices against violence, repression and persecution, against injuries to their human dignity. But to the extent that human rights are accepted as a transcultural language, disagreements over their appropriate interpretation between cultures have only intensified. Insofar as this intercultural discourse on human rights occurs under conditions of reciprocal recognition, it also has the potential of leading the West toward a decentered understanding of a normative construct that no longer remains the property of Europeans, and can no longer mirror the particularities of one culture.[24]

---

[22] I have addressed the philosophical problems associated with these assertions else-where. See for example Sanusi, 2003[a] and 2000.
[23] Habermas, 2002, 147-167.
[24] Ibid., 153.

And later:

> Individual cultures can only make a positive contribution to the rise of a world culture if they are respected in their own, stubborn individuality. This tension needs to be *stabilised*, not resolved, if the net of intercultural discourse is not to be torn."[25]

It seems to me that the missing element in the West's attempt at dialogue remains its unwillingness to conduct this dialogue "under conditions of reciprocal recognition," and respect the right of other cultures to "their own, stubborn individuality." In a world of independent nations, globalisation brings the powerful West into direct contact with other cultures and civilisations. The context of discourse is fundamentally altered through the decentering of the background consciousness and the resultant relativisation of each culture's individual perspective. This cognitive presupposition is necessary for the achievement of meaningful dialogue, and the refusal of the West to accept the relativity of its concepts is itself some form of "fundamentalism," a refusal to recognize what Habermas calls "the cognitive limits of *modern* life."[26]

The difficulty the West faces in finding friends and allies among Muslims is not limited to political and religious leaders, or to the masses of the people. Progressive Muslim intellectuals have been unable to agree with the West and offer it co-operation in its opposition to *shari'ah* for additional reasons. As noted earlier, a defining element in post-structuralist criticism is its belief in the ultimately determining character of the economic instance, and many radical Muslims hold on to some variant or another of post-structuralist thought (Althusser, Foucault, Gramsci, for example). The great economic inequalities in Nigeria have been made possible by a combination of official corruption and the pursuit of economic policies inspired by the so-called "Washington Consensus." These policies have led to the death of industry and increased unemployment, the devaluation of the currency and national assets,

---

[25] Ibid., 155.
[26] Ibid., 151.

the disappearance of the middle class, economic distortions that favour importers of products from the West and middle-men, etc. Progressive Muslims, like other progressive intellectuals, believe in the necessity and urgency of confronting these economic programs and the pursuit of programs that are more oriented toward the people, programs that are not in the interest of the West and its multinational corporations. In their confrontation with the dominant elements in the *shari'ah* discourse, Muslim critics recognize these elements, correctly, as a sub-set of a national hegemony which itself is acting in the economic interest of the West. The crimes for which *shari'ah* courts have pronounced the so-called "primitive" sentences tend towards proliferation in an environment of poverty and joblessness. Poor men tend to steal if they cannot find employment. Poor women tend to sell their bodies for small material rewards. By this logic, the Muslim critic sees the West as actively *complicit in the very thing it condemns*.

THE OTHER SIDE OF THE DIALOGUE AND THE WAY FORWARD

We now turn to the other side of the argument, with a view to understanding the dominant mind-set and making suggestions on the best options for dialogue. It is clear from the above that any criticism of Muslim law from a perspective of human rights discourse, and any call on Muslims to abandon religious law in the name of secularism, will fail. The jealous protection of religious authenticity is not peculiar to the Muslims. It is, rather, symptomatic of the age we live in, where due to "accelerating homogenisation and simultaneous manufacture of difference . . . religions are articulated as the last refuge of unadulterated difference, the last reservoir of cultural autonomy."[27] It is therefore to be expected that attempts by the West to impose its values on the Muslim world will be met with fierce resistance.

But internal Muslim criticism has its own problems. As mentioned earlier, Muslim critics of *shari'ah* as discourse all too often attribute to the Northern political establishment a definitive ideological position. Religious discourse is seen as merely one element

---

[27] Mendieta, 2002, 1.

in the ideological apparatus of the state, whose objective is the legitimation of an existing social formation characterized by fundamental inequalities in the economy, polity, and society. On reflection, it appears that while this may indeed be the case among the more intellectually sophisticated or the less pious segments of the establishment, it does not necessarily apply to everyone. This is not to deny the fundamental role of religious interpretation in supporting the dominant discourse. The distinction I seek to make is between two questions: whether the interpretation of religion from the perspective of power happens *because* the subject deliberately manipulates knowledge to serve its interest (à la Edward Said), or whether it happens *in spite* of the subject's desire to objectively interpret and apply God's authorial intent in legislation (à la Michel Foucault).[28] In other words, do the manifestations of what critics view as political violence *necessarily* result from a deliberate attempt by the interpreter to legitimate his preferred state of affairs, or do they result from the necessary intrusion of historical conditions on the interpretive process, intrusions of which the interpreter may not even be conscious?

This is an engaging philosophical question,[29] and one that assumes added relevance in the context of the subject of this paper. The *shari'ah* discourse in Northern Nigeria has, with justification, been criticised for its injustices against the poor and women. The post-structuralist view, as in Althusser and Said, would suggest that the interpretations of this law are ideological, and thus that the *Subject* is somehow implicated in a deliberate process of legitimating alienation. But if Foucault is correct, and if the *Subject* is itself a product of its history, the blanket allegation that this injustice is the result of a deliberate ideological strategy by the establishment *as a whole* would be incorrect, and the vigorous protestations of the defenders of the discourse may indeed reflect genuine indignation felt at what they themselves consider to be unjust aspersions cast on their motives.

---

[28] For a discussion of the differences between Said and Foucault, see Walia, 2001, especially 28-31.
[29] This is a subject of debate in the French tradition between Foucault and Althusser. See Lecourt, 2001, 33-44 and 188-203.

The standard response of criticism would be to dismiss this argument in its entirety. Let me explain with an example. There are many *hadith*s, now widely considered in Muslim thought to be racist fabrications, that were nevertheless reported and endorsed by respected scholars, discrediting black and Sudanic peoples in their entirety.[30] We are told that the Prophet said, "choose suitable partners for your children, but avoid marrying blacks for they are a deformed race (*fa innahu lawnun mushawwah*)."[31] Another report claims that the Prophet said, "Blacks live guided by their private parts and stomachs" (i.e. they are only good in fornication and gluttony).[32] Ahmad Ibn Hanbal reports that God created the white race (*dhurriyya bayda'*) from Adam's right shoulder and the black race (*dhurriyyah sawda'*) from his left shoulder, then He decreed that those on the right will enter heaven and those on the left will enter hell.[33] These *hadith*s have been condemned as racist by many scholars, notably Ibn al-Qayyim and the Wahhabi scholar Nasir al-Din al-Albani.[34] However, they were reported by respected scholars like Ibn Hibban, Ibn Hanbal and al-Hakim, and authenticated by scholars as recent as al-Suyuti. It is almost certain that those who rejected these *hadith*s did so because of their self-evident immorality and racism.[35]

If any Muslim thinker today were to rely on the evidence even of a respected early scholar to justify a Muslim society based on racism he would be roundly condemned. The question whether he was using the traditions to support an antecedent ideology of racism, or whether his racist beliefs were rather derived from his faith in the authenticity of the traditions, would be immaterial. The same argument applies to the criticism of the manner in which *shari'ah* is applied in Northern Nigeria. In the final analysis, it does not matter whether those who endorse amputation for goat thiefs but not for corrupt public servants, or who approve *different standards* of proving adultery for a man and a woman who committed the crime *together* (thus ensuring conviction of the woman and acquittal of the man), do this as a

---

[30] For several of the references below I am indebted to El-Fadl, 2001, 247-250.
[31] Al-Hindi, *Kanz ul-'Ummal*, 16: 295.
[32] See ibid., 9: 86-87; al-Tabarani, *al-Mu'jam al-Kabir*, 11: 153.
[33] Ibn Hanbal, *Musnad*, 6: 492.
[34] Al-Albani, *Silsilat*, 2: 158.
[35] El-Fadl, 2001, 248.

matter of antecedent ideology or of derivation from faith. The end result is the same: and the immorality and injustice of that result must be exposed and resisted, just as one would condemn and resist any attempt to justify a Muslim society based on racism.[36]

Ironically, this conclusion is implicit in Foucault's critique of the role given to ideology in Althusserian thought. He argues that

> the problem does not consist in drawing the line between that in a discourse which falls under the category of scientificity or truth, and that which comes under some other category, but in seeing historically how effects of truth are produced within discourses which in themselves are neither true nor false.[37]

This much is true, but it seems to me that we cannot be indifferent as to these effects, and our endorsement of, or resistance to them implies the adoption of a certain standard of judgement, hence of truth. It is this fact that pitches subversive trends against dominant discourses, and sets the stage for the dialectical confrontation that is the subject of discussion. It would seem that, on this point, Said and Althusser are correct, for all *practical* purposes.

However, it is true that many Muslims, irrespective of class and gender, do not question the implicit truth-claims of the *shari'ah* discourse. For these persons, the exercise is an act of piety, not one of manipulation. This seems to me to be corroborated by certain scholarship that considers ideological positions as truth-claims so long as they are considered in the objective context of a "cultural domain." On this reading, such positions can be defended so long as we recognise as their context a given "cultural system or consciousness."[38] I will not discuss the merits and demerits of this argument here. What is clear is that the blanket condemnation of the *shari'ah* project as some form of conspiracy by men and the elite to oppress women and the poor has elicited a defensive response on the part of the men and the elite, and a stiffening of their stubborn

---

[36] One lesson from the example of the racist *hadith*s is that once the Muslims are convinced of the essential immorality or injustice of a position, they are less likely to resist its repudiation or reform.
[37] Quoted in Lecourt, 2001, 194.
[38] See Oruka, 1998, 58-62.

tendency to resist change. Dialogue with them can be facilitated through recognition of, and respect for, the honesty and good intentions of at least some, and perhaps many of them. This dialogue could be situated within an on-going process in the wider Muslim world that has led to reforms in criminal and personal laws.

There is a general recognition in Muslim scholarship that strict adherence to the interpretation of a particular scholar or school of law (*taqlid*) is not the Islamic ideal. Most Muslim nations have driven reforms through the introduction of flexibility in and diversification of sources of legislation, usually within the constraints of the totality of the early tradition. For example, some of the historico-cultural factors that influenced legal scholarship may be addressed through the *salafi* insistence on the primacy – and exclusivity – of the Qur'an and authentic traditions as sources of legislation. Every view expressed by a scholar is to be weighed against these two sources and rejected if it contradicts them. A second approach is choice (*takhyir*) among the opinions of various schools. This would, for instance, open up the possibility of examining Maliki rulings against those of the Hanafi, Shafi'i and Hanbali schools, in addition to the views of individual jurists like al-Tabari and Ibn Hazm. Within the Maliki tradition itself, flexibility can take the form of a broadening of source literature to include the works of Ibn 'Arabi,[39] al-Qurtubi,[40] Ibn Rushd,[41] al-Shatibi,[42] Ibn 'Abd al-Salam[43] and Ibn 'Abd al-Barr,[44] among others. Many new interpretations of the law are to be found in these sources. These scholars differ in their approaches to exegesis and it is to be expected that the decision on the preferred opinion will be influenced by the rules of authentication. For example, Ibn Abd al-Barr shows strong tendencies towards giving weight to the authentic *hadith*s in legislation, while al-Shatibi and Ibn Abd al-Salam show a great appreciation for the general interest (or *maslahah*). A fruitful case may be made within traditional scholarship for the need to give due

---

[39] Such as his commentary on the *Muwatta'* of Imam Malik, *Al-Qabas*.
[40] *Al-Jami'a l-Ahkam al-Qur'an*.
[41] *Al-Bayan wa'l-Tahsil*.
[42] *Al-Muwafiqat*.
[43] *Qawa'id al-Ahkam*.
[44] *Al-Tamhid* and *al-Istidhkar*.

weight to the overall interest of the Muslim community in its present circumstances while prioritising our options.

In the area of criminal law, critical theorists can draw attention to a much-neglected area, that of *ta'zir* (deterrence), which in fact holds the greatest potential for dynamism and social re-engineering. Many of the imbalances complained about in the punishments for theft and adultery, for instance, can be redressed through the instrument of *ta'zir*, which provides for a wide range of sanctions depending on the estimation made by the judge of the gravity of the particular offence. The failure of the system to provide effective sanctions for the *khiyana* – breach of trust – of the elite is therefore not a failing of the *shari'ah*, but a result of the inability or the deliberate refusal of police, prosecutors, and judges to take full advantage of its provisions in this regard. Similar arguments have been applied by Muslim nations in the areas of personal and civil law when promoting legislation protecting the rights of women in marriage, divorce and custody, as well as their right to education and work.[45]

A final area in which critics of the discourse have failed is in the concentration of their effort on criticising punishments in Muslim law. It is true that this is a natural response to the manner in which the political leaders of Northern Nigeria have limited their contribution to the introduction of the fixed punishments or *hudud*. However, critics have also been major contributors to the excessive focus on this area. The *shari'ah* is primarily about the actualisation of the objective norms of the Muslim religion, and the constitution of a society of human beings living a life guided by a Divine moral code. Specific differences in definition notwithstanding, most Muslims would agree that the *shari'ah* is about promoting education, honesty, justice and fairness, good-neighbourliness, charity, compassion for the poor, care for the weak (particularly the elderly, the woman and the child) and loyalty to the community. Whole works have been written on the core values of political leadership in Islam, based on the intellectual legacy of the leaders of the 19th century *jihad* in Northern Nigeria.[46] It seems to me that while Muslim critics are correct to censure the focus of "*shari'ah* implementation" on

---

[45] See Sanusi, 2002.
[46] See for example Tukur, 1999.

punishments to the exclusion of other areas like social justice, education, poverty alleviation and moral reform, they have failed to make constructive suggestions as to how these other areas should be addressed. In other words criticism has too often only condemned what is being done wrongly, while too seldom shining the light in a positive direction. Criticism also often fails to recognize actual steps taken in the direction of societal re-orientation and reform, and to give allowance for a learning curve, particularly given the extent of the moral decay permeating Nigerian society.

CONCLUSION

I have in this paper tried to put down some of my reflections on the intercultural dialogue about *shari'ah*. The exercise has presented for me a challenge in that it compelled me to reflect critically on the views of my ideological opponents as well as my own. While my views are largely unchanged, the paper has led to a reconsideration of strategy and tactics in the critical engagement with *shari'ah* discourse. I have tried to ground this contribution within the broad theoretical nexus of the hermeneutical tradition, drawing not only on the dialogic approach of Hans Georg Gadamer but, and perhaps more partially, on the critical hermeneutics of Jürgen Habermas. In any case, I have tried to make the following points.

First, that dialogue offers an opportunity for progress, through reciprocal absorption of the ideas and viewpoints of the *Other*. By adopting a dialogic approach to social problems we are able to move the views of the *Other* towards our own while we in turn find our own views fashioned or altered somewhat through contact with foreign views.

Second, that *shari'ah* in Northern Nigeria, understood as the contemporary ascendant political discourse in the region, has been subjected to criticism from two sources. One source is the West, which has carried into Northern Nigeria its policy of demanding the capitulation of other cultures to its own values and concepts, without respecting their right to insist on their own identity. This may not apply to all Europeans or Americans, but it does apply to the official discourse coming from the West, including the views of secular and clerical civil society. I have shown that the approach of the West will not lead to fruitful dialogue precisely because of its failure to recognize the authenticity of Islam and to respect the sensitivities of Muslim peoples to what is viewed as a grand conspiracy aimed at destroying Islam. The fact that globalisation is viewed as a conquering, predatory movement from the West also makes its humanitarian claims suspect, in view of the great poverty and human destruction that comes in its wake.

The second source of criticism is internal to the Muslim community in Northern Nigeria, and is spearheaded by Western-educated Muslims who have ideological leanings of a radical or progressive nature, and who therefore resist what they view as an attempt to legitimate ideological reaction through the appropriation of religious symbols. I have argued that this group is in reality part of the "Western" tradition, to the extent that its ontological presuppositions reflect the "*West*-oxification" of its intellect. However, its healthy scepticism for the geo-political and strategic designs (not to speak of the supremacist pretensions) of the Occidental tradition ensure a critical appropriation of Western thought, and this places the group in the unique position of interlocutor and facilitator of dialogue.

Let me be more specific on the last point. Muslim critics need first to be more critical of their own views and recognise the influence of Western rationalist pre-suppositions on their re-interpretation of the Muslim world-view. Secondly, they need to apply the distinction in post-structuralist thought between those who consciously manipulate religion for ideological ends and those who genuinely believe they are implementing God's law and who seek no material reward for their effort. This would entail contextualising religious interpretation and practice within a "cultural domain," thus refraining from the wholesale judgment of Muslim society by the standards of Western capitalist societies. The latter are driven by a conscious and deliberate effort to control nature, to improve material conditions of living, and to exploit all resources – including human beings – in the quest for attaining those objectives. By making this distinction, it becomes possible to have a meaningful discussion within the Muslim intellectual tradition that will lead to a more liberal, egalitarian and progressive application of Muslim laws. Finally, Muslim critics need to emphasise the objective norms of Muslim law and offer constructive comments aimed at using Islam as a driver of social justice and human development, as opposed to the present pattern of constant criticism of the negative aspects of the *shari'ah* discourse.

In this way, I believe, the *shari'ah* discourse can be brought to implement much-needed reforms without giving up its own identity and seeming to capitulate to the demands of Western culture and civilisation. Confronted by a powerful and global discourse, which seems bent on its own "transcendentalisation"[47] as the only *reality*, and which is determined to attain a coagulation of diverse and particular histories into reincarnations of itself as the model for the universe, the Muslim world can preserve essential elements of its own authenticity by selective adoption of those modern values that satisfy the yearnings of the modern Muslim for emancipation, justice and equity. This selective adoption, it is understood, will only occur to the extent that the modern values in question can be accommodated by a new understanding of Islam's sacred texts, reflecting the exegesis of the contemporary (i.e. modern) interpretive community. In this way a stable synthesis emerges not through complete "Westernisation" of Northern Muslim states, which would be a capitulation to the negation of *shari'ah* discourse, but through reforms of the discourse. These reforms would represent, in Hegelian terms, the dialectical synthesis of the discourse with its negation.

REFERENCES

Al-Albani, *Silsilat al-Ahadith al-Dha'eefah wa 'l-Maudhu'ah*, Riyadh: Maktabat Ma'arif, 1996.

Al-Hindi, *Kanz ul-'Ummal*, Haidarabad ad-Dakkan: Da'irat al-ma'arif al-'uthmaniyyah, since 1970, 22 vol.

Al-Qurtubi, *Al-Jami' al-Ahkam al-Qur'an*, Beirut: Muassasa Manahil al-'Irfan, n.d.

Al-Shatibi, *Al-Muwafiqat*, Beirut: Darul Ma'rifah, n.d.

Al-Tabarani, *al-Mu'jam al-Kabir*, Beirut: n.p, n.d.

Althusser, Louis, *Lenin and Philosophy and other essays*, New York: Monthly Review Press, 1971.

---

[47] I have borrowed this term from Serequeberhan, 1998, 68.

Bowie, Andrew, *Introduction to German Philosophy from Kant to Habermas*, Cambridge, UK: Polity Press, 2003.

El-Fadl, Khaled Abou, *Speaking in God's Name: Islamic law, authority and women*, Oxford: Oneworld, 2001.

Fanon, Frantz, *The Wretched of the Earth*, New York: Grove Weidenfeld, 1968.

Grondin, Jean, *Introduction to Philosophical Hermeneutics*, New Haven: Yale University Press, 1994.

_____, *Hans-Georg Gadamer: A biography*, New Haven: Yale University Press, 2003[a].

_____, *The Philosophy of Gadamer*, Montréal: McGill-Queen's University Press, 2003[b].

Habermas, Jürgen, *Religion and Rationality: Essays on reason, God, and modernity*, Cambridge, Mass.: MIT Press, 2002.

Hasan, Hasan Ibrahim, *Tarikh al-Islam al-Siyasi*, Beirut: Dar al-Jil, 1991.

Hays, Gregory, "Introduction", in: Marcus Aurelius, *Meditations*, New York: Modern Library, 2002, vii ff.

Honneth, Alex, "The social dynamics of disrespect: situating critical theory today", in Peter Dews (ed.), *Habermas: A critical reader*, Oxford, UK & Malden, Mass.: Blackwell, 1999, 320-337.

Ibn 'Abd al-Barr, *Al-Tamhid li ma fi Muwatta' min al-Ma'ani wa'l-Asanid*, Rabat: al-Warashat al-'Arabiyyah li'l-Tajdid al-Fanni, 1967.

_____, *al-Istidhkar*, Beirut/Damascus: Dar Qutaiba, 1993.

Ibn 'Abd al-Salam, *Qawa'id al-Ahkam*, Beirut: Dar al-Kutub al-'Ilmiya, n.d.

Ibn 'Arabi, *Al-Qabas*, Dar al-Gharb al-Islami, 1992.

Ibn Hanbal, *Musnad*, Beirut: Dar al-Kutub, 1985.

Ibn Qayyim, *Ahkam Ahl al-Dhimmah*, Beirut: Dar al-'Ilm li 'l-Malayin, 1983.

Ibn Rushd, *Al-Bayan wa'l-Tahsil*, Beirut: Dar al-Gharb al-Islam, 1984-1991.

Ibn Taimiyyah, *Iqtidha' as-Sirat al-Mustaqim Mukhalafah Ashab al-Jahim*, annotated by Nasir b. Abd al-Karim al-'Aql, n.p., 1984.

Imam, Ayesha, "Fighting the polical (ab)use of religion in Nigeria", http://www.whrnet.org/fundamentalisms/docs/doc-wsfmeeting-2002.html.

Jameson, Frederic, "Introduction", in Louis Althusser, *Lenin and Philosophy and other essays*, New York: Monthly Review Press, 1971, vii-xiv.

Lecourt, Dominique, *The Mediocracy: French philosophy since the mid-1970s*, London & New York: Verso, 2001.

Lyotard, Jean François, *The Postmodern Explained: Correspondence, 1982-1985*, Minneapolis: University of Minnesota Press, 1993.

McCarthy, Thomas A., *The Critical Theory of Jürgen Habermas*, Cambridge, Mass.: MIT Press, 1978.

Mendieta, Eduardo, "Introduction", in: Jürgen Habermas, *Religion and Rationality: Essays on reason, God, and modernity*, Cambridge, Mass.: MIT Press, 2002, 1-36.

Oruka, H. Odera, "Ideology and culture: the African experience", in: P.H. Coetzee and A.P.J. Roux (eds.), *Philosophy from Africa: A text with readings*, Oxford University Press, 2002, 58-63.

Said, Edward W., *Orientalism*, New York: Pantheon Books, 1978.

Sanusi, Sanusi Lamido, "Non-Muslims in a contemporary Islamic state", www.gamji.com/sanusi.htm, 1998.

———, "Between *shari'ah* and barbarism", www.gamji.com/sanusi.htm, 1999.

———, "Woman and political leadership in Muslim thought: a critique", www.gamji.com/sanusi.htm, 2001.

———, "The politicisation of ontological questions: discourses, subjectivities and Muslim family law in Northern Nigeria", www.gamji.com/sanusi.htm, 2002.

———, "Democracy, rights and Islam", www.gamji.com/sanusi.htm, 2003[a].

———, "Muslim communities in multi-religious milieux: some reflections on the Madinan constitution", www.gamji.com/sanusi.htm, 2003[b].

Serequeberhan, Tsenay, "The critique of eurocentrism and the practice of African philosophy", in: P.H. Coetzee and A.P.J. Roux (eds.), *The African Philosophy Reader*, London & New York: Routledge, 1998, 64-78.

Shaykh, Sa'diyya, "Transforming feminisms: Islam, women and gender justice", in Omid Safi (ed.), *Progressive Muslims: On justice, gender and pluralism*, Oxford: Oneworld, 2003, 147-162.

Thompson, E.P., *The Poverty of Theory & Other Essays*, New York: Monthly Review Press, 1978.

Tukur, Mahmud M., *Leadership and Governance in Nigeria: The relevance of values*, London: Hodder & Stroughton, 1999.

Walia, Shelley, *Edward Said and the Writing of History*, Cambridge, UK: Icon Books, 2001.

Warnke, Georgia, *Gadamer: Hermeneutics, tradition and reason*, Cambridge, UK: Polity Press, 1987.

Weinsheimer, Joel, *Philosophical Hermeneutics and Literary Theory*, New Haven: Yale University Press, 1991.

Commentary

I.

Umar H.D. Danfulani

A BRIEF SUMMARY OF SANUSI LAMIDO SANUSI'S PAPER

In his paper Sanusi Lamido Sanusi sets out to achieve four things. First, a methodology grounded in the hermeneutical traditions of Jürgen Habermas and the dialogic approach of Hans-Georg Gadamer. Second, to extol the virtues of dialogue in the discourse on *shari'ah* in Nigeria. Third and fourth, to discuss two criticisms that the *shari'ah* discourse has so far attracted. The first of these, the official discourse from the West, is the view of secular clerical civil society. This approach, according to Sanusi, cannot lead to fruitful dialogue because it does not respect the sensibilities of Muslims, who view it as a grand conspiracy to destroy Islam. Thus most Northern Nigerian Muslims demonise globalisation as an all-Western conquering predator, which leaves poverty in its wake. Its human rights claims are considered suspect. Finally, there is also an internal self evaluation of the *shari'ah* expansion from within, spearheaded by Western-educated Muslims who have ideological leanings of a radical progressive nature and who resist *shari'ah* re-implementation because they view it as an attempt to legitimise ideological reaction through appropriating religious symbols/space. These Muslim critics, according to Sanusi, have been thoroughly Westernised since their intellectual output is a product of Western thought or has been (in his word) *westoxicated*. Their hermeneutics of Muslim cosmology (worldview) is tainted by Western rational pre-suppositions. Sanusi differentiates between those who manipulate religion for power, food and shelter, and pious/righteous Muslims who view themselves as implementing the laws of God. The second group seek to explore the laws of God for creating a better society with better living conditions for its citizens but they have very clearly failed. He ends by stressing that liberal or progressive Muslim critics should be more constructive in analysing the *shari'ah* re-implementation project going on in Northern Nigeria and that they should focus on its virtues rather than on the negative aspects as is the case today.

THE POWER OF COSMOLOGY AND THE CULTURAL MATRIX

Sanusi clearly states that the Muslim world, including Northern Nigerian Muslims, have over the years developed great hatred for the West. The question that is germane to our discussion here is why this is the case. In other words, why does most of the Muslim world disagree with, reject and even hate most Western ways of doing things? Why is the socio-economic capitalist system and political machinery of the West unacceptable to most of the Islamic world? Why are Western ways, religions, and cultures not acceptable to Muslims? Why does the Muslim reject Westernisation and term globalisation *Americanisation*? This is essentially the case because Westerners share different cosmologies from those of most Muslims, and certainly from most African Muslims, and it is because though there are overlapping areas in their world views, there are also yawning differences.

In Nigeria, how many Christians became Christians by converting from Islam? How many Muslims were born and brought up as Christians before they crossed the carpet over to Islam? Indeed most Nigerians are born and brought up through generations of their respective faiths. Thus most Muslims and Christians in Nigeria were born, not made. Many people on the Jos Plateau for example, would have remained adherents of various traditional religions if not for the *jihad* wars which affected a few pockets and later the more influential activities of Christian missions. Yet, returning to the Western example we have greatly criticised, some beautiful concepts exist within it which we are ignoring. Westerners behave as if the rest of the world does not exist just because they are Westerners and they do not hide the fact. Western cosmology or way of looking at the rest of the world constitutes the raison d'être of Western culture, hence the cultural matrix here is uniquely and positively Western, American, British and/or German among others, which ensures that such Western or national interests are protected throughout the world. A question we should address is this: do Nigerians possess a cultural matrix that is uniquely positive and can equally protect the interests of Nigeria and Nigerians anywhere and everywhere in the world? *Americanisation* ensures that Americans are not only proud of being American, but are protected throughout the world. We may call it selfish and even hate it, but this does not change the fact that any threat to the life of a single American causes insecurity in the whole American nation.

Do Nigerians possess such patriotism? Have they evolved such spirit and built it into their body politic? Is such a spirit of nationalism strong enough to build a virile nation where Nigerian Muslims and Christians can live together peacefully and which they can truly and proudly call their own? Or are the matters of religion more important for Nigerian Muslims and Christians than the nation state? When I try to elicit answers to these questions I shudder with fear for generations of Nigerian children yet unborn, because, while the West has moulded the notion of nationhood into a majority of its citizens by making it a part of its civil myths, cosmology and thus the cultural matrix, Nigeria has failed woefully in that direction. In the US for example, notions of liberty, civil society, rule of law, equity and freedom have been mythologised, and symbolically and ritually engraved on the society as a part of its civil religious programme.

While Western cosmology has been harnessed towards patriotism to nationhood at all cost, the Nigerian mythical and cosmological frequency has been tuned towards patriotism for religion – sect/denomination and ethnic group, among others. Here lies the power of the cultural matrix. Thus when I say "I love Nigeria," it may merely relate to or mean that I love a particular region, local government area, village, religious culture, ethnic group and/or a section of the town. While in the West, citizens freely live where they choose, in Nigeria they are considered settlers and/or treated as second class citizens on the grounds of ethnicity – so called "sons of the soil" or they are regarded as *unbelievers*, *kafir* or *arna* when the religious card is flashed. Solving this issue is one of the greatest challenges facing the Nigerian nation. While the West forges ahead in the area of closer ties (G8, European Union and NATO) and explores the possibilities of forging a single human community and coinage amidst a great deal of cultural, national, political, social, economic, and religious diversities, Nigerians bask in the empty glory of their derisive and divisive pluralisms. The day Nigeria sheds off its scales and cloaks of ethnicity and the settler mentality and provides the enabling environment for its citizens to settle anywhere without ethnic, religious and/or cultural prejudice, without being treated as second class citizens in their own country, one of the great sources of crises and dehumanisation would greatly diminish because the backbone of ethnicity and religious discrimination and other grounds of differences would have been broken.

THE FEAR OF MUSLIM EXTREMISTS OR FUNDAMENTALISTS

As observed by Sanusi, liberal Muslims who are Western trained are very critical of the on-going exercise of expanding the jurisdiction of *shari'ah* laws. This also means that perhaps there are other voices among Northern Nigerian Muslims discussing the *shari'ah* issue. What are these voices saying? Are Muslims satisfied with this on-going process of expansion? If not, at what stage of the expansion will they be satisfied? If so, then why do we have other groups coming out to demand for a more strict type of *shari'ah* such as the recent self-styled Taliban or *Hijrah* group of Yobe State? We should recall the recent incident whereby Islamic fundamentalists and fanatics sacked several villages in Yobe, particularly Kanamma, overrunning police stations – symbols of civil society and law and order – all in the name of putting in place a better *shari'ah* government. This exhibits their disenchantment and disappointment with the on-going *shari'ah* expansion exercise going on in the state.

What actually happened in Kanamma? In December 2003, Nigerian security agents attacked the members of the self-appointed government of a group referring to itself as the *Hijrah*, which had earlier-on overrun Kanamma and its environs, making the inhabitants to run helter-skelter. They had been erroneously labelled *Maitatsine* and/or *Taliban*. Both the *ulama* and their students, including Muslims and Christians, did not fully comprehend the Maitatsine movement of the 1980s. Perhaps, because the *ulama* failed in performing their duties, persons such as Mohammdu Marwa Allah Maitasine felt that with their own interpretation of the Qur'an and Sunnah, they could produce a *mujtahid, mujaddid* (reformer) or even *Mahdi*, ('chosen one', 'sent one') together with a society ruled by their own brand of misguided *shari'ah*. We all know that Islam goes far beyond what Mohammdu Marwa Allah Maitasine taught and stood for. The same fact could be said about the *Hijrah* group of Kanamma in Yobe State. They ironically migrated (performed *hijrah*) by isolating or separating themselves from the rest of society. They performed this act of *hijrah* after the fashion of migration of eighty-three families of the early Muslim community in Mecca to the Christian Emperor of Abyssinia and the *hijrah* performed after the first of *Aqabah* (in the 11th year of Muhammad's prophethood). This was later performed by the West African *mujtahid* Sheikh Usman Dan Fodio from Degel to Gudu in 1804, and repeated by *al-Takfir wa'l-Hijrah*, the militant offshoot of the Egyptian *Ikhwan al-Muslimin*. The Kanamma *Hijrah ummah* or community of Yobe State was indeed seeking for an ideal— the utopian society promised by politicians in *shari'ah*-complaint states, but which has remained elusive since such a society cannot be realised anywhere today in the world. They sought to establish a separate society free from corruption, lack of accountability and injustice. They sought in its place a transparent society, with upright leaders who are not day-light thieves and robbers. This end product should indeed be envisaged as *shari'ah* law is being expanded all over the larger portion of Northern Nigeria. We may then ask how far and to what extent *shari'ah* law should be expanded today. It is clear that various Muslim groups/sects will draw the line differently and some extremist "Islamic revivalists" may well never have enough of *shari'ah*!

Thus, if the governments of the *shari'ah*-complaint states are not watchful, they will soon find themselves once more being caught within the jaws of the vicious cycle of violence led by some so called *Hijrah* conservatives or even un-Islamic groups whom we can truly term fundamentalists as was the case with the Maitatsine uprisings of the 1980 and 1990s. This destructive and dehumanising type of "Islamic revivalism" and Talibanisation process must be avoided at all costs and all pious Muslims must stay away from this path so that we can together denounce those who would choose to trek on it in the future. I think when scholars such as Sanusi Lamido Sanusi and Abdullahi A. An-Na'im criticise the on-going expansion exercise in Nigeria, they are merely cautioning against this type of excess in the name of implementing *shari'ah* in the stricter sense employed such as the Taliban government of Kabul in Afghanistan.

THE MISAPPLICATION OF *SHARI'AH*

Most Muslims in Nigeria in particular and Africa in general are ignorant of what *shari'ah* is all about. This ignorance is even heavier where Christians are concerned. That being the case, what do we expect of the West which is even more ignorant and may not have the patience and the will to learn about it? When the Westerner is confronted with something s/he does not understand the tendency for him/her is to reject it with a contempt and arrogance that may not necessarily stem from any theory of grand conspiracy. The onus lies on us (Nigerians) to at least educate ourselves (Christians and Muslims) through the dialogue proposed by Sanusi, so that we will have the proper perspective and orientation on what *shari'ah* is all about and stem the tide of misunderstanding and misapplication of *shari'ah* going on in society. The point has been made elsewhere by myself and by many other scholars including Sanusi, and rightly so, that there is nothing wrong with the nature, virtues and values of *shari'ah*. Most of these are found in the Jewish Torah (see Exodus 19-20, and the Decalogue) of the Christians Bible. The problems inherently associated with the *shari'ah* are with the wide-ranging misapplication of the laws by those responsible for their implementation. It is only when they are thus misapplied that they appear unacceptable to the majority of Christians and Westerners. I should also add that this misapplication we are referring to primarily affects the underdogs in society. *Shari'ah* is applied by non-experts on both Muslims and non-Muslims alike in a gendered society where the weak are not protected in accordance with the injunctions of the Qur'an and the traditions of the Prophet, to the exclusion of the "powerful and wealthy" or sacred cows in society.

THE REALITY OF POVERTY AND UNDERDEVELOPMENT

It is not enough to state that "the great economic inequalities in Nigeria have been made possible by a combination of official corruption and the pursuit of economic policies inspired by the so called 'Washington Consensus'" as stated by Sanusi. It is time for us to stop moaning, wining and shouting foul against the West and accusing it for every failure in our system. If Western "policies have led to the death of industry and increased unemployment, the devaluation of the local currency and national assets, the disappearance of the middle-class, economic distortions that favour importers of products from the West and middle-men," as Sanusi says, what part have we Nigerians played in this saga? It is not fair to blame our poverty, joblessness, etc., etc., on others so many years after independence!

POVERTY AND THE REDISTRIBUTION OF WEALTH

Sanusi reminds us about the principles of the Qur'an and the Sunnah, which enjoin society to develop the spirit of brother/sisterhood in the *ummah* to foster an egalitarian existence.[1] The Qur'an in *Suratul Hashr* enjoins rich Muslims not to hoard wealth but to take care of "the next of kin and orphans and the needy and the wayfarer."[2] The Qur'an in *Suratul Taubah* strongly condemns Jewish rabbis and Christian monks who "hoard gold and silver," saying that in hell fire

> their foreheads and their flanks and their backs will be branded therewith: "Here is that which you hoarded for yourselves. Now taste of what you used to hoard."[3]

Wealth is supposed to be distributed in accordance with carefully laid down procedures provided by the *zakat* institution such that nobody would be poor within an Islamic state. Islam condemns corruption even as the Prophet said in a *hadith*: "He is not a true Muslim who eats his fill when his next door neighbour is hungry"[4] and "the administrator who rules over the affairs of Muslims but remains indifferent to their plight, needs and poverty, Allah will also be

---

[1] This subsection, and parts of my conclusions, are based on Sanusi, 2001.
[2] Qur'an 59:7, quoted in Sanusi, 2001.
[3] Qur'an 34:5, quoted in Sanusi, 2001.
[4] Al-Bukhari, *al-Adab al-Mufrad*, quoted in Sanusi, 2001.

indifferent to his own plight, needs and poverty."⁵ Furthermore, the Prophet declared that, "Any ruler who is responsible for the affairs of Muslims but does not strive sincerely for their well being will not enter paradise with them."⁶ The responsibility for the collection of *zakat* and its equitable distribution is aimed at the elimination of poverty from the Muslim *ummah*. Thus Caliph Umar stressed that all in the *ummah* including the Caliph have an equal right to the wealth of the community. Similarly, Caliph Ali observed that God made it obligatory for the wealthy to provide for the poor. Thus if the masses are hungry, naked or troubled, it is because the rich have deprived them and God will punish them for it.⁷

An excellent warning to rulers, particularly the contemporary political *shari'ah*-ists of Northern Nigeria readily comes from Abdullahi Dan Fodio, the brother of Sheikh Usman, who in 1809 was so appalled at the enormity of the greed of some of the officers serving under him that he wrote in his treatise, *Tazyn Al-Waraqat (A Revolution Betrayed)*,

> Their affairs had become confused because of their preoccupation with the world . . . liars who say that which they do not do, and follow their desires, And follow avarice in everything incumbent upon them; And who has broken with his own people and scorned knowledge, And who has preferred the crown of rabble to his own relations, Whose purpose is not the affairs of the mosques, Nor the schools of learning, nor even the affairs of the Qur'an schools, But whose purpose is the ruling of the countries and their people in order to obtain delights and acquire rank, according to the customs of the unbelievers, and the titles of their sovereignty and devouring of the gifts of sanctity, and booty, and bribery and lutes, and flutes and the beating of drums; And the collecting of concubines, and fine cloths and horses that gallop in the towns, not the battle fields.⁸

---

⁵ Abu Dawud, *Suman*, quoted in Sanusi, 2001.
⁶ Sahih Muslim, 1987, 1/126.
⁷ Sanusi, 2001.
⁸ Hodgkin, 1975, 260; cf. Kukah, 1993, 2, Kukah and Falola, 1996, 101, 118 f.

Hausa poets criticised such abuses by rulers and politicians in much the same way in which Sheikh Usman Dan Fodio once spoke of the *Habe* courts, "Do not act proudly because of this world, do not strive for wealth . . . . Do not practice confiscation as the courtiers do, galloping, galloping upon their ponies, they seized by force from the peasants and leave them, With nothing save the sweat of their brow."[9]

LIVING CONDITIONS OF THE MASSES IN NORTHERN NIGERIA

The Northern Region of Nigeria was not ready for impendence from the British in 1957 or even earlier because it was generally backward in all areas of development and the presence of civil society. Today the economy of the North has been thoroughly destroyed by years of ethno-religious riots and civil unrest that annually moved from one city/town to the other. This has had the net effect of creating an atmosphere of political instability and the general feeling of lack of personal and collective security with criminality on the increase. Unfortunately too, the *shari'ah* reforms have not substantially improved the living conditions of the *talakawa* masses or *fellahems* in these areas. Mohammed, Adamu and Abba set out to address this issue when they wrote:

> The fundamental issue of the relationship between these reforms and the living conditions of the tens of millions of Nigerian citizens of the Muslim faith who are mostly directly affected is almost completely ignored. Many of the politicians, journalists and clerics on both sides of the controversy seem to want to turn the whole matter into one of a 'jihad' or a 'crusade', in wanton disregard of what will be the grim consequences to millions of innocent men, women and children of both the Muslim and Christian faiths who have been living together peacefully, amicably and fraternally, and whose living conditions are daily deteriorating irrespective of their religious faiths.[10]

---

[9] Isichei, 1983, 206.
[10] Mohammed, Adamu and Abba, 2000, 2.

First is the problem of abject poverty in the Northern states. The enormity of the challenges of justice as envisaged by the *shari'ah* is still to be fully comprehended and appreciated by Nigerians, including Muslims themselves who have chosen to live under it. Thus the impression we get from many current advocates of *shari'ah* is that it is an essentially punitive, political arrangement dealing with alcoholic beverages, the dress code, the amputation of limbs and the refurbishment of mosques,[11] and if I may add, the flogging of fornicators and stoning of adulterers, whereas it goes beyond all these. The grim realities of the conditions under which the *talakawa* in Northern Nigeria are living are bad and getting worse. These are caused by poverty, hunger, destitution, ignorance and/or lack of education, lack of health facilities, inadequate housing, cruel economic realities and political instability. These militate against the people's ability to meet the harsh conditions of *hudud*-related punishments and other aspects of their religious obligations. Once politicians settle in office, the issues concerning the living conditions of Muslims are ignored by the *shari'ah avant garde*. The issue of poverty defines whether or not a Muslim can live and lead a meaningful life in a *shari'ah* state. The *shari'ah* is holistic to the life of the Muslim. It covers his/her faith, prayer life, education, health, housing, nutrition, employment, environment, commerce, transportation and communication, among other requirements needed for existence. Legal systems are not mere abstract notions in the minds of lawyers and in books, but concretely apply to the living conditions of persons. Thus *shari'ah* propagandists in Nigeria must be concerned with the stark realities of the living conditions of the *talakawa* masses.[12]

Moreover, the economy is controlled by a few rich people, leaving 70% of the population to live on less than $1 a day. The reality on ground, particularly in Northern Nigeria, is that the governments are not providing these needs.[13] The socio-economic condition in Nigeria is not yet ripe or conducive for the introduction of *shari'ah* law. Take for instance the case of Safiya Husseini, a mother of four, who said she was enticed and tempted into adultery because

---

[11] Ibid., 8.
[12] Ibid., 2000, 6-7.
[13] Sanusi, 2001.

of the "occasional gift" she got from her farmer-fisherman boy-friend Yakubu Abubakar. Yet she was sentenced to be stoned to death by the very society that failed to cater for her by putting in place a social welfare scheme that would have solved most of her problems. The living condition of the *talakawa* is so wretched that it militates against the application of *shari'ah*. Most Muslim families live in such appalling and poverty-stricken ghetto-communities that it negates the most modest situation and/or environment they would normally need to adhere to some of the tenets of their religion, particularly *shari'ah* as a way of life. Lack of decent housing conditions and much needed privacy, which should prevail in the near ideal Muslim community, tends to promote *zina*. It is commonplace in the cities for a family of seven or nine to live in a dilapidated two-room shack, sharing a compound with many other such families. Since there is no privacy in such homes, parents are forced into intimacy with each other in the presence or within hearing of their kids. Such children are thus forced to become adults before their time. This gives rise to high incest rates, rape, pre-marital sex, lesbianism, homosexuality and *zina* in the cities.[14]

Thus the seeds of moral decay and decadence are sown in the homes even before the children are ripe for sex education and exposure to the need for such intimate relationships. Poverty and low status inhibits against the effective exercise of women's fundamental rights and freedoms.[15] Women's poverty is directly related to the absence of economic opportunities and autonomy, lack of access to economic resources, including credit and land ownership.[16]

Second is the problem of ignorance and lack of education. The level of illiteracy is very high in the far North of Nigeria.[17] The Northern *shari'ah*-compliant states are also behind in secondary school enrolment.[18] Furthermore, aside from the general backwardness of the North in the area of education, there is a general discrimination in girls' access to education. This has persisted owing

---

[14] Mohammed, Adamu and Abba, 2000, 32.
[15] Ladan, 2003, 78.
[16] Ibid., 78-79
[17] Mohammed, Adamu and Abba, 2000, 28-29 citing Federal Office of Statistics, 1997, 183, table 132.
[18] Ibid.

to customary attitudes such as early and/or forced marriage, high incidence of teenage pregnancy, inadequate gender sensitisation, gender-biased teaching and educational materials, sexual harassment and inaccessible educational facilities. Girls and young women are expected to simultaneously manage both educational and domestic responsibilities, often resulting in poor or dismal performance in scholarship, and early school leaver (drop out) syndrome.[19] Bint Badamasiuy stresses the marginalised position of women, their ignorance due to lack of education, and the limitation of their roles to childbearing, which makes them a burden to the Muslim *ummah*.[20] Moreover, the necessary awareness campaign and education concerning the meaning of *shari'ah* law is still lacking at the grassroots level. For this to occur sufficiently, the general literacy and education of the masses must be raised through adult literacy and education programmes.

Third is the problem of health and nutrition. The problem of stunted growth, wasting and under-weight have persisted in the Northern states as compared to their Southern counterparts.[21] While 63.5% of children surveyed were affected by stunting in the North, it also recorded 31.2% for underweight children. The survey revealed that 23.9% of the children in the Northeast and 25.7% in the Northwest suffered from diarrhoea, which is a direct result of poor sanitary conditions, poor water supply, lack of safe water and lack of sanitary toilet facilities.[22]

In the area of prenatal care, the North is disadvantaged. Prenatal care is available to only 47.6% of expectant mothers in Northwest and 45% in the Northeast. Furthermore, only 10.4% of women in the Northeast and 9.7% in the Northwest have access to the health care delivery facilities. While only a mere 17.7% of children in the Northwest and 15.7 in the Northeast have access to vaccination in

---

[19] Ladan, 2003, 79.
[20] Badamasiuy, 1998, 1.
[21] Mohammed, Adamu and Abba, 2000, 10.
[22] Ibid., 12, 19, and 21. Cf. USAID, 1995, Federal Office of Statistics, 1990, 101, table 8.11, and UNDP, 1997, 108. In the Federal Statistics, an analysis by state displays highest incidence of this disease in the Northern states. Adamawa recorded 14.6%, Kano 10.3% and Niger 9%, compared to the lower figures of Ogun 0.12%, Abita 0.14%, Imo 0.46%, and Rivers 0.56%

1990. Infant mortality is high in the North, recording 87.7 for every 1000 live births in the Northeast and 109.8 for every 1000 live births in the Northwest. Thus a large proportion of the children born in the Northern states will not live beyond age five. This, however, is not due to lack of agricultural resources since the North leads in the production of grains, legumes and potatoes.[23] as well as in the cultivation vegetables and meat.[24]

The *talakawa* are economically restricted and oppressed by the authorities, the wealthy, and powerful in society who exert a great deal of weight, exactions and extortion on them through the use of a great number of middlemen between producers and consumers, great disadvantages in the value of exchange between local and manufactured goods, exploitation of land, labour and needs. Nigeria has one of the lowest charges on the labour potentials of its citizens in the world today.[25]

Aside from these problems, the population suffers from ravages of diseases particularly childhood killer diseases such as cholera, meningitis, diphtheria, typhoid fever, malaria, poliomyelitis and whooping cough, among others. In fact the effort to rid Nigeria of poliomyelitis has met with a brick wall from some governors from *shari'ah*-compliant states under the pretext that the drugs being dispensed free of charge to the public by some WHO agents were fake or expired. While these common infections and diseases kill the people, the scourge of sexually transmitted diseases (STDs, or sexually transmitted infections – STIs), particularly HIV/AIDs is on the increase.

Finally, there is the problem of the Human Development Index (HDI). The United Nations Development Programme (UNDP) predicates general HDI on factors that essentially deal with long life resulting from improved health, acquisition of knowledge, development of skills, and access to resources needed for a decent standard of living and income. The HDI is generally low in Nigeria (0.400), being ranked 137th out of 174 countries in the world in 1993. The HDI for most of the Northern states is much lower than those

---

[23] See Usman, 1994, 36; Federal Office of Statistics, 1984/85 and 1986/86, 36-37, table 3.6.
[24] Yazid, 1994, 142.
[25] Mohammed, Adamu and Abba, 2000, 13.

for the rest of the country. While life expectancy in Lagos is 61.4 years and Imo is 60 years, the life expectancy in Kaduna is as low as 36.6 years, and Bauchi and Borno, 36.7 and 37 years, respectively.[26] The UNDP stated in 1997 that regional disparities in GDP, income per capita, mean years of schooling and educational level, in Nigeria were among the worst in the world. However, while Edo and Delta States' HDI of 0.666 would have ranked 90th in the world if they were separate countries, the states with low HDI in Nigeria are concentrated in the North. There are thus wide disparities in HDI (based on education, longevity and income) between the South and the North.[27]

This wide disparity persists in the area of economic development, industry and energy.[28] In fact 53% of the industries are located in the Southwest, 27.16% in Southeast and only 19.84% in the North. In the North, 324 industries (79.6%) out of a total of 407 are located in just three cities – Kaduna, Kano and Jos.[29] Thus very few jobs are generated in the industrial sector for skilled Northerners.[30] Energy is crucial for large scale industrialisation, cottage industries and household usage.[31] While only 34% of Nigerian households have access to electricity, less than 10% of the citizens in Jigawa, Kebbi, Sokoto, Zamfara, and Taraba have access to electricity. In Bauchi, Adamawa and Yobe one-fifth of the households have access to electricity, but the figures are much higher for the Southwest. In rural areas, less than 8% of the people enjoy electricity in the North.[32]

Ahmad, therefore, rightly concludes that "the challenge facing *shari'ah* critics is to modernise Islamic law, not banish it from public life."[33] Ahmad accepts the death penalty and amputation in theory, though in practice he believes that *shari'ah* implementers do not reflect the truth that much crime stems from poverty and desperation. He thus concludes that amputation for thieves should

---

[26] Ibid., 15-16; UNDP, 1997, 2.
[27] Mohammed, Adamu and Abba, 2000, 17-18; UNDP, 1997, 4.
[28] Mohammed, Adamu and Abba, 2000, 17-18.
[29] UNDP, 1997, 101.
[30] Mohammed, Adamu and Abba, 2000, 24-25.
[31] Ibid., 26.
[32] Ibid.
[33] Ahmad, 2002, 14.

not be executed until the poor are better provided for.³⁴ The socio-economic and political conditions for the full implementation of *shari'ah* are clear. Maududi, a contemporary Muslim jurist, constitutional expert and thinker also accepts the Islamic prescription of a hundred lashes for fornication and stoning to death for *zina*, but such punishments are not meant for a society experiencing moral filth, sexual excitement, nudity, pornography and carousing on cinema, but

> It applies to a society wherein every trace of suggestiveness has been destroyed, where mixed gatherings of men and women have been prohibited, where public appearance of painted and pampered women is completely non-existence, where marriage has been made easy, where virtue, piety and charity are current coins and where the remembrance of God and the thereafter is kept ever fresh in men's minds and hearts.³⁵

This work contends that such conditions are totally absent in contemporary Nigerian Muslim societies and in the so-called *shari'ah*-compliant states of Northern Nigeria. *Shari'ah* is and has been part and parcel of Islam, and one can not divorce one from the other. I agree with Sanusi when he asserts:

> The Islamic movement, as a political movement, is to be judged primarily on the basis of its success in formulating an ideology, articulating a programme and implementing (successfully) strategies that promote the interest of the Muslim *Ummah*. By *Ummah*, I do not mean Muslim emirs and chiefs, or *qadi*s and imams, or petty-bourgeois academic and middle-class elite, even though each of these rightfully belongs to the *Ummah*. I mean rather the bulk of the *Ummah*, those poor people called the masses whose illiteracy, ill-health, penury, degradation and despair cry out for a liberator. What strategies have been adopted to protect their interest? What publications have addressed their plight? Where is their voice in the public

---

³⁴ Ibid.
³⁵ Ladan, 2002, 75; cf. Maududi, 1986, 55.

discourse? What education has been given that can help them change their pathetic circumstances?[36]

CONCLUSION: THE WEST AND THE REST

In this comment on Sanusi's paper, I have urged the need for Nigerians to develop common national myths, cosmology, civil society and morality based on cohesive national symbols, unity and common goals, shared aspirations, destiny and collective human problems. There is a great deal Muslims and Christians can do to stem the tide of the HIV/AIDS pandemic, which is currently ravaging and wasting the youthful human resources of Nigeria. Fortunately, HIV/AIDS is not killing Nigerians along religious or ethnic lines. Furthermore, the problem of status and class is suffered by both Muslim and Christian *talakawa* alike, while the rich who in the words of the Prophet Amos "trample upon heads of the poor" are also Muslims and Christians; likewise those dealing in human spare parts, child labour, drug trafficking, 419 scams, trafficking in women (in red light districts where rings of commercial sex workers are operated) and children as paedophiles. There is the urgent need to recognise the human being and accord him/her with the complete and holistic worth and dignity with full and equal rights before the law and before God. The same should hold for the rule of law.

I have also observed that while Islamic revivalism of some sort is being pursued by *shari'ah*-compliant states in the North, great caution must be exercised so that government does not abdicate its responsibility of maintaining law and order by allowing Muslim extremist and fundamentalists such as the *Hijrah* group of Kanamma in Yobe State or the Maitatsines of the 1980s and 1990s to take over the reins of power in the name of pursing a more strict and utopian type of *shari'ah*. In fact, the emergence of such groups has been made possible in the first place because the *ulama* have failed in their responsibilities in leading the *ummah* towards *shari'ah* expansion, leaving a vacuum which has been utilised by politicians towards political goals.

---

[36] Sanusi, 2001.

I agree with Sanusi that *shari'ah* in its expanded form and practice has suffered misapplication in a number of areas. The problem with empirical application very often comes from failure of some *qadi*s in adjudicatory aspects owing to ignorance of and low education in *shari'ah* law itself. Islam has beautiful rights available to women under it, but it is not enough as is often done, to merely state that these rights are also violated in other religious traditions and societies. It is better to say that women are practically receiving better justice towards their fundamental rights not only because Muslims have chosen to live under *shari'ah* law but because they are Muslim women.

Finally, I have also examined favourable socio-economic conditions necessary for expansion of Islamic laws to cover criminal aspects. To this end, I agree with Sanusi and Mohammed, Adamu and Abba that the application of *hudud* punishments on erring Muslims in society are anachronistic not because the laws are faulty, but because the prevailing socio-economic circumstances of Nigerian Muslims is still detrimental towards true *ibada* worship.

REFERENCES

Ahmad, Ali, "In defence of Islamic *shari'ah*", *Viewpoint Manawatu Evening Standard*, Palmerton North, New Zealand, Friday, October 25, 2002.

Badamasiuy, Juwayriya Bint, *Status and Role of Women Under the Shari'ah*, Kaduna: Zakara Publishing Co. Ltd. and Baraka Press and Publishers Ltd, 1998.

Federal Office of Statistics (Nigeria): *Rural and Agricultural Sample Survey*, Lagos: Government Printing Office, 1984/85 and 1985/86.

Federal Office of Statistics (Nigeria): Demographic and Health Survey, Lagos: FOS and DHS, Government Printing Office, 1990.

Federal Office of Statistics (Nigeria), *Annual Abstracts of Statistics*, Abuja: Government Printing Office, 1996 and 1997.

Hodgkin, Thomas, *Nigerian Perspectives: An historical anthology*, London: Oxford University Press, 1975.

Isichei, Elizabeth, *A History of Nigeria*, London/Lagos/New York: Macmillan, 1983.

Kukah, Mathew Hassan, *Religion, Politics and Power in Northern Nigeria*, Ibadan: Spectrum Books Limited, 1993.

Kukah, Mathew Hassan and Toyin Falola, *Religious Militancy and Self Assertion: Islam and politics in Nigeria*, Aldershot/Brookfield/Hong Kong/etc.: Avebury Publications, 1996.

Ladan, Mohammed Tawfiq, "Women's rights under *shari'ah* in Northern Nigeria: a case study of Safiya", in: *Protection of Women's Rights Under Shari'ah Law: Safiya Tugartudu Husseini – a case study*, a publication of the Friedrich Ebert Stiftung, Lagos: Frankad Publishers, 2002.

Ladan, Mohammed Tawfiq, "Women's rights and access to justice under the *shari'ah* in Northern Nigeria", in: Joy Ngozi Ezeilo and Abiola Akiyode Afolabi (eds.), *Shari'ah & Women's Human Rights in Nigeria: Strategies for action*, a publication of the Women Advocates Research & Documentation Centre (WARDC) and Women's Aid Collective (WACOL), Lagos: Frankad Publishers, 2003, 37-88.

Maududi, Sayyid A.A., *Islamic Law and Constitution*, New Delhi: Taj Company, 1986.

Mohammed, Abubakar Siddique, Sa'idu Hassan Adamu, and Alkasum Abba, *The Living Conditions of the Talakawa and the Shari'ah in Contemporary Nigeria*. Zaria: Centre for Democratic Development, Research and Training, Occasional Publications No. 2, 2002.

Muslim ibn Hajj-aj al Qushayr-i, *Sahih Muslim*, (4 vol.), translated by Abdul Hamid Siddiqi, Lahore: Sh. Muhammad Ashraf, 1971-75.

Sanusi, Sanusi Lamido, "Basic needs and redistributive justice in Islam: the panacea to poverty in Nigeria", www.gamji.com/sanusi.htm, 2001.

UNDP, *Human Development Report: Nigeria*, Lagos, 1996.

UNDP, "Nigeria: selected health indicators by region", *Nigerian Human Development Report*, Lagos, 1997.

USAID, *Integrated Baseline Health Survey*, Abuja, 1995.

Usman, Yusufu Bala, *Katsina State in the Nigerian Federation: The basic realities*, Kaduna: Dansa Publications, 1994.

Yazid, Imrana, "The role of agriculture in the development of Nigeria", in: A. Mahadi et. al. (eds.), *Nigeria: The State of the Nation and the Way Forward*, Kaduna: Arewa House, 1994.

II.

Is-Haq Oloyede

The current encounter between Islam and the West has been the subject of many works, fora and conflicts. Yet there is no appreciable understanding between the two distinct perspectives to a common concern of humanity – harmonious co-existence despite differences in philosophy, ideology and approach. It has largely been, in our view, a "dialogue" between two unequal and mutually suspicious parties who, in an attempt to act as partners, which they ought to be, suppress, more often than not, their real feelings, the substance of the matter and the actual objectives of the encounter between them, by digressing into secondary issues and gigantic co-operative projects, which are realisable only with a firm foundation of sincerity, genuine dialogue and mutual respect. The present conference on *shari'ah* has all the elements, which probably account for the poor state of intercultural relationships between the West and Islam.

THE CONFERENCE AS AN ILLUSTRATION OF THE NATURE OF THE CONTEMPORARY DIALOGUE BETWEEN THE WEST AND ISLAM – INSENSITIVITY OF THE WEST TO MUSLIM CONCERNS

The organisers of this conference on "Comparative Perspectives on *Shari'ah* in Nigeria" by their declaration intend a comparative analysis of the two perspectives on *shari'ah* – that of the West and that of Islam or the Muslims. The other alternative is that it is intended as comparative analysis in the sense that the situation elsewhere in the world is to be compared with the situation in Nigeria on the *shari'ah*. In either case, the need for authentic expression of the Nigerian situation is critical. Muslims in Nigeria are almost unanimous in suspecting the motives of the organisers, particularly when the USA's involvement is alleged. A little sensitivity to the feelings of the Muslims would have made, in our view, the difference. However, the choice of the main speakers, apparently inadvertent, hardly supports the proclaimed mission. ALL the actors in the promulgation and implementation of *shari'ah* in Nigeria are effectively excluded from making major input into the proceeding and probably eventual product of the conference. There is no doubt that the West is adequately represented in the team of main speakers while Islam is made to be represented by those whose opinions on *shari'ah* implementation in Nigeria are known not to be representative of the majority of Muslims in Nigeria. The agenda-setting posture of the West is also evident from the topic of the main study which gave birth to the conference, "The *Shari'ah* Debate and the Shaping of Muslim and Christian Identities in Northern Nigeria." Muslims argue that the topic appears to be an intuitive articulation of the real goal of the study. It is observed that secularism, which has de-Islamised the Muslims in the south-western part of Nigeria for instance, does not attract such study, but the very recent development of implementation of the *shari'ah* is so disturbing to the West that many conferences have to be funded apparently to nip it in the bud.

A group of Muslims, irrespective of their declared good intentions, who sponsor a debate or conference on the Trinity, for example, cannot claim to have obtained Christian perspectives on the matter if the majority of the speakers are Muslims and the Christian speakers belong to a distinct Christian group such as the Jehovah's Witnesses. It is like taking the Seventh-Day Adventists' view on the Sabbath as an adequate representative of the Christians. It can be argued that the participants are objective scholars who, not being involved in the *shari'ah* project, are sufficiently detached to critically analyse the situation about *shari'ah* in Nigeria and provide detached comparative perspectives of the development of *shari'ah* in Northern Nigeria. Nevertheless, the reality, as far as we know, is that such claim of objectivity is a product of subjectivity. We agree with Sanusi Lamido Sanusi when he declares in his paper that such is pretentious and unhelpful:

> To pretend to any form of universalisation of the local, totalisation of the partial, externalisation of the historical or objectivisation of the subjective would be counterintuitive to the project of criticism.

As Sanusi also says:

> It is ... correct to say that reflecting on a debate and presentation of opposing arguments, will remain the best path to arriving at mutually acceptable solutions to social crisis.

If *shari'ah* is considered as a threat to the West, a one-man debate may not be a solution. It is indeed "a discussion with the dumb."

SOME SALIENT ISSUES

In his paper Sanusi has defined the two terms of "the West" and "*shari'ah*" in clear and certain terms that do not require extensive elucidation. Our concept of "West" and "Islam" is neither restrictive nor over generalised as it is common in many contemporary discourse on Islam and the West. The "West" is not monolithic in idea and it excludes "Western" Muslims as well as the few non-Muslims who, in their commitment to sincerity, fairness, and objectivity continue to raise objections to demonisation of Islam by the West. Islam, on the other hand, incorporates both those considered as moderate/modern and those designated as traditionalist/conservatives. We are in agreement that whenever the West discusses *shari'ah*, Islam is meant.

In his characteristic frankness, Sanusi has clearly placed on the table the real underpinnings which are primary to the discourse on the encounter of Islam by the West. One area of disagreement with his submission, is his repeated remarks on sectarian and intra-faith dialogue among Muslims which, in our view, is irrelevant to the subject of this discourse, given its nature as an inter-faith encounter. Impression ought not to be created that the "Western-educated" Muslims are representatives of the West among Muslims or are partners of the West in its self-styled reformative efforts of reshaping the *shari'ah* or Islam. The fact, as can be gathered elsewhere in Sanusi's paper, is that all Muslims have sufficient reasons to consider contemporary America in particular, if not the West, as a foe because Muslims believe that America detests Islam and Muslims. And that in reality, today, America is the leader of, if not the West.

It would be unfortunate to regard all Muslims who are critical of some interpretations of some sacred texts or certain *shari'ah* implementation-strategies as agents of the West, or closer to the West, than other Muslims. The reality, in our opinion, is that while there might be apparent agreements in conclusions reached by such Muslims and the West, the processes, reasons and objectives in most cases are different. On the other hand, one cannot deny the fact that there are a number of Muslim scholars whose modernization of Islamic thought is being propelled and guided by Western civilization and the urge to comply with Western standards even if *shari'ah* would have to be abandoned in the process.

Certain critical facts emerge from Sanusi's paper. One is that certain fixations and stereotypes exist in the perception of each other by Muslims and the West. In the West Muslims are demonised. The Prince of Wales confessed that:

> We, in the West . . . regard Islam as a threat – in medieval times as a military conqueror, and in modern times as a source of intolerance, extremism and terrorism.[1]

On the other hand, Muslims consider the West as generally hypocritical, deceptive, exploitative and unjust. Any discourse between the two which fails to take cognisance of this mutual distrust and deep-rooted hatred is at best superficial.

History is replete with facts to support Sanusi's assertion that the animosity is contemporary. In fact, what the West considers as recent Muslim fundamentalism might as well be, in Professor Anderson's words,

> . . . a two-sided phenomenon: on the one hand, a very understandable revolt against dominance, and (until recently) the colonialism, of Western powers; on the other hand, a reaction against what might be termed the Western philosophy of life which, although basically founded upon Christian faith and ethics, has become so engulfed in liberalism and agnosticism that it has largely lost both its cutting edge and persuasive power.[2]

It has been insinuated that the implementation of *shari'ah* in Northern Nigeria is discriminatory against women and the poor. While one or two of the often-quoted illustrations of the assertion may border on interpretation of the text, a large number are, in our view, based on unpreparedness of the critics to understand the justification of such provisions.

For example, proof is essential in criminal law. A proof of sexual cohabitation is pregnancy and thus, a pregnant female accused of *zina* (adultery, or fornication) has to plead one of: legitimacy of the cohabitation, coercion, or state of unconsciousness to avoid sentence. On the part of the male, in the absence of confession, the prosecutor needs to establish *ab initio* the involvement of the male in a sexual cohabitation beyond reasonable doubt. The fact that a female fornicator alleges that a particular man is her partner in crime cannot

---

[1] Quoted in Yamani, 1997, 91.
[2] Anderson, 1987, 351, quoted in Noibi, 2001, 195.

be taken as conclusive proof against him. It is this natural situation that is being misconstrued by some as deliberate discrimination in the implementation of the *shari'ah* in Nigeria.

Secondly, the issue of distinction between breach of trust and theft is fundamental. It has its root in the definition of crime. The three essential elements of a crime in a court of law are definition of the crime, the ingredients (proof) and the penalty. Many assume that in every crime, all systems of law disagree only on the penalty. This is not so.

Furthermore, breach of trust is applicable to both the poor and the rich and that explains why an employee who commits fraud in resources entrusted to him or her is not, in the *shari'ah*, to be a thief whose hand is to be amputated because Allah has forewarned human beings not to place trust in the hands of the unworthy.

Justice in Islam is class-blind. The Qur'an says:

> O ye who believe, stand out firmly for justice, as witnesses to Allah, even as against yourselves, parents, kin, and whether it be (against) rich or poor for Allah can best protect both.[3]

In the same vein, theft is not the exclusive preserve of the poor. The rich also steal or sponsor theft.

The third argument is that a penalty ought not be applied because the ideal atmosphere conducive to its application has not been created or because those charged with the implementation also commit crime. The fact that a policeman, judge or governor steals is not, in our view, excuse to allow thieves to go unpunished. What Umar did by suspending amputation during drought is still operative today as proof of being forced to steal is acceptable from an accused thief under the *shari'ah*.

One fundamental difference between Islam and the West, is that the West generally give the impression of discarding God to an extent that whatever scriptures stipulate is subject to the pleasure of man, whereas in Islam, Allah's explicit stipulations are incontestable and sacred. What the West considers as manifestations in Islam are, more often than not, the kernel of Islam itself. The remark of Francis

---

[3] Qur'an 4:135.

Lamand on the provocative ban on Muslim students wearing headscarfs in French public schools is apposite:

> The decision by the French Ministry of Education bans the wearing of "all ostentatious religious symbols" in public schools but the controversial point is that, in this decision, the ministry assumes that wearing a headscarf is ostentatious in itself as opposed to wearing a cross. Therefore, the Muslim girl who is wearing a scarf has no possibility of showing her intentions: she is simply assumed to be provocative. This gives the impression that France doesn't understand the meaning of the scarf, or *hijab*, as part of religious practice and not only as a religious sign.[4]

The earlier the West realises that the *shari'ah* is in fact the practice of Islam, the better for humanity that is being threatened by unnecessary and unfounded fear of Islamism.

One recurrent point in Sanusi's paper is that *shari'ah* should be used for social re-engineering. This is very apt. Apart from the culpability of the West in the pauperisation and victimisation of Muslims, the West's apparent lack of interest in genuine dialogue of action between it and Islam, is what Muslims consider as another negative contribution of the West to the welfare of the downtrodden.

It is our candid view that inter-faith projects on religion and poverty alleviation, economic development, transparency and responsible governance, girl-child education, women, etc. would go a long way in harnessing the resources of the global community for the development of humanity. In addition, such collaboration may generate and promote mutual understanding and respect between the two world-views of Islam and the West.

The consensus in the West that *shari'ah* is a violation of human rights and liberties is one area of conflict in the discourse between Islam and the West on the *shari'ah*. Muslims are understandably angered by the use of Western prejudices and customs to evaluate and adjudge another legal system (the *shari'ah*). The repugnancy doctrine of the Western law which condemns some *shari'ah* provisions and

---

[4] Quoted in Yamani, 1997, 93-94.

declares them as universally unacceptable since they are considered, by the West, as incompatible with Western 'natural' justice, equity, fair play and Western promulgations is inhibitive to meaningful dialogue between Muslims and the West on the *shari'ah*.

It is, in our view, incorrect to accuse operators of the *shari'ah* in Northern Nigeria as victimising the poor simply because *hudud* are being applied. There is no dispute that Allah commands the amputation of a hand of a convicted thief. It is equally true that theft is different from "abuse of trust." Both should be punished but the prescribed punishments differ. Theft is amputation while that of "abuse of trust" is as promulgated or determined through *ta'zir*. Muslims ought to continue to insist on good governance in conformity with the *shari'ah* but cannot, in our view, make it an excuse for abrogation or suspension of *hudud*.

In agreeing with the observation that Muslims consider the West's claim of protecting the interests of Muslim women and masses in its campaign against the *shari'ah* as self-serving and porous, Table 1 is provided to vividly illustrate one of many evils of greed-propelled globalisation (Americanisation) on the poor nations of the world which include all Muslim nations.

Table 1[5]

Country	Gross Domestic Product (GDP) at Current US Dollars (in millions) Using Market Exchange Rate			
	1978	1985	1989	1995
Top 20 nations in terms of GDP (in descending order as of 1995)				
USA	2,218,910	3,946,600	5,132,001	6,952,020
Japan	971,322	1,327,900	2,834,232	5,108,540
Germany	639,781	624,970	1,176,632	2,415,764
France	483,623	510,320	955,175	1,536,089
UK	321,958	454,300	845,350	1,105,822
Italy	298,749	358,670	865,826	1,086,932
Canada	209,974	346,030	538,245	568,928
Spain	146,743	164,250	375,102	558,617

---

[5] Adapted from Beg, 2000, 92, citing the World Bank *World Development Reports* for 1987 and 1997, and the United Nations' *Trends in International Distribution of Gross World Product*, 1993.

Netherlands	137,250	124,970	225,895	395,900
Australia	123,593	162,490	283,765	348,782
Switzerland	84,829	92,690	181,125	300,508
Belgium	95,033	97,080	152,992	269,081
Austria	58,004	66,050	126,775	233,427
Sweden	91,819	100,250	191,298	228,679
Denmark	56,460	57,840	104,845	147,220
Norway	40,649	57,910	90,954	145,954
Finland	34,825	54,030	115,219	125,432
Israel	15,543	20,270	46,428	91,965
Ireland	12,969	18,430	34,170	60,780
New Zealand	17,487	22,140	40,069	57,070
Top 20 total GDP	6,059,521	8,589,190	14,316,098	21,762,510
World total GDP	8,985,000	12,455,496	20,052,000	27,846,241
Top 20 GDP as % of world GDP	64.44	68.95	71.39	78.15
Rest-of-world GDP as % of world GDP	32.56	31.05	28.61	21.85
Top 20 population as % of world population				14.23

The table shows that despite the fact that the top 20 nations that are the beneficiaries of globalisation constitute only about 14.23% of the world population, they control 78.15% of the total world GDP as at 1995. Studies have shown that globalisation increases astronomically the fortunes of the advantaged states while it ensures escalation of the impoverishment in developing nations.[6]

In addition, Muslims are not impressed by the materialistic basis of the West for opposition to *shari'ah*. Allah cautions as follows:

> Have you not seen one that takes as his/her god, his/her own vain desires? Allah has left him astray, and sealed his hearing and his heart and put a cover on his sight; who then will guide him besides Allah. Will you not be admonished?[7]

---

[6] Momin, 2001.
[7] Qur'an 45:23.

Despite the obvious destabilizing plot propaganda against the *shari'ah*-compliant states in Northern Nigeria, appreciable improvement has been made to the socio-economic life of the citizens of some of the states. Kano, for instance, is witnessing in recent times, a rapid transformation in social services due to good governance. While more can still be done to improve the welfare of Zamfara citizens, the state government is, by our assessment, more responsive than many other states to the yearnings and aspirations of her citizens. This observation does not obliterate or reduce the import of Sanusi's clarion call for the utilisation of *shari'ah* for rapid emancipation of the disadvantaged segments of the community.

While it is true that adherents of the theory of *taqlid* still exist in large number among Muslims, it can be safely asserted that the majority of Muslims, at least in theory, agree that *ijtihad* as opposed to *taqlid*, is the veritable avenue to making Islam and the Muslims relevant to the contemporary world. A study of the different *shari'ah* enactments in the twelve *shari'ah*-compliant states of Northern Nigeria reveals the move towards *ijtihad* as a tool for providing legal solutions to contemporary problems through the instrumentality of the *shari'ah*.[8]

CONCLUSIONS

1. No genuine dialogue is going on between Islam and the West on the *shari'ah*. What the West seeks is the capitulation of Islamic culture, ethics and law to its own norms and values.
2. The relationship between the West and Islam has degenerated to a level that unless urgent steps are taken by both parties, dialogue may be impossible.
3. *Shari'ah* is an integral part of Islam, and the opposition to the *shari'ah* by the West is, in Muslims' view, a ploy to eliminate Islam.
4. The Western debate on the *shari'ah* cannot be meaningful to the Muslims until the West purges itself of arrogance and the domineering stance of imposing its own values and norms as universal standards.

---

[8] Oloyede, 2000.

5. Operation of *shari'ah* in Northern Nigeria is based on the resolve of Muslims to obey Allah in conformity with the Qur'anic prescription that:

It is not fitting for a Believer, man or woman, when a matter has been decided by Allah and His Messenger, to have any opinion about their decision; if anyone disobeys Allah and His Messenger, he is indeed on a clearly wrong path.[9]

REFERENCES

Anderson, Norman, "Islamic law today: the background to Islamic fundamentalism", *Arab Law Quarterly* 2/4, 1987, 339-351.

Beg, Tahir, "Globalization vulnerabilities and the response of Islamic economies", *American Journal of Islamic Social Sciences* 17/3, 2000, 70-94.

Momin, A.R., "Pluralism and multiculturalism: an Islamic perspective", *American Journal of Islamic Social Sciences* 18/2, 2001, 115-146.

Noibi, M.A., "The *shari'ah* in the Nigerian legal system", in: M.O. Abdul-Rahmon, *Perspectives in Islamic Law and Jurisprudence*, Ibadan: National Association of Muslim Law Students, 2001, 174-228.

Oloyede, I.O., *Shari'ah versus Secularism in Nigeria*, Lagos: IPB, 1990.

———, "*Shari'ah* in the North, concerns of the South: renewed controversy over the *shari'ah* in Nigeria", in: I.A.B. Balogun, *Islamic Tenets and the Shari'ah*, Ibadan: Sam Books Publishers, 2000, 129-153.

Yamani, M.A., "Islam and the West: the need for mutual understanding", *American Journal of Islamic Social Sciences* 14/1, 1997, 87-98.

---

[9] Qur'an 33:36.

Religion: Source of Conflict or Resource for Peace?[1]

Gerrie ter Haar

INTRODUCTION

Religion is often viewed today as having a negative role in world politics, particularly in cases where a religious revival is perceived to be taking place. After decades during which religion seemed to be largely and effectively relegated to the private realm, religious activists are staking out a new claim for religion as a central feature of public life. The wish to restore religion to what is considered its rightful place at the heart of society is the most notable common denominator of today's religious fundamentalist movements.[2] In order to achieve their aim, members of such movements may employ several tactics, including violent ones. They justify their use of violence by reason, often referring to a perception that we are not living in normal times, and that exceptional circumstances ask for exceptional measures.[3] As a result, an unusual alliance has been forged in many cases between religion and politics, as we will come to see.

The emergence of certain interest groups that do not shun violence and seem to be inspired by a particular religious ideology has tempted many observers, notably in the West, to assume an intrinsic connection between religion and violence. Hence, it is common today to consider religion as a source of conflict rather than a resource for

---

[1] This paper is a preliminary version of the more extensive exploration of the subject by the same author which has appeared as the introductory chapter to Ter Haar and Busuttil, 2005, 3-34.
[2] See the various contributions to Ter Haar and Busuttil, 2003. There are many scholarly books on the subject of fundamentalism, but the most comprehensive study is the so-called Fundamentalism Project that has resulted in five volumes edited by Martin Marty & R. Scott Appleby, see Marty and Appleby, 1993-95.
[3] This point was made by R. Scott Appleby during a seminar at the Institute of Social Studies in May 2000.

peace. The logical conclusion then is to try and reduce the influence of the religious factor in the political arena. Typically in such a view, religion is deemed to be a private affair, something between individual believers and their god(s), a relation that should not spill over into the public domain. Whereas religion is expected to limit itself exclusively to regulating humans' relations between the visible and invisible worlds, it is politics, on the other hand, which is deemed solely responsible for regulating their relations with the state that they live in. The formal separation between the fields of religion and politics has been the hallmark of Western democracies for centuries and was also introduced to other parts of the world, notably those which were colonised by Europe, and, by extension, countries that were long under the influence of Western Europe and North America. The world-wide resurgence of religion is increasingly seen as challenging the basis of the secular state.[4]

Many commentators, at least in the West, have lamented the fact that religion is reassuming a public role, bringing together again two fields of operation that in the Western tradition of the Enlightenment have long been kept apart. To them, this is why religion has become a deadly weapon in the political struggles that are fought out in so many places. The examples abound. One may look, for example, at Nigeria, which has made international headlines with religion-related riots that have left hundreds of people dead; or at India, where many people have lost their lives in recent years in violent conflicts between Hindu and Muslim believers; or at Northern Ireland with its longstanding, bloody conflict between Protestants and Catholics. We may also think of the participation of Buddhist monks in the recent political and military struggle in Sri Lanka.[5] Often in such situations political violence becomes legitimised through religion, if necessary with due reference to the founding charters of the respective religious traditions.

In a way, religion and politics are always in an uneasy relationship because they are rivalling powers. In fact, they constitute two alternative sources of power, based in the spiritual and material

---

[4] Cf. Westerlund, 1996.
[5] Seneviratne, 2003.

spheres respectively.[6] While in most countries in the South religion historically had a role to play in the governance of their societies, in most countries in the northern hemisphere, notably Western Europe and North America, religion has long been denied such a role. In most parts of the world, however, religion remains a social and political force of great importance. Most current religious revivals have a historical basis in the – often post-colonial – societies where they emerge, to the extent that these may be said to represent a form of decolonising the mind by reconnecting with the past.[7] The argument can equally be applied to the current discussion on the *shari'ah* as an alternative and religion-based system of law in many countries, including Nigeria. The Western denial of religious realities in other parts of the world is further based on two misconceptions that are contradictory but nevertheless often expressed: first, that religion in itself, that is, by its very nature, is an obstacle to peace, as is deemed evident from all the conflicts in the world today; and second, that when religion *becomes* a significant factor in a particular conflict, it is in fact being used contrary to its essential nature, which is deemed to be intrinsically good. As one can see, these are in fact two incompatible positions: while the former opinion (religion is a negative force) is based on what people may *experience* in practice, the latter view (religion is basically good) is based on what some commentators *believe* it ought to be. These contrasting positions are in fact reflections of a common discrepancy between theory and practice, that deserves further attention.

If it is true that a widespread theoretical assumption (that religion is something good) contradicts a widespread experience (that religion is in actual fact usually bad), then this reflects the ambiguous nature of religion itself. For religion is neither inherently peaceful, nor does it automatically or inevitably lead to conflict. From a social science perspective – which, I should emphasise, is different from the theological perspective of individual believers – religion is a human construct, something which has grown among human communities and serves human interests, which are in many cases conflicting ones. As such it becomes a tool in the hands of human beings that can be

---

[6] See Ellis and Ter Haar, 2004.
[7] Cf. ibid. Ch. 9, notably pp. 182-7.

used for good or not-so-good purposes, for constructive or for destructive aims and objectives. Hence, for a scholarly analysis of religion it is necessary to examine religion as a *social* trend that can be analysed in the same way as any other important trend in society, such as the economy, education, or public health. All of these are products of human endeavours aimed at regulating society, with more or less success, and with a greater or lesser degree of self-interest. By analysing religion in a similar way we will find that, just as in the case of other social trends such as those mentioned, religion too has the potential to be used at the expense of particular groups, or employed for the common good. From a social science perspective there is nothing divine about the final outcome of such processes, which is entirely the work of humankind. This is not to deny in any way the validity of a theological perspective. While the former (social science perspective) represents an outsider's point of view, the latter represents an insider's point of view. The two should be seen not as exclusive viewpoints, but as complementary angles from which one may legitimately view the subject matter under discussion.

Due to recent conflicts in which religion also played a role, and notably after the events of September 2001, religion is often associated in the West with violence. The question is, however, are we simply dealing here with religious conflict, as is so often suggested, or has religion become a suitable instrument for political mobilisation, providing a resource that – like any other – can be effectively exploited for rather mundane purposes. This is an argument that has a certain relevance for Nigeria too, where the *shari'ah* discussion has become highly politicised. For anybody to answer that question, it is of vital importance to analyse the role of religion in society, and to do so from a historical perspective. This is important, first, to be able to understand today's world better; and second, in order to analyse the specific properties, and therefore the potential, of religion. Only then does it become possible to determine whether religion is indeed a source of conflict, or whether it may equally be considered a resource for peace. In the following I will look at these two sides of the same religious coin.

RELIGION AS A SOURCE OF CONFLICT

The tendency to associate religion rather uncritically with conflict is particularly notable in the West where, as I suggested, specific historical conditions have led to a separation of church and state, that is of the secular and spiritual powers operating in society, thus decreasing the role of religion in the public realm. What one might refer to as the privatisation of religion, however, appears to have reached its limits in a world that has undergone such dramatic changes since the end of the Cold War. The ideological changes resulting from it created new space for religious ideologies, which have gradually come to replace the secular ones that many people had become so familiar with. While until recently the main ideological divides were between secular ideologies – such as between capitalism and Marxism – today they are more likely to occur between religious ideologies. The most obvious example of the latter is the growing sense of a fundamental antagonism between Christianity and Islam. This has become even more manifest after the recent events in the United States, resulting in an on-going "war on terror" that is more and more depicted as a "clash between civilisations," along the lines of Samuel Huntington's well-known analysis.[8]

The ideological changes that have taken place since the 1990s have profoundly altered the relationship between religion and politics, in such a way as to give substance to the widespread idea that where there is religion there is conflict. This is not surprising, in the sense that whenever there is political conflict this becomes reflected in the dominant ideology, which today is often a religious one. Just like their secular counterparts, religious ideologies have their own –theological – justifications for the use of violence, which are part and parcel of their histories. Christianity, for example, boasts a history in which the notion of a just war is not only accepted, but also provides justification for current right-wing Christian revivalist groups to declare war on both their religious and secular enemies. It should not be left unmentioned, in this context, that Christian liberation theology, as frequently embraced by the political left, is in fact a modern elaboration of the just war theory, resulting in another form

---

[8] Huntington, 1996. Huntington's analysis has had a great influence on US thinking.

of "exceptionalism." Similarly, in Islam the concept of *jihad*, a spiritual idea that may be carried over on to the material plane under particular conditions, notably for the purpose of self-defence, has proved helpful in justifying and rationalising the use of violence in modern times. Founders of Hamas, for example, have expanded the notion of self-defence beyond individuals' physical well-being to include the defence of their dignity and pride. In Judaism too, allowance is made for the need to fight a just war in certain circumstances, but in a similar manner a reinterpetation of historical sources takes place in such a way as to justify, for example, the current violence against Palestinians. In fact, it appears that all major religious traditions, notably the book religions, make allowance for the use of violence;[9] an idea, we may add, that has left its traces in secular societies that legitimise the use of violence in the exceptional situation known as war, and which also provides the legitimisation of the current global "war on terror."

Yet there is no evidence that religious ideology is more harmful than any other ideology. In fact, the opposite may be true. If we look at recent history, we see that the greatest bloodshed has been associated with secular, and not religious, ideologies. The largest conflicts in the world in the twentieth century, which resulted in genocides on a previously unheard-of scale, were all connected with ideologies that were, or in some cases still are, rooted in secular values. We may refer here to the racist ideology of Nazi Germany, which resulted in millions of dead during World War II; one may think of the millions of dead caused by Stalinist and Marxist ideological purges notably in the former Soviet Union, or by the Pol Pot regime in Cambodia; or of the countless dead in China, inspired by the political ideology of Chairman Mao during the Cultural Revolution; and – more recently – one may also think of the Rwanda genocide, which no one will seriously claim was in any way religiously inspired, even though massive crime may be religiously legitimised, which is a different matter. Zbigniew Brzezinski, the former US National Security Adviser, estimated in 1993 that at least 167 million lives had been "deliberately extinguished through politically motivated

---

[9] See Juergensmeyer, 2003.

carnage" since the beginning of the twentieth century.[10] He noted that this was done in the service of "coercive utopias" that had largely replaced religion. Ten years and a number of politically-motivated conflicts since Brzezinski made his estimate have significantly added to the loss of human lives.

Hence, we may conclude, historical evidence points in a different direction than many seem to assume these days. It shows that *all* ideologies, whether recognised to be purely man-made or believed to be divinely inspired, are ambiguous in nature, although the precise character of this ambiguity may differ. All of them can be used, and are used in fact, to serve human interests. One such major interest is in the field of politics. The political manipulation of, and mobilisation through, religion is probably the most frequent way in which religion is used, or misused, in present times. The political manipulation of religion has been evident, for example, in the recent Balkan wars in Europe, forging a dangerous link between religion and nationalism. We see a similar process at work in India, in the form of Hindu nationalism.[11] Other examples of religious extremism from other parts of the world could easily be added, and from all major religions, as the American scholar Mark Juergensmeyer has notably shown in his recent analysis of religious violence, and as case studies by others equally prove. All these are examples of situations in which religion is used to justify the use of violence in settling conflicts. They have in common a proven capacity to create havoc through the indiscriminate and, at times, massive use of violence. In that respect religious extremists do not differ from other ideological extremists (like the sort just mentioned). The examples show that conflict is often exacerbated when religion becomes a tool in the hands of politicians or political interest groups, and is thus used to create, maintain, or strengthen a factional position. This is what causes secularists to mistrust religious-based arguments, in the same way as religious believers may question the secular ideology of the state, arguing that this is the root cause of, rather than the solution to, religious violence, since it fails to take the religious values of its citizens into account.[12]

---

[10] Brzezinski, 1993, 17.
[11] Ram-Prasad, 2003.
[12] Ter Haar, 2000, 12.

Yet, it is useful to realise that religious extremism is by no means representative of any one particular religion. Most religions are characterised by a great diversity of views and trends, and the vast majority of religious believers in the world are not located at the extreme ends of any given spectrum of religious opinions, but rather in the centre, just as most people take a centre position in politics. Often such middle-of-the-road believers themselves become targets of their extremist co-religionists whose means and methods they reject. Moderates and extremists of course may, and often do, share some political objectives, as in the current conflict between the Western-Christian and the Muslim world. The 9/11 attacks have been instrumental in uniting Muslim opinion around a number of unresolved political issues, including notably the Israeli-Palestinian conflict, the presence of US troops in Saudi Arabia – and hence control of access to the Muslim holy places – and the question of sanctions against Iraq.[13] Muslims worldwide tend to feel more and more that their political grievances are not recognised by the Western world; they see that Western governments are not shy in supporting oppressive and even brutal regimes, including brutal Muslim regimes, if and when it suits them; and they are aware of the dominating power of the West in almost every aspect of life today. The global expansion of Western power has in effect widened the gap between the rich and the poor in the world, creating large populations who are marginalised and excluded as they have no access to any sources of wealth and power. According to some, the experience of exclusion – economically, politically and culturally – has become a major reason for the rise of religious extremism worldwide.[14]

While acknowledging the importance of such mundane facts, we should avoid becoming reductionistic in our explanations and acknowledge the potency inherent in religion itself and in the religious imagination. Ideas of martyrdom, for example, and self-sacrifice, images of an alternative world believed to exist beyond the visible one, are deep-rooted and may provide extremely powerful motives to

---

[13] See also the unreleased interview with Osama Bin Laden (21 October 2001), published in *Religioscope*, www.religioscope.com/info/doc/jihad/ubl_int_1.htm. The last two issues have been resolved by now, but in a rather unsatisfactory manner. The Iraq war, in particular, has created even greater political problems.
[14] Cf. Muzaffar, 2005.

those who feel attracted to them. Mark Juergensmeyer has coined the term 'performance violence' to explain the theatrical and dramatic character of a religious extremist act. These are dramatic statements, he argues, which are not intended to serve a particular strategic goal, but to impress the audience by their symbolical significance. Hence, they can be fruitfully analysed in the same way as any other symbol, ritual or sacred drama.[15] From such a perspective, the 9/11 attacks too can be seen as primarily designed as a drama intended to have an impact on the several audiences that were affected. The role of the media, as one of the most powerful globalising forces, is of unmistakeable importance in all this. Juergensmeyer goes as far as claiming even that such acts are increasingly performed for a television audience around the world. Though not all might agree with that, the understanding of religious-related violence in terms of a sacred drama and public performance, or as a social event with both real and symbolic aspects, is helpful in the analysis of religion as a source of conflict.

In conclusion to this consideration we may say that although in actual practice religion often proves an obstacle to peace, this by no means implies that it *has* to be that way, as if religion could not be used differently, namely in such a way that it becomes an instrument for the promotion of social harmony and peace. I will turn to this now.

RELIGION AS A RESOURCE FOR PEACE

The current association of religion with international peace and social harmony, it is worth remembering, is a historically recent development that reflects the change in worldview that has taken place over time. This development has gone hand in hand with secular developments to strive for peace, such as those that led to the United Nations Universal Declaration of Human Rights, which is itself an example of how different ideologies, both of a secular and a religious nature, can negotiate for the common good. It is important to realise, in this respect, that the Universal Declaration is the product of a process in which a team of Western and non-Western drafters,

---

[15] Juergensmeyer, 2003, 125-6.

standing in different religious traditions, worked together. The core group of drafters included representatives of such diverse countries as Australia, Chile, China, France, Lebanon, the former Soviet Union, the United Kingdom and the United States of America. There was a significant influence of Muslim drafters, as well as of Latin American socialists, to whom we owe the inclusion of social, economic and cultural rights in the Declaration.[16]

The attempt to establish a legitimate foundation for religion as a resource for peace is actively pursued in certain religious circles by highlighting those aspects of sacred scripture and tradition that are conducive to a positive valuation of religion in public life. Hence, it is important to identify and subsequently propagate those elements in a particular religious tradition that have the potential to make a significant contribution to the solution of social and political conflicts, and thus to establishing peace. This is an exercise in which many responsible leaders are actively engaged. As part of that process, several human rights declarations or similar statements have been drafted over the years that base themselves explicitly on a particular religious creed, such as the Universal Islamic Declaration of Human Rights; or highlight specific cultural values, such as the Bangkok Declaration, which contains a statement from some forty states from the Asian and Pacific regions reflecting Asian values in human rights; but also a Declaration of Human Rights by the World's Religions, to mention only a few.[17] Whatever one may think about specific details of such texts, their primary importance lies in the fact that all are the result of a conscious attempt to root certain universal values in particular cultural and religious traditions.

If we look at the so-called book religions – those that base themselves on a written authority such as the Torah, Bible, or Qur'an – it is apparent that the humane worldview on which many people strive to base their actions today did not exist at the time that these books were written. In those days the use of violence was commonly accepted and even encouraged in certain circumstances, while peace and tolerance were usually limited to a particular circle of people.

---

[16] See Morsink, 1999, notably Ch. 1: "The drafting process explained".

[17] For the full texts of these and similar human rights documents, see Ter Haar & Busuttil, 2005, Part IV: "Documentary Resources on Religion, Violence and Peace".

Those who fall outside the category of belonging could be dealt with differently, and often harshly. If we look with modern eyes at the Bible, for example, to limit ourselves to the Judeo-Christian tradition that has shaped the Western world, we find a shocking degree of violence perpetrated in the name of a god who protects his own children but has their enemies killed, including women and children. Similar examples can be taken from other holy books. In many religious traditions there is originally a limited understanding of the common good, which is restricted to one's own family or clan. This may lead to an attitude that can still incite what we would refer to today as ethnic violence. Judaism, Christianity and Islam in particular are of an exclusive nature in that they promote the worship of gods who do not tolerate the presence of any rivals; their intrinsic monotheism may lead to aggressive evangelisation or conversion campaigns that are not conducive to the creation of religious tolerance. All this makes the reinterpretation of sacred traditions in their present context an absolute necessity in the modern world.[18] The first responsibility for that lies with religious leaders and those who train them, including in departments for the study of religion.

Both from a practical and intellectual perspective it seems logical to argue that all the human resources in a given society are usable for political purposes – not only material and intellectual resources, but also religious and spiritual ones. Such aims and objectives include the protection of human rights, but one may also think of other challenges, such as the protection of the environment, the fight against poverty, and similar challenges that pose threats to world peace. For the same reason, it is important to try and mobilise religious communities, but also to interact with them for the common good. Through religion one can reach large constituencies and maximise resources. The positive potential of religion is often underutilised, including by state actors, and it is therefore worth exploring its resources, notably those elements that have the potential to make a significant contribution to the solution of social and political conflicts, and thus to establishing peace.

Religious resources are contained in the four main elements of which religions consist: religious ideas (content of belief), religious

---

[18] For examples of this, see Ter Haar & Busuttil, 2005.

practices (ritual behaviour), social organisation (religious community), and religious experiences (psychic attitudes). These occur in most if not all religious traditions, although in various forms, and with one or the other element perhaps favoured. These various dimensions of religion can all be used for the purpose of a human striving for peace. Below I will quickly examine each of them.

Religious ideas that contain the seeds for a peaceful approach to conflict situations can be strengthened: this can be done through identifying and stressing the importance of such ideas and by giving them new layers of meaning. The re-interpretation of religious ideas is a prime responsibility of religious leaders and other specialists; it includes the development of new theologies that address contemporary issues. During an international workshop on religion and human rights in Ghana in 2002 it was suggested, for example, that a theology of the "other" is sorely needed, as well as a theology of "transformation."[19] These are concrete suggestions that link up with key ideas in many religious traditions. Although they are not unique in this, religious ideologies, notably those of an exclusivist nature, tend to ascribe all sorts of evil to those who are not considered "people like us." The resulting process of "othering" has given rise in recent years to forms of religious and ethnic cleansing in various parts of the world.[20]

Religious practices, or ritual behaviour, also contain an underutilised potential. For example, it is worth exploring the ritual potential in "rites of passage," known to most human societies, to enhance human dignity and status. Such rites are designed to help people make the transition from one important phase of life to another. To give one example, some charismatic churches in Liberia, a country devastated by the experiences of the war, use the ritual means at their disposal to re-integrate child soldiers into the community, encouraging them to effect a change of life with the help of God. Young ex-combatants give public testimony of the often horrific acts they committed during the civil war. Such testimonies assume the character of a public confession, providing enormous psychological

---

[19] See the policy recommendations on p. 10 of the report of the International Workshop on Religion and Human Rights, held from 4-8 November 2002 at the Marina Hotel in Dodowa, Ghana.

[20] See Ter Haar, 2000, notably pp. 17-18.

relief to these young fighters. At the same time they are encouraged by the community of believers that with the help of God they can make a new start with their lives. The church opens up a new horizon for youth, providing them with spiritual tools, including such techniques as building faith through prayer and fasting, to increase their determination to effect a change of life.[21] Their acceptance by the community is of crucial significance to these young ex-fighters, whose anti-social deeds cannot easily be forgotten and forgiven. We know of similar initiatives in the traditional-religious sphere in the post-war reconstruction process in Mozambique. Outside Africa, rites of peace have been recorded as an effective instrument of conflict resolution in the Lebanon, for example, where the indigenous ritual of *sulha* is an integral part of communal traditions throughout the Middle East, whether Muslim, Christian, Jewish or Druze.[22] Anthropological research in Latin America has drawn attention to yet another model for the avoidance of violent conflict, that of symbolic confrontation, which provides a culturally accepted way to condemn the behaviour of others without resorting to physical violence. One example is through devil mythology, or spiritual warfare theology, which is particularly popular among Pentecostal groups.[23]

These are also examples of how religious communities, as a type of social organisation, can be used to help turn conflict into peace, in this case by facilitating people to live together peacefully. Their spiritual approach to conflict resolution is a valuable complement to secular approaches which are often externally initiated. This is particularly important in circumstances where a profound breach of relations has occurred, even to the point of seeming beyond repair. The Truth and Reconciliation Commission in South Africa, which has been an example to many other countries,[24] although not a religious initiative *stricto sensu*, was supported by the various religious communities in the country, quite apart from being characterised by a religious approach in its dealings and procedures. Also in South Africa, the concept of *ubuntu*, a concept that cannot easily be

---

[21] This is based on my personal observations during a reseach trip to Liberia in October 2000.
[22] King-Irani, 2000.
[23] Miguez, 2005.
[24] These include, for example, Ghana, Nigeria, and Sierra Leone.

translated into English, is explored for its conflict resolution potential. Literally, *ubuntu* means "collective personhood" or "the art or virtue of being human."[25] In other parts of Africa too, and other parts of the world for that matter, traditional or culture-specific methods to manage conflicts or restore peace have been revived.[26]

Religious experiences, finally, have been crucial in the foundation and subsequent spread of many religions, and are a powerful inspiration notably for those who normally lack power, often women, and often the poor. One may think of divine revelation, dreams, and visions, or the experience of a miracle in one's life. Examples of this abound in the history of Africa and apply to its various religious traditions, indigenous and imported. All these constitutive elements of religion – ideas, practices, organisation, and experience – can be explored and used, not only by believers but also by others who may be motivated by secular ideals. Part of a tolerant (world) society is the acceptance that different paths may lead to the same goal, in this case a humane and peaceful society. In my view, this also applies to the *shari'ah* debate, in which the whole world seems to have a stake today. Whereas certain aspects defy universal standards of human rights, this is no reason to suggest that *shari'ah* as a whole should be rejected or that it cannot be made compatible with the requirements of modern times.[27]

There are many individuals and groups today who use their religious resources (as located in ideas, practices, organisation, and experience) to further the cause of peace. Well-known examples include inter-religious organisations such as the World Conference on Religion and Peace and the Parliament of the World's Religions, but also peace organisations within a single religious tradition such as Pax Christi and Justice and Peace, or peace movements that are political in nature but have been religiously inspired, such as the All Party Hurriyet ('Freedom') Conference in Kashmir, established by a young Muslim leader (*Mirwaiz* Umar Farooq). One may also refer to the 1999 The Hague Appeal for Peace, in which many individuals, notably including a large number of women, participated on the basis of their

---

[25] Masina, 2000, 170.
[26] Cf. Zartman, 2000.
[27] Cf. An-Na'im, 2003.

individual religious conviction. In the painful conflict between Israel and Palestine religious women have set up peace groups, as such women have also done in the long-standing conflict in Sudan. These are only some random examples.

All this does not mean that the religious dimension can, or should, be dissociated from the social and political problems that often underlie religious-based violence. Religious solutions, it has been observed by others, must address the same social and psychological needs (such as for identity, dignity etc.) that contemporary militant formulations of religious traditions address.[28] Without reducing the degree of social and economic inequality in the world, showing a willingness to share the world's resources, there will always be a breeding ground for extremism, whether religious or secular in its orientation. Secular people must be aware of the multifold functions of religion, which provide such powerful motives for believers to act in the way they do. Religion provides people with a life orientation and a moral point of reference; it is also a cultural anchor that provides them with a social identity and places them in a social framework that becomes a safety-net if and when the need arises. A core problem in the relations between believers and non-believers, or religionists and secularists, is the lack of understanding among secularists of what religion means to believers and the power – spiritual power – they derive from it.

CONCLUSION

Religion itself is neither good or bad, it is simply there; it is a reality, whether one likes it or not. Religion is a social fact, that rather than being lamented, dismissed or ignored should be turned to the advantage of humankind by considering how it can be used for constructive purposes. Contemplating the destructive side of religion, I have argued, does not require an analyst to be a religious believer him- or herself. Nor is it necessary, by the same token, to believe in any religious doctrine in order to appreciate efforts to highlight those aspects of religion that can be developed as a positive resource. Evidence points to the fact that the majority of people in the world

---

[28] See Kelsey and Twiss, 1994, 15.

are religious in some shape or form, in the sense that they believe in an invisible world inhabited by invisible beings (such as spirits or deities, etc.) to which they ascribe an effective power over their lives. It follows then that such a power expresses itself in the lives of believers, in positive or negative ways. It becomes a negative power, as suggested above, when it is used for the oppression and exploitation of others. But it is positive, for example, when it is used for healing purposes, or as an inspiration to resolve conflicts and bring about peace.

Religion is an (often powerful) instrument in the hands of those who use it. These are not necessarily always believers alone. They may also include others, such as politicians, who manipulate religion effectively. It is worth noting that many politicians in the world, at least in those parts of the world where people are overwhelmingly religious (in the defined sense of the word), have already discovered this potential and use it for their own, often factional purposes, in ways that prevent the establishment of peace. They are acutely aware that both the realm of politics and the realm of religion are connected with power, whether religiously defined (in terms of spiritual power, located in the transcendental sphere) or in secular terms (located in the material sphere). Religion and politics are distinct but not separate categories in the discussion about conflict and peace in the world. Politicians therefore find it important to try and extend their influence and control into the religious realm. Such political manipulation of religion can have disastrous consequences, such as has been the case, for example, at the time of the Rwandan genocide, in which Christian believers and even priests and nuns, took an active part. We also see it in places where human differences are exacerbated by representing them in religious terms, whether it is in Northern Ireland or Nigeria, in India or Pakistan. We see it also in Western tendencies to consider the "war against terrorism" as a war against Islam.

In conclusion, I would like to stress two points. First, as I mentioned at the beginning of this paper, it is important to realise that religion and politics are related, in the sense that both of them call on, and make use of, a source of legitimate power (whether spiritually or materially defined); at the same time this turns them into rivals.

Religious and political leaders are potential rivals and may actually become so in reality, as we see for example in the case of Iran, where the worldly leader Khatami and the religious leader Khamenei have been competing for power. We may also think of some historical examples including Martin Luther King, Archbishop Desmond Tutu and other religious leaders who made their reputations by effectively challenging the worldly powers of their time. It is no surprise, then, that both political and religious leaders are concerned, and engage themselves, with questions of conflict and peace.

Secondly, I want to stress once again the ambiguous nature of religion, which may turn it into either a source of conflict or a resource for peace. It is up to those dealing with religion, whether as believers or policy-makers and other interest groups, to help steer its course in one or the other direction.

REFERENCES

An-Na'im, Abdullahi Ahmed, "Islamic fundamentalism and social change: neither the 'end of history' nor a 'clash of civilizations'", in: Ter Haar and Busuttil, 2003, 25-48.

Brzezinski, Zbigniew, *Out of Control: Global turmoil on the eve of the twenty-first century*, New York: Charles Scribner's Sons, 1993.

Ellis, Stephen and Gerrie ter Haar, *Worlds of Power: Religious thought and political practice in Africa*, London: Hurst & Co./New York: Oxford University Press, 2004.

Huntington, Samuel, *The Clash of Civilizations and the Remaking of the World Order*, New York: Simon & Schuster, 1996.

Juergensmeyer, Mark, *Terror in the Mind of God: The global rise of religious violence*, Berkeley/Los Angeles: University of California Press, 2003.

Kelsey, John and Sumner B. Twiss (eds.), *Religion and Human Rights*, New York: The Project on Religion and Human Rights, 1994.

King-Irani, Lauri E., "Rituals of forgiveness and processes of empowerment in Lebanon", in Zartman, 2000, 129-40.

Marty, Martin and R. Scott Appleby (eds.), *The Fundamentalism Project*, Chicago: Chicago University Press, 1993-95. Vol. 1: *Fundamentalisms Observed*; Vol. 2: *Fundamentalisms and Society: Reclaiming the sciences, the family, and education*; Vol. 3: *Fundamentalisms and the State: Remaking polities, economies, and militance*; Vol. 4: *Accounting for Fundamentalisms: The dynamic character of movements*; Vol. 5: *Fundamentalisms Comprehended*.

Masina, Nomonde, "Xhosa practices of *ubuntu* for South Africa", in: Zartman, 2000, 169-81.

Miguez, Daniel, "From open violence to symbolic confrontation: anthropological observations of Latin America's southern cone", in Ter Haar and Busuttil, 2005, 81-118.

Morsink, Johannes, *The Universal Declaration of Human Rights: Origins, drafting and intent*, Philadelphia: University of Pennsylvania Press, 1999.

Muzaffar, Chandra, "Religious conflict in Asia: probing the causes, seeking solutions", in Ter Haar and Busuttil, 2005, 57-79.

Ram-Prasad, Chakravarti, "Being Hindu and/or governing India? Religion, social change and the state", in Ter Haar and Busuttil, 2003, 159-96.

Seneviratne, H.L., "The monk's new robes: Buddhist fundamentalism and social change", in Ter Haar and Busuttil, 2003, 143-58.

Ter Haar, Gerrie, *Rats, Cockroaches and People like Us: Views of humanity and human rights*, The Hague: Institute of Social Studies, 2000.

Ter Haar, Gerrie and James J. Busuttil (eds.), *The Freedom to Do God's Will: Religious fundamentalism and social change*, London: Routledge, 2003.

Ter Haar, Gerrie and James J. Busuttil (eds.), *Bridge or Barrier: Religion,violence and visions for peace*, Leiden: Brill, 2005.

Westerlund, David (ed.), *Questioning the Secular State: The worldwide resurgence of religion in politics*, London: Hurst & Co., 1996.

Zartman, I. William (ed.), *Traditional Cures for Modern Conflicts: African conflict "medicine"*, Boulder/London: Lynne Riener, 2000.

Commentary

J. D. Gwamna

It is with much delight and every sense of privilege and honour that I respond to our distinguished senior colleague and an erudite scholar of world renown, Professor Gerrie ter Haar, of the Institute of Social Studies, the Hague. Ter Haar's paper, "Religion: Source of Conflict or Resource for Peace?", is not only apt and timely, but it captures the contemporary discourse of religion at the global scene today, and calls for critical reflections. Global conflicts and wars that have religious underpinnings are becoming more evident and recurring. It is in order to address these issues that ter Haar's paper is situated. It provides further insights into our understanding of religion *sui generis*, and critical lenses towards the appraisal of *shari'ah* and its implementation in Nigeria.

Ter Haar's paper is divided into four parts: introduction, religion as a source of conflict, religion as a resource for peace, and conclusion. I will comment on each of these in turn.

INTRODUCTION

Religion today is gradually assuming a defining role in public life across the globe, sometimes with trails of violence especially when it is related to politics. It is easy to see religion more as a source of conflict than as a resource for peace. The separation of the state from religion, part of the Western democratic tradition, is fast becoming old fashioned, particularly after the end of the Cold War. Religion seems to be staging a come-back, challenging the theory of the secular state as is happening in Nigeria presently. Ter Haar has recognised that religion and politics are two rival powers. While in the West religion and politics are separated, the Arab world, typified by Islam, recognises the mixture of both.

She points out that religion today is on the political agenda worldwide, in large part because of the September 11, 2001 attacks on the World Trade Centre and other targets in the United States of America. Most people in the West see the events of 9/11 as the handiwork of religious extremists who misuse religion for political ends. This singular event has created a gulf between the Western-Christian and the Arab-Muslim Worlds. Today, in the West, religion is easily associated with violence. And indeed, religion has become a deadly weapon in Nigeria, India, Northern Ireland and Sri Lanka, among others. In these nations, political violence has been legitimised using religion.

Ter Haar notes, though, that religion is by nature ambiguous, neither inherently peaceful nor inevitably leading to conflict. What matters is its use, or misuse, or even its application. She maintains that from a social science perspective, religion is a human construct, which serves human interests, including conflicting ones. This Durkheimian position sees religion as having in-built functional and dysfunctional roles in the society. This implies that religion needs to be studied just as other human institutions like economies, systems of education, or public health. The issue is to investigate how and why religion has become an instrument for political mobilisation and a resource that can be exploited for mundane activities.

RELIGION AS A SOURCE OF CONFLICT

Ter Haar states that it is in the West that religion is associated more with conflict, though uncritically, particularly where historical conditions have favoured the separation of church from the state. In the West, religion has literally been "privatised." This trend has changed with the end of the Cold War, following the collapse of the erstwhile secular ideology particularly of Marxism. A new space for religious ideologies has emerged, manifesting itself, globally and in many locales, as a fundamental antagonism especially between Christianity and Islam. This has resulted in more tension in political and religious relationships around the world. Like secular ideologies, religious ideologies have their own theoretical justifications for the use of violence. This is true of Christianity (exemplified in Liberation Theology), Islam (exemplified in the concept of the *jihad*), and Judaism (exemplified in the concept of the just war).

Thus, it appears that all the monotheistic religions make allowance for the use of violence, providing justification sometimes even in secular societies for legitimising violence, as in the case of the current global "war on terrorism." As ter Haar points out, though, secular ideologies produced far more bloodshed in the 20th century than religious ones. The slaughters of World Wars I and II; the mass deaths occasioned by the ostensible quest for Communist utopias in the Soviet Union, Mao's China, and Pol Pot's Cambodia; the Rwandan genocides: it is estimated that one hundred and sixty-seven million people died in these 20th century disasters, which were brought on not by religious conflict at all but by purely secular ideologies and concerns.

Ter Haar believes that secular and religious ideologies both almost always end up in the service of politics. Thus, political manipulation of and mobilisation through religion is probably the most frequent way in which religion is used, or in the view of some, misused in present times.

She notes that the 9/11 attacks have united the Muslim world on common issues such as the Israeli-Palestinian conflict, the presence of US troops in Saudi Arabia, and US support of brutal Muslim regimes, among others. She also notes that the global expansion of Western influence has widened the gap between the rich and the poor, creating conditions for discontent and the rise of religious extremism worldwide. Ter Haar sums up this section by stating that in practice, religion has often proved to be an obstacle to peace, but can also be used differently to forge social harmony and peace.

RELIGION AS A RESOURCE FOR PEACE

Monotheistic religions promote exclusivism to the extent that violence is promoted in the name of God. These religions project a God who does not tolerate rivals. This in-built intolerance reflects in their evangelism and conversion campaigns, which create conditions for religious intolerance. But some attempts have been made to root universal values in particular religious traditions, such as the Universal Islamic Declaration of Human Rights, the Bangkok Declaration, and the Declaration of Human Rights by the World's Religions, among others.

It is ter Haar's opinion that religion has the potential to solve social and political conflicts and to build peace. Religious resources contain four important elements that can serve these purposes: religious ideas, ritual behaviour, social organization and religious or spiritual experiences.

1. Religious ideas contain seeds for peaceful approaches to conflict situations, which could be promoted through religious leaders. This involves the development of theologies that address contemporary issues, while guarding against exclusivistic theologies which seek to segregate and alienate people and thus to justify various forms of religious and ethnic cleansing.
2. Religious behaviour or ritual can be turned to purposes of social reconciliation and the building of inter-faith community. For example, one could explore the ritual potential in rites of passage in order to enhance human dignity and status. In Liberia, this was achieved where ex-combatants were re-integrated into society through building faith and determination to effect change in life. The same was achieved in the post-war reconstruction process in Mozambique. Rites of peace have also been effective in

Lebanon, where the ritual of *sulha* has become popular in the Arab world, even among differing faiths.
3. Religious communities can also be used to help the wider community learn to live together peacefully and in mutual toleration. The Truth and Reconciliation Commission experimented with this in South Africa.
4. Religious experiences also provide avenues for evolving peace blocks. For example, several religious bodies today have been established to promote peace. They include; The World Conference on Religion and Peace, The Parliament of the World's Religions, and Justice and Peace, among others.

CONCLUSION

Gerrie ter Haar concludes her paper by stating that religious solutions must address both social and psychological issues, such as identity and dignity. Conditions must be created to reduce social and economic inequalities in the world in order to reduce factors that breed extremism, whether secular or religious.

Religion, she notes, can be used by both believers and non-believers: we are all too familiar with cases in which cynical and unbelieving politicians exploit religion for their own purposes. In parts of the world where people are religious, religion is easily manipulated for factional purposes, as is the case in Nigeria. Religion and politics are relevant in discussing conflict and peace in the world. Politicians easily use it in their quest for power. This can be dangerous as was the case with the Rwandan genocide where Christian believers, including priests and nuns took active part. The same case has been true in Northern Ireland, Nigeria, India and Pakistan. We see it also in the West where the war against terrorism is almost always seen as a war against Islam.

Religion and politics use various sources of power to legitimise their holds, sometimes turning into rivals as witnessed in Iran where the worldly leader Khatami and the religious leader Khamenei are competing for power. Martin Luther King and Desmond Tutu are examples of two religious leaders who challenged the worldly powers of their time.

PERSONAL CRITIQUE

Global events have changed the religious map of the world very significantly in the last decades. Gerrie ter Haar captures the issues well when she notes that religion is a two-faced coin, capable of serving both negative and positive functions. Religion is a potent force that has assumed a global influence of late and this will likely continue for some time to come. Religion has factionalised the world into the West, which some tag as Christian, and the Arab world which some see as symbolising Islam. Ter Haar believes that the use of religion has nothing divine about its final outcome but is entirely the work of humankind.

While religion can be a strong mobilising force, it can also be manipulated for negative purposes. The manipulative tool of religion and some exclusive postures (as exemplified in monotheistic faiths) have created negative effects of religion generally, across the world. Thus, religions must resist all forms of injustices perpetrated around the world in order to reduce tension and wars, instead of fanning them.

Religion needs to be contextualised within our contemporary experience through the development of theologies that are more open, more tolerant, and less exclusive. The tension between religion and politics needs to be balanced so that religion can serve mankind to forge a global human community of peace, instead of being used as a tool of political expedience to promote conflict and war which has been the unfortunate lot of some nations in the past years. Religion must be elevated above the level of the "opium of the oppressed" by those who manipulate it, to a positive force which meet people's needs and promotes development and human fulfilment. It is my conviction that a secularised view of the world devoid of "true religion" can only produce misery, conflict and war, as was the case in the 20th century.

In conclusion, however, it is pertinent to draw the attention of the author to some salient posers which still remain to be addressed. Ter Haar does not seem to state exactly the prospects for religion and its relevance in the future. Will the manipulation of religion, for example, likely continue, and to what extent? How does the Western world convince the rest of the world that they are not fighting Islam or the Arab world? Can the Arab world purge and insulate Islam from violence and terrorism, which some see as having serious connections? What concrete international instruments of peace can be used to wage a global "war against war"? Is it not correct also to note that politicians who manipulate religion are not necessarily "unbelievers" as they share in the faith, or at least profess a faith within which they hide and easily mobilise for their own ends? Are the religious bodies discussed in ter Haar's paper effective to forge religious peace around the world? What is their common platform? Do individual nations have a part to play in evolving mechanisms for promoting peace through religion, as it is the case in Nigeria? These, and other similar puzzles need further reflection and clarification.

The Future of *Shari'ah* and the Debate in Northern Nigeria

Abdullahi Ahmed An-Na'im

INTRODUCTION

Shari'ah does indeed, in my view, have a most important future in Islamic societies and communities for its foundational role in the socialization of children, sanctification of social institutions and relationships, and the shaping and development of those fundamental values that can be translated into general legislation and public policy through the democratic political process. But it does not have a future as a normative system to be enacted and enforced as such by the state as positive law and public policy. That is, whatever is enacted or enforced is not *shari'ah* as such, and should not be described in those terms at all. This paper is a preliminary and tentative inquiry into this delicate *mediation* of the public role of *shari'ah* in present Islamic societies, with special reference to Northern Nigeria. The term 'mediation' is used here to emphasise the need for balancing competing claims, instead of asserting either the categorical fusion of *shari'ah* and the state or its total exclusion from the public domain.

To avoid any confusion, I emphasise from outset that the thesis and argument presented here are proposed **only** for the public role of *shari'ah* (*mu'amalat*), and **not** matters of religious beliefs and worship practices (*'aqidah* and *'ibadat*). The reason for this specification of the subject of my thesis is that the latter matters are not affected by the drastic social, political and economic transformations of the context in which the *mu'amalat* aspects of *shari'ah* have to operate in present Islamic societies. In particular, my focus in this essay is on the actual role of *shari'ah* in the public life of present and future Islamic societies, rather than the study of the subject as a historical phenomenon. In other words, the following analysis assumes that *shari'ah* will continue to have a role in the public life of Islamic societies, and attempts to clarify and facilitate that role from the particular theoretical perspective explained below.

The main question I am addressing here is how to reconcile the profound and persistent commitment of Muslims to what is commonly known as *shari'ah* with the needs of present and future Islamic societies at home, as well as their need for peaceful and cooperative international relations with other societies. This framing of the question is of course relevant to a wide range of Islamic societies, whether Muslims constitute the majority of the population of a state, or they are a minority asserting the right to have *shari'ah* personal or family law, as is the case in India and Israel, for instance. The specific relevance of this question to the present situation in Northern Nigeria, the occasion for this volume, can further be clarified as follows.

It seems clear to me that the present political situation in Nigeria, especially since the first re-introduction of long-dormant aspects of *shari'ah* by Zamfara State in 1999, clearly indicates a dangerously high degree of confusion, misunderstanding, and suspicion regarding the terms in which the national and regional debate over the implementation of *shari'ah* in twelve Northern states is being conducted.[1] This state of affairs is of course due to a complex web of historical and contextual factors that can be traced to the pre-colonial history of the wider West Africa region, as well as developments in Nigeria since independence, including the civil war of the late 1960s. Without going into a discussion of that broader historical and political context, which is beyond the scope of this essay, I am suggesting here that the present confusion, misunderstanding, and suspicion surrounding *shari'ah* are partly due to the fundamental ambiguity of demands by the Muslims of the Northern Nigerian states which tend to attract negative reactions from Christians and other citizens of Nigeria.

As an observer of this debate over the last four years, from the vantage point of someone who has participated in a similar debate in Sudan, my home country, since the mid 1960s, I believe that the grossly inflated rhetoric and exaggerated demands by many Muslim Nigerians tend to draw a hostile response from Christian Nigerians,

---

[1] See Ostien, 2002, especially 170-173.

which leads, in turn, to even stronger rhetoric by Muslims, and the vicious cycle of confrontation and recrimination continues. It is therefore critically important, I believe, to clearly define realistic positions on both sides of the debate over the role of *shari'ah* in the public life of *any* state in Nigeria, regardless of the respective percentage of Muslim and non-Muslim citizens. In particular, the positions of both sides must be clearly and publicly stated in terms of the minimum constitutional and political requirements of a united, stable, pluralistic, and democratic country.

To begin with, the fundamental right of Muslims to freedom of religion regarding matters of belief and practice is not in any way whatsoever in question or under any sort of attack. It is also beyond dispute that Muslims also enjoy every possibility of voluntary personal and communal compliance with *shari'ah*. Since we are only concerned with the demands of some of the Muslims of Northern Nigeria that *shari'ah* should be enforced by the state, the question is which aspects of this vast legal and ethical tradition are Muslims demanding should be enforced as a matter of positive state law and official policy? Does this include such aspects of *shari'ah* as the *dhimmah* system, whereby Christian Nigerians will be relegated to the status of second-class citizens in their own country? Will those subscribing to non-scriptural beliefs (commonly known now as Traditional African Religions) who are deemed to be unbelievers by *shari'ah*, not be accepted as legal persons at all, except under the discretionary status of temporary safe conduct (*aman*)? Are Muslims calling for state enforcement of the *shari'ah* law of apostasy (*riddah*), whereby a Muslim who repudiates his or her belief in Islam is subject to the death penalty? Are they calling for the legal prohibition of charging or receiving interest on loans (*riba*), and speculative contracts (*qarar*), thereby outlawing modern banking and insurance contracts? To reiterate: the question is whether the state should enforce these aspects of *shari'ah* as a matter of positive law or official state policy, and not whether Muslim Nigerians are free, for example, to refrain from interest-based banking or insurance contracts.

This fundamental ambiguity in the position of Nigeria's Muslims confronts the country as a whole with a critical dilemma. On the one hand, if Muslims are in fact demanding the total and comprehensive implementation of *shari'ah*, including the aspects mentioned above, they leave no basis for the equality before the law of those Nigerian citizens who are not Muslims. A demand for the application of the totality of *shari'ah* would be tantamount to an invitation to civil war. On the other hand, if Muslims are not calling for the total and comprehensive implementation of *shari'ah* in this way, they must explain how they choose those parts of *shari'ah* they do want enforced. What basis or criterion do they use to select those aspects of *shari'ah* they want the state to implement, and what justification is there for such selection, from a *shari'ah* point of view? Unless these questions are answered, how can those Nigerians who are not Muslims know the precise extent of what Muslim Nigerians are demanding, and how are they to assess its full implications for their rights as citizens of the same country? If the criterion of selection is either unclear, or unjustified from a *shari'ah* point of view, Christian Nigerians would fairly and reasonably think that Muslims are being tactical by demanding now only what they think they can get, until they are able to demand and get more later on.

The thesis and analysis I present in this essay focuses on such underlying issues, rather than examining such technical questions as whether the Northern states have the constitutional power to extend the application of *shari'ah* in the ways they have done, or discussing the rationale or reasons for the inclusion of such a power in the constitution of 1999.[2] In my view, the issues I am raising are of more fundamental constitutional concern. Without going into the provisions of the Nigerian constitution in detail, it is clear as a matter of basic constitutional doctrine that no state can have the power to enact legislation or implement any policy that violates the fundamental rights of any citizen or group of citizens. Since, as explained below, certain aspects of *shari'ah* are simply inconsistent with basic constitutional government altogether, the enactment of such principles into law, or their adoption as official state policy, is inherently unconstitutional, even if the explicit text of the constitution might seem to indicate otherwise. By addressing such issues, I hope to contribute to the clarification of the terms and implications of the *shari'ah* debate in Nigeria today. However, these

---

[2] As to which see, for example, Illesanmi, 2001.

issues and reflections clearly apply to a wide range of Islamic societies and communities around the world, now and in the near future.

From this perspective, I will argue that the state should not claim, or be accepted by the public as having, the authority to enforce any aspect of *shari'ah* as positive law or official policy. This does not mean that no principles of *shari'ah* can or should be included in the law of the state, or implemented by its administrative organs. Indeed, it is most probable that wherever Muslims constitute the majority or even a significant minority of the population, *shari'ah* principles will influence the law and policy of the state. Rather, my point is that whenever that happens, it should be done as a matter of ordinary legislation or policy of the state, and not in the name of *shari'ah* as such. In view of the various ways in which *shari'ah* will continue to influence state policies and pubic institutions and practice, I refer to this approach as "the religious neutrality of the state." As I will attempt to explain in the next section, this does not mean the total banishment of Islam from the public domain, which is the charge often raised against "secularism," wrongfully in my view. The issue for me is one of mediation of competing claims about the relationship of religion and the state, rather than simplistic categorical separation of the two which is neither possible nor desirable in my view.

This approach is necessary it seems to me because of a basic dilemma. On the one hand, prevalent traditional interpretations of *shari'ah* are profoundly problematic for constitutional governance, political stability and economic development in present Islamic societies. In addition to the well-known problematic aspects of those prevalent interpretations such as discrimination against women and non-Muslims,[3] the nature of *shari'ah* itself precludes its enforcement by the state as positive law or official policy, as I will explain below. On the other hand, the religious commitment of Muslims to some sort of public role for *shari'ah* in their societies makes its total relegation to the so-called private domain neither viable, nor desirable in my view.

One possible response to the first part of this dilemma is the call by the late *Ustadh* Mahmoud Mohamed Taha of Sudan for a paradigm

---

[3] On those issues see An-Na'im, 1990, 86-91,

shift in *ijtihad* and revision of *usul al-fiqh* (the classical science of understanding the sources of *shari'ah*) in order to reformulate those problematic aspects of *shari'ah*.[4] This approach consists of two parts. First is the premise that there is need for a paradigm shift, and second, the specific methodology for achieving that shift and its outcomes. I remain convinced of the validity of the premise, as well as the legitimacy and viability of the specific methodology proposed by *Ustadh* Mahmoud. But the two can be distinguished, so that one can accept the premise while proposing an alternative methodology than of *Ustadh* Mahmoud, provided it can achieve the same objectives.

But accepting or rejecting that or any other proposed approach does not resolve the question of the public role of *shari'ah* in Islamic societies today, particularly in relation to the state, and regarding international relations. That is, whether or not one believes in the need and a method for re-interpreting *shari'ah* sources does not resolve the issue of the enforcement of such new principles by the state, which is the subject of this essay. In particular, I will argue that the inherent nature of *shari'ah* as necessarily the product of human interpretations of the Qur'an and Sunnah of the Prophet means that whatever formulations one prefers to adopt should not be enforced by the state as such.

From this perspective, I am concerned here with how to mediate between the need for "the religious neutrality of the state," on the one hand, and the legitimate demand of Muslims for the strong influence of Islam in the social and political life of predominantly Islamic societies, on the other. I will begin in the next section of this essay with a brief clarification of the terms *shari'ah* and *fiqh*, to emphasise that human interpretation is integral to any process or method of formulating the religious law of Islam, the divine guidance/commands of God for human beings, whether as individual persons or as whole communities or societies. Next I will challenge the idea of an Islamic state that enforces any interpretation of *shari'ah* as positive law or official policy, as opposed to a state in which Islam influences law and policy in less direct ways as indicated above. The final section is devoted to a tentative discussion of the proposed

---

[4] See, generally, Taha, 1987 and An-Na'im, 1990.

mediation between the religious neutrality of the state and the influence of Islam in the politics of Islamic societies.

INEVITABILITY OF HUMAN INTERPRETATION, WHETHER OF *SHARI'AH* OR OF FIQH

The main premise of my argument in this section is that what is commonly known among Muslims as *shari'ah*, was in fact the product of a very slow and gradual process of interpretation of various parts of the Qur'an and Sunnah during the first three centuries of Islam. This process was conducted by scholars and jurists who developed and applied the sources or methodology (*usul al-fiqh*) *completely independently* of the state, albeit with due regard to the circumstances and concerns of their communities and political institutions. The deeply contextual nature of that process is illustrated by the fact that al-Shafi'i changed some of his views when he moved from Iraq to Egypt. Moreover, as is to be expected, there was a lot of disagreement among those "founding" scholars on the sources, the methodologies they developed, and the conclusions they drew from their respective interpretative efforts.

These significant differences continue to the present day among Sunni and Shi'a schools of Islamic jurisprudence (*madhahib*), as well as within each school, with serious practical consequences. For example, the Maliki, which prevails in North and West Africa today, is the only one that accepts the pregnancy of an unmarried woman as proof of *zina* (illicit sexual intercourse), which is punishable by stoning to death if the woman was *muhsanah* (having been married before). Thus, a woman can be sentenced to stoning to death on the basis of this "proof" if she happens to live in a place where the Maliki school prevails, like Northern Nigeria, as illustrated by some recent cases. In contrast, under the Hanafi, Shafi'i, Hanbali and Ja'fari (Shi'a) schools, basing a charge of *zina* on such evidence alone is grounds for the other *shari'ah* offence of *ghadhf* (unproved accusation of illicit sexual intercourse). In other words, not only would a woman be acquitted of a charge of *zina* that is based only on her pregnancy, if she happens to live in a place where any of those other schools prevails, but also her accuser can face the serious criminal charge of *ghadhf*.

In current debates about the application of *shari'ah* in the modern context, a distinction is often made between *shari'ah* and *fiqh*, whereby the former is said to be enacted by God while the latter is legal understanding by human beings.[5] While this distinction can be meaningful in contrasting principles or rules that are the product more of speculative thinking than textual sources from the Qur'an and Sunnah, it cannot mean that these divine sources are not subject to human interpretation as well.

> Although the law is of divine provenance, the actual construction of the law is a human activity, and its results represent the law of God *as humanly understood*. Since the law does not descend from heaven ready-made, it is the human understanding of the law – the human *fiqh* [literally meaning understanding] – that must be normative for society.[6]

For our purposes here, therefore, human interpretation of divine sources is always necessary, whether the outcome is called *shari'ah* or *fiqh*. In other words, while *fiqh* principles can be changed more easily when they lack textual support from the Qur'an or Sunnah, disagreement on the meaning and normative significance of those divine sources cannot be avoided.

This point was so clear to the founding scholars of *shari'ah* that they strongly resisted imposing their views through state authority, even at the risk of torture and imprisonment. In fact, none of the founding scholars of the major Sunni schools held any judicial or other official office, except Abu Yusuf of the Hanafi School who held the position of Chief Judge under the Abbasid Caliphate. Instead, those scholars accepted diversity of opinion as a healthy and creative feature of their work, while seeking to enhance consensus among themselves and their communities. Thus, every single principle of *shari'ah* (not only *fiqh*) became established through *ijma'* (consensus) and voluntary compliance by Muslims at large, and never through an institutional authority, whether official or non-official. There was

---

[5] Weiss, 1998, 120.
[6] Ibid, 116.

never a council or formal meeting, even among scholars privately convened, where various views of *shari'ah* principles were debated in order to recognise some and reject others once and for all. Instead, the validity and binding authority of any *shari'ah* principle or rule was always the product of the free and unfettered choice of generations of Muslim scholars and communities, over a long period of time.

It is also relevant to note that voluntary and inter-generational *ijma'* among Muslims at large is in fact the fundamental foundation of all sources and techniques of *shari'ah*, past, present and future. In standard manuals, and according to the common knowledge of Muslims in general, the sources of *shari'ah* are said to be the Qur'an, Sunnah, *ijtihad* (juridical reasoning), *ijma'* and *qiyas* (reasoning by analogy to previously established rulings on a similar matter). But in fact, all of these sources, and their priority and application, are the product of *ijma'*. Even the text of the Qur'an is known and accepted as such by virtue of the consensus of generations of Muslims since the time of the Prophet. The collection and recording of Sunnah into authoritative compilations (known as *sihah* or reliable books like those by Muslim and Bukhari) happened through voluntary consensus among many generations of Muslims. The possibility of *ijtihad* and *qiyas*, and the legitimacy of their implementation to produce specific principles of *shari'ah* or *fiqh*, are also the product of *ijma'* of Muslims at large. The development and survival of different schools of thought, and extinction of others, was also the product of *ijma'*. For example, the views of Abu Hanifa or Malik evolved into separate and successful *madhahib* only because generations of Muslims accepted and implemented them by their own free choice. The development of *usul al-fiqh*, and its systematic compilation by al-Shafi'i, as well as his own school of jurisprudence, survived and became established by virtue of *ijma'*.

It is true that there have always been clear difficulties with the principle and process of *ijma'*. To begin with, how is the field or subject upon which *ijma'* may operate to be decided, and by whom? Some Muslims maintain that certain matters are so settled by the direct and categorical text of the Qur'an or Sunnah that there is no question of competing human interpretations that can be adjudicated though *ijma'* (*la ijtihad fi ma fihi nass*, that there can be no *ijtihad* in any matter governed by a categorical text of scripture). What those who hold this view fail to appreciate, is that even the opinion that a given matter is governed by categorical text is itself already a product of human judgment, authoritative only to the extent that it itself is supported by the *ijma'* of those who hold the same opinion. And then there is the question of whose *ijma'* makes an interpretation binding. Some have wanted to confine the binding force of *ijma'* to consensus among a select group of jurists; questions facing those who hold this view include how to agree on the criteria for identifying the jurists whose *ijma'* is binding, and how to identify and verify their opinions. If one is to say that the authority of *ijma'* is to come from the consensus of the Muslim community at large, the question still remains how to determine and verify that this has happened on any matter. Whether the consensus is supposed to be of a select group of jurists or of the community at large, why should the view of one generation bind subsequent generations?

Moreover, whatever solutions one may find for such methodological and practical difficulties will, again, always themselves be the product of human judgment and voluntary choice. Thus, the very idea of *shari'ah*, its sources and content, are inherently and permanently embedded in human understanding; and this necessarily means both the inevitability of differences of opinion and the possibility of error, whether among scholars or the community in general. Any conceivable view of *shari'ah* could not have been established, and cannot remain authoritative into the future, except through *ijma'*, which is necessarily the product of human judgment and voluntary acceptance of countless generations of Muslims, and not of some institutional authority that has the prerogative power to define religious doctrine for the community of believers.

For our purposes here in particular, the profoundly decentralised, voluntary, and inter-generational nature of any understanding or knowledge of *shari'ah* make it inherently incompatible with any notion of institutional enactment or enforcement. *Shari'ah* is binding on Muslims as a matter of religious belief, and one cannot be bound in one's belief by what he or she does not personally accept as a valid interpretation of relevant texts of the Qur'an and Sunnah through application of other sources and techniques of *shari'ah*. Given the diversity of opinions among Muslim jurists, whatever the authorities in control of any state may elect to enforce as *shari'ah* through positive law or official policy, is bound to be objectionable to some Muslims or other as a matter of personal religious conviction. In other words, the alleged enforcement of *shari'ah* by the state inevitability entails the violation of the fundamental freedom of religion for Muslims themselves, in addition to whatever other objections may be raised against particular principles, as outlined below.

The basic conclusion of this section is the inevitability of *human agency* in the interpretation of all religious texts, the Qur'an and Sunnah in the case of Islam. I use the term 'human agency' here to indicate that human beings are the primary agents of social change, for both good and bad, without denying the impact of cultural, structural, environmental and other factors. My use of this term also takes due account of religious or other motivations people may have in acting or refraining from action, and is not meant to suggest that all human beings are equally able and willing to play a proactive role in religious discourse. This usage is also consistent with the religious belief of Muslims that God is the ultimate creator and actor in the world, because God always acts through human beings through their apparently autonomous wills and in their respective contexts, rather than by direct "divine" intervention. To emphasise the role of human agency is – without disputing or undermining the belief that God is the ultimate creator – to call on people to take responsibility for the relevance and meaning of their religious beliefs to their own lives, instead of perceiving themselves as passive objects of manipulation by forces beyond their control.

It is clear to me, moreover, that the human agency of some actors not only tends to diminish the social and political "space" in which the human agency of others may operate freely, but also that the outcome of the agency of every actor is likely to be objectionable from some point of view or another. Yet, for the human agency of some people to counter the negative manifestations of the agency of others, the space for religious, social and political dissent and disagreement must be maintained as free and as open as is humanly possible. That is why I am particularly concerned about the dangers of allowing the coercive powers of the state to be used, or rather abused, to the advantage of some religious views or against others. Moreover, the tendency of Islamic discourse to cast every difference of opinion over *shari'ah* into charges of apostasy and heresy makes it imperative to avoid allowing political differences to assume a religious dimension. I will therefore devote the next two sections to a discussion of issues of the nature of the state and the dangers of the political use of charges of apostasy or heresy.

THE ILLUSION OF AN ISLAMIC STATE TO ENFORCE *SHARI'AH*

The main problem with the idea of an Islamic state that can enforce *shari'ah* as positive law or official policy is that, in view of the inherent subjectivity and consequent diversity of all interpretations of the Qur'an and Sunnah, such an effort will necessarily rely on the specific interpretation accepted by those in political power, to the exclusion of other interpretations which would be equally valid for other believers. In other words, the impossibility of the enforcement of *shari'ah* by the state is due to the nature of *shari'ah* as a religious normative system, and nature of the state as a political institution. Yet, the paradox persists: On the one hand, Muslims not only continue to aspire, in theory at any rate, to the illusion of a pure Islamic state in which *shari'ah* is enforced as the only law, but many of them even regard opposition to the idea of an Islamic state as tantamount to apostasy – a capital crime punishable by death. On the other hand, the vast majority of post-colonial Islamic societies have in fact avoided the enactment of *shari'ah* as the legal system and basis of public policy in their own independent states, and the very few countries that have tried it, like Iran, Pakistan, and Sudan, are encountering severe problems in making it work in practice. In sum, Islamic societies seem neither willing to abandon the illusion that *shari'ah* could and should be the only law under which they live; nor are they willing – or able – to actually implement it through the institutions of the state as such.

This paradox can be mediated, it seems to me, by providing an Islamic rationale for the religious neutrality of the state, whereby *shari'ah* can play a positive role in the public domain, without being enforced by the state as positive law and public policy. Since the religious neutrality of the state and its institutional separation from religious authority is commonly called "secularism," and viewed with hostility by many Muslims, my argument must include a rebuttal of what I believe are misconceived objections to this concept.

In support of this proposition, I would first emphasise that the states that have ruled over Muslims throughout history have always in fact been secular, and could not have been otherwise. Secularism should be understood as a particular type of deeply contextual relationship between religion and the state, varying from one setting to another, that enables the state to claim religious legitimacy without enabling it to appropriate religious authority as such.

The second argument against the fallacy of an Islamic state that purports to enforce *shari'ah* as positive law is that it is more damaging than a secular state for the freedom of religion and integrity of religious experience of Muslim as well as non-Muslim citizens of the state. To begin with, while Muslims have always continued to aspire to the model of the Prophet's state in Medina (622-632 CE), it is clear that that experience can neither be repeated, nor logically compared to any other period in Islamic history or the future of Islamic societies. In addition to the extraordinary fact of the actual existence of the Prophet, who continued to receive and explain revelation throughout that period of time and to exercise his personal charisma and moral leadership, the state in Medina consisted of close-knit tribal communities of highly motivated new converts who lived within an extremely limited space. In other words, the state of Medina was based more on the moral authority of the Prophet and of social conformity within a small, close-knit community than on the coercive power of the state as in other human societies. The model of the Prophet's state in Medina cannot be applied in the present context of any Islamic society because it was a unique phenomenon that ended with his death.

Regarding the rest of Islamic history, it is also clear that the Islamic legitimacy of the state has always been a cause of conflict and civil war since the death of the Prophet Muhammad in 632. The majority of Sunni Muslims believe that the reigns of the first four Caliphs of Medina (the seat of the first state in western Arabia) continued the ideal Islamic state and community of the time of the Prophet. But according to Shi'a Muslims, the first three of the Medina Caliphs were illegitimate usurpers of the position to which only Ali (the Prophet's cousin, who became the fourth Caliph of

Medina) and his decedents from Fatima (the Prophet's only surviving child) were rightly entitled. Throughout his reign as the fourth Caliph (656-61), Ali was locked in bitter civil war against the Umayyad clan and other factions, including some of his own supporters, known as al-Kawarij (the breakaway group), who condemned him for accepting mediation with the Umayyad. Upon Ali's assassination by one of al-Kawarij in 661, the Umayyad clan established a monarchy that ruled the expanding Muslim Empire from Damascus, Syria, until 750. The Abbasid launched their successful challenge to the Umayyad dynasty in the name of Islamic legitimacy, but the Abbasid state (750-1258) was also a monarchy that ruled from Baghdad, Iraq, more in accordance with political expediency than *shari'ah* principles. The same has been true of the other states of various seizes and durations that have ruled Islamic societies ever since: from Spain, North and West Africa, and Central Asia to India, including the Ottoman Empire that was finally abolished in 1923-24.

The tension between Islamic legitimacy and political expediency was usually mediated at different phases of history through mutual accommodation between *al-umara* (rulers) and *al-ulama* (scholars of *shari'ah*) whereby the former acknowledged the theoretical supremacy of *shari'ah* and the latter conceded the practical political authority of the rulers. Occasionally, some rulers professed commitment to more rigorous implementation of *shari'ah*, as happened during the early Abbasid dynasty, the Ibadi Khariji kingdom of Tlemsen, Morocco (761-909), the Almoravids in Morocco and Spain (1056-1147), and the Isma'ili Shi'a Fatimati dynasty in parts of North Africa (969-1171). It is difficult to assess the scope and efficacy of those episodes of *shari'ah* application because of the lack of independent and sufficiently detailed historical sources. But it is reasonable to assume that the highly decentralised nature of the state and of the administration of justice at those times in history would not have permitted the sort of systematic and comprehensive application of *shari'ah* as is demanded or expected by the Muslims of the Northern Nigeria in the modern context.

One of the basic difficulties that has frustrated efforts to establish a state that can effectively implement *shari'ah* has been the lack of political and legal institutions to ensure compliance by the state itself, and its officials, with the demands *shari'ah* makes on them. While the *ulama* were supposed to be the guardians of *shari'ah*, they had no resort except appealing to the moral and religious sentiments of the rulers. Another factor was that the *ulama* were too concerned with safeguarding the unity of their communities, and the maintenance of peace and public order, to forcefully press their demands on rulers, especially in times of internal strife and external threat. The few scholars who expressly addressed constitutional and legal matters, like al-Mawardi (died 1058) in *Al-Ahkam al-Sultaniyyah* (Principles of Government), and Ibn Taimiyyah (died in 1328) in *al-Siyasah al-Shar'iyyah* (Islamic Public Policy), confined themselves to elaborations of what *ought* to happen, in the form of advice to the ruler, without addressing what should happen when the ruler fail to comply with the application of *shari'ah* as an obligation of the state. Consequently, those episodes of aspirations to an ideal state that would faithfully and impartially implement *shari'ah* as a total way of life were continuously frustrated by such mundane factors as political expediency and security concerns. When the balance tilted too much in favour of the latter, however, the intensity of demands for the application of *shari'ah* would rise, usually as a local or regional movement that might succeed in seizing power for a brief period of time, as illustrated by the rare examples cited above.

It seems clear to me from this brief review that the states that have ruled over Muslims throughout their history have been secular, in the sense of a mutual accommodation between *al-umara* (rulers) and *al-ulama* (scholars of *shari'ah*). In particular, the difficulties those states had in enforcing *shari'ah* were due to the inherent nature of *shari'ah* itself, and could not be overcome over time. Neither *al-umara* nor *al-ulama* could combine the two functions of exercising coercive political authority and being the scholarly guardians of *shari'ah* at the same time. In other words, there is no historical precedent for a so-called "Islamic state" in Islamic history, and the model will be even more unworkable in the future, partly because of the inherent nature of *shari'ah* as a religious normative system.

The idea of an Islamic state is conceptually incoherent, and practically very dangerous for the integrity of the religious experience of Muslims themselves, in addition to its serious violations of the rights of women and non-Muslims, which are not addressed here. The idea is incoherent in that a state is necessarily a political institution, and not a natural person who is capable of belief in Islam or any other religion. In other words, 'Islamic' may be used to refer to states where Muslims constitute a clear majority of the population, but the adjective 'Islamic' logically applies to a people, rather than to a state as a political institution. The fact that a state calls itself Islamic by proclaiming Islam to be the state religion, or alleging that it is making *shari'ah* a formal source of legislation does not accurately reflect an Islamic quality of the state itself as a political institution. Unless one is willing to accept every claim by a state to be Islamic, the question becomes one of who has the authority to determine the quality of being Islamic, and according to which criteria. Thus, neither is Saudi Arabia likely to accept the claim of the present government of Iran that it is an "Islamic" republic, nor is Iran likely to accept that the Saudi monarchy can ever be "Islamic," regardless of its claim to enforce *shari'ah* as the sole legal system of the land.

Finally, it is clear that the forms of political and social organisation by which all Muslims live today, and the types of economies they have to operate and depend on for their survival, make even the much more recent history of the Ottoman and Mughal imperial states of the Middle East and India too alien to be revived or resurrected in the present post-colonial world of global economic and political interdependence and integration. Accordingly, claims to establish an Islamic state to enforce *shari'ah* today are dangerously naive, if not cynical and manipulative. Yet, as noted earlier, opposing this unprecedented and untenable notion is routinely construed as tantamount to apostasy in Islamic discourse throughout the region. As I will attempt to show in the next section, the tendency to intimidate and suppress dissent that is characteristic of public debates around the idea of an Islamic state or enforcement of *shari'ah* is inherent to the discourse itself. This profoundly problematic tendency makes it even more urgent to repudiate the illusion of an Islamic state and claims of the enforcement of *shari'ah* by the state. Such claims undermine the protection of critically important fundamental rights, and in the process render national constitutional governance, political stability and economic development increasingly untenable.

ISLAMIC DISCOURSE AND THE PROSPECTS OF CONSTITUTIONALISM

The main point I wish to make in this section is that the inherent nature and terms of Islamic discourse around the enforcement of *shari'ah* by the state has far reaching negative consequences for the prospects of constitutionalism, stability and development in the whole country. Throughout Islamic history, up to the present in Northern Nigeria for instance, the debate around the enforcement of *shari'ah* has always tended to be cast in absolute terms of religious salvation and paradise for those who are "right" versus apostasy and eternal hell for those who are "wrong." But the problem is that such absolute terms are not only inherent to the subject itself, but also seriously detrimental to the possibilities of civic participation in public affairs, for Muslim and non-Muslim citizens alike. When the stakes are cast in terms of either fulfilling or frustrating God's will for humanity, the consequences of being right or wrong will necessarily be equally absolute. The main problem from the perspective of this essay is the threat to the fundamental rights of all citizens is much more serious when such judgments are being made in the name of the state, with its enormous and far-reaching coercive powers. In the final analysis, the idea of the protection of the constitutional rights of political and religious dissidents, indeed all who disagree with the government of the day, itself becomes an untenable heresy.[7]

The irony is that, like the idea of an Islamic state or formal enforcement of *shari'ah* by the state discussed in the preceding section, the concept of apostasy and related notions are profoundly problematic from an Islamic perspective. In addition to its incompatibility with individual religious liberty, there are two objections to the notion of apostasy in Islamic jurisprudence itself, namely, the vagueness and fluidity of the concept, and the ambiguity of the basis for its legal consequences as a capital crime. The vagueness and fluidity of the concept of apostasy relate to its

---

[7] This does not of course address other reasons for the suppression of political dissent, as happens under dictatorial or authoritarian regimes. But I believe that denying such regimes any religious pretext or justification for their policies is necessary for sustainable constitutionalism and protection of human rights in Islamic societies today.

definition and punishment, as well as its close association with several equally problematic related concepts in Islamic jurisprudence, such as unbelief (*kufr*) blasphemy (*sabb al-rasul*), heresy (*zandaqah*), and hypocrisy (*nifaq*).

The Arabic word *riddah*, commonly translated as apostasy, literally means to 'turn back', and *murtadd*, the active participle from *irtadda*, means one who turns back. In Islamic jurisprudence, *riddah* is understood to be reverting from the religion of Islam to *kufr* (unbelief) whether intentionally or by necessary implication.[8] In addition to an open repudiation of his or her belief in Islam, apostasy is said to apply whenever a person is deemed to have reverted from Islam, by an intentional or blasphemous act or utterance, whether or not it was said mockingly, out of stubbornness, or out of conviction.

An obvious problem with the notion of apostasy is that, while the Qur'an repeatedly condemns apostasy as a religious sin, it does not provide any punishment for it in this life, as can be seen in verses 2:217, 4:90, 5:54 and 59, 16:108, and 47:25.[9] In fact, the Qur'an clearly contemplates situations where an apostate continues to live among the Muslim community, rather than being put to death. For example, verse 4:137 of the Qur'an can be translated as follows: "Those who believed, then disbelieved, then believed, and then disbelieved [once more] and became more unbelieving; God will not forgive them or guide them to the righteous pathway." Nevertheless, classical Islamic jurisprudence imposes the death penalty on the basis of some Sunnah reports; other negative legal consequences also follow, for instance, concerning inheritance. According to one report, the Prophet said that "the life of a fellow Muslim should never be taken except these three: an adulterer, a murderer, or one who abandons Islam after having embraced it."

Since apostasy means to be openly reverting to disbelief in Islam after having freely embraced it, an obvious association is with disbelief (*kufr*) – open and complete rejection of the message of Islam itself. Although it repeatedly speaks of belief and disbelief, and

---

[8] The following review of classical Islamic jurisprudence of apostasy is based on Ibn Rushd, vol. 2, n.d., and Nu`man Abd al-Razid al-Samar`i, 1968. In English see Rahman, 1972.

[9] The Qur'an is cited here by giving the number of the chapter (*surah*), followed by the number of the verse (*ayah*).

related terms, the Qur'an does not provide clear guidance on what these terms mean beyond the basic sense of either accepting or rejecting the confession of the faith – that "There is no God but God, and Muhammad is his messenger." For example, the Qur'an frequently links belief to performing worship rituals like prayer and fasting during the month of Ramadan and doing good deeds, but does not say what should happen to those who fail to live up to these obligations other than punishment in the afterlife. Moreover, the Qur'an does not expressly state the consequences of questioning the precise meaning of the confession of the faith itself. For instance, what does it mean to affirm that "There is no God but God"? What do believers know, or what should they know, about God? What are the imperative consequences of belief in the unity of God for the personal practice or behaviour of Muslims, whether at the private personal level or in relation to public socio-economic and political institutions and processes? Who has the authority to adjudicate the inevitable disagreements about these and other matters after the death of Prophet, and how?

It is clear that the Qur'an leaves Muslims to struggle with all these issues for themselves, with whatever guidance they can draw from the Sunnah of the Prophet, which also has its own uncertainties and ambiguities. The consequent major differences among Islamic scholars include the role that actions or deeds (*amal*) play in the definition of belief (*iman*). Whereas some scholars were willing to accept as sufficient an apparent confession of the faith for a person to be considered a Muslim, others insisted that professed belief must be expressed in specific action or deeds. For those who hold the latter view, the question becomes what to do about people who claim to be Muslims but fail to act accordingly. But then, who decides whether or not a person has acted according to the requirements of the faith, and what consequences should follow from such a determination? These debates and their violent manifestations have raged from the times of the al-Khawarij during the civil wars of the seventh century, to the arguments about the status of the Ahmadiyya in Pakistan since 1950s, to Usama bin Ladin's call today to vindicate belief in Islam by any means possible, including international terrorism. As already noted, the field is further complicated by ambiguities and disagreements about other concepts, including the following.

Blasphemy is the use of foul language primarily about the Prophet Muhammad, known as insulting the Prophet (*sabb al-rasul*), God, or any of the angels or prophets, and is punishable by death. At a later stage, this offence was extended to cover using foul language against the Companions of the Prophet. This extension was probably intended to penalise some dissidents among Muslims, like al-Khawarij and Shi'a, who were reviling leading figures of the early Muslim community in the context of the civil wars of the seventh and early eighth centuries. The punishment for blasphemy appears to be based on certain incidents in the lifetime of the Prophet, as there is no clear Qur'anic instruction on the matter. Even when the Qur'an uses the term *sabb*, as in 6:108, it only commands Muslims not to revile the deities of non-Muslims lest they revile God, but without any reference to punishment in this life. However, during the time of the Prophet, some Muslims killed a number of non-Muslims who reviled the Prophet. Since all those killed in these incidents were among the staunchest opponents of Islam, and some of them had fabricated certain stories about the Prophet, as well as about the Muslim community in general, it is difficult to identify the precise reason used to justify killing them. But it is clear that neither the Qur'an nor the Prophet declare the existence of an offence called 'blasphemy' or a specific punishment for it.

The term 'heresy' (*zandaqah*) is applied in classical Islamic jurisprudence to a heretic, whose teachings become a danger to the state, thereby rendering him liable to the death penalty. However, the term and its derivatives do not appear in the Qur'an at all, and seem to have come into Arabic from Persian.[10] This term was apparently used for the first time in connection with the execution of Ja'd bin Dirham in 742 – more than a century after the Prophet's death. "In practice, the polemics of the conservatives describe as a *zindik* (one who is guilty of *zandaqah*) anyone whose external profession of Islam seems to them to be not sufficiently sincere."[11] Yet, instead of agreement among scholars on a general definition of these terms, one finds a variety of views about the type of conduct that constitutes *zandaqah*, or makes a person a *zindiq*. According to one view, for

---

[10] See the article "*Zindik*" in Gibb and Kramers, 1991, 659.
[11] Ibid.

instance, a *zindiq* is a person who outwardly pretends to be a Muslim while inwardly adhering to his former religion.

Assuming that one accepts this definition, the question then becomes how the fact of *zandaqah* is to be known or proved in specific cases? Some scholars were prepared to infer it from the accused's advocacy of indulgence in various acts that are prohibited in Islam, such as *zina* or drinking wine. The ambiguity of the concept appears to have been both caused by, and grossly abused in the context of, the large-scale conversion of people to Islam following the Muslim conquests of the first two centuries of Islamic history. In other words, the emergence and expansion of this concept may have been prompted by fears of infiltration of the Muslim community and state by non-Muslims who may have been using Islam for personal gain or to escape discrimination. But the vagueness of the concept and the difficulty of proving its application in specific cases also permitted its abuse for political ends by rulers, and even by some scholars against their theological or intellectual rivals. Yet, a clear definition is critical for distinguishing it from apostasy since some scholars, of the Hanafi and Maliki schools in particular, would not grant a *zindiq* a chance to repent, as they would an apostate.

The third term associated with apostasy is hypocrisy (*nifaq*), referring to those who openly profess belief in Islam, while harbouring disbelief. Again, while the Qur'an repeatedly condemns such hypocrisy (2:8-10), promises hypocrites punishment in hell in the afterlife (9:68), and warns the Muslim community against the dangers of having hypocrites in their mist (2:8-10, 9:68) it does not prescribe any punishment in this life. In verse 9:73, the Prophet is commanded to engage in *jihad* against the hypocrites and unbelievers, but that cannot mean imposing criminal punishment as such, since punishment can be executed only within the jurisdiction of a stable and effective state, away from the context of *jihad*. Nevertheless, Muslim scholars, especially of the Hanafi and Maliki schools, decided to impose the death penalty on a *zindiq* as a hypocrite who professes Islam but secretly holds contrary belief.

As this brief review clearly shows, there has always been a substantial degree of confusion and fluidity in these concepts and in how they were to be defined, as well as uncertainty about the basis of imposing criminal punishment on those "convicted" of holding such beliefs. Since the Qur'an neither defined these concepts in legal terms, nor imposed a punishment for any of them in this life, the Muslim communities could have chosen simply to view them as matters of freedom of conscience, instead of punishing them as capital crimes. Indeed, the Prophet himself set an example for that by refusing to question the beliefs of anyone who claimed to profess Islam as a religion. Yet, those purported offences and their punishment became entrenched in classical Islamic jurisprudence, probably for political reasons disguised with an alleged religious rationale.

The general conclusion here is that these notions are totally inconsistent with the fundamental human right of freedom of thought, conscience, and religion – a right entrenched in the constitutions of the vast majority of the countries in the world today. But the more specific conclusion for my thesis and analysis about the future of *shari'ah* is that such confused and arbitrary charges are the unavoidable result of mixing issues of private religious belief with public constitutional and political questions. If such charges are available as part of enforceable law, it is totally unrealistic to expect politicians to refrain from making them when they find it expedient to do so in order to suppress political opposition. Even the risk of that happening will greatly inhibit the excise of the critical freedoms of opinion, expression, and association in the political realm, to the detriment of the essence of constitutional governance, political stability, and economic development in the country. In other words, the enforcement of *shari'ah* by the state will necessarily and inevitability result in serious damage to the political and economic health of any modern society, doing damage far beyond the immediate scope of the field in which it is supposed to apply.

MEDIATION OF THE RELIGIOUS NEUTRALITY OF THE STATE AND A PUBLIC ROLE FOR ISLAM

Yet, I am calling for a mediation of the public role of *shari'ah*, rather than for its total and immediate relegation to the so-called exclusively private domain. This qualification is critically important because opposition to the enforcement of *shari'ah* by the state is immediately equated by many Muslims with a call for "secularism," which is regarded with extreme hostility as anti-religious, or at least as a Western colonial imposition. It is therefore necessary for the political viability of what I am calling for to attempt to clarify the confusion around the term 'secularism' in order to avoid the negative connotations associated with that term.

Etymologically, the word 'secular' derives from the Latin word *saeculum*, meaning "great span of time" or more closely "spirit of the age." Later, the word came to mean "of this world", implying more than one world, eventually translating into a concept of the secular and the religious derived from the idea of the temporal and the spiritual.[12] The term also evolved in the European context from "secularisation" as privatisation of church lands, to "secularisation" of politics and later of art and economics.[13] This line of development is reflected in the Webster's dictionary definition of the word 'secularism' as "indifference to or rejection or exclusion of religion or religious considerations."[14] Another definition sees it as "the doctrine that morality should be based solely on regard to the well-being of mankind in the present life, to the exclusion of all considerations drawn from belief in God or in a future state."[15] Shiner identified and distinguished between five definitions of secularism as (1) decline of religion, (2) conformity to the present world, (3) disengagement/differentiation of society from religion, including separation of church and state, (4) transposition of religious beliefs and institutions (shift from divine sources of power to human capability and creation), and (5) desacralisation of the world and subsequent sacralisation of rationality.[16]

From my perspective, all these views are simply reflections of how the concept has evolved in various European and North American settings, each in its own way. Secularism is in fact a "multidimensional concept,"[17] reflecting elements of the historical, political, social, and economic landscape of a particular nation. In the United States, it has come to mean a purported "wall of separation

---

[12] Engineer and Mehta, 1998, 25.
[13] Mcleod, 2000, 1.
[14] *Merriam-Webster's Collegiate Dictionary*, 10th edition, 1994.
[15] Engineer and Mehta, 1998, 2.
[16] Shiner, 1967, 215.
[17] Engineer and Mehta, 1998, 25.

between church and state." Mexican secularism requires such a strict separation of religion and politics that priests are not allowed to vote. In the "secular" Republic of Ireland, the Catholic Church wields so much power politically that abortion is still illegal on the grounds that it violates Church doctrine. France's unique secularism is defined as a rigidly guarded separation of religion and the state. Essentially, "each country has its own specificity as far as the concept of secularism is concerned. This specificity depends on its historical evolution as well as on contemporary social conditions."[18]

I would therefore define secularism as a principle of public policy that seeks to secure the institutional separation of religion and the state, while acknowledging and seeking to mediate the unavoidable and desirable interaction of religion and politics. Given the nature of *shari'ah*, as a comprehensive normative system, and the persistent commitment of Muslims to its implementation, secularism in the Islamic context should seek to mediate the public role of *shari'ah*, rather than attempt simply to relegate it to the private domain. In other words, secularism for Islamic societies must account for the religious dimension of the lives of local communities, instead of being seen as an effort to impose preconceived notions of what the term "must mean."

In this light, it is therefore misleading to speak of complete separation or total union of any religion and the state.[19] Any state is conceived and operated by human beings whose religious or philosophical beliefs will necessarily be reflected in their thinking and behaviour. Total separation between religion and the state is not possible, or desirable in my view, because of the impossibility of separating religion from politics. How can one prevent people from acting politically according to their religious or other beliefs? Even if such a demand is made, how can one monitor its application in practice, while maintaining the integrity and legitimacy of the political process itself? At the same time, however, one must address the question whether secularism, as a principle of public policy for organising the relationships between religion and the apparatus of the state, including politics, in a specific context, is compatible with *any*

---

[18] Ibid, 202.
[19] An-Na'im, 2000, 37-39.

relationship, or does it have to have certain minimum requirements? Do some forms of this relationship achieve more optimal synergy and interdependence among religion, human rights and secularism than others do?

If it is true that the relationship between religion and the state should not be one of either complete fusion or categorical separation, then one would expect a continuum of "secularisms" between these two extremes. Drawing on the premise that secularism is indeed dynamic and deeply contextual, a study that examined the relationship between religion and the state in the United States, The Netherlands, Australia, England and Germany, concluded that a minimum requirement for a positive relationship between religion and the state is that people are neither advantaged or disadvantaged by their adherence to any religious or other faith or belief, or none at all.[20] The state should be neutral, and neither favour nor disfavour one particular religious tradition over another.[21] The problem with this clearly necessary requirement is that no public policy is ever completely neutral because of the unavoidable relationship between religion and politics.

To summarise and frame the issue: In view of the nature of *shari'ah*, as historically understood by Muslims, the modern territorial state should neither seek to enforce it as positive law and public policy, nor claim to interpret *shari'ah* doctrine and principle for its Muslim citizens. At the same time, the organic relationship between *shari'ah* and the culture and politics of each Muslim society mean that *shari'ah* principles will remain relevant to varying degrees to matters of public policy and legislation. That is, as *shari'ah* principles will continue to strongly influence the moral sensibilities of Muslims from early childhood, those principles are bound to find expression in the public policy of their state, and rightly so. It is simply not possible, and not desirable in my view, to attempt to prevent *shari'ah* from influencing the political and public behaviour of Muslims. But that cannot mean the direct enforcement of *shari'ah* principles as such through the official institutions of the state for the reasons stated in

---

[20] Mosma and Soper, 1997, 208-209.
[21] Ibid, 209.

the preceding section. In other words, what is problematic is for *shari'ah* principles *as such* to be enforced as positive law, but the ethical principles and values of religion are indeed necessary for the proper functioning of society at large.

The underlying tension therefore relates to how people can excise free democratic choice in accordance with their own religious or other beliefs, while ensuring the neutrality of the state. As I see it, the answer lies in transforming people's understanding of *shari'ah* so that their free democratic choices are still respectful of the principles of constitutional democratic government, and of the full rights of other human beings everywhere. That is, Muslims must interpret *shari'ah* in ways that do not confront them with a choice between fidelity to their religion, on the one hand, and upholding the principles of constitutionalism and peaceful coexistence with non-Muslim citizens on the other, in the interest of the stability and development of their own country. To this end, I am calling for significant reform to reformulate problematic interpretations of *shari'ah* through an Islamic methodology that is both sufficient and acceptable. The proposed methodology has to be sufficient in the sense of achieving the necessary degree of change in popular interpretations of *shari'ah*. But a good methodology is not much useful if Muslims are not willing to accept and implement it in practice.

The dilemma facing the proponents of reform in Islamic societies today is whether to seek their objectives through the existing corpus and methodology of classical Islamic jurisprudence, or to attempt to avoid the limitations of that approach by bringing in such European and North American notions as secularism and separation of religion and the state. While the vast majority of Islamic societies today are struggling with the first approach, several have attempted varying forms or degrees of the second, with Turkey being the most extreme example of authoritarian imposition of European secularism by the state under the ideology of Mustafa Kamal Ataturk and his successors. By briefly explaining the limitations of both approaches in the following remarks, I am suggesting the need for a comprehensive theory of Islamic reform that can contribute to mediating that basic dilemma by questioning the underlying assumptions of a dichotomy between the religious and the secular. Such a theory is necessary, I believe, for reformulating the structure and methodology of classical Islamic jurisprudence in order to make it more relevant and useful in the modern context of Islamic societies.

The basic limitation of reform within the framework of what is known as classical Islamic jurisprudence is that it cannot achieve the necessary degree of change in some of the most basic issues, like the abolition of the notion of apostasy and related concepts. Classical Islamic jurisprudence cannot achieve the desired degree of reform because of the limitations of its own methodology, *usul al-fiqh*, which does not permit changing any rule of *shari'ah* that is based on an explicit and categorical text of Qur'an or Sunnah.[22] As noted earlier, while the Qur'an strongly condemns apostasy, without providing a specific punishment for it in this life, the Sunnah has been cited as the basis of such punishment. To abolish the criminal punishment of apostasy through secular law and policy, without some form of Islamic justification, will neither redress the civil (family law) consequences nor their inhibiting power in Islamic discourse.

At the same time, an assertion of separation of Islam and the state is unlikely to be accepted by Muslims unless it is presented with an Islamic rationale or justification. Otherwise, such a separation will have to be imposed on the community, which means the negation of the objectives of democratisation and protection of fundamental human rights, which are usually cited as the justification of such imposition. The negative consequences of authoritarian imposition of secularism can be seen in the case of Turkey, where the secularisation of the state continues to be enforced by the army since it was imposed by Ataturk in the 1920s. Moreover, even if *shari'ah* is not enforced by the state as such, it will still be influential in shaping law and policy through the political processes of the country. For instance, as long as Muslims believe apostasy to be a capital crime, they will probably continue to act on that belief by supporting political leaders who will enact laws to that effect. In other words, secularisation in the formal sense of separation of Islam and the state will not be enough without a transformation of the content of *shari'ah*, as it is known and accepted by Muslims.

---

[22] See, generally, An-Na'im, 1990, especially chapter 4.

It is therefore critical, in my view, to combine these two approaches by clarifying the relationship between Islam and the state, while at the same time seeking to achieve fundamental reform of certain aspects of *shari'ah* because of its powerful influence on Muslims everywhere, even when it is not enforced by the state as such. My argument for the first part of this combination is that the idea of an Islamic state to enforce *shari'ah* as positive law is conceptually untenable and practically counter-productive from an Islamic point of view. This idea is untenable because once principles of *shari'ah* are enacted as positive law of a state, they cease to be the religious law of Islam and become the political will of that state. Moreover, allowing the state to invoke such Islamic sanctity for its policies will violate the freedom of religion of Muslims as well as non-Muslims.

The possibility of drastic reform of the content of *shari'ah*, even as a religious normative system, requires the fundamental reformation of *usul al-fiqh*, as emphasised earlier. This reformation is both necessary and possible because every interpretation of the Qur'an and Sunnah, in the past, present, or future, is necessarily a product of the historical context of the Muslim society of that time and place. One possible approach is the one proposed by *Ustadh* Mahmoud Mohamed Taha, cited at the beginning of this essay. In his view, given the radical transformation of the political, social, and economic context of Islamic societies today, as compared to what used to prevail when traditional understandings of *shari'ah* were developed, the methodology of interpretation must respond to these present realities to produce modernist formulations of *shari'ah*. Re-examining the rationale for enacting certain passages of the Qur'an and Sunnah into *shari'ah* principles, and for de-emphasising others as inapplicable in the context of early Islamic societies can do this, for example. Once it is appreciated that the selection of which passages should be emphasised and which downplayed was made by human beings, rather than decreed by direct divine command, it becomes possible to reconsider the question of which texts are to be enacted today, and which are to be de-emphasised in the present context. But other approaches are certainly possible, like those which focus on the underlying purposes or objectives of *shari'ah* over strict interpretation of the scriptural texts,[23] though one might question whether they will go far enough.

However, there is also a political or contextual dimension to this internal theological debate. A reformer's ability to gain the confidence of a constituency, and authority among its members, depends on his or her understanding of all the complexity of their history and immediate context, concerns, and aspirations. Therefore, in addition to the availability of a credible theological methodology for reform, one must still appreciate the political consequences of whose interests are undermined or promoted by one interpretation or another. The more the political and/or religious elite of a society feel threatened by internal or external forces and factors, the more they become entrenched in their conservative views for fear of losing their power and privilege. Other considerations include how personal or psychological, as well as broader political, economic, and sociological factors influence people's understanding (or willingness or ability to understand) the Qur'an and Sunnah in one way or another.

One should also appreciate the influence of broader geo-political or security concerns on a community's ability or willingness to be open to challenge to its basic moral and metaphysical precepts. That is, are such concerns likely to make the community more defensive and conservative, or to help in overcoming the defensiveness and conservatism of these elites? The state has a critical role in these processes, not only by itself refraining from purporting to enforce *shari'ah* as such, but also through the educational system, and by promoting critical thinking in the media and in general securing the political and social "space" for dissent and free debate. But the state itself, and the international community at large, can also be part of the problem. The required political and social liberalisation may appear to be, or in fact be, threatening for the elite who control the state, even when they claim to be secular in their political orientation, as can be seen in such countries as Egypt and Syria. Other states may also be supportive of oppressive regimes in Islamic countries, or pursue hostile foreign policy objectives that provoke conservatism and defensiveness in Islamic societies, instead of the confidence and sense

---

[23] See, generally, Baderin, 2003.

of security that would encourage internal political and social liberalisation.

Thus, especially in the aftermath of the invasion and colonisation of Iraq by the United States, with the support of the United Kingdom, the previous colonial power of the region, it is critical to show that the proposed conception of the religious neutrality of the state is not a Western imposition of secularism on Islamic societies. Indeed, my argument is that secularism cannot be imposed by external powers: it can only evolve out of the actual historical experiences and practical circumstances of each society, consistently with its own religious beliefs and cultural values. The Islamic argument for secularism I am trying to develop and substantiate is unlikely to be accepted unless it is also able to account for the political and security apprehensions of Islamic societies about Western hegemony and economic globalisation.

To conclude on the debate in Northern Nigeria over the enforcement of *shari'ah* by the state, I would first recall my opening remarks about the imperative importance of clarifying the terms of the debate itself. Since it is the Muslims of the Northern Nigerian states who are taking this initiative, they should begin by clarifying the precise terms of their demands, and consider the implications for the unity and stability of the country as a whole. Once they do that, I am sure they will realise and appreciate the need for the religious neutrality of the state, regardless of whether they would accept the term 'secularism' to describe the outcome. One would also hope for non-Muslim Nigerians throughout the country to appreciate the underlying concerns and aspirations of Muslim citizens. As emphasised above, the political dimensions of the process are as important as its theological or legal aspects. It may therefore be difficult for Nigerian Muslims to initiate their own internal discourse, or to begin to transform their interpretation of *shari'ah*, or the relationship between Islam and the state, without strong and sustained support by non-Muslim Nigerians too.

REFERENCES

An-Na'im, Abdullahi Ahmed, *Toward an Islamic Reformation: Civil liberties, human rights and international law*, Syracuse: Syracuse University Press, 1990.

———, "Shari'ah and positive legislation: is an Islamic state possible or viable?", in: Eugene Cotran and Chibli Mallat (eds.), *Yearbook of Islamic and Middle Eastern Law*, The Hague: Kluwer Law International, 2000, 29-42.

Baderin, Mashood A., *International Human Rights and Islamic Law*, New York: Oxford University Press, 2003.

Engineer, Asghar Ali and Uday Mehta (eds.), *State Secularism and Religion: Western and Indian experience*, Delhi: Ajanta Publications, 1998.

Gibb, H.A., and J.H. Kramers (eds.), *Shorter Encyclopaedia of Islam*, Leiden: EJ Brill, 1991.

Ibn Rushd, *Bidayat al-Mugjtahid*, Cairo: Dar al-Fikr al-Arabic, not dated.

Illesanmi, Simeon O., "Constitutional treatment of religion and the politics of human rights in Nigeria", *African Affairs*, 100, 2001, 529-554.

Mcleod, Hugh, *Secularisation in Western Europe*, New York: St. Martin's Press, 2000.

Mosma, Stephen V. and J. Christopher Soper, *The Challenge of Pluralism: Church and state in five democracies*, Lanham: Rowman & Littlefield, 1997.

Nu'man Abd al-Razid al-Samar'i, Ahkam, *al-Murtad fi al-Shari'ah al-Islamiyyah*, Beirut: al-Dar al-Arabiya, 1968.

Ostien, Philip, "Ten good things about the implementation of *shari'a* in some states of Northern Nigeria", *Swedish Missionlogical Themes*, 90/2, 2002, 163-174.

Rahman, Shaikh Abdur, *Punishment of Apostasy in Islam*, Lahore: Institute of Islamic Culture, 1972.

Shiner, Larry, "The concept of secularization in empirical research", *Journal for the Scientific Study of Religion*, 6, 1967, 207-220.

Taha, Mahmoud Mohamed, *The Second Message of Islam*, Syracuse: Syracuse University Press, 1987.

Weiss, Bernard, *The Spirit of Islamic Law*, Athens: University of Georgia Press, 1998.

Commentary

I.

Ali Ahmad

SHARI'AH AND STATE

Debates over the proper role of *shari'ah* in the public life of modern Muslim societies are not new, but they are attracting increasing attention since the current religious reawakening the world over. This is more so in the case of Nigeria since the extension of *shari'ah* implementation beyond the traditional personal law realm to the public sphere. Unless we are able to evince a theoretical clarification of the relationship between religious law and public affairs in a modern state, we will neither be able to effectively understand and anticipate the future of *shari'ah* in the public life of Muslim societies nor to rationalise decisions and activities of public officers. A defined theoretical perspective and accurate assessment of this role of *shari'ah* is important given the profound commitment of Muslims to *shari'ah* on the one hand, and on the other their needs for socio-economic development and constitutionalism.

Many commentators on this subject are wont to equate *shari'ah* with religion and on that basis compare the public role of *shari'ah* in Muslim societies to the dominant discourse of "church and state." But *shari'ah* is not *religion* only or *law* only; it is at the minimum law with a basis in religion. The opposition between "church and state" or "religion and state" is not universal to all cultures; and although it may be an appropriate analytical tool in many societies including Muslim ones, failure to locate the proper status of *shari'ah* in Muslim societies is bound to lead to analytical error.[1]

Reasons abound for suggesting that examination of the role of *shari'ah* in the public life of Muslim societies cannot be limited by, or restricted to, the "church and state" straitjacket. In my view, it is only the Jewish *halaka* or religious law that is comparable to *shari'ah* and not the Christian canon law even though the latter also derives from

---

[1] Sedgwick, 2003, 40.

religion or religious authorities. Canon law does not seem to enjoy the level of commitment from Christians that many Jews have for the *halaka* or Muslims have for the *shari'ah*.[2] Scholars of Islam may be said to have reached a consensus lately, based upon historical development of their various societies, that a wall can hardly be erected between religion and state in Muslim societies.

If "church and state" seeks to analyse institutionalised religion in relation to the state, "religion and politics" analysis is of limited importance in societies that are deeply religious. "Religion and politics" analysis examines the extent and ways in which religiously grounded moral beliefs affect political choices.[3] This does not mean that religious participation in politics is not problematic but that it is not given to easy regulation or monitoring in the sorts of thoroughly religious societies that exist all over Africa.

Quite apart from the nature of *shari'ah* as an animating factor in the debate in Muslim societies, the religious explosion in the world following the collapse of communism is leading a growing number of liberal democracies to make a rethink on privatising religion. In the United States for instance, not many people realise that the rigid separation of church and state is no longer the law of the land. In the past two decades or so, the United States Supreme Court in a series of cases has abandoned some of its earlier harsh rulings that tended to discriminate against public religion. Thus, religious groups can now

---

[2] Newspapers widely reported that Zamfara State Governor Ahmed requested Christians in the state to submit any part of their religious law that they wanted promulgated and enforced by the state. To this day and to my knowledge, Christians in the state have not responded to the call. Similarly, another governor in the East of Nigeria promised to turn his state, overwhelmingly populated by Christians, into a Christian one by enacting and enforcing canon law, but many years have passed without the governor or any of the Christian leaders or groups working toward that. However, the fact that Christians are indifferent to canon law in public affairs does not mean that they are less committed to other aspects of their religion. In contrast, Muslims' commitment to *shari'ah* is often tempered but not completely eliminated by the situational reality either of being a minority group or by normative constraints such as a constitution.

[3] For the latest work by one of the leading scholars in the field of religion and politics, see Perry, 2003.

gain equal access to public facilities and funds that were already opened to other civic groups.[4]

AN-NA'IM'S PAPER

This paper is intended as a commentary to a paper by eminent senior international human rights scholar and Professor Abdullahi A. An-Na'im on the public role of *shari'ah* in Muslim societies. I will explain An-Na'im's proposal and arguments and then contextualise them through experiences of Muslims in Nigeria to show their limited viability in this country.

Professor An-Na'im is unwavering in his proposition that Islamic law should never be relegated to the sphere of personal status and private law matters in Muslim countries and that public law as well should be based on Islam. The basis is that Muslims are highly devoted to *shari'ah* and are unlikely to accept any assertion of separation of Islam and state unless it is imposed on them and guarded by the military as in the case of Turkey, which he roundly condemns. Accordingly, he is saddled with confronting the problems arising from any application of a religious law in contemporary territorial states – entities that are mere unifying rubrics for citizens with differing identities and often conflicting interests.

Many commentators who have addressed the subject matter have not gone beyond rehearsing popular sentiments, without raising and thoroughly addressing the relevant issues affecting the daily lives of Muslims. An-Na'im goes beyond reactive and apologetic "defence of Muslims" that is the bane of Muslim writers on the subject matter. The challenge now is for others to evaluate his proposal and offer alternatives.

Professor An-Na'im recognises the dilemma that Muslims face in not letting go of application of *shari'ah* in the public sphere and the incongruity that results from such application in a contemporary society. Today, Muslims do not live in a constitutional vacuum and they have legitimate economic and social interests to which they aspire in addition to their commitment to *shari'ah*. The Professor's panacea in seeking to balance the commitment to *shari'ah* with the

---

[4] Witte, 2001, 766.

modern needs of Muslims (needs for security and economic development, peaceful coexistence with others, constitutionalism and cooperative international relations) lies in his proposed theory of mediation in place of current political expediency that Muslim rulers or leaders have chosen over the years. Political expediency as a policy for public involvement of *shari'ah* is unwise because it is whimsical and antithetical to any idea of law or order. Any unprincipled choice must be rejected especially when it is likely to be anchored on religious legitimacy.

Sceptical whether classical *shari'ah* can address all the vital concerns or needs of contemporary Muslim societies, An-Na'im has always advocated for a shift in methodology of independent reasoning represented by *usul al-fiqh* (the classical science of understanding the sources of *shari'ah* and through which *shari'ah* principles are formulated and developed). According to him, *usul al-fiqh* is too limited by its own scheme and technique to be deployed in addressing several contemporary issues that cannot be swept under the carpet. In the specific context of the relationship between *shari'ah* and the state, he advocates a mediatory approach between total exclusion of religion in public life and complete fusion of religion and state.

SHARI'AH AND STATE: THE THEORY OF MEDIATION

An-Na'im dismisses the dominant discourse of exclusion of religion from public affairs of a state. Apart from the fact that it is not in practice anywhere, secularism as a public policy for excluding religion is undesirable in Muslim-majority countries. This, however, raises the issue of whether *shari'ah*'s role in the public affairs of a Muslim-majority state is limitless. Reference to a Muslim-majority state implies existence of non-Muslim *citizens*. The idea of citizenship and its constitutional and international implications, among others, introduces a variable unfamiliar to *usul al-fiqh* and therefore to classical *shari'ah*, and has partly informed An-Na'im's conclusion about complete fusion of *shari'ah* and state.

His response is a proposal that is capable of addressing issues that each Muslim state has to confront – religious pluralism, the principle of non-discrimination, socio-economic expectations, international relations, etc. His proposal seeks to reconcile religion, human rights, and state neutrality. Creating optimal synergy among these three concepts is central to An-Na'im's proposal if *shari'ah* is to play a satisfactory role in the public affairs of Muslim nations.

Irrespective of any theoretical postulation that may be put forward for explaining or understanding what the role of *shari'ah* is or should be in the public affairs of Muslim countries, An-Na'im's fears about the fusion of religion and state are real. When the enormous power of the modern nation state is combined with the aura and imprimatur of religious authority, the calamitous effect on the citizenry is better left to imagination. Politicians or other human beings will be the ones to exercise religious authority and human history has shown that those in authority misuse enormous powers to satisfy their interests unless there is an external frame of reference put in place to check the excesses. An-Na'im's proposal provides such external frame of reference to mediate the enormous influence that religion and the modern nation state confer on human agents. Even if the early history of Islam or that of pre-colonial Northern Nigeria appears to support a theory of fusion between "state" and religion (referred to popularly as *din wa daulah*), such an argument appears to be overblown in comparing loose territories with modern nation states and the pervasive powers which the latter possess. The nation state is a modern construct and analyses are mistaken that tend to equate its organic structure, components and privileges with pre-modern, loose and amorphous territories.[5] In pre-modern times separation or fusion was possible and easy, today neither is.

SHARI'AH AS POSITIVE LAW

Intent to limit misuse of state power on the basis of religion or misuse of religious authority sanctioned by state power, An-Na'im however anchors his proposal for mediating the problems of religion and state on an argument that is more controversial than the proposal being supported. It is an argument that draws conclusions from the historical operation and status of *shari'ah*. An-Na'im concludes that the modern territorial state should neither seek to enforce *shari'ah* as

---

[5] Jackson, 2003, 786.

positive law or public policy, nor seek to interpret the doctrine and principle of the law for its Muslim citizens. State non-enforcement of religious law guarantees state religious neutrality, a major theme in An-Na'im's mediating factors.

This argument of state non-enforcement of *shari'ah* is based on the fact that historically it was jurists, who were totally independent of the state and its institutions, who fully developed *shari'ah* and its methodology as known to us today. The more a jurist got closer to governmental agents, the more he risked undermining his acceptability and authority. This milieu of intellectual freedom resulted in multiple juristic views on a given legal point. Within the generally accepted framework, each jurist chose his sources and determined their hierarchy, precedence, or interpretive methodology. Thereafter, compatible legal views would coalesce under the leadership of more renowned jurists while other views would fizzle out, without any input or interference from the state. The four Sunni schools that we have today survived because of the prominence, popularity and piety of the founding jurists.[6]

However, we cannot be oblivious to the fact that once a school of law enjoyed certain level of popularity, the state adopted and enforced the school's legal views. To the extent that the state in a given time or location in Islamic history enforced views of a particular school of law that had crystallised and become accepted by the generality of the people of the area, the over-broad sweep of An-Na'im's statement denying any form of state enforcement becomes obvious. Successive governments in Islamic history declared their allegiance to *shari'ah* and were ready to enforce its rules irrespective of the fact that they had little enforcement to do because of high incidence of what An-Na'im refers to as "voluntary compliance" by the people.

Voluntary compliance did not preclude the state from, or excuse its duty of, enforcing the rules of *shari'ah* in accordance with the school of law it had chosen to support. Compliance is as a result of fear of sanction, either in this world or in the hereafter; and voluntary compliance cannot be sustained where deviant behaviour, however rare, is not expected to be punished. Records abound of historical

---

[6] Powers, 1993, 102.

court proceedings (courts that were established and supported by the government) enforcing *shari'ah* rules on sale of goods, domestic relations, real property and of course crime and tort.

One will agree with An-Na'im that historically, the Islamic state had nothing to do with the exposition and development of what a *shari'ah* rule should be on a point, but the wall of separation ended at that stage. Once the rules crystallised, the state implemented them through its machinery. The Fodio and Kanem dynasties in Northern Nigeria and some Muslim kings in western Nigeria enforced the *shari'ah* before the period of colonialism. There is therefore little Muslim historical support for the argument of non-enforcement of *shari'ah* by the state.

An-Na'im's argument implies that he is opposed to *any* enforcement of *shari'ah* by the state, whether in its jurist-centric form, or developed as a policy or enacted as positive law. The fact that enactment is a modern phenomenon or at least unknown to traditional Islam, validates An-Na'im's objection about positive law as a mechanism of enforcement. It is an obvious fact that the act of enactment is an innovation or *bid'ah* in Islam. It is also true that enactment of any rule or principle of *shari'ah* changes to a large extent the *shari'ah* characteristic of that rule.

If one appreciates An-Na'im's rejection of legal positivism as an enforcement mechanism, one cannot say the same for his denunciation of any and all enforcement by the state. Granted that enactment is unknown to Islam, this presents no support for the assertion that a modern nation state cannot enforce *shari'ah* in its jurist-based form which is known to Islam. In the context of the *shari'ah* debate in Nigeria, the positive law argument is relevant in the field of criminal law, which is the only area of *shari'ah* that is so far enacted.

But even if governments choose to enact any other rule of *shari'ah* or base their entire enforcement of *shari'ah* on enactment, I do not share Professor An-Na'im's principled objection. Nothing in *shari'ah* precludes enactment as such, since it is not everything unknown to *shari'ah* that is prohibited. As a matter of fact, nothing in *shari'ah* provides that it should or must be jurist-based. The fact that development of *shari'ah* was jurist-based could have been dictated or facilitated by the socio-political currents of the time. But the fact also should not be lost that *shari'ah* began with the revelation of the Qur'an, which by no account was jurist-based.

Thus, although *shari'ah*'s development owed a lot to the jurist-based method, it began as a textual process akin to enactment. Any enacting state could be made to appreciate the changed characteristic of the enacted rule and the traditional *shari'ah* principle on the point, so that when the enacted rule freezes the *shari'ah* content and becomes radically transformed over time through principles of statutory interpretation, the enacting state reserves the right of re-enactment in accordance with *shari'ah* principles.

I believe An-Na'im's worthy proposal deserves serious consideration on its merits, and that it does not have to be anchored on a controversial argument that is of questionable validity. It is possible to develop a proposal for seeking reconciliation in Islam between religion, state neutrality and human rights that is not based on sweeping conclusions drawn from historical facts that do not support them. State enforcement of *shari'ah* per se (either juristic-based *shari'ah* as we have long practised in Nigeria or as enactment as recently introduced in the field of criminal law) would not make such reconciliation impossible.

VIABILITY IN NIGERIA

Professor An-Na'im's proposal is fascinating as one possible platform for resolving the tension created by the public role of *shari'ah*. One does not find many writers squarely addressing all the socio-political issues raised by the involvement of *shari'ah* in the public polity of *modern* Muslim-majority states. Such issues are ignored or merely treated as unimportant. But even if An-Na'im's argument in support of the proposal is valid and legitimate, it is not viable in the Nigerian context, if it is anywhere in the contemporary world.

The positive-law argument seems to break down if it is realised that only Islamic criminal law was enacted in all the Northern states where *shari'ah* has been implemented. All other aspects of *shari'ah* apply in the traditional form without intervention on its content from the state. One appreciates An-Na'im's point to the extent that the *shari'ah*-implementing states might have been literally compelled by the constitutional provision mandating enactment of crime and punishment in the country.[7] Traditional *shari'ah* has to respond and sometimes give in to some claims of modernity or statehood, but in the situation of application of *shari'ah* in Nigeria enactment is so far the exception rather than the rule.

An-Na'im's positive-law argument is better understood when its two components are separated. There is the "state non-enactment" on the one hand and on the other the "state non-enforcement." The former is plausible; and it is defendable at least historically in Islam but whether it is feasible anywhere in the contemporary world is arguable. The latter, state non-enforcement, is untenable historically and unviable now. It has been mentioned that when norms that were developed by jurists crystallised and became accepted as part of *shari'ah* in what An-Na'im calls "intergenerational consensus," Islamic governments throughout history enforced those norms. Even historical states, loose as they were, could not function without enforcing some values or norms, in this case the *shari'ah*. That there is a high incidence of voluntary compliance with *shari'ah* norms does not derogate from the state's reserved power of enforcement. To a greater extent today in Nigeria, state non-enactment or state non-enforcement particularly of *shari'ah* will send the law into complete oblivion.

How can *shari'ah* play *any* public role as An-Na'im himself advocates if it is unsupported in a modern state that was built on a neo-liberal colonial super-structure under doctrinaire anti-*shari'ah* currents? How can the *shari'ah* play any role when the state spends so much public resources to stifle it? Today the state is so powerful and overwhelmingly intrusive that its non-support of a policy such as the *shari'ah*, not to mention its objection, is enough to render that policy permanently mute. State non-support or minimal support might be tenable if Northern Nigeria had not been colonised and the structures of *shari'ah* were not forcibly skewed in favour of the worldview of the colonisers. Indeed, an equal state intervention is required to bring back *shari'ah* not necessarily to its pre-colonial status, but to enable it

---

[7] Section 36(12) of the Nigerian Constitution, 1999, providing in relevant part that "a person shall not be convicted of a criminal offence unless that offence is defined and the penalty therefor is prescribed in a written law; and in this subsection a written law refers to an Act of the National Assembly or a Law of a State, any subsidiary legislation or instrument under the provisions of a law."

to withstand the demands of modernity and compete among other contending civic values. Professor Witte is a strong advocate of modern-nation state support for public religion:

> Today's state is an intensely active sovereign from whom complete separation is impossible. Few religious bodies can now avoid contact with the modern welfare state's pervasive network of education, charity, welfare, child care, health care, family, construction, zoning, workplace, taxation, security, and other regulations. Both confrontation and cooperation with the modern welfare state are almost inevitable for any religion.[8]

STATE NEUTRALITY AND NIGERIA

The rhetoric of state neutrality is misplaced where the state structure, its organs and processes are biased. Neutrality is a mere façade where vestiges of colonialism and foreign currents of globalisation run amok in the land. In reality, examination of any concept or declared practice of neutrality shows that it is always placed upon, determined or dictated by, a certain parochial value clothed with the garb of impartiality and objectivity.

The concept of neutrality aims at addressing and minimising incidences of discrimination. Non-discrimination is an essential rule for any modern state where citizenship or nationality now transcends traditional bases and ties of union. By its sectarian nature, religion is a source of discrimination rather than the opposite. An-Na'im seriously doubts the ability of *shari'ah* or any other religion to address discrimination. Apart from the fact that discrimination is still rampant in government policies and practices despite the non-discrimination clause of the Nigerian constitution,[9] one has a feeling of unease from attempts to create symbolic equality between Christianity and Islam in Nigeria. State discrimination against religious groups that are non-Christian and non-Muslim seems to be permanent and irreversible.[10] With regard to state patronage or access for Muslims and Christians, Nigeria is actually bi-religious rather than multi-religious. As between

---

[8] Witte, 2003.
[9] Section 42 Nigerian Constitution, 1999.
[10] US Department of State, International Religious Freedom Report 2003.

the two, the attempt to eradicate discrimination is commendable but not exemplary. Although corresponding categories are needed in order to achieve common goals, one easily notes equal treatment by government of issues of unequal theological or spiritual significance in the two religions.

Islam, for example, unlike Christianity, has no symbols, images, or icons which it particularly venerates. Thus in Islam no symbol is accorded the solemnity and reverence Christians have for the cross – not the crescent, not the scarf, nor the sword. Nevertheless in Nigeria, in order to put the two religions formally on a par, symbols of both must be accorded equal treatment; hence the Muslim crescent, which only signifies the lunar timings upon which Islamic rituals are calculated, is elevated publicly to the same status as the Christian cross.

The way Nigeria has come to treat certain religious issues across the board shows the need for more logical reconsideration. The example of religious holidays, pilgrimages and religious laws will vividly illustrate the point. Christians naturally enjoy three different religious holidays in a year. To create equality in number of holidays for Muslims, government considered the choice between the birthday of Prophet Muhammad, upon whom be peace, and the first day of the Islamic calendar year. Government chose the Prophet's birthday in addition to the two Islamically recognised holidays of Ramadan and the Eid of Sacrifice.

By this act, Government has created for Nigerian Muslims a parallel between the Prophet's birthday and Christmas in order to ensure that both groups enjoy the same number of holidays annually. This is done without regard to the view of some Muslims that marking the Prophet's birthday has no theological basis and could in fact be unorthodox. One Christian holiday of Christmas, rooted in the Christian faith (even if its religious pedigree has been de-emphasised in some Western countries to show its religious neutrality), over and above Muslims' is not too much where there is no equally religiously significant holiday in Islam.

Similarly, there is no equivalence of the scriptural imperative for the Muslim *hajj* in Christianity. Nigerian Muslims had made *hajj* on donkeys and horses long before the advent of automobiles and airplanes. Not discounting the importance of pilgrimage to Jerusalem for modern Nigerian Christians, there is no corresponding theological imperative on Christians supported by historical facts to undertake pilgrimage to Jerusalem. Undoubtedly, pilgrimage to Jerusalem is highly recommended in Islam and was undertaken by Muslims, just as lesser *hajj* or *umrah* is, but both are not on the same plane with the *hajj*. Attempt to equate pilgrimage to Jerusalem with *hajj* (instead of with *umrah*) can only be explained in relation to pretentious equality.

Likewise, the most recent attempt by some Christian leaders to equate canon law with the *shari'ah* and draw a parallel is misleading. The claim is that since Christians do not demand that government implement the canon law, Muslims should also not demand that government implement the *shari'ah*. In his keynote address to participants of this very conference, Dr. Danny McCain states: "If *shari'ah* were voluntarily practiced only within the Muslim community and did not have the threat of state enforcement, most Christians would have little objection to its implementation."[11] But the other side of the argument is that since government spends resources to implement *shari'ah* for Muslims it should, in reflecting the principle of equality and non-discrimination, also implement canon law for Christians. The reason I believe this argument is not attractive to Christians is that they do not feel equally strongly about the canon law. They do not feel so because there is no equivalent theological basis providing a significant role for the canon law in public affairs and in governance.

It is plausible that the Nigerian state is biased against the *shari'ah*. This is because with the benefit of hindsight, it is difficult to find a single incident where Muslims have tried to be *shari'ah*-compliant without such efforts being vigorously resisted, even if it will result in little or no adverse effect to non-Muslims.

Recently, for example, the Nursing and Midwifery Council of Nigeria has officially permitted female Muslim nurses who so wish to wear veils and trousers.[12] A few years back, it was a bitter fight between Muslim advocates and non-Muslims who argued that the dress pattern was part of the nursing profession worldwide. Similar

---

[11] McCain, this volume, 16.
[12] See the news story "Muslim Nurses Can Now Wear Veils—Council" in *The Triumph*, May 3, 2002, 1.

argument was put forward in the North of the country during the agitation of an Islamically-compliant dressing mode for Muslim schoolgirls. In the year 2004, Muslims in Oyo State still encounter this resistance on dressing mode for Muslims from government officials in the state's Ministry of Education. Today, it may seem commonplace, but taking time off on Friday to attend the weekly congregational prayer and come back to duty posts, was no less a struggle. Thus, confrontation rather than reason, sentiments rather than rationality, will likely be deployed in support of otherwise worthy causes.

An-Na'im's proposal involving state religious neutrality is preferable to secularism, foisted upon us from other societies. But even the current volte-face by the Christian clergy, in contradistinction to ordinary Christians, on the issue of whether Nigeria is or should be a secular state, speaks volumes. "Nigeria is not a secular state, it is a multi-religious one", is now a popular catchphrase among the leading Christian intelligentsia. Many Nigerian Christians now denounce secularism as inappropriate for the country. Dr. McCain's incisive comment captures it all:

> Although Islam has led in the opposition to secularism, Christians should stand shoulder to shoulder with their Muslim brothers and sisters and oppose it because it is not in the best interest of our society and it is certainly not the best interest of either Christianity or Islam. An English proverb states that sometimes a person will "cut off his nose to spite his face." Christians must not so react against *shari'ah* that we hinder or own ability to publicly practice our religion. It is better to make some concessions to accommodate Muslim convictions and preserve the opportunity to practice our own religion publicly than to lose our religious soul to the godless forces of political correctness and secularism.[13]

It is heartening that Christians and Muslims are now reaching a consensus on the issue of secularism in addressing matters raised by religion and state. But with the benefit of hindsight, the initial approach taken by Christians and the current volte-face do little in

---

[13] McCain, this volume, 15.

instilling honest debates in future. Christians should have empathised with their Muslim fellows that Islam mandates the *shari'ah* and then sought how to protect Christian interests in that regard. Muslims in turn would have reciprocated the gesture in some way and Nigeria would have been able to teach the rest of the world and present a contemporary model of involving religion in the public sphere.

If any advocacy for state neutrality is to be taken seriously in the Nigerian context, one will hope to see an "affirmative state action" disproportionately empowering structures for the enforcement of the *shari'ah* in relation to other competing policies for some time to come so that *shari'ah* is raised to a comparable level in the polity. An affirmative action is justified to redress previous discrimination and denial that have been unleashed on *shari'ah* since the colonial period.

This is not to say that the current widespread arrangement in Nigeria is the best where the executive arm of government, rather than the people or at minimum the learned jurists, determines what emerges as *shari'ah* criminal law. And since government may embark on future enactment of other specific areas as it deems fit, everyone should be concerned about the process to be adopted. The current practice of what emerges or could emerge as the official *shari'ah* confirms An-Na'im's fear about fusion of religion and state and the tendency for repression of minority views. Government may facilitate but should have no hand on what emerges as an enacted *shari'ah*.

CONCLUSION

There is no question among Muslim scholars that *shari'ah* will continue to have a role in the public life of Muslim societies, the relevant question for Muslims is: what role? What role should the state play with regard to religion(s); or what role should religion(s) play in the formal affairs of the state or of its officials? There seems to be no one model that is suitable for any two regions. Certainly, the Western model on religion and state is not suitable for Nigeria.[14] What should inform preference for a single model for countries of a region or for minimum acceptable criteria to be adopted by all Muslim-majority countries? Apparently, Professor An-Na'im shows

---

[14] Ostien and Gamaliel, 2002, 27.

preference for the minimum criteria option while additionally advocating the reinvention of *usul*.

It is inescapable that present and future Muslim societies will need to continuously evaluate the *shari'ah* through *usul* given emerging social and economic realities. But if *usul al-fiqh* must be reinvented it should be done in a manner that maintains the Islamic character of the process. Otherwise the debate about mediating the public role of religion becomes meaningless and Muslim societies could as well embrace the principle of secularism. It is gratifying that An-Na'im himself recognises that the argument to substantiate his proposal is unlikely to be accepted by the majority of Muslims because of the justifiable fear of their socio-political and economic vulnerability to the neo-colonial powers and Western hegemony.

There should be means other than abandoning the *usul* or seeking for state non-enforcement of *shari'ah* in arriving at reconciliation among the enormous influence of religion, the need to guarantee protection of human rights of all citizens, as well as ensure religious neutrality of the ever intrusive nation state. The ultimate objective of any modern state, including Muslim-majority states, is to devise means to ensure non-discrimination against minorities or dissenters and to guarantee protection of their rights by limiting the powers of the state in relevant areas. This achievable task is the current challenge of scholars of Islam.

REFERENCES

Jackson, John H., "Sovereignty-modern: a new approach to an outdated concept", *American Journal of International Law* 97/4, 2003, 782-802.

McCain, Danny, "Which road leads beyond the *shari'ah* controversy? a Christian perspective on *shari'ah* in Nigeria", this volume, 7-26.

Ostien, Philip and J.D. Gamaliel, "The law of separation of religion and state in the United States: a model for Nigeria?", in: S.O.O. Amali et al. (eds.), *Religion in the United States*, Ibadan: American Studies Association of Nigeria, 2002, 14-32.

Perry, Michael J., *Under God? Religious faith and liberal democracy*, Cambridge: Cambridge University Press, 2003.

Powers, David S., "Legal consultation (*futya*) in medieval Spain and North Africa", in: Chibli Mallat (ed.), *Islam and Public Law: Classical and contemporary studies*, London/Boston: Graham & Trotman, 1993, 85-106.

Sedgwick, Mark, "Is there a church in Islam?", *ISIM* Newsletter, 13, December 2003, 40-41.

Witte, John, Jr., "A Dickensian era of religious rights: an update on *Religious Human Rights in Global Perspective*", *William and Mary Law Review* 42/3, 2001, 707-770.

———, "A new freedom of public religion", Editorial Opinion, *Emory Report*, September 2, 2003.

II.

Andrew F. Walls

The richness of Professor An-Na'im's thought-provoking paper deserves a fuller response than can be given here; and ideally such a response should reflect the different fields and disciplines to which the paper relates: philosophy, theology, history, and political science among them, not to mention law. The aspect of the paper that particularly strikes me from the perspective of my own field of the history of religions is the remarkable degree of parallelism that it suggests between the issues surrounding *shari'ah*, as Professor An-Na'im enunciates them, and some aspects of the Christian tradition. Professor An-Na'im has forced me to think again about things I have said and written, and to resolve in future at least to say them differently. I have argued that there is a structural difference between a religion where revelation is based on prophecy and a religion where revelation is based on incarnation. The former, I urged, had an inbuilt tendency to absolutise the conditions under which the original prophecy was given; the latter, while not exempt from the temptation to absolutise a particular period of history, had an inbuilt tendency to seek embodiment in changing conditions.[1] I argued that these processes produced on the one hand the continuing Islamic concern for *shari'ah*, and on the other the absence of any Christian equivalent. Reflection on Professor An-Na'im's paper suggests that I was over-

---

[1] Walls, 1996, 26-42.

confident on both issues; he persuades me that Islam does not *necessarily* absolutise the conditions of seventh century Arabia; and reflection suggests that some circumstances in Christian history have produced attempts to install a system with analogies to *shari'ah*, and to seek its enforcement by the state. It seems to me that the logic of Professor An-Na'im's argument applies as much to Christian as to Islamic attempts to realise the divine will in human society; and that in Christianity, as he argues is the case in Islam, there is an internal contradiction involved in making the state the instrument of such attempts at realisation.

So there may be comparative perspectives on *shari'ah* within the history of religions, as well as comparative perspectives from different regions of the world. I propose to explore further the parallelism suggested by Professor An-Na'im's argument, taking in turn the three pillars of his analysis: the place of human agency in the transmission of revelation; the internal contradiction involved in seeking the enforcement of *shari'ah* by the state; and the need for revelation and its social implications to be mediated in the public sphere in states that are neutral in matters of religion.

THE PLACE OF HUMAN AGENCY IN THE INTERPRETATION OF REVELATION

All religions claiming a basis in divine revelation have to face this issue. The *immediacy* of revelation (whether prophetic word, theophany or incarnation) belongs to an event in the past. The revelatory event also occurred (at least in Islamic and Christian conviction, where history is taken seriously) within a particular historic setting. All attempts to interpret the revelatory event, or to apply it within another historical setting, are inevitably human constructs. Revelation is always at least one remove away from its interpretation or application. Were it otherwise the unique status of the revelation would be called into question. One may believe, as Muslims and Christians have in different ways always believed, in some principle of divine guidance of the believing community, but that principle is always of a different order from that of the original revelatory Word (spoken or lived). Christians, like Muslims, have historically seen consensus as an indication of guidance; the principle of catholicity distinguishes what is universally affirmed among Christians from purely local formulations. But the process of reflection from which consensus arises must inevitably make use of the intellectual and cultural traditions of a particular time and place. These are the materials with which reflection is done. With the wide geographical expansion that both Christianity and Islam have seen comes a wide range of intellectual and cultural materials through which the original revelatory event is mediated in a continuing process. The process is dynamic, not a transmission of static tradition. The variety of intellectual and cultural materials enables aspects of the revelation that passed unnoticed in one time and place to be recognised in another time or place, and applications to be seen that were previously hidden from view. To impose one framework of interpretation (which means one set of intellectual and cultural materials) is to absolutise the conditions of one time and place, and thus to localise what was meant to be universal. This is to usurp the proper sphere of revelation by imposing upon it a man-made screen or filter; it is an interference with the immediacy of revelation.

These principles apply to the process of constructing theology as well as law, for theologians and jurists use analogous methods. Theology and law are interpretive processes involving human reflection, and in the nature of the case they are unfinished, open-ended processes. When Christians have tried to make absolute the formulations of a particular time and place (as happened, for instance, in the Western Church in the later Middle Ages), this was to fix a particular moment in the interpretive process as the final one, to identify a particular part of the process as uniquely the vehicle of divine guidance. Such attempts are inevitably disruptive. What its proponents were doing in this case was not (as they thought and intended) safeguarding purity of doctrine, but isolating themselves from fellow-believers whose faith and practice had developed under different conditions.

Interpretation is a human process that at best results in approximation. It can rarely produce unanimity; not only because of the possibility of error and perversion, but because of the way in which humanity is constructed. There is no generalised humanity, only the infinite variety of culture-specific humanity, different segments of social reality in time and space. It is the totality of these segments that constitutes the human auditorium that is the theatre of revelation, the setting where it is transmitted. Different social segments, belonging to different times and places, are like different seats in a theatre, offering different views of the stage – and even different views of the rest of the auditorium. People seated in one part of the auditorium see things that are unseen by people sitting somewhere else. There is no seat or block of seats that can claim to offer the sole, complete and authentic view.

There will always be a temptation to try to close off the process, to fix the view of one time and place – one segment of social reality, one block of seats in the theatre – as the "authentic" view. Christians have often succumbed to this temptation. To do so is to give to human construction the attributes of divine revelation.

Christians, like Muslims, believe in revelation, and revelation implies the immediacy of the divine action. What becomes clear from the paper is that Muslims, like Christians, recognise the *mediated immediacy* of revelation. After the immediacy of the unique revelatory event, the revelation reaches humanity in mediated form, mediated under the conditions of another time and place. When Professor An-Na'im speaks of the need for a "deeply contextual" view of *shari'ah* I take it that he is indicating that the process of mediation must take full account of the context, the particular segment of social reality, in all its *depth*. Here Christians are in the same position, confident of revelation, but interpreting and applying its immediacy in mediated form. This is not to relativise revelation; merely to recognise the conditions under which we receive it. And those conditions should lead the believer, not to despair, but rather to respect for the medium that God has chosen for the purpose. That medium is a diversely culture-specific humanity.

THE INAPPROPRIATENESS OF THE STATE AS THE VEHICLE OF ENFORCEMENT

Professor An-Na'im sketches the history of *shari'ah* in relation to the different forms that Islamic communities have taken over the centuries, pointing out how different was the community around the Prophet in Medina (the one situation where it can be argued that the immediacy of revelation gave the ground for state enforcement) from such complex entities as the Ummayyad and Abbasid caliphates; how different again were these from the nation state of modern times, operating within an international community. Once again, it is interesting to pursue the Christian parallel.

The earliest Christian community consisted of Jews who recognised Jesus as Messiah. As the Gospel spread into Greco-Roman society, and former pagans responded to it, the Christian church had to hold together two quite different styles of Christian life. There were Jewish believers who still kept the Torah and lived within Jewish culture, and there were ex-pagan believers who lived in a society where it was impossible even to keep the Sabbath, and who were not subject to the Torah. Men and women entered the community as individuals or family groups (rather as did those who responded to the early preaching of the Prophet). The church was a society within the wider society of the Greek, the Roman, and the Arab worlds, often attracting the hostility of the state. As the church grew larger, and attracted more of the elite and eventually of the powerful, state hostility was replaced by state favour. People flocked into the church as Christianity became the majority and eventually the official religion, and the church began to enter the political process. The scene was set as early as 325 CE, when the first of the great councils was called at Nicea, under the aegis of the Emperor Constantine, himself not yet baptised. The church had a religious and theological agenda for this as for later councils; it was to gain consensus in the clarification of central Christian teaching. The Roman state had a political agenda, which was imperial unity. This was not in itself an illegitimate or unworthy aim, but it belonged to a different motivation from the ecclesiastical concern for doctrinal clarification. It appeared at the time that these parallel agendas could be pursued simultaneously. In fact, the church was to pay heavily for the combination of its own agenda with that of the state. One result of combining the agendas was to introduce the principle of compulsion into Christian practice, a principle wholly at variance with all that the Messiah had taught, and wholly alien to previous Christian experience. A second distressing result appeared only with the later councils, and it was probably not recognised at the time how damaging it was. The church had originally thought of itself as "catholic", universal, worldwide, and this was remembered at Nicea when leaders from beyond the Roman Empire attended. But as the church's intersection with the imperial state became more regular, the church in the Roman Empire – a large part of the worldwide church, but far from the whole of the Christian community – began to think in imperial terms. The later councils no longer invited leaders from churches beyond the Empire, and gradually the Christians in the Empire gradually lost touch with believers beyond the Empire. These processes, combined with the principle of compulsion, issued eventually in a permanent breach between believers who thought in Latin or Greek and those who thought in Coptic or Syriac. Combining with the state agenda had permanently altered the international character of the church.

A further development followed as the Gospel spread to the northern and Western barbarians from whom my people are descended. Stories of the conversion period in northern Europe sometimes feature councils of elders and military leaders, the decision – makers of the community, deliberating whether or not to adopt Christianity into the code of customary law and practice of the community. The decision to adopt Christianity involved agreement to worship God rather than the gods. It involved establishing the Christian festivals, especially Christmas and Easter, as the community's high days. It involved abolishing certain traditional customs, such as abandoning female children – a means of population control in a harsh environment. These things and others like them became the law and custom of the community, binding on everyone born within it. Over the years law and custom were elaborated and extended and codified. In early Christian times men and women had chosen to join the Christian community and those who were already members of the Christian community had chosen to accept them. Among the northern peoples, it was the existing communities that were reconstituted by adopting Christian custom as their own. Over centuries, as more and more communities made this choice (or sometimes had it imposed upon them), virtually the whole of Europe became territory subject to Christian law and custom. As a result, European Christians came to think of Christianity territorially: as "Christendom," the area subject to the law of Christ, where public rituals were Christian, where Christian princes ruled as vassals of the

King of Kings and were under obligation to ensure that no idolatry, heresy or blasphemy occurred within their dominions.

But of course, although these dominions were in theory subject to the law of Christ, in practice the law of Christ was constantly being ignored, travestied or flouted by Christian rulers, until devout lovers of the Messiah cried out in distress. Nor were even devout lovers of the Messiah always wise or just when they called upon the state to enforce what they believed to be the divine will. The state machinery was constantly used to secure uniformity of belief, of worship, of Christian practice. Use of the state machinery brought death, distress, division; it never brought unanimity.

It was colonialism that started the decline of Christendom and thus the secularisation of Europe. From the late fifteenth century a confident, expansive Europe, now secure in its appropriation of Christianity, came into contact with a non-Western world that it had not previously known. That world included lands where Christianity had once been prominent but was now in eclipse. The first instinct of European Christians, used to conceiving Christianity in terms of territory marked by Christian worship and subject to Christian laws, was to try to bring this new world into Christendom, to make it subject to the law of Christ. The Spanish sought to carry this out in Central and South America, at terrible cost to the good name of Christianity. The Kingdom of Congo became one of the states of Christendom; but in most of Africa and Asia the task of making the nations subject to Christian law proved impossible. Western rulers could see, however, that there were huge commercial and economic advantages to be gained from continued engagement with the non-Western world. So the European powers effectively abandoned the goal of religious propagation and concentrated on security and profit. The economic and political interests of the powers that made up Christendom became increasingly separated from their religious profession. The Portuguese, the Dutch, and most of all the British, without abandoning the rhetoric of Christendom, abandoned any attempt to propagate it by the state machinery. In India the British administration, to the distress of many of the devout in Britain, repeatedly announced its neutrality in matters of religion.

In Europe itself, the situation was different. The sixteenth and seventeenth centuries saw Europe engulfed by war as the states of

Europe settled on different formulations of Christianity. But rarely could the religious settlements, achieved at such cost by the powers at home, be successfully exported to their overseas colonies. The Protestant British state established and endowed the Catholic Church in its newly acquired colony of Quebec at a time when there were discriminatory laws against Catholics in England and Ireland. By the nineteenth century, the British government was accepting guardianship in Sri Lanka of the temple of the Buddha's tooth, and with it responsibility for appointing the Buddhist priesthood there. Christian experience has been that the enlistment of the state in the enforcement of religion brings about its secularisation. I am not arguing that colonialism was the sole cause of Western secularisation and the retreat from Christianity which has been such a marked feature of Western life in the twentieth century. But it was one of the earliest factors working to that end, and it set in train the decline of Christendom, the idea of Europe as Christian territory.[2] By the late twentieth century Europe could be best described as post-Christian.

In the course of the twentieth century the cultural and demographic composition of Christianity changed completely. By the beginning of the twenty-first century the majority of Christians were living, no longer in Europe and North America, but in Africa, Asia and Latin America. Western formulations, Western priorities, even Western resources, seem likely to become less and less important in Christianity. Africa (where Christianity has had a continuous presence for most of its two thousand years of existence), some parts of Asia and Latin America will increasingly be its most important theatres of activity. The reality of the twenty-first century is a post-Christian West and a post-Western Christianity.

MEDIATION IN THE RELIGIOUSLY NEUTRAL STATE

I have wrestled with Professor An-Na'im's use of the word mediation in this context, but if I understand him aright, it seems that once again Christians and Muslims find themselves in similar positions, not least with regard to the post-Christian West. Christendom is dead.

---

[2] I have argued this in Walls, 2002, 27-48.

The European Union cannot even agree whether Europe's Christian past should be recognised in its constitution, even as a historical fact. Christianity is increasingly becoming a non-Western religion, with Africa gradually moving into the leading place once occupied by Europe. And Christians, like Muslims, believe in the transcendence of God. The modern state increasingly leaves no public space for the recognition of transcendence of any kind beyond itself. In these circumstances the human propensity for worship and aspiration takes other forms. The state may come to worship itself, or its leaders or its achievements, and the ghastly results of that process are well known. Or it may encourage the worship of idols, such as Mammon, the god of money, whose altars are more grisly than those of many divinities that demand human sacrifice. Those, whether Christian or Muslim, who believe that God is Compassionate and Merciful, and believe in that Day when the murdered child will enquire why it was slain, may need to confront strange divinities, more seductive than Al-Lat and Al-Uzza, within states that proclaim their religious neutrality. Perhaps both communities need to recall the injunction of the old prophet of the Torah: Do justly. Love mercy. Walk humbly with your God.

REFERENCES

Walls, A.F., *The Missionary Movement in Christian History*, Maryknoll NY: Orbis, 1996.

———, The Cross-Cultural Process in Christian History, Maryknoll NY: Orbis, 2002.

About the Authors

AHMAD, Ali is a Lecturer and Head of the Department of Public Law at Bayero University, Kano. He holds an LL.M. from Harvard and an S.J.D. from George Washington University. His writings on the relationship between *shari'ah* and public law include *Cosmopolitan Orientation Of International Environmental Law: An Islamic Law Genre* (2000). He is a Fellow of the Islam and Human Rights Programme at the Emory University School of Law, Atlanta.

ALLI, Warisu O. is a Professor in the Department of Political Science, University of Jos. He is a graduate of Kiev State University, Kiev, Ukraine, where he earned his masters and doctoral degrees. He has published widely on Nigerian politics and foreign policy.

AN-NA'IM, Abdullahi Ahmed is Charles Howard Candler Professor of Law at Emory University. He studied law at the University of Khartoum, the University of Cambridge, and the University of Edinburgh (Ph.D. 1976). He taught at the University of Khartoum until 1985, and subsequently held several visiting appointments before becoming the Executive Director of Africa Watch in 1993. He joined the Faculty of Emory Law School in 1995. He is the author or editor of several books and numerous articles, and the Director of the Religion and Human Rights Project at Emory University.

DANFULANI, Umar H.D. is Associate Professor, History of Religions at the University of Jos, where he also serves as Dean of Students. Among his numerous publications the most recent is *Understanding Nyam: Studies in the History and Culture of the Ngas, Mupun and Mwaghavul in Nigeria* (2003). He was a Senior Researcher in the project on *The Shari'ah Debate and the Shaping of Muslim and Christian Identities in Northern Nigeria* and presented a paper at its conference in Bayreuth.

DURHAM (Jr.), W. Cole is the Susa Young Gates University Professor of Law at Brigham Young University, Logan, Utah. A leading authority on the relationship between religion and state, he is the Director of the

International Center for Law and Religion Studies at BYU. He is also a recurring visiting professor of Law at the Central European University in Budapest, Hungary. His has served as Secretary of the American Society of Comparative Law, and is an Associate Member of the International Academy of Comparative Law. For the past several years, he has served as a Co-Chair of the Advisory Panel on Freedom of Religion and Belief of the Organization for Security and Cooperation in Europe.

ELAIGWU, J. Isawa, Professor Emeritus of Political Science at the University of Jos, is President of the Institute of Governance and Social Research (IGSR), Jos. His first degree is from Ahmadu Bello University; he also holds MA and Ph.D. degrees from Stanford University. He served as Director General and Chief Executive of the National Council on Intergovernmental Relations (NCIR) in Abuja from 1992 to 1996. He also served as Chairman of the Board of Trustees for the United Nations Institute of Training and Research.

GAIYA, Musa A.B. is a Reader in Church History at the University of Jos, where he has been teaching for the past fourteen years. He was a Senior Researcher in the project on *The Shari'ah Debate and the Shaping of Muslim and Christian Identities in Northern Nigeria* and presented a paper at its conference in Bayreuth.

GWAMNA, Je'adayibe Dogara is a Senior Lecturer in the Department of Religious Studies, University of Jos. He specializes in New Testament studies and contextual theology. He was a Researcher in the project on *The Shari'ah Debate and the Shaping of Muslim and Christian Identities in Northern Nigeria* and presented a paper at its conference in Bayreuth. He is the editor of the *Gbagyi Journal,* devoted to the study of the Gbagyi (Gwari) people of central Nigeria.

HACKETT, Rosalind I. J. is a Distinguished Professor in the Humanities at the University of Tennessee, Knoxville. She spent the academic year 2003-04 as a Rockefeller Visiting Fellow at the Joan B. Kroc Institute of International Peace Studies at the University of Notre Dame. She has published widely on new religious movements in Africa, religious pluralism, art, and religion in relation to conflict, gender, the media, and human rights. She is currently Vice President of the International Association for the History of Religions.

KENNY, Joseph (Rev. Fr.) of the Order of Preachers, has worked in Nigeria since 1964. A specialist in Arabic and Islamic Studies (Ph.D., Edinburgh, 1970), he has lectured widely and written extensively on this and other subjects. He was a Professor in the Department of Religious Studies, University of Ibadan, 1979-2001, and is now attached to the Dominican Institute, Ibadan. He is a member of the Interreligious Dialogue Commission of AECAWA, and serves as Vice Chairman of its Catholic Bishops' Conference of Nigeria counterpart.

KOGELMANN, Franz is Research Fellow of the German Institute for Middle East Studies in Hamburg, Germany. He is also affiliated with the University of Bayreuth, Germany, where he earned degrees in Islamic Studies, Social Anthropology and African History. He has published on modern Islamic movements in the Middle East, the development of Islamic foundations (auqaf) and on Muslims outside the Arab world. He was the German co-ordinator of the project on *The Shari'ah Debate and the Shaping of Muslim and Christian Identities in Northern Nigeria.*

MAHDI, Saudatu Shehu, a leading women's rights activist in Nigeria, is Secretary General of the Women Rights Advancement and Protection Alternative (WRAPA), an NGO devoted to the promotion and protection of the human rights of women through education, political advocacy, and the provision of legal services. Educated at Ahmadu Bello University and the Administrative Staff College of Nigeria, she was a teacher and public school administrator before joining WRAPA. From 2001 she has been closely involved in the defence of women who have been victims of the *shari'ah* legal system now operational in twelve states of Northern Nigeria.

MANGVWAT, Monday Y. is Vice-Chancellor of the University of Jos. He is a historian, educated at Ahmadu Bello University (B.A. 1976, Ph.D. 1984), where he also began his teaching career. He joined the University of Jos in 1990. In addition to his teaching and research responsibilities at Jos, he has served on the Board of the University's Consultancy Services Division, on the governing Council of the University, and as Dean of the School of Postgraduate Studies. He is the author of numerous articles and the editor or co-editor of four books.

MCCAIN, Danny is Associate Professor of Biblical Theology at the University of Jos. He also is the Africa Director of the International

Institute for Christian Studies, a US-based organisation that helps to develop and enhance academic Christian studies in public universities. He has worked closely with the Federal Ministry of Education and a joint Christian-Muslim coalition to develop a faith-based AIDS awareness programme for the secondary schools of Nigeria. He has lived with his family in Nigeria since 1988.

NASIR, Jamila M. a Reader in Law at the University of Jos, is currently acting as Dean of the Law Faculty. She has lectured and written extensively in the areas of intellectual property law, human rights, and the rights of women under *shari'ah*. She was a Senior Researcher in the project on *The Shari'ah Debate and the Shaping of Muslim and Christian Identities in Northern Nigeria* and presented a paper at its conference in Bayreuth. She is an active member of a number of human rights organisations working in Nigeria.

OLOYEDE, Is-haq is currently the Deputy Vice-Chancellor (Academic) of the University of Ilorin, where he has been teaching for the past two decades. A Professor of Islamics, his first degree is in Arabic and his Ph.D. is in Islamic Studies. He is a fellow of the Islamic Academy in Cambridge and a member of the Nigeria Institute of Management. Among his many other publications, he is the author of *Sharia Versus Secularism in Nigeria* (2003).

OSTIEN, Philip is a Reader in Law at the University of Jos. His Ph.D. is from the University of Pennsylvania, in philosophy; he also holds J.D. and LL.M. degrees from the University of Iowa. He formerly taught in the University of Iowa and practised law in Des Moines, Iowa. Born in Jos, he joined the University of Jos Law Faculty in 1991. He was the Nigerian coordinator of the project on *The Shari'ah Debate and the Shaping of Muslim and Christian Identities in Northern Nigeria*.

PETERS, Ruud teaches Islam and Islamic law at the University of Amsterdam. From 1982 to 1987 he was the director of the Netherlands Institute for Archeology and Arabic Studies in Cairo, Egypt. Since his Ph.D. thesis (*Islam and Colonialism: The Doctrine of Jihad in Modern History*, 1979), he has published numerous articles and books on Islam and politics and on Islamic law, including *Islamic Criminal Law in Nigeria* (2003).

About the Authors

REITZ, John is the Edward L. Carmody Professor of Law and the Associate Dean of International and Comparative Law Programs at the University of Iowa College of Law, where he also chairs the LL.M. program in International and Comparative law. He specializes in comparative law, studying especially Eastern and Western European legal systems. He is the co-editor, along with Kenney and Reisinger, of *Constitutional Dialogues in Comparative Perspective* (1999).

SADA, Ibrahim Na'iya teaches law in Ahmadu Bello University. He was formerly the Head of Department of Islamic Law and Dean of the Faculty of Law. He served as Legal Adviser to the President of Zanzibar from 1998-2000. He is presently the Director of the Centre for Islamic Legal Studies of Ahmadu Bello University, Zaria. He is called to the Nigerian Bar and specialises in Islamic Law.

SANUSI, Sanusi Lamido is well-known in Nigeria as an active participant in the debates among Muslims about *shari'ah*; he has also gained increasing international recognition and has been invited to speak in numerous international conferences in Africa, Europe, and the United States. He has degrees in economics from Ahmadu Bello University and in Islamic law from the International University of Africa, Khartoum. Before starting on a banking career in 1985, he taught economics at ABU. He is now the Head, Risk Management, at United Bank for Africa Plc.

TAYOB, Abdulkader does research on Islam and public life in Africa, and on modern Islamic thought. He is the author, among others, of *Islam in South Africa: Mosques, Imams and Sermons* (1999) and *Islam, a Short Introduction* (1999). Currently based at the International Institute for the Study of Islam in the Modern World and the University of Nijmegen, The Netherlands, he formerly taught at Cape Town University.

ter HAAR, Gerrie is Professor of Religion, Human Rights and Social Change at the Institute of Social Studies, The Hague. She is a specialist in the religious traditions of Africa and has written a number of books on the subject. She has also published widely on broader issues, including several edited works. She is one of the founding members of the African Association for the Study of Religions (AASR), and is currently Deputy Secretary General of the International Association for the History of Religion (IAHR).

WALLS, Andrew is Honorary Professor in the Universities of Edinburgh and Aberdeen, Scotland. He was Head of the Department of Religion in the University of Nigeria, Nsukka 1962-1965, and was the founding editor of the *Journal of Religion in Africa*. A specialist in the history of Christianity in Africa, he also established the Centre for the Study of Christianity in the Non-Western World at Edinburgh and is the author, among many other books and articles, of *The Missionary Movement in Christian History: Studies in the Transmission of Faith* (New York & Edinburgh, 1996).

YADUDU, Auwalu Hamisu attended the School for Arabic Studies, Kano, Ahmadu Bello University, and the Harvard Law School (Ph.D. 1985) He has taught at Bayero University, Kano since 1980, where he has served as Dean of Law and Deputy Vice-Chancellor (Academic). He was a member of the Constitution Review Committee of 1987-88 and the Constituent Assembly of 1988-89. He has been a Visiting Scholar at Harvard Law School and an Adjunct Professor at Emory Law School. He is the author of numerous scholarly articles and the editor or co-editor of several books.

YAHYA, Muslih Tayo is a Professor of Arabic in the Department of Religious Studies, University of Jos. He holds a B.A. in Arabic Language and Literature from the University of Damascus (1974) and M.A. and Ph.D. degrees from the University of Ibadan (1980, 1986). His teaching and research is focussed on the twin disciplines of Arabic and Islamic Studies, particularly in the areas of Arabic/Islamic Literature in West Africa, and interfaith relations.

Index

Abington School District v. Schempf (US), 214
Abubakar, Atiku, 72
Abubakar, Muhammad Daud, xxiv
Abu-Zayd, Nasr Hamid, 136, 139
Adamu, Sa'idu Hassan, 55, 283, 291, 292
Adegbenro v. Akintola and Aderemi (Nigeria), 149
Ado-Kurawa, Ibrahim, xxxvi, xxxix
Afghanistan, 22, 127, 131, 146, 253, 261, 280
African Charter on Human and Peoples Rights, 245
African Traditional Religion, 15, 26, 154, 248, 276, 329
Agostini v. Felton (US), 161-62, 216
Ahmad, Ali, 266, 288, 291, 358, 383
Al-Albani, 266, 272
Albie, Sachs, 34, 53
alcohol, 21, 69, 72, 124, 131, 137, 284
Al-Gaddafi, Mu'ammar, 123
Algeria, 4, 146
Al-Halabi, Ibrahim, 110, 134
Al-Hindi, 266, 272
Alli, Warisu O., 57, 383
Al-Mawardi, 176, 341
Almond, Gabriel, 94, 95
Al-Muhairi, B.S.B.A., 133
Al-Qurtubi, 272
Al-Shatibi, 272
Alston, Philip, 148, 166
Al-Tabarani, 272

Althusser, Louis, 251, 258, 263, 265, 267, 272-73
Al-Wasewi, Ibrahim Harun Hasan, xxxv, xxxvi, xxxix
Ambali, M.A., 49, 53, 65
amputation, 44, 123, 125-26, 138, 169, 252, 266, 284, 288, 297, 299
Anderson, Norman, 96, 296, 302
An-Na'im, Abdullahi A., xxix, xxxiii, 79, 89, 92, 94, 279, 316, 319, 327, 331, 332, 350, 353, 357, 360-67, 370-76, 380, 383
apartheid, 32, 36, 57, 66, 91, 94
apostate, apostasy, xxxiii, 71, 329, 338, 342-44, 347, 353
Appleby, R. Scott, 76, 79, 94-95, 172-73, 303, 319
Arjomand, Said Amir, xiv, xxxix
Arkoun, Muhammad, 136, 139
Armstrong, Karen, 81, 95
arrogance, xix, 259, 261-62, 280, 301
Asad, Talal, 87, 89, 95, 103
Ashmawy, Muhammad Sa'id, 139
Aste v. Brooks (US), 209
Attorney-General Bendel State v. Attorney-General of the Federation (Nigeria), 149
Australia, 99, 146, 150, 300, 312, 351
Awal, Rahmat, xxiv

B. v. Children's Aid Society of Metropolitan Toronto (Canada), 209

Badamasiuy, Juwayriya Bint, 286, 291
Baderin, Mashood A., 355, 357
Bahrain, 3, 146
Bakari, Mohammed, 60, 66
Bangkok Declaration, 312, 323
Bangladesh, 4, 146
Barber, Putnam, xiv, xxxix
Barker, Eileen, 95
Barkindo, Bawuro M., 53
Barry, Brian, 92, 95
Bashir, Amina, 40, 53
Bauchi, xxxvi, 25, 62, 288
Baxi, Upendra, 92, 95
Bayreuth
    conference on "The *Shari'ah* Debate and the Shaping of Muslim and Christian Identities in Northern Nigeria", xxv-xxvi
    University of, ix-x, xxii, xxiv, xxxii
Beckford, James, 29, 53
Beck-Peccoz, Roberta A., 119, 133
Beg, Tahir, 299, 302
Bellah, Robert N., 27-28, 53, 68
Bello, Ahmadu, 49, 169
Bello, Mohammed, 169, 174
Bendjilali, Boualem, xiv, xxxix
Berman, Harold J., 205-06, 242
Berner, Ulrich, xxii
Beyer, Peter, 77, 95
Bhargava, Rajeev, 89, 95
Bible, 10, 18, 24, 161, 189-90, 280, 312
Bilder, Richard, 148, 166
Bin Laden, Osama, 19, 310
blasphemy, 124, 344, 346, 379
Blazek, Jody, xiv, xl
Blood Transfusion Case (Germany), 207, 210, 229, 236

Board of Educ. of the Westside Community Schools (Dist. 66) v. Mergens (US), 161, 214
Bolling v. Sharpe (US), 195
Borno, 62, 288
Bowie, Andrew, 273
Braunfeld v. Brown (US), 192-93
Brenner, Louis, 53-54, 56-57
Brown, Beverly B., 53
Brunei, 4
Bruni, Frank, 213, 242
Brzezinski, Zbigniew, 308, 319
Buddhist, Buddhism, 97, 99, 304, 320, 380
Buhari, Muhammadu, 72
Bush, George W., 83, 98, 261
Busuttil, James J., 173, 303, 312-13, 319-20

Cachalia, Firoz, 34, 53
Canada Civil Liberties Ass'n v. Ontario (Canada), 214
Canadian Charter of Rights and Freedoms, 191-92, 196, 200, 206, 208, 235
canon law, 138, 358-59, 369
Cantwell v. Connecticut (US), 179, 197, 204, 240
Carter, Stephen L., 81-82, 95
Casanova, Jose, 29, 53, 68, 77, 96
Castells, Manuell, 77-78, 96
Catholic Charities of Sacramento, Inc. v. Superior Court of Sacramento County (US), 232
Centre for Islamic Legal Studies (ABU, Zaria), x, xxv, 387
Chandokhe, Neera, 89, 96
Chaves, Mark, 86, 96
Chesnut, R. Andrew, 90, 96
Chidester, David, 29, 53, 91, 96
China, 146, 308, 312, 322
Christelow, Allan, 50, 54

Christian Association of Nigeria (CAN), 48, 54
Church of Lukumi Babalu Aye, Inc. v. City of Hialeah (US), 179, 184, 186, 198-99, 228, 235, 238, 239
City of Boerne v. Flores (US), 156, 228, 239-40
civil religion, 27-30, 41-43, 45, 47, 53-54, 68, 174
civil rights, 76, 82, 91, 193
civil society, 29-30, 38, 53, 58, 91, 94, 179, 270, 275, 277-78, 283, 290
Classroom Crucifix II Case (Germany), 213-215, 217, 220, 223, 237
Clinton, Bill, 81
codification. *See shari'ah*: codification of
coercion, 137, 191, 207, 213-14, 215, 223, 232, 236, 296
colonial, colonialism, 38-39, 48, 55, 57, 59, 65, 78, 87, 91, 113, 123, 127, 169-70, 255, 296, 328, 349, 356, 362, 364, 366-67, 371-72, 379-80
compulsion, 16, 215, 377
Connolly, William E., 84, 96
conscience, 17, 82, 144, 154, 163-65, 179-82, 189, 200, 215, 230, 245, 348
conscientious objector, 156, 181, 225
consensus, 15, 23, 31, 84, 180, 234, 236, 252, 253, 260, 298, 334-36, 359, 366, 370, 374, 377
Constantin, Francois, 42, 54
conversion, 7-8, 313, 323, 347, 378
Cook, Rebecca, 93, 96, 146

Cooper v. Eugene School District No. 4J (US), 224
corruption, xxxii, 20, 24-25, 64, 126, 137-38, 171, 253, 255, 259, 263, 279, 281
Cox, Brian, 80, 96, 101
Cross, F.L., 26
cults, 28, 95, 99, 247
custom, 113-15, 378
customary law, 108, 115, 148, 378

Dahlab v. Switzerland (ECtHR), 222
Dan Fodio, Abdullahi, 282
Dan Fodio, Usman, 176-77, 279, 282-83
Danfulani, Umar H.D., xi, xxiv, xxvi, xxxix, 275, 384
Davis, Derek, 98, 148, 166
Dawson, John P., 98, 230, 242
De la Hera, Alberto, 155, 166
De Vries, Hent, 77, 96
Declaration of Human Rights by the World's Religions, 312, 323
Declaration on the Elimination of all Forms of Intolerance and of Discrimination Based on Religion or Belief, 166
democracy, 27, 31, 34, 38, 54, 56, 58, 65, 67-68, 77, 81-82, 84-85, 91, 105, 176, 181, 372
democratisation, xxx, 27, 45, 53, 57, 62, 68, 73-74, 82, 90, 94, 97, 130, 353
dhimma, 329
Diamond, A.S., 152, 166
dignity, human dignity, 3, 5, 24, 34, 145, 189, 191, 201, 208, 262, 290, 308, 314, 317, 323, 324
discrimination, 10, 26, 154, 159, 162, 183-85, 187, 191-92, 194,

196, 198, 206, 216, 218, 220,
   226, 229, 235, 239, 242, 246,
   248-49, 278, 285, 297, 347,
   361, 367, 369, 371-72
disestablishment of religion, 47,
   89, 154, 167
dissent, 112, 117, 213-15, 219-20,
   226, 337, 342-43, 355, 372
diversity
   among federating states, 141,
      224
   cultural, 91, 98, 248
   of opinion, 84, 86, 309, 334,
      336, 338
   religious. *See* religious
      pluralism
diyah, 132, 138, 142, 169
Docherty, Jayne Seminare, 79, 96
Downie, Mark, xvi, xxxix
Durham, W. Cole, Jr., xxviii, xxx,
   xxxiv, xli, 95, 144, 151-52,
   166-69, 172-73, 183, 217, 243,
   383
Durkheim, Émile, 27-28, 56, 68
Düstur, 115, 134

Ebert, Hans-Georg, 134
Eco, Umberto, xix, xxxix
education, 56, 76, 91, 94, 99, 104-
   05, 128, 150, 155, 161, 205,
   208, 212, 216, 219, 221, 223-
   24, 226, 238, 246-47, 255, 257,
   269, 284-85, 288, 290-91, 298,
   306, 319, 321, 367, 385
Egypt, 4, 11, 87, 113, 115-16,
   119-20, 122, 124, 134, 146,
   256, 333, 355, 386
Eickelman, Dale F., 74, 96
Elaigwu, J. Isawa, 66, 384
El-Fadl, Khaled Abou, 80, 266,
   273
Ellis, Stephen, 304, 319
Elshtain, Jean Bethke, 93, 96

Employment Division v. Smith (US),
   14, 156-57, 161, 186, 194, 197-
   99, 204, 207, 226-29, 231-33,
   236, 238-42
endorsed religion, 153-54, 159
Engel v. Vitale (US), 161, 214
Engineer, Asghar Ali, 3, 5, 349,
   357
equal protection, 179, 195-196,
   198, 225, 228, 242
equality, 34, 70, 93, 156, 158, 160,
   256-57, 259, 330, 367-69
established religion. *See* state
   religion
Establishment Clause (US), 157,
   161-63, 165, 192, 216-17
Ethiopia, 2, 4, 146, 150
ethnic cleansing, 314, 323
European Convention for the
   Protection of Human Rights
   and Fundamental Freedoms,
   166, 181, 196, 200, 202-04,
   206-08, 222, 225, 229, 235
evangelism, 49, 323

faith-based programmes, 22, 24-
   25, 79, 83, 386
Falola, Toyin, 55, 282, 291
Fanon, Frantz, 255, 273
Feierman, Steven, xiv, xl
feminist, feminism, 256, 274
Ferrari, Silvio, 155, 166
fiqh, 34, 58, 110, 112, 115-17, 127,
   135-36, 141-42
   distinguished from *shari'ah*, 33,
      110, 135, 334-38
flogging, 44, 125, 284
Foucault, Michel, 258, 263, 265,
   267
Foundation Center (US), xiii-xv,
   xl-xli
foundations, xi-xvi
   awqaf. *See waqf, awqaf*

Carnegie, xi, xiii-xiv, xvi-xvii
Ford, xi, xiii-xiv, xvi
Gates, xii-xiv, xvi, xxxiv
MacArthur, xi-xiv, xvi
Rockefeller, xi, xiii, xvii
Volkswagen, ix, xvii-xxiv, xxviii, xxxii-xxxiii, xxxvi
France, 13, 92, 95-97, 146, 150, 159, 168, 224, 242-44, 298-99, 312, 350
Frazee v. Illinois Department of Unemployment Security (US), 187
Free Exercise Clause (US), 161, 195-98, 208, 226-28, 240
freedom of religion, xxx, 31-32, 82-83, 85, 94-97, 99, 137, 144-46, 148, 150-52, 154, 156, 158-159, 162, 166-167, 174, 176, 178-242, 244-47, 249, 329, 337, 339, 354
fundamentalist, fundamentalism, 49, 78, 94-95, 174, 253, 261, 263, 273, 278-79, 290, 296, 302-03, 319-20
Fwatshak, Sati, xxiv

Gaffney, Edward M., Jr., 178, 190, 197, 209, 240-41, 243
Gaiya, Musa A.B., xxiv, 168, 384
Galaskiewicz, Joseph, 86
Gamaliel, J.D., 47, 56, 161, 167, 175, 177, 216, 243, 371, 372
Gambia, 3
Garba, Ahmad, xxxvi, xxxviii, xl
Gedicks, Frederick M., 216, 239, 241-43
gender justice. *See* women's rights
genocide, 308, 318, 322, 324
Germany, ix, xvii-xxi, 66, 92, 96, 146, 150, 155, 162-64, 174, 207, 211, 215-18, 222, 229-33, 235-36, 243-44, 299, 308, 351, 385

ghadhf, 333
Ghana, 4, 146, 150, 314-15
Ghanim, Ibrahim al-Bayumi, xiv, xl
Gibb, H.A., 346, 357
Gifford, Paul, 30, 54, 78, 82, 97, 101
Gill, Anthony, 90, 97
Gillette v. United States (US), 182
globalisation, 94, 253, 257, 261, 263, 271, 275-76, 299- 300, 356, 367
Goldman v. Weinberger (US), 224
Gombe, 62
Gombrich, Richard, 89, 97
Gonzalez v. Roman Catholic Archbishop (US), 165
Good News Club v. Milford Central School (US), 161
Gopin, Marc, 79, 97
Gordley, James Russell, 231, 244
Gravelle, Kent Benedict, 5
Greece, 146, 201-02, 205
Grondin, Jean, 252, 273
Gruchy, J.W. de, 91, 97
Gumi, Abubakar, 49, 55, 63
Gunn, T. Jeremy, 92, 97
Gwamna, J.D., xxiv, xxvi, 320, 384

Habermas, Jürgen, 29, 37, 68, 74, 97, 252, 262-63, 270, 273-75
Hackett, Rosalind I.J., xxviii, 74, 91-94, 97, 100-03, 385
hadd, hudud, 125, 127, 132, 134, 269, 284, 291, 299
hadith, xxxi, 3-5, 108, 122, 129, 135, 257, 281
hajj, 13, 48, 56, 129, 368
Hammond, Phillipp E., 53
Hannum, Hurst, 167
Harneit-Sievers, Axel, xxxviii, xl
Harnischfeger, Johannes, 46, 54

Harris v. McRae (US), 165
Harun, Abdulhakeem, 103, 106
Hasan and Chaush v. Bulgaria
 (ECtHR), 165
Hasan, Hasan Ibraheem, 273
Hassan, Ahmed Issack, 54
Hays, Gregory, 260, 273
headscarf, 13, 92, 220-22, 224,
 235, 242-43, 298, 369
Headscarf Case (Germany), 221-23,
 237, 243
Hefner, Robert W., 91, 97
Henkin, Louis, 148, 167
heresy, heretics, 187, 338, 343-44,
 346, 379
hermeneutics, 110, 112, 252, 254,
 257-58, 270, 275
hijab. *See* headscarf
hijrah, 278-79, 290
Hilmi, Omer, 116, 134
Hindu, Hinduism, 76, 89, 304,
 309, 320
Hirsch, Susan F., 39, 54
hisbah, xxiv, 171, 252
HIV/AIDS, xii-xiii, xv, xxxii, 22.
 24-26, 287, 290, 386
 APIN (AIDS Prevention in
  Nigeria), xii-xiii, xvi
Hodgkin, Thomas, 282, 291
Hodgson, Marshall G.S., xiv, xl
Hogg, Peter W., 191, 206-07, 214,
 243
Honneth, Alex, 260, 273
Hoover, Dennis R., 83, 97
Hopkins, Bruce R., xiv, xl-xli
Humphrey, John, 167
Huntington, Samuel, 76-77, 97,
 101, 307, 319
Huquq-i A'ile Qararnamesi, 117,
 134
Husseini, Safiya, xxv, 69, 261,
 284, 292
Hutchison, William R., 171, 174

hypocrites, hypocrisy, xxxv, 15,
 296, 344, 347

Ibn 'Abd al-Barr, 268, 273
Ibn 'Abd al-Salam, 268, 273
Ibn,'Arabi, 268, 273
Ibn Hanbal, 266, 273
Ibn Qayyim, 260, 273
Ibn Rushd, 268, 273, 344, 357
Ibn Taimiyyah, 176, 260, 273,
 341
Idris, Muhammad al-Khamis,
 xxiv
ijma', 334-36
ijtihad, 3, 122, 136, 301, 332, 335
Ilchman, Warren F., xiv, xxxix, xl
Illesanmi, Simeon O., 29-30, 54,
 330, 357
illiteracy, 24, 253, 285, 289
Imam, Ayesha, 54, 273
imams, 19, 36, 43-45, 58, 62-63,
 109-111, 289, 387
India, 4, 75, 88, 131, 146, 150,
 304, 309, 318, 320-21, 324,
 328, 340, 342, 379
indigenous cultures and religions,
 90, 205, 315-16
Indonesia, 2, 4, 91, 97, 146
Interdenominational School Case
 (Germany), 216, 219
International Bible Society, xxv
International Covenant on Civil
 and Political Rights, 146, 172
intolerance, 26, 28, 94, 170, 296,
 323
Iran, 2, 4, 48, 88, 114, 119, 122,
 131-34, 141, 151-52, 261, 318,
 324, 338, 342
Iraq, 4, 131, 146, 253, 261, 310,
 333, 340, 356
Isichei, Elizabeth, 283, 291
Islam and the West, xxiii, xxx,
 xxxiii-xxxv, 88, 118, 123, 125,

174-77, 251-74, 276, 292-302, 310, 321, 324-25, 356, 372
Islamic law. *See shari'ah*
Islamisation, re-Islamisation, xxix, 50-52, 119, 122, 124-25, 133, 141
Islamist, Islamism, 49-50, 53, 119, 122-25, 128-29, 136, 253, 298
Israel, 4, 11, 261, 300, 316, 328

Jackson, John H., 362, 372
Jama'atu Nasril Islam, x, 24
Jameson, Frederic, 258, 273
Jehovah's Witnesses, 201, 204, 294
Jenkins, Philip, 78, 97
Jigawa, xxxvi, 62
jihad, 61, 269, 276, 283, 308, 310, 322, 347
Joda, Asmau, 45, 54
Johnston, Douglas, 77, 79, 95, 97, 101
Jordan, 2, 4, 147
Jos, 45, 276, 288
    conference on "Comparative Perspectives on *Shari'ah* in Nigeria", vii-ix, xxii, xxvi–xxxviii; and see xxxix-xli for citations to reviews of the conference
    crises of 2001-02, vii, xxiii, 45
    University of, vii-x, xxiii, xxxii, xxxiv, xxxvii, 24, 383-88
Juergensmeyer, Mark, 89, 98, 308-11, 319

Kabo, Shaykh Ibrahim, xxxvii
kadhi's courts. *See* Kenya: *qadi*'s courts and the constitution
Kaduna, 8, 21, 25, 45, 62, 72, 250, 288, 291-92

Kano, xxxiii, xxxvi-xxxvii, 53, 62, 71, 142, 286, 288, 301, 383, 388
Kano State Shári'ah Implementation Advisory Committee, xxiii, xxxiv-xxxvii, xxxix
Kaplan, Robert D., 76, 98
Kaşıkçı, Osman, 116, 134
Katsina, 62
Katz, Stanley N., xiv, xxxix, xl
Kebbi, 62
Keddie, Nikki R., 88-89, 98, 103
Kedroff v. Saint Nicholas Cathedral (US), 165
Kelly, J.M., 134
Kelsey, John, 317, 319
Kenny, Joseph, 30, 54, 135, 137-39, 384
Kenya, xxx, 31, 51-55, 64-65, 68
    qadi's courts and the constitution, 37-44, 58-61
Kenya National Church, 39-44, 55
Kenyatta, Jomo, 38
Kilani, Abdul Razaq, 48, 55
King, Martin Luther, 319, 324
King-Irani, Lauri E., 315, 319
Kishwar, Madhu, 89, 98
Kogelmann, Franz, ix, xiv, xvi, xl, 385
Kokkinakis v. Greece (ECtHR), 200-01, 203-04, 207, 211, 235
Kommers, Donald P., 189-90, 207, 209, 213, 215-19, 236, 243
Kozlowski, Gregory C., xiv, xl
Kramers, J.H., 346, 357
kufr, kafir. See unbelief, unbelievers
Kukah, Matthew Hassan, 46, 55, 282, 291
Kumo, Suleiman, 169, 174

Kuwait, 2, 4, 147

Ladan, Mohammed Tawfiq, 6, 285-86, 289, 292
laïcité. *See* secularism
Lampman, Jane, 83, 98
Larissis and Others v. Greece (ECtHR), 204
Larsen, Lena, 94, 98
Last, Murray, 47, 55
Lawal, Amina, xxv, 20, 54, 69, 261
Lebanon, 4, 147, 312, 315, 319, 323
Lecourt, Dominique, 265, 267, 273
Lederach, John Paul, 79, 99
Lee v. Weisman (US), 192, 214
Leukfeld, Carl G., xv, xli
Levine, Daniel H., 76, 90-91, 98, 101
Liberia, 147, 150, 314-15, 323
Libya, 2, 4, 119, 123, 131, 133, 147
Lillich, Richard B., 149, 167
Lindholm, Tore, 95, 167, 243
Livingstone, E.A., 13, 26
Locke v. Davey (US), 226
Loimeier, Roman, 49, 55
loya jerga, 22
Ludwig, Frieder, x-xi, xxi-xxii, xxvi, xxxix-xl
Lyotard, Jean François, 257, 273

MacEoin, Denis, 6
Madan, T.N., 89, 98
madhhab, madhahib, 110, 115, 135, 333, 335
   Hanafi, 4, 110, 112, 115-18, 121, 268, 333-34, 347
   Hanbali, 4, 120, 268, 333
   Ja'fari (Shi'a), 333

   Maliki, 4, 116, 121, 135, 143, 268, 333, 347
   Shafi'i, 4, 116, 268, 333, 335
Mahdi, Saudatu Shehu, xxv, xxxi, 1, 6, 51, 55, 385
Mahlmann, Matthias, 221-22, 243
Mahmud, Tayyab, 188, 243
Maitatsine, 278-79, 290
Malaysia, 4, 147
Maldives, 4
Mangvwat, Monday Y., vii, 385
Manoussakis v. Greece (ECtHR), 203, 211, 235-36
Markus, Hazel, 93, 96, 99
Marquis, Christopher, 224, 243
Martin, S., 97
Marty, Martin, 87, 303, 319
Masina, Nomonde, 315, 319
maslahah, 136, 268
Massey, James, 89, 98
Maududi, Sayyid A.A., 289, 292
Mazrui, Ali, 65-66, 101, 103, 106
Mbiti, John, 15, 26, 172-74
McCain, Danny, xxxii, 7, 24, 26, 369-370, 372, 385
McCarthy, Thomas A., 252, 273
McCollum v. Board of Education (US), 216
McCutcheon, Russell T., 82, 98
McGowan v. Maryland (US), 192
Mcleod, Hugh, 349, 357
mediation, 95, 327, 331, 333, 340, 348, 361, 376, 380
Mehdi, R., 132, 134
Mehta, Uday, 349, 357
Mendieta, Eduardo, 262, 264, 274
Merrills, J.G., 167
Metropolitan Church of Bessarabia v. Moldova (ECtHR), 165
Meyer, Birgit, 74, 97-98
Meyssan, Thierry, 102, 106
Miguez, Daniel, 315, 319
Minow, Martha, 93, 96, 99

missionaries, 206, 248
Mohammed, Abubakar Siddique, 55, 283, 291-92
Momin, A.R., 300, 302
Monsma, Stephen, 182-83, 190, 215-16, 233-34, 243
Moosa, Ebrahim, 33, 55
Moosa, Najma, 33-34, 36, 55
Morocco, 2, 4, 69, 114, 147, 340
Morsink, Johannes, 312, 320
Mosma, Stephen V., 351, 357
Moyers, Bill, 93, 98
Mozambique, 147, 150, 315, 323
Mukhtasar, 135
multiculturalism, 84, 92, 95-96, 99, 302
Muslim ibn Hajj-aj al Qushayr-i, 292, 335
Muzaffar, Chandra, 310, 320

Nasarawa, xxiv, 62
Nasir, Jamila M., ix-x, xl, 244, 386
natural justice, equity, and good conscience, 37, 52, 113, 169, 272, 277, 299
Netherlands, 99, 147, 300, 351, 386, 387
neutrality. *See* state neutrality between religions
Newman, Graeme, 127, 134
Nichol v. ARIN Intermediate Unit 28 (US), 224
nifaq. *See* hypocrites, hypocrisy
Niger Delta, 48, 55
Niger State, 71
Nigeria
  Christian-Muslim relations, xxxii, 7-26, 45, 48, 55-56, 106, 139, 328, 368-71
  crises related to religion, vii, 8, 21, 44, 72, 244, 278-80

shari'ah and the constitution, 47, 144-66, 168-72, 174-77, 183, 211, 232, 244-50, 330
shari'ah implementation in twelve states, ix-xi, xxi-xxv, xxix-xxxi, xxxiii, xli, 44-51, 64, 70-73, 275-92, 365-66
Noibi, M.A., 296, 302
Noonan, John T., Jr., 178-80, 182, 189-90, 197, 209, 240-41, 243
Noorani, A.G., 89, 98
Northern Ireland, 23, 304, 318, 321, 324
Nowak, John E., 195-96, 243
Nowak, Manfred, 204, 243
Nu'man Abd al-Razid al-Samar'i, Ahkam, 357
Nussbaum, Martha C., 93, 97-98

Obasanjo, Olusegun, 71-73
Obeyesekere, G., 89, 97
Oded, Arye, 42-43, 55
Odinkalu, Chidi Anselm, 78, 98
O'dua People's Congress (OPC), 71
Ogugu v. State (Nigeria), 148-49
Okike, Benedict Ohadughiro, 30, 46, 55
Okpu, Ugbana, 170, 174
Oloyede, Is-Haq, xxiii, xxxv, xli, 292, 301-02, 386
Olupona, Jacob Obafemi Kehinde, 29, 54, 56
Oman, 2, 3, 147
Oruka, H. Odera, 267, 274
Ostien, Philip, ix-xi, xxxix, xli, 47, 56, 61, 63, 66, 160-61, 167, 169-70, 174-75, 177, 216, 243, 328, 357, 371-72, 386
Ottoman Empire, 109-10, 113-18, 131, 134, 340, 342

Pakistan, 4, 119, 123, 131-34, 141, 147, 188, 210, 236, 243, 318, 324, 338, 345
Palestine, 4, 261, 318
Parekh, Bhikhu, 92, 98
Parliament of the World's Religions, 316, 324
Peebles, Jane, xli
Perry, Michael J., 359, 372
persecution, 151, 154, 159, 178, 188, 197, 262
Peters, Ruud, xiv, xxix, xxxiii, xli, 44, 56, 107, 119, 125, 132, 134-35, 140, 386
Philippines, 4, 147, 150
Philpott, Daniel, 77, 80, 96, 98
Pickering, W.S.F., 28, 56
Piscatori, James, 77, 99
Plang, Danladi, 245, 250
Plateau State, xii-xiii, xxiv, xxxvi, 25, 276
Plesner, Ingvild T., 94, 98
polygamy, 121-22, 197, 199
post-colonial, 52, 75, 305, 338, 342
poverty, 63, 124, 253, 257, 264, 270-71, 275, 281, 284-85, 288, 292, 298, 313
Powers, David S., 363, 372
Presbyterian Church v. Mary Elizabeth Blue Hull Mem'l Presbyterian Church (US), 165
progressive Muslims, xxxi, 32, 51-52, 254, 257, 260, 263, 274-75
proselytism, 92, 144, 167, 200, 202-05, 210, 225, 233, 235, 237, 246
public sphere, 27, 29, 31, 57, 74, 77, 86, 94, 96, 100, 102, 104-05, 223, 232, 358, 360, 371, 374; *see also* religion in the public sphere

qadis, qadis' courts, 37-44, 52, 57-62, 108-09, 112, 289, 291
Qadri Pasha, Muhammad, 116-17, 134
Qatar, 2, 3, 147
qisas, 132
qiyas, 335
Queen, Edward L. II, xiv, xxxix, xl
Qur'an, xxxi, 3-5, 20, 24, 33, 40, 49, 108, 122, 125, 129, 135-36, 256-57, 268, 272, 278, 280-82, 297, 300, 302, 312, 332-38, 344-48, 353-55, 365

R. v. Big M Drug Mart, Ltd. (Canada), 191-93, 206, 211, 235
R. v. Edward's Books (Canada), 193
R. v. Oakes (Canada), 207
Rahman, Shaikh Abdur, 344, 357
Ram-Prasad, Chakravarti, 309, 320
Rautenbach, Christa, 36, 56
Registered Trustees of the Rosicrucian Order, Amorc (Nigeria) vs. Henry O. Awoniyi & 3 Ors (Nigeria), 247
Reichmuth, Stefan, 49, 56
Reitz, John C., xxx, 178, 218, 244, 245, 387
religion
    as resource for peace, xxx, 7, 10, 25, 79, 81, 95, 99, 311-17, 323-24
    as source of conflict, xxx, 81, 93, 306-11, 321-22, 339
    in public schools, 21, 25, 85, 92, 105, 155, 175, 212-16, 219-25, 228, 232, 234, 237, 298

in the public sphere, xxviii, 14-15, 27, 29-31, 39, 45, 48, 51-54, 57, 74-100, 102, 105, 288, 303-304, 321, 327, 331, 338, 348-56, 358-72, 376-81
privatisation of, 13, 15, 29, 75-77, 83, 87, 102, 157, 159, 162, 172, 176, 223, 232, 303-04, 307, 322, 331, 348, 350, 359
Religious Freedom Restoration Act (US), 156, 240-42
Religious Land Use and Institutionalised Persons Act (US), 241-42
religious minorities, 9, 12-13, 16, 48, 50, 61, 64, 75, 85, 89, 91, 93, 96, 98, 166-67, 169, 174, 243, 372
Religious Oath Case (Germany), 189-90
religious pluralism, 6, 30, 33-34, 58, 68, 87, 90-91, 98, 222, 274, 361, 385
religious rights. *See* freedom of religion
Renz, Loren, xv, xli
revelation, 108, 316, 339, 365, 373-76
Reynolds v. United States (US), 74, 196-99, 210
riba, 133, 329
Richardson, James T., 92, 99
ridda. *See* apostasy
Ries, Joanne B., xv, xli
Risala, 135, 139
Robert, Jacques, 27-28, 53, 97-98, 223, 244
Robertson, A.H., 167
Robertson, Roland, 99
Rotunda, Ronald D., 195-96, 243

Rousseau, Jean Jacques, 27-28, 37, 56, 68
Rudolph, Susanne H., 77, 99
rule of law, 6, 41, 67, 180-81, 215, 277, 290

sabb al-rasul. *See* blasphemy
Sada, Ibrahim Na'iya, xxiii, xxv, xli, 174, 387
Said, Edward W., 258, 265, 267, 274
Salamon, Lester M., xiv, xli
Salvatore, Armando, 96
Sampson, Cynthia, 77, 79, 97, 99, 101
Sani, Governor Ahmed, 44-46, 62, 71, 137, 359
Sanusi, Sanusi Lamido, xxv-xxvi, xxx-xxxi, xxxiii, xli, 46, 56, 251, 257, 259, 261-62, 269, 274-76, 278-82, 284, 289-92, 294-96, 298, 301, 387
Saudi Arabia, 2, 3, 120, 123, 126, 134, 310, 322, 342
Schacht, Joseph, 116, 134
Schlesinger, Rudolf B., 231, 244
Schneiter, Paul H., xv, xli
School Dist. of Abington Township v. Schempp (US), 161
School Prayer Case (Germany), 212, 214-15, 218-20, 223, 229-30, 237
schools of Islamic jurisprudence. *See madhhab, madhahib*
secular state, 30, 41, 47, 52, 55, 75, 88, 98, 160, 168, 182, 184, 304, 321, 339, 370
secularisation, 76, 89, 102, 123, 349, 353, 357, 379, 380
secularism, xxiii, xxxii, 13-15, 33, 44, 58, 65, 82, 84, 86-89, 95, 97-98, 102-04, 159-60, 163, 166, 175, 182, 244, 264, 294,

331, 338, 348-53, 356, 361, 370, 372
Sedgwick, Mark, 358, 373
Senegal, 4, 147, 150
separation of religion and state, xxvii, 2, 13, 42, 56, 65, 77, 151, 157, 167, 177, 182, 216, 232, 243, 304, 306, 349, 359, 372
September 11, 2001, 75, 78, 83, 98, 102, 106, 177, 310-11, 321-22
Serbian E. Orthodox Diocese v. Milivojevich (US), 165
Serequeberhan, Tsenay, 257, 272, 274
Serif v. Greece (ECtHR), 165
Sharia Courts of Appeal (Nigeria), 61, 72, 170-71, 245
shari'ah
  and human rights, xxxi, xxxiii, 5, 32-37, 64, 72, 254, 260, 264, 298, 316, 331, 341-43, 352
  and non-Muslims, 20-21, 25, 46, 64, 137, 176-77, 259, 274, 280, 331, 341, 346, 354, 369
  codification of, 107, 113-19, 128, 130, 136, 143
    criminal law, 4, 116, 119, 123-24, 126-27, 131, 176, 364, 371
    personal law, xxxi, 3-5, 34, 122, 131, 269
  distinguished from *fiqh*, 33, 110, 135, 334-38
  enactment as positive law, xxix, 3, 140, 301, 330-56, 364-65
  reformation of, 1, 35, 58, 91, 118, 136, 267, 352-55
  sources of. See *usul al-fiqh*

"*Shari'ah* Debate and the Shaping of Muslim and Christian Identities in Northern Nigeria", project on, ix, xxi-xxvi
Shaykh, Sa'diyya, 256-57, 260, 274
Shaykhzade, 110, 134
Sherbert v. Verner (US), 193, 198, 238
Shi'a, Shiites, 259, 333, 339-40, 346
Shiner, Larry, 349, 357
Shweder, Richard, 93, 96, 99
Silk, Mark, 83, 95, 98-99
Singapore, 4, 33-34, 55, 147
Sivan, Emmanuel, 94-95
Smith, David, 26
Smith, Steven D., 167
Sohn, Louis B., 167
Sokoto, 6, 47, 62, 71, 169, 288
Somalia, 2, 4
Soper, J. Christopher, 182-83, 190, 215-16, 233-34, 243, 351, 357
South Africa, xxx, 41, 43, 45, 51-56, 64-65, 68-69, 91, 94-97, 99, 105, 315, 319, 324
  Muslim personal law and the constitution in, 31-37, 57-58
Sri Lanka, 4, 88, 97, 99, 147, 304, 321, 380
Stahnke, Tad, 144, 167
state neutrality between religions, 150, 153, 155-61, 163-64, 168, 182-86, 216-18, 220, 223-24, 231-32, 235-37, 243, 331-32, 338, 352, 356, 362-63, 365, 367-72, 379, 381
state religion, xxviii, 40, 47, 105, 144, 147-48, 150-52, 154-55,

157, 159-60, 163, 169, 174, 176, 342
Stegeby, E. Kenneth, 154, 167
Steinfels, Peter, 233, 244
Stephens, Laura, 86
Steyn, H. Christina, 91, 99
Stone v. Graham (US), 214
stoning, 44, 126, 138, 169, 252, 261, 284, 289, 333
Stout, Jeffrey, 84, 99
Sudan, xxxiii, 2, 4-5, 119, 123, 125, 131, 133, 141, 316, 328, 331, 338
Sunnah, 3, 33, 108, 122, 125, 129, 256, 278, 281, 332-38, 344-45, 353-55
Sunni, Sunnites, 259, 333-34, 339, 363
Sweden, 94, 147, 167, 300
Syria, 4, 147, 340, 355

ta'zir, 132, 269, 299
Taha, Mahmoud Mohamed, xxxiii, 331-32, 354, 357
Tahanawi, Muhammad, 108, 134
Tahzib-Lie, Bahia, 93, 95, 99, 167, 243
takhyir, 268
talakawa, 283-85, 287, 290
Talbi, Muhammad, 136, 139
Taliban, 127, 137, 278, 280
Tambiah, Stanley J., 89, 99
Tangban, O.E., 48, 56
Tanko, Sani B., xxxv-xxxvi, xli
Tanzania, 4
taqlid, 268, 301
Tayob, Abdulkader, xxix, 27, 29, 56-59, 62-63, 65, 68-69, 91, 99, 387
Tellenbach, S., 132, 134
Ter Haar, Gerrie, x, xxx, xli, 173, 303-304, 309, 312-14, 319-26, 387

terrorism, 296, 318, 322, 324-25, 345
theocracy, 64, 152, 159, 176
Thomas v. Review Board (US), 226
Thornberry, Patrick, 149, 167
Tobacco Atheist Case (Germany), 189
Toffar, A.K., 33-35, 56
tolerance, toleration, 30, 73, 79, 85, 88, 94, 153, 171, 222, 243, 312-13, 324
Torah, 280, 312, 377, 381
Troper, Michel, 223-24, 244
Truth and Reconciliation Commission (South Africa), 315, 324
Tukur, Mahmud M., 269, 274
Tunisia, 2, 4, 147, 256
Turaki, Yusufu, xxv, 46, 56
Turkey, 2, 119, 147, 150, 160, 168, 352-53, 360
Tutu, Desmond, 319, 324
Twiss, Sumner B., 317, 319

ulama, xxiv, 112, 114, 118, 128-30, 136, 143, 278, 290, 340-41
Umar, Khadijah Abdullahi, xxiv
Umar, Muhammad Sani, 50, 57
ummah, 1, 172, 279, 281-82, 286, 289-90
unbelief, unbelievers, 11, 277, 282, 326, 329, 344, 347
United Arab Emirates, 2, 3, 127, 133
United Kingdom, 113, 151-52, 311, 356
United States, 47, 56, 65, 76, 81-82, 86, 97, 99, 102, 147, 150-51, 156-57, 160-65, 167, 175-79, 183-85, 192-96, 199, 207-08, 211-18, 224-31, 233, 235, 238-39, 243-44, 261, 277, 299, 307-08, 310-11, 321-22, 349,

351, 356, 359, 367, 372, 386-87
US Embassy, Abuja, xxxiii-xxxiv, xxxvi
United States v. Ballard (US), 190
United States v. Board of Education for the School District of Philadelphia (US), 224
Universal Declaration of Human Rights, 144, 146, 148-49, 166-67, 172-73, 311, 320
Universal Islamic Declaration of Human Rights, 312, 323
Usman, Yusufu Bala, 176-77, 279, 282-83, 287, 292
usul al-fiqh, 135, 332-33, 335, 353-54, 361, 372

Van der Veer, Peter, 78, 99
Van der Vyver, Johann, 99, 166, 242-44
Vogel, Frank E., 120, 134
Volkswagen Foundation. *See* foundations: Volkswagen
Von Mehren, Arthur T., 231, 244
Vospernik, Tanja, 204, 243

Wa Mutua, Makau, 205, 244
Waldock, Humphrey, 167
Walia, Shelley, 265, 274
Wallace v. Jaffree (US), 214
Walls, Andrew F., 373, 380-81, 388
Walz v. Tax Comm'n of New York City (US), 186
waqf, awqaf, xiii-xiv, xvi, xl, 116, 119
Warnke, Georgia, 252, 258, 274
Watson v. Jones (US), 165, 187
Weinsheimer, Joel, 256, 274
Weiss, Bernard, 334, 357
Weiss, Holger, xiv, xli
Weithman, Paul, 84-86, 99, 105

West and Islam. *See* Islam and the West
Westerlund, David, 55, 169, 174, 304, 320
Westernisation, xxxiii, xxxv, 119, 272, 275-76
of Islamic legal systems, xxix, 107-18, 128
Williams, Pat T., 66
Wisconsin v. Yoder (US), 189, 197, 205, 208
Witte, John Jr., 82-83, 100, 102, 166, 242-44, 360, 367, 373
Witters v. Washington Dept. of Servs. for Blind (US), 162
Women Rights Advancement and Protection Alternative (WRAPA), xxv, 385
women's rights, xi, xvi, xxxv, 1-5, 6, 32, 36, 39, 50-55, 58-59, 69, 96, 98, 112, 121, 252, 254, 256, 269, 273-74, 285-86, 291-92, 331, 341, 385
World Conference on Religion and Peace, 316, 324

Yadudu, Auwalu Hamisu, 139, 388
Yahya, Muslih T., 100, 106, 388
Yamani, M.A., 296, 298, 302
Yazid, Imrana, 287, 292
'Yan Izala, 49, 55
Yemen, 4, 120, 133
Yick Wo v. Hopkins (US), 239
Yobe, 62

Zaheeruddin v. State (Pakistan), 188, 210, 236
zakat, xxiv, 69, 120, 133, 281
Zamfara, 6, 44, 50, 54, 62, 70-72, 136, 169, 288, 301, 328, 359
zandaqah, zindiq. See heresy, heretics

Zartman, I. William, 316, 319, 320

zina, xxv, 44, 70, 169, 266, 269, 284-85, 289, 296, 333, 347

Zylberberg v. Sudbury Board of Education (Canada), 214